Immigration Law and the Family

Sixth Edition

Sixth Edition

IMMIGRATION LAW AND THE FAMILY

A Practical Guide to Family-Sponsored Immigration

Edited by Charles Wheeler

AMERICAN IMMIGRATION LAWYERS ASSOCIATION

Website for Corrections and Updates

Corrections and other updates to this and other AILA publications can be found at **www.aila.org/errata.** If you have any corrections or updates to the information in this book, please let us know by sending a note to the address below, or email us at **books@aila.org.**

This publication is designed to provide accurate and authoritative information in regard to the subject matter covered. It is distributed with the understanding that the publisher is not engaged in rendering legal, accounting, or other professional service. If legal advice or other expert assistance is required, the services of a competent professional should be sought.

—from a Declaration of Principles jointly adopted by a Committee of the American Bar Association and a Committee of Publishers

Proceeds from the sales of AILA publications are reinvested in the association to help support member programs and services in the areas of federal and state advocacy, government liaison, practice assistance, ethics education, media outreach, and timely dissemination of members-only information via www.aila.org. In addition, contributions are made to the American Immigration Council (AIC).

Printed in the United States of America

ISBN 978-1-57370-467-0

Stock No. 54-67

AILA Titles of Interest

AILA's Occupational Guidebooks

Immigration Options for Investors and Entrepreneurs

Immigration Options for Artists, Entertainers, and Athletes

Statutes, Regulations, Agency Materials & Case Law

Immigration & Nationality Act

Code of Federal Regulations

Core Curriculum

Navigating the Fundamentals of Immigration Law

Immigration Practice Pointers

Toolbox Series

AILA's Immigration Practice & Professionalism Toolbox

AILA's Immigration Litigation Toolbox

AILA's Immigration Practice Toolbox

AILA's Toolbox for Immigration Paralegals

AILA's Focus Series

EB-2 & EB-3 Degree Equivalency
by Ronald Wada

Private Bills & Pardons in Immigration
by Anna Gallagher

The Child Status Protection Act
by Charles Wheeler

Online Research Tools

AILALink

Treatises & Primers

Kurzban's Immigration Law Sourcebook
by Ira J. Kurzban

Business Immigration: Law & Practice
by Daryl Buffenstein, Bo Cooper, Kevin Miner, and Crystal Williams

AILA's Asylum Primer
by Dree K. Collopy

Immigration Consequences of Criminal Activity
by Mary E. Kramer

Representing Clients in Immigration Court
edited and updated by CLINIC

Litigating Immigration Cases in Federal Court
by Robert Pauw

Immigration Law & the Family
edited by Charles Wheeler

Immigration Law & the Military
by Margaret D. Stock

Essentials of Immigration Law
by Richard A. Boswell

Provisional Waivers: A Practitioner's Guide
by Charles Wheeler

Public Charge and Affidavits of Supoort: A Practitioner's Guide
by Charles Wheeler

Other Titles

The Consular Practice Handbook

The Diplomatic Visas Handbook

The Waivers Book: Advanced Issues in Immigration Law Practice

AILA's Guide to U.S. Citizenship & Naturalization Law

The International Adoption Sourcebook

Build and Manage Your Successful Immigration Law Practice
by Ruby L. Powers

About the Editor

Charles Wheeler is an attorney with Catholic Legal Immigration Network (CLINIC) in San Francisco and directs its Training and Legal Support section. CLINIC conducts training, provides technical support and legal analysis, and produces legal reference materials for immigration attorneys and other nonprofit agency staff throughout the United States. It also advocates on behalf of low-income immigrants at the local and national level and co-counsels federal litigation. Prior to joining CLINIC, Mr. Wheeler directed the National Immigration Law Center in Los Angeles (1985–96) and the Farmworker Program of Colorado Rural Legal Services in Denver (1979–84). He has been specializing in immigration law and aliens' rights issues for 40 years. He is considered an expert in several aspects of immigration law, as well as immigrants' eligibility for public benefits. He was the 2002 recipient of the Daniel Levy Memorial Award for Outstanding Achievement in Immigration Law, awarded by Matthew Bender LexisNexis. He was a 1989 recipient of the Carol King Award for Achievement in Litigation, awarded by the National Immigration Project of the National Lawyers Guild. He is a graduate of the University of Virginia and the University of Maryland School of Law.

Acknowledgments

I want to acknowledge and thank the many people who assisted in the unfolding of this book from its inception as a basic training manual to its current status as a comprehensive, yet practical, reference tool for immigration practitioners. During that 20-year period, several staff from the Catholic Legal Immigration Network, Inc. (CLINIC), as well as other practitioners, assisted with creating and revising various chapters. The following is a catalogue of those who played a significant role. The portions of this book that first appeared in the publications identified below are reprinted with permission.

I originally wrote chapters 1–5 and 8. For the current edition I updated chapters 1–3, 5, 7 and 8. CLINIC attorney Kristina Karpinski updated chapter 4 and assembled the appendices pertaining to those chapters. CLINIC managing attorney Susan Schreiber updated chapters 6, 9, and 10.

Portions of chapter 5 first appeared in 90-03 *Immigration Briefings* (Mar. 1990), and evolved into a chapter in the *Immigrants' Rights Manual*, co-authored by CLINIC and the National Immigration Law Center (NILC). Portions of chapter 6 were originally written by NILC's Daniel Levy and first appeared in 91-08, 91-09 *Immigration Briefings* (Aug., Sept. 1991). This was later updated by NILC's Linton Joaquin and evolved into another chapter of the *Immigrants' Rights Manual*.

Juan Osuna, when he was editor of *Interpreter Releases*, contributed the portion of chapter 7 on waivers to health-related grounds of inadmissibility, while I wrote other portions. CLINIC attorneys Kristina Karpinski and Jennie Guilfoyle expanded and updated this chapter for the second edition.

Chapter 8 was adapted from several articles that originally appeared in AILA's *Navigating the Fundamentals of Immigration Law* (2008–09); 11 *Bender's Immigr. Bull.* 857 (Aug. 1, 2006); AILA's *Immigration & Nationality Law Handbook* (2002–2005 eds.); 6 *Bender's Immigr. Bull.* 772 (Aug. 1, 2001); 5 *Bender's Immigr. Bull.* 125 (Feb. 1, 2000); 4 *Bender's Immigr. Bull.* 97 (Feb. 1, 1999); AILA's *INS Forms for Applications and Petitions* (4th ed.); 98-06 *Immigration Briefings* 1 (June 1998); and 74 *Interpreter Releases* 1581 (Oct. 20, 1997).

Chapter 9 was adapted from an article written by former CLINIC attorney Anne Marie Gibbons that originally appeared in AILA's *Handbook on Waivers and Relief from Removal*. The chapter was later expanded by former CLINIC attorney Evangeline Abriel. Former CLINIC attorney Laurie Joyce wrote chapter 10, portions of which first appeared in 02-06 *Immigration Briefings* (June 2002), and later in *Affidavit of Support and Sponsorship Requirements: A Practitioner's Guide*, published by CLINIC and NILC. This chapter was updated and revised for the second edition by Debbie Smith and former CLINIC attorney Mary McClenahan. Thanks to all of you!

Charles Wheeler

August 2020

Preface

When I started dabbling in immigration law four decades ago, times were simpler. Family-based immigration was not a major component of any AILA member's law practice. Some immigration attorneys even steered their clients to local nonprofit agencies and self-help guides rather than charging them a separate fee to complete the paperwork necessary to immigrate the client's family members.

Those were the days before conditional residents, employment authorization documents, widow petitions, relief for survivors of domestic violence, humanitarian reinstatement, unlawful presence, reinstatement of removal, permanent bars, grandfathering under INA §245(i), binding affidavits of support, adjusted age determinations to preserve child status, service centers, and the National Visa Center—to name just a few of the intervening changes.

Back then we had local district offices staffed by employees of the Immigration and Naturalization Service who would receive and adjudicate petitions, interview our clients, and grant or deny them benefits. When problems arose in a case, we called the agents up and usually straightened them out. Times have changed.

The impetus for this book was to address the complexities of family-based immigration in a straightforward and step-by-step approach—to boil them down to their fundamentals and offer practical advice for those representing clients in this process.

It was not my intention that this book serve as an in-depth legal reference tool. Rather, it was meant to summarize the law in this area and steer the practitioner to a successful outcome. Included in this book are sample motions and waivers, as well as useful recommendations for problem solving. Use it as an economical guide to the process for immigrating family members and a quick resource for answers to the most common questions.

This area of immigration law has evolved over time into a serious subspecialty; this book is meant to help illustrate and justify the respect it now deserves.

Charles Wheeler

August 2020

SUMMARY OF CONTENTS

IMMIGRATION LAW AND THE FAMILY, 6TH ED.

Detailed Table of Contents

Immigration Law and the Family, 6th ed.

About AILA

The American Immigration Lawyers Association (AILA) is a national bar association of more than 15,500 attorneys who practice immigration law and/or work as teaching professionals. AILA member attorneys represent tens of thousands of U.S. families who have applied for permanent residence for their spouses, children, and other close relatives for lawful entry and residence in the United States. AILA members also represent thousands of U.S. businesses and industries who sponsor highly skilled foreign workers seeking to enter the United States on a temporary or permanent basis. In addition, AILA members represent foreign students, entertainers, athletes, and asylum seekers, often on a pro bono basis. Founded in 1946, AILA is a nonpartisan, not-for-profit organization that provides its members with continuing legal education, publications, information, professional services, and expertise through its 39 chapters and over 40 national committees. AILA is an affiliated organization of the American Bar Association and is represented in the ABA House of Delegates.

American Immigration Lawyers Association

www.aila.org

Chapter 1

FAMILY-BASED IMMIGRATION: IMMEDIATE RELATIVES AND THE PREFERENCE SYSTEM

Family reunification has been the principal policy underlying U.S. immigration law since at least 1965. Family-based immigration allows close relatives of U.S. citizens and lawful permanent residents (LPRs) to immigrate to the United States.[1] Family members immigrate either as "immediate relatives" of U.S. citizens or through the family preference system as relatives of U.S. citizens or LPRs.

Immigrating as Immediate Relatives

Immediate relatives include spouses of U.S. citizens, unmarried minor children of U.S. citizens, and parents of U.S. citizens age 21 or older.[2] The benefit of immigrating as an immediate relative is that there is no cap, or quota, on the number of visas available each year.

Immigrating Under the Family Preference System

The family preference system allows the following family members to immigrate:

- Adult children (unmarried and married) of U.S. citizens;
- Brothers and sisters of U.S. citizens age 21 or older; and
- Spouses and unmarried children (both minor and adult) of LPRs.[3]

A limited number of visas are available every year under the family preference system.

Legal immigration to the United States is controlled by numerical limitations called quotas, which are applied to the family-based category and to the overall number of legal immigrant (permanent resident) visas distributed per country, per year.[4] Backlogs develop because there are more applicants in some countries and categories than there are visas. There are also the non-quota immigrants, such as immediate relatives, who are exempted from the yearly limitations.

---

1 Lawfully admitted for permanent resident means being classified as a lawful permanent resident and being admitted to reside in the United States on a permanent basis. Immigration and Nationality Act (INA) §101(a)(20).

2 INA §201(b)(2)(A)(i).

3 INA §203(a).

4 INA §201(c).

U.S. consulates abroad issue immigrant visas.[5] In addition, U.S. Citizenship and Immigration Services (USCIS) or the Executive Office for Immigration Review may adjust an applicant's status to LPR within the United States.[6] Whether applicants for immigrant visas are eligible to adjust status or must go through the consular process depends on several factors, including whether they made a lawful entry to the United States, whether they violated the terms of their nonimmigrant visa, when they filed the Petition for Alien Relative, and whether they are immigrating as an immediate relative or through the preference system.[7]

In most cases. all citizens or LPRs who wish to petition for a family member must have an income of at least 125 percent of the federal poverty level and must execute a legally enforceable affidavit in which they agree to support their family member. If they have insufficient income, they will have to secure the assistance of a joint sponsor.[8]

Requirements for Family Relationships

Many of the terms used in defining eligibility for a family-based visa are technical and are set forth in the statute and regulations. The following are the most important terms and requirements:

- Petitioner—the family member who is either a U.S. citizen or an LPR.[9] Proof of LPR status is possession of a Form I-551, the Permanent Resident Card, commonly called a "green card." Some family members may self-petition, such as widows/widowers, battered spouses and children of U.S. citizens and LPRs, certain Amerasian children, and special immigrant juveniles.[10]
- Beneficiary—the family member seeking permanent resident status who is related to the U.S. citizen or LPR petitioner.[11] The beneficiary could be a principal (on whose behalf the relative petition is filed) or a derivative (spouse or unmarried child of the principal beneficiary in the preference categories).
- Spouse—the spousal relationship must be legally valid and recognized in the place where the relationship was created.[12] It must not be a sham marriage, i.e., one entered into primarily for immigration purposes. There

5 INA §§221, 222.

6 INA §245.

7 INA §245(a), (i).

8 INA §213A.

9 INA §204(a).

10 8 CFR §204.1(a)(1)–(5).

11 8 CFR §204.1(a).

12 *See Matter of Bautista*, 16 I&N Dec. 602 (BIA 1978).

is a presumption that the marriage is a sham if the couple gets divorced within two years of the noncitizen's obtaining LPR status based on the marriage. In addition, even if the marriage is valid in the foreign country, it must not violate federal or state public policy. Polygamous, incestuous, and proxy marriages (unless later consummated) are not recognized for immigration purposes.[13] Some states recognize common-law marriages. The marriage must be in existence—i.e., not legally terminated—at the time the permanent residency application is adjudicated, although the marriage need not be "viable."[14] If the parties are separated, more proof will be required to demonstrate that the marriage was bona fide at the time it was entered. If the parties married while the beneficiary was in immigration proceedings, they will have to establish through clear and convincing evidence—as opposed to a mere preponderance of the evidence—that the marriage is bona fide.[15]

- Parent—must meet the definition in the statute, Immigration and Nationality Act (INA) §101(b)(2), and may include a stepparent, an adoptive parent, and a parent of a child born out of wedlock (though the applicant may have to establish the "parent-child relationship" by blood tests, evidence of cohabitation, support, and communication).[16]
- Brother or sister—each sibling must show that he or she is the "child" of at least one common parent.[17]
- Child—must meet the definition in the statute, INA §101(b)(1), and must be unmarried and under 21; "son or daughter" refers to children who are 21 or over or who are of any age and married.
  - *Legitimacy*—a child who was born in wedlock.[18] Children born out of wedlock may obtain immigration benefits from the natural mother[19] or from the father if the child was legitimized before age 18 while in the father's custody.[20] Marriage of the natural parents is the most common form of legitimation. Children born out of wedlock may also obtain immigration benefits from the natural father so long as they have established a "bona fide parent-child relationship," i.e., cohabitation and provision of support, before age 21.[21]

---

13 INA §101(a)(35).

14 *See Matter of McKee*, 17 I&N Dec. 332 (BIA 1980).

15 INA §245(e)(3).

16 8 CFR §204.2(c).

17 *See Matter of Mahal*, 12 I&N Dec. 409 (BIA 1967).

18 INA §101(b)(1)(A).

19 INA §101(b)(1)(D).

20 INA §101(b)(1)(C).

21 *See Matter of Vizcaino*, 19 I&N Dec. 644 (BIA 1988).

- *Stepchildren*—eligible to immigrate through stepparent if child was under 18 at the time of the marriage creating the relationship.[22] It is irrelevant whether the stepchild was born in wedlock or out of wedlock. The stepchild relationship may continue even after the natural parent dies or divorces the stepparent, provided the stepparent has maintained active parental interest.[23] Stepchildren who are U.S. citizens age 21 or over may serve as petitioners and immigrate their stepparents to the United States.

- *Adopted children*—eligible to immigrate if adopted before age 16 and have been in the legal custody of, and resided with, the adoptive parent for at least two years.[24] The two years can be counted in the aggregate. The adoption must be legally valid in the jurisdiction where it took place.[25] Natural siblings of the adopted child also are eligible to immigrate if adopted while under 18 by the same adoptive parent.[26] Adoptions are available under the Intercountry Adoption Act of 2000,[27] which the United States enacted to comply with its obligations under the Hague Convention.[28] U.S. citizens seeking to adopt and emigrate a child from one of the convention member countries must satisfy certain requirements.[29] The immigration procedure for an adopted child pursuant to the Hague Convention is covered in chapter 2.

- *Orphans*—a U.S. citizen can sponsor an orphan under age 16 if legal requirements are met under INA §101(b)(1)(F). Both parents must have died, disappeared, or abandoned the child. If there is a sole or surviving parent, he or she must be incapable of providing for the child and irrevocably release the child for emigration or adoption.[30] The child must be under 16 and unmarried at the time the petition is filed on his or her behalf to qualify as an immediate relative. The petitioner must be a U.S. citizen. Natural siblings of the orphan also are eligible to immigrate if adopted abroad while under 18 by the same adoptive parent.

---

22 INA §101(b)(1)(B).

23 *See Matter of Mowrer*, 17 I&N Dec. 613 (BIA 1981).

24 INA §101(b)(1)(E).

25 8 CFR §204.2(d)(2)(vii)(C).

26 INA §101(b)(1)(E).

27 Pub. L. No. 106-279, 114 Stat. 825 (Oct. 6, 2000).

28 Convention on Protection of Children and Cooperation in Respect of Intercountry Adoption, May 29, 1993, S. Treaty Doc. 105-51 (1998), 32 I.L.M. 1139. For in-depth guidance on international adoption issues, see *The International Adoption Sourcebook* (AILA 2008); visit http://agora.aila.org and search "adoption."

29 INA §101(b)(1)(G); 22 CFR §42.24.

30 8 CFR §204.3(d)(1)(iii).

- *Unmarried*—not married at the time the Form I-130, Petition for Alien Relative, was filed, at the time the application for adjustment of status or an immigrant visa was filed, and at the time of admission to the United States as the unmarried son or daughter of a U.S. citizen or LPR, whether or not previously married. If immigrating as the beneficiary of a second-preference petition, the person must be unmarried from the filing of the petition until admission as an LPR. If the beneficiary marries at any time during that period, the petition is automatically revoked.[31]

Immediate Relatives and the Preference System

Immediate Relatives

The term "immediate relative" includes the following family relationships: spouse, child (unmarried, under 21), and parent of a U.S. citizen.[32] In the case of a parent, the U.S. citizen petitioner must be at least 21 years of age. The definition also includes widows or widowers of U.S. citizens who were not legally separated at the time of the spouse's death, filed an application within two years of the death, and did not remarry before acquiring the immigrant status.[33] Immediate relatives immigrate outside the numerical restrictions and thus are not subject to the long waiting period that exists in many of the preference categories. Nevertheless, there is often a backlog at the USCIS service centers that adjudicate the relative petitions and at USCIS district offices that schedule adjustment interviews. This means that even immediate relatives can expect to wait a year or longer to receive their immigrant status.

Preference System

Relatives immigrating through an LPR, as well as some immigrating through a U.S. citizen, are subject to numerical restriction. The following are the family preference categories:

- First: unmarried son or daughter (age 21 or over) of U.S. citizen parent ("F-1");[34]
- Second:
  - Spouses or unmarried children (under 21) of LPR ("F-2A");[35]

---

31 8 CFR §205.1(a)(3)(i)(H), (I).

32 INA §201(b)(2)(A)(i).

33 INA §204.2(b)(2)(A)(i), as amended by FY2010 Department of Homeland Security Appropriations Act, Pub. L. No. 111-83, 123 Stat. 2142, §568(c)(1) (Oct. 28, 2009).

34 INA §203(a)(1).

35 INA §203(a)(2)(A).

- Unmarried sons or daughters age 21 and over of LPR ("F-2B");[36]
- Third: married sons and daughters of U.S. citizens ("F-3");[37]
- Fourth: brothers and sisters of U.S. citizens age 21 or over ("F-4").[38]

Quota System

Congress has placed a limit on the number of foreign-born individuals who are admitted to the United States annually as family-based immigrants: 480,000 persons per year.[39] A formula that imposes a cap on every family-based immigration category, with the exception of "immediate relatives" (spouses, minor unmarried children, and parents of U.S. citizens), governs family-based immigration. The formula allows unused employment-based immigration visas in one year to be dedicated to family-based immigration the following year, and unused family-based immigration visas in one year to be added to the cap the next year. This formula means that there are slight variations from year to year in family-based immigration. Because of the numerical cap, there are long waiting periods to obtain a visa in most of the family-based immigrant preference categories.[40]

There is no numerical cap on the number of immediate relatives admitted annually to the United States as immigrants.[41]

The following are the number of visas available in each of the four family-based preference categories:

- First preference (unmarried sons and daughters of U.S. citizen)—23,400 visas per year, plus any visas left over from the fourth preference;[42]
- Second preference (F-2A) (spouses and minor children of LPR)—87,900 visas per year, plus any visas left over from the first preference;[43]
- Second preference (F-2B) (unmarried adult children of LPR)—26,300 visas per year, plus any visas left over from the first preference;
- Third preference (married adult children of U.S. citizen)—23,400 visas per year, plus any visas left over from the first and second preferences;[44]
- Fourth preference (brothers and sisters of U.S. citizen over 21)—65,000

36 INA §203(a)(2)(B).

37 INA §203(a)(3).

38 INA §203(a)(4).

39 INA §201(c)(1)(A)(i).

40 INA §202(e).

41 INA §201(b).

42 INA §203(a)(1).

43 INA §203(a)(2)(B).

44 INA §203(a)(3).

visas/year, plus any visas left over from the previous preferences.[45]

- The primary source of information on visa availability is the *Visa Bulletin*, available from the U.S. Department of State, Bureau of Consular Affairs, Visa Services, found at https://travel.state.gov/content/travel/en/legal/visa-law0/visa-bulletin.html. A copy of the *Visa Bulletin* for June 2020 is included as Appendix 1.[46]

You will need to become familiar with how to read the *Visa Bulletin* to determine how long a particular visa application will take. You must be familiar with the following concepts:

- *Priority date*—Under the quota system, family-based immigrant visas are distributed on a chronological basis, determined by the date on which the Form I-130, Petition for Alien Relative, was properly filed with USCIS. That filing date becomes the "priority date."[47] To be properly filed, the application must be completed, signed, and submitted with the appropriate filing fee.[48]

  The priority date may or may not be "current," a term indicating that applications filed before that date are not subject to any further wait. If the priority date is not current, it is often risky to estimate how long it will be before the priority date becomes current and a visa or adjustment of status becomes available. Compare the priority date against the date indicated in the section, Application Final Action Dates, in the most recent monthly *Visa Bulletin*, taking into consideration the preference category and the foreign national's country of origin. The priority date must be *before* the date listed under Chart A, Application Final Action Dates, to be considered current. For example, a Mexican LPR who is immigrating his unmarried son in the F-2B visa category will look at the most recent *Visa Bulletin* for that preference category under the column for Mexico. In June 2020, the date on the *Visa Bulletin* for that category and nationality was February 15, 1999. Only applicants whose I-130s were filed before that date are considered current.

  Beginning in October 2015, the Department of State began publishing a separate chart called Chart B, Dates for Filing Family-Sponsored Visa

---

45 INA §203(a)(4).

46 You can request to be sent the *Visa Bulletin* by e-mail; send your request to listserv@calist.state.gov. In the body of the message type "subscribe Visa Office Bulletin," followed by your first name and last name. Alternatively, you may call the State Department for a recording on the status of priority dates, (202) 663-1541, or visit its website at https://travel.state.gov/content/travel/en/legal/visa-law0/visa-bulletin.html. *Visa Bulletins* are also posted to www.aila.org.

47 8 CFR §204.1(c).

48 8 CFR §204.1(d).

Applications, which indicates when a person may file an application for adjustment of status or when the National Visa Center (NVC) can start consular processing. For example, the same son of the Mexican LPR could file for adjustment of status beginning on June 1, 2020, if the priority date was before September 22, 1999, and USCIS permitted use of the Dates for Filing Family-Sponsored Visa Applications for filing purposes. Each month USCIS will indicate whether adjustment-of-status applicants are permitted to use the Dates for Filing Family-Sponsored Visa Applications or whether they must use the Application Final Action Dates.

- *Cross-Chargeability*—If the principal and derivative beneficiaries were born in different countries, it may be possible to apply cross-chargeability principles. Visas are usually chargeable to the country of the principal beneficiary's place of birth.[49] But a basic tenet of family-based immigration is keeping the family intact. If one family member was charged to a country that is oversubscribed, while the other family members in the same preference category were charged to countries that are current, this would result in separation and undue hardship. To remedy this potential problem, the law allows in some situations for the family to elect whichever foreign state is more beneficial. The law seems to limit application of this cross-chargeability, however, to the third– and fourth-preference categories and to situations in which it is necessary to prevent the separation of spouses or separation of children and parents.[50] For example, if a U.S. citizen is petitioning for his married Mexican son, the son and his Guatemalan spouse can elect to have their visas charged to Guatemala, since the third preference for Mexicans is backlogged further than for Guatemalans. Similarly, if a U.S. citizen is sponsoring his Japanese brother, the brother's Filipino wife would elect to be charged to her husband's country of birth.

Derivative Beneficiaries

Family members on whose behalf the I-130 petition is filed are considered "principal beneficiaries." If they are being petitioned for in one of the preference categories and have minor, unmarried children or a spouse, those family members also may qualify to immigrate as "derivative beneficiaries."[51] In other words, a derivative beneficiary is the spouse or unmarried child of a principal beneficiary in the preference category.[52]

---

49 INA §202(b).

50 22 CFR §42.12.

51 INA §203(d).

52 9 *Foreign Affairs Manual* (FAM) 502.2-3(C).

Derivative beneficiaries, by definition, do not have separate Form I-130 petitions filed on their behalf. In fact, except for the F-2A preference category, they do not qualify to have a separate Form I-130 filed on their behalf. If the family member is immigrating as an immediate relative, he or she must have a separate Form I-130 petition on file.[53]

Derivative family members are accorded the same preference status as the principal beneficiary. These derivatives may either accompany the principal beneficiary or "follow-to-join," which means immigrate more than six months after the principal beneficiary.[54]

Retention of Priority Dates

A lot can happen between the time the petitioner files an I-130 petition and the beneficiary adjusts status or immigrates. For example, the beneficiary might marry, divorce, turn 21, or die. In addition, the petitioner might divorce, naturalize, lose LPR status, or die. There also might be after-acquired children to consider. Similar events could happen in the lives of the derivative beneficiaries. When a new Form I-130 needs to be filed, sometimes the beneficiary can retain the original priority date. Let us review the effects in all these situations.

General Principles. The basic principle is that one can retain an earlier priority date if the same petitioner is filing for the same beneficiary in the same preference category and the prior I-130 petition was not terminated or revoked.[55] If the Form I-130 was lost by the agency and the petitioner needs to refile, he or should be able to retain the priority date from the original petition.

Marriage. If the beneficiary is an immediate relative, marrying will convert him or her to the third-preference category.[56] If the beneficiary is already over 21 and started out in the first-preference category, then he or she also converts to the third preference.[57] There is no need to file a new Form I-130; simply notify the appropriate USCIS service center, the National Visa Center (NVC), or the consulate of the automatic conversion to third preference. The priority date for the third-preference visa petition would remain the same since no separate petition was filed.[58]

This conversion to third preference does not occur if the beneficiary is in the second-preference category. The child/son/daughter of an LPR cannot marry without automatically revoking the I-130 petition. If a second-preference category (F-2A or

53 8 CFR §204.2(a)(4).

54 22 CFR §40.1(a)(1).

55 8 CFR §204.2(h)(2).

56 8 CFR §204.2(i)(1)(ii).

57 8 CFR §204.2(i)(1)(i).

58 8 CFR §204.2(i)(1)(i), (ii).

F-2B) beneficiary marries before immigrating or adjusting status, the I-130 petition is revoked.[59]

Divorce. Divorce tends to work the opposite way from marriage. The third-preference beneficiary converts to the immediate-relative category (if under 21) or the first preference (if 21 or over).[60] Again, there is no need to file a new Form I-130, and the priority date remains the same. Inform the appropriate USCIS service center, the NVC, or the consulate of the automatic conversion from third to first preference or immediate-relative and enclose proof of termination of the marriage.

If the second-preference beneficiary divorces, he or she cannot regain the status of an F-2A or F-2B preference holder because the Form I-130 was automatically revoked. The LPR petitioner must file a new Form I-130 and cannot retain the earlier priority date. If the beneficiary obtains an annulment, however, that might serve to reinstate the second-preference status. Courts have determined that an annulment serves to void the marriage *ab initio*.

If the U.S. citizen or LPR petitioner is the one to divorce after filing a Form I-130 petition for a spouse, the petition is automatically revoked.[61] If the petitioner had filed a Form I-130 for a stepchild based on that marriage, in most cases the divorce severs the relationship and the I-130 petition is revoked. But those stepchildren who can establish an ongoing relationship with the stepparent may be able to proceed with their petition.[62] Divorce between the principal beneficiary and the derivative spouse in the third– or fourth-preference category terminates the derivative status of the spouse.

Naturalization. When the LPR petitioner naturalizes, principal beneficiaries under 21 convert from the F-2A category to the immediate-relative category. If the beneficiary is already 21 or older and in the F-2B category, he or she would convert to the first preference. There is no need to file a new Form I-130; the priority date remains the same.[63] Inform the appropriate USCIS service center, the NVC, or the consulate of the automatic conversion from second preference to first preference or to immediate relative and enclose a copy of the naturalization certificate.

The F-2B category is sometimes more favorable than the first-preference category, particularly for Mexico and the Philippines. Fortunately, the Child Status Protection Act (CSPA)[64] neutralizes any negative effect that the petitioner's naturalizing might

59 8 CFR §205.1(a)(3)(i)(I).

60 8 CFR §204.2(i)(1)(iii).

61 8 CFR §205.1(a)(3)(i)(D).

62 *Medina-Morales v. Ashcroft*, 371 F.3d 520, 531–32 (9th Cir. 2004).

63 8 CFR §204.2(i)(3).

64 Child Status Protection Act (CSPA), Pub. L. No. 107-208, 116 Stat. 927 (2002). For in-depth guidance on the CSPA, see *AILA's Focus on the Child Status Protection Act* (2014); visit http://agora.aila.org and search "CSPA."

have on these F-2B sons and daughters by allowing them to opt out of the automatic conversion to the first preference. The effect of naturalization on the beneficiary is covered in greater detail in the section below on CSPA.

Second-preference (F-2A) beneficiaries under 21 when the petitioner naturalizes are not allowed to opt out of this conversion to the immediate-relative category. This could work a hardship if the beneficiary has derivative children. When the principal beneficiary converts to the immediate-relative category, he or she will not be able to include those children as derivatives.[65]

Derivative beneficiaries who are the children of the LPR petitioner in the F-2A category are affected. When the petitioner naturalizes, they will lose derivative status and will be required to have a separate I-130 petition filed on their behalf. When the newly naturalized U.S. citizen petitioner files this separate I130 petition for the unmarried child, the beneficiary should be able to retain the original priority date.[66] This is usually irrelevant because, as an immediate relative, the beneficiary is not subject to any annual quotas and the CSPA freezes the beneficiary's age.[67] But if the beneficiary marries before obtaining LPR status, the earlier priority date might prove helpful. Request the original priority date in the cover letter for the second Form I-130, cite the regulatory authority, and include proof of filing the original Form I-130.

Death of the Petitioner. Death of the petitioner automatically revokes the Form I-130.[68] But there is possible relief for widows and widowers of U.S. citizens who have not remarried and who file a Form I-360, Petition for Amerasian, Widow(er), or Special Immigrant, within two years of the citizen spouse's death. The widow or widower adjusts or immigrates as an immediate relative, and unmarried children under 21 are classified as derivative beneficiaries. The process for self-petitioning as a widow or widower is covered in more detail in chapter 5.

In addition to the spouses of U.S. citizens, other surviving family members may continue to receive immigration benefits from a pending or approved Form I-130 after the petitioner has died.[69] If INA §204(*l*) applies, it acts to nullify the petitioner's or the principal beneficiary's death. Those who cannot satisfy the requirements of section 204(*l*) may qualify for "humanitarian reinstatement." These are discussed in greater detail in chapter 2.

---

65 9 FAM 502.2-3(C).

66 8 CFR §204.2(i)(3).

67 INA §201(f).

68 INA §201(b)(2)(A)(i), as amended by FY2010 Department of Homeland Security Appropriations Act, Pub. L. No. 111-83, 123 Stat. 2142, §568(c)(1), (Oct. 28, 2009).

69 INA §204(*l*), as amended by FY2010 Department of Homeland Security Appropriations Act, Pub. L. No. 111-83, 123 Stat. 2142, §568(d)(1), (Oct. 28, 2009).

Death of the spouse/parent usually terminates the stepparent–stepchild petition, except when the parties establish an ongoing relationship.

Age-Out. The CSPA has addressed the age-out problem for many beneficiaries. This will be explained in greater detail later in this chapter. But prior to the CSPA, turning 21 meant (and for those few who cannot take advantage of the law, still means) one of the following: (1) converting from the immediate-relative to the first-preference category; (2) converting from F-2A to F-2B; or (3) converting from derivative beneficiary and possibly losing status (derivatives in the F-2A preference category still convert to F-2B). It is important to remember that if the CSPA is found not to apply—for example, if the child fails to comply with the one-year filing requirement—the rules prior to the CSPA will apply.

Prior to the CSPA, children who were under 21 at the time the Form I-130 was filed on their behalf by a U.S. citizen parent automatically converted from immediate relative to the first-preference category upon turning 21.[70]

Prior to the CSPA, children who were under 21 at the time the Form I-130 was filed on their behalf by an LPR parent automatically converted from the F-2A category to the F-2B category upon turning 21.[71] Derivative beneficiaries in the second-preference category automatically lost their derivative status when they turned 21. But if they were the unmarried children of an LPR parent, they were able to convert from the F-2A to the F-2B category when the LPR petitioner filed a separate Form I-130 on their behalf. Fortunately, they were also able to retain the original priority date.[72] However, if they were the children of a principal beneficiary who was the unmarried child of an LPR, they lost their derivative status upon turning 21. That is because the LPR petitioner cannot petition for his or her grandchildren.

Derivatives in other preference categories also lost their derivative status when they turned 21. Unlike the children of LPRs, who converted automatically from the F-2A to the F-2B category, these sons and daughters did not automatically convert to another category upon turning 21. They had to start over again after their parent immigrated or adjusted status. The LPR parent then filed a new I-130 petition on their behalf. Prior to the CSPA—and even according to current USCIS interpretation after implementation of the law—these former derivative beneficiaries did not retain the original priority date.

Pre-1977 Western Hemisphere Priority Dates. When Congress changed the immigration law at the end of 1976 that established the current family-based preference categories for Western Hemisphere immigrants (North America, Central America, South America, and adjacent islands), it allowed pending applicants—

70 8 CFR §204.2(i)(2).

71 9 FAM 503.3-3(B)(2).

72 8 CFR §204.2(a)(4).

called registrants—to use their old, unused priority dates.[73] It also allowed any derivative beneficiaries in existence on the date of original filing (registering) to use their unused priority dates for later applications. Derivatives include spouses and unmarried children under 21 on the date of original filing, as well as children born later from a marriage that existed on that date. This means that children born after January 1, 1977, can still qualify as derivatives if their parents were married and had filed (registered) before that date. The savings clause in the 1976 amendment allows the beneficiaries and derivatives to use the original date of filing (registering) for later Form I-130 applications. Once established, the priority date is retained by the derivatives, even if they subsequently marry or turn 21. The priority date can be used in conjunction with any properly approved visa petition filed on behalf of the applicant.

The Child Status Protection Act

The CSPA went into effect on August 6, 2002. Since that date, USCIS and the Department of State (DOS) have together issued more than a dozen memoranda interpreting the statute and providing information on how they interpret it. The CSPA helps many unmarried children of U.S. citizens immigrate faster than they would have under the prior law. It provides a more limited form of relief for the unmarried children of LPRs and derivatives in the preference categories.

Children of U.S. Citizens

The children of U.S. citizens can preserve the status they held when their parent filed the I-130 petition. If they were immediate relatives on that date—unmarried and under 21—they will still be considered immediate relatives should they turn 21 before they obtain permanent residency.[74] In other words, they will never "age out." Under the prior law, they would have automatically moved into the first-preference category upon turning 21. The CSPA does not change their status, however, should they marry before immigrating. In that case, the son or daughter still converts to the third-preference category.[75]

The children of LPR parents who naturalize also can to take advantage of the CSPA. If the children are unmarried and under 21 on the date of the petitioning parent's naturalization (i.e., they are direct beneficiaries in the second-preference F-2A category), they then convert to immediate-relative status. They preserve that status if they subsequently turn 21 before immigrating.[76] Some LPR petitioners filed only one Form I-130 for their spouse with the intention that their children would

---

73 Immigration and Nationality Act Amendments of 1976, Pub. L. No. 94-571, 90 Stat. 2703; 9 FAM 503.3-4(A).

74 INA §201(f)(1).

75 8 CFR §204.2(i)(1)(ii).

76 INA §201(f)(2).

immigrate as derivatives. Keep in mind that when these parents naturalize, they will need to file a separate I130 petition for each child, because the children will lose their derivative status.[77] The current USCIS position is that these children will need a separate Form I-130 on file before they turn 21 to preserve their immediate-relative status.

The married children of U.S. citizens (i.e., direct beneficiaries in the third-preference category) also benefit from the CSPA. If they divorce before turning 21, they convert to immediate-relative status. They will preserve that status even if they turn 21 before immigrating, since it is their age at the time of the termination of the marriage that controls.[78] If they divorce after turning 21, the CSPA does not affect their status—they would still convert to the first-preference category.

Children of LPRs and Derivatives

The CSPA provides a different form of relief to children of LPR parents who do not naturalize, and to derivative children in the preference categories. Children in the second-preference category previously would have converted from the F-2A to the F-2B category upon turning 21. Derivative children in the family-preference categories previously would have lost their derivative status upon turning 21. But under the CSPA, their age for purposes of determining their preference category and derivative status will be reduced by the period of time the I-130 petition was pending.[79] In other words, look at the biological age of the second-preference child, son, or daughter at the time the F-2A preference category becomes current for the priority date. If they are over 21, they still might qualify, depending on how long their I-130 petition was pending.

For example, take the case of an LPR who files a Form I-130 for his son. If USCIS took one year to approve the I-130 petition, subtract that period from the son's biological age (or add that period to the son's date of birth) to arrive at his "adjusted age." Use the son's adjusted age on the date the second-preference F-2A category becomes current to determine if he is under 21. If he is under 21, he will be considered in the F-2A category (even though his biological age is over 21) and he will retain that status, assuming he does not marry.

Such children will preserve their F-2A status provided they seek to acquire lawful permanent resident status within one year of visa availability.[80] USCIS has defined

77 8 CFR §204.2(a)(4).

78 INA §201(f)(3).

79 INA §203(h)(1).

80 INA §203(h)(1)(A).

that to mean filing for adjustment of status.[81] DOS has defined it to include: (1) submitting a completed Form DS-260, Application for Immigrant Visa and Alien Registration; (2) paying the immigrant visa fee; (3) paying the affidavit of support fee; or (4) filing a Form I-824, Application for Action on an Approved Application or Petition.[82] This latter form is most commonly used by principal beneficiaries who adjusted status but have derivative family members who will be consular processing. In a published decision, the Board of Immigration Appeals (BIA) has found that an applicant may satisfy the "sought to acquire" requirement by filing one of the forms, paying the filing fees, or by establishing "extraordinary circumstances" that prevented filing within the one-year window. Such circumstances might include retaining an immigration attorney and completing the application within the one-year period, but then having the attorney unnecessarily delay the filing.[83]

USCIS issued a memo on the issue of what might constitute "extraordinary circumstances" for failing to satisfy the one-year filing requirement.[84] The memo states the general rule that the child must demonstrate: (1) that the circumstances were not created by him or her through his or her actions; (2) the circumstances were directly related to the child's failure to make a timely filing; and (3) the delay was reasonable under the circumstances. The memo then lists examples of "extraordinary circumstances" during the one-year period that may warrant a favorable exercise of discretion: serious illness or mental or physical disability; legal disability (mental impairment); ineffective assistance of counsel; timely filing that was rejected by the USCIS, corrected, and returned within reasonable time; and death or serious illness/incapacity of the applicant's representative or a member of the applicant's immediate family.

The same age-adjusting principle applies for derivative beneficiaries.[85] Look at the date that the principal beneficiary's priority date becomes current. If the derivative beneficiary is under 21 using his or her adjusted age, then he or she retains derivative status, even if he or she subsequently turns 21.

For example, take the case of a U.S. citizen who files a third-preference petition for his married son. The son's wife and minor daughter are derivatives. When the

---

81 INS Memorandum, J. Williams, *The Child Status Protection Act—Memorandum Number 2* (Feb. 14, 2003), AILA Doc. No. 03031040, *replaced by* USCIS Memorandum, D. Neufeld, *Revised Guidance for the Child Status Protection Act (CSPA)* (May 6, 2008), AILA Doc. No. 08050669.

82 Child Status Protection Act of 2002: ALDAC #2, State 015049 (Jan. 2003), AILA Doc. No. 03020550.

83 *Matter of O. Vasquez*, 25 I&N Dec. 817 (BIA 2012).

84 USCIS Memorandum, *Guidance on Evaluating Claims of "Extraordinary Circumstances" for Late Filings When the Applicant Must Have Sought to Acquire Lawful Permanent Residence Within 1 Year of Visa Availability Pursuant to the Child Status Protection Act* (Apr. 15, 2015), AILA Doc. No. 15073010; Minutes from Visa Office Attendance at IIUSA 2015 EB-5 Regional Economic Advocacy Conference, AILA Doc. No. 15041466.

85 INA §203(h)(2)(B).

daughter turns 21, she loses derivative status, and the only way for her to immigrate is through a separate petition filed by her father or mother after they immigrate. But use the derivative child's adjusted age (biological age minus the time the I-130 petition was pending) on the date the third-preference visa became current to determine if the child retains derivative status. To preserve derivative status, the child must seek to adjust status or consular process within one year.

To determine the adjusted age, it will be necessary to know the priority date and the date on the Form I-797 approval notice. It also will be necessary to know when the F-2A category—or other family– or employment-preference category for derivatives—first became current for the specific priority date using Chart A, Final Action Dates. The date that a visa number becomes available is the first day of the month in which the *Visa Bulletin* indicates availability of a visa for that preference category.[86]

The CSPA codifies prior policy when a beneficiary ages out from the F-2A into the F-2B category. It now formally states that "the alien's petition shall automatically be converted to the appropriate category and the alien shall retain the original priority date issued upon receipt of the original petition."[87] The USCIS interpretation, which was upheld by the BIA[88] and the U.S. Supreme Court,[89] is that this provision applies only to second-preference F-2A derivatives who age out and thus convert automatically to the F-2B category. Other derivatives who age out, for example in the third or fourth preference, would need to be petitioned for by one of their parents once the parent has obtained LPR status. That petition would be in the F-2B category and the son or daughter would not retain the earlier priority date for the petition filed on behalf of their parent.

The agency has issued instructions clarifying that when a derivative beneficiary in the F-2A category ages out before the priority date becomes current, he or she automatically converts to the F-2B category and no second petition needs to be filed.[90] When the priority date in the F-2B category becomes current, the beneficiary can proceed to file for adjustment of status or an immigrant visa. Should the LPR petitioner elect to file a second I-130 petition for the son or daughter in the F-2B

---

86 *Visa Bulletins* dating back to February 1995 can be accessed at https://travel.state.gov/content/travel/en/legal/visa-law0/visa-bulletin.html.

87 INA §203(h)(3).

88 *Matter of Wang*, 25 I&N Dec. 28 (BIA 2009).

89 *Scialabba v. Osorio*, 573 U.S. 41 (2014).

90 Updated Guidance to USCIS Offices on Handling Certain Family-Based Automatic Conversion and Priority Date Retention Requests Following the Supreme Court Ruling in *Scialabba v. Cuellar de Osorio*, AILA Doc. No. 15063009; Guidance to USCIS Offices on Handling Certain Family-Based Automatic Conversion and Priority Date Retention Requests Pending a Supreme Court Ruling on *Mayorkas v. Cuellar de Osorio*," AILA Doc. No. 13112251.

category, he or she will retain the original priority date for the first petition.[91] This is true even if the petitioner has naturalized and the second petition is being filed in the F-1 category.

Relief for F-2B Beneficiaries When the Petitioner Naturalizes

The first-preference category is often backlogged further than the second-preference F-2B category. Therefore, when the petitioning parents naturalize, and the sons and daughters over 21 converted from F-2B to first preference, they actually extend the time they need to wait for their visa to become current. The CSPA eliminates this disparity and penalty by allowing these beneficiaries to elect whether they want to convert automatically to the first preference or opt out and stay in the F-2B category.[92] Applicants for adjustment of status "should file a request in writing with the District Office having jurisdiction over the beneficiary's residence."[93] For those residing in the United States, that will be the local district office. For those who will be consular processing, DOS advises them to seek opt-out from the USCIS by emailing the agency at opt-out@uscis.dhs.gov. USCIS will then send an automatic reply approving the request. The applicant should use that automatic reply to notify NVC that the opt-out request has been approved.[94]

Relief for Some F-2A Beneficiaries Over 21 When the Petitioner Naturalizes

The Ninth Circuit has held that children who were over 21 using their biological age but under 21 using their adjusted age could still convert to the immediate relative category when their petitioning parent naturalizes.[95] The case turned on the interpretation of INA §201(f)(2), which states that the child's eligibility for immediate relative status is determined by "the age of the alien on the date of the parent's naturalization." The Ninth Circuit applied traditional rules of statutory construction and found that "age" does not mean biological age but rather "statutory age," which is the adjusted age after applying the CSPA formula for those in the F-2A category.

---

91 8 CFR §204.2(a)(4).

92 INA §204(k).

93 USCIS Memorandum, D. Neufeld, *Revised Guidance for the Child Status Protection Act (CSPA)* (May 6, 2008), AILA Doc. No. 08050669.

94 The automatic response currently reads: "United States Citizenship and Immigration Services received a request from the beneficiary of the referenced petition to "opt-out" of automatic conversion from classification under section 203(a)(2)(B) of the Immigration and Nationality Act (the Act) to classification under section 203(a)(1) of the Act pursuant to section 204(k)(2) of the Act. The request for "opt-out" is hereby granted and the above referenced beneficiary will remain classified as the unmarried son or daughter of a lawful permanent resident, as though the petitioning parent did not naturalize."

95 *Tovar v. Sessions*, No. 14-73376 (9th Cir. Feb. 14, 2018).

This holding conflicts to a large extent with a prior decision from the BIA, *Matter of Zamora-Molina*,[96] which held that children in those situations could not convert to the immediate relative category, even if they were under 21 using their CSPA age. The BIA based that on CSPA §2,[97] which only allows conversion to the immediate relative category if the child was under 21 using his or her biological age.

The question before the BIA in the *Zamora-Molina* was not whether children in that situation could convert to the immediate-relative category when the petitioner naturalizes. It was whether they would be able to opt out of automatic conversion to the F-1 category and remain in the F-2A category, given that the F-2 category is preferable to the F-1 for all nationalities. The BIA held that while CSPA §6 allows children in the F-2B category to opt out of conversion to the F-1 category, this same protection is not extended to children over 21 but still in the F-2A category.

Effective Date

At the time of passage, the CSPA potentially affected thousands of cases pending before USCIS and DOS. Section 8 of the CSPA states unequivocally that the new law applies to I-130 petitions, adjustment of status applications, and immigrant visa applications pending before the agencies on August 6, 2002. It also applies to I-130 petitions approved before August 6, 2002, provided no final determination had been made on the subsequent adjustment or immigrant visa application. USCIS and DOS originally took the position that the CSPA required the filing of an application for adjustment of status or an immigrant visa prior to August 6, 2002, for those children who had approved I-130 petitions but who turned 21 before August 6, 2002. In other words, the agencies' position was that if such children did not have an application or petition pending on that date, the CSPA did not apply. But after a precedent BIA decision held that the CSPA applied retroactively,[98] the agencies reversed their prior positions.[99] Now, according to the agencies, as long as the child had not received a final denial on an application by August 6, 2002, the CSPA principles will apply.

Authority

Statutes

The following statutory cites provide legal authority for the issues discussed above:

- INA §201—the immigrant-visa selection system
- INA §202—numerical limitations and distribution of second-preference

96 25 I&N Dec. 606 (BIA 2011).

97 INA §201(f)(2).

98 *Matter of Avila-Perez*, 24 I&N Dec. 78 (BIA 2007).

99 USCIS Memorandum, D. Neufeld, *Revised Guidance for the Child Status Protection Act (CSPA)* (May 6, 2008), AILA Doc. No. 08050669.

visas

- INA §203—family-based preferences and order of consideration

Regulations

The following regulatory citations provide legal authority for the issues discussed above:

- 8 CFR §204.1—substantive basis for immediate-relative and family-preference petitions; evidentiary and documentary requirements
- 8 CFR §204.2—elements to be proven and the documentation to be submitted to establish each type of family relationship
- 22 CFR §40.1—definition of terms
- 22 CFR Part 42—documentary requirements

Agency Guidelines

The following guidelines provide additional authority for the issues discussed above:

- *USCIS Policy Manual*—a comprehensive "how to" manual detailing policies and procedures for all aspects of the adjudications program. USCIS employees follow these detailed procedures and the agency's interpretation of the law when adjudicating petitions and applications. It is currently accessible on the USCIS website at www.uscis.gov/policy-manual and through AILALink. The predecessor to the *Policy Manual* is the *Adjudicator's Field Manual* (AFM). Much of the AFM's content has been superseded by the *Policy Manual*, and the provisions that have not been superseded have been appended to the *Policy Manual* pending their ultimate incorporation.
- *Foreign Affairs Manual* (FAM)—provides guidance and interpretation of regulations for DOS officials. The FAM defines qualifying relationships, provides guidelines regarding immigrant visas, and availability of foreign documents. The portions relating to immigrant visas are located in volume 9.[100]

---

[100] Volume 9 of the FAM is available at https://fam.state.gov/Fam/FAM.aspx?ID=09FAM. FAM volumes 7 and 9 are also available on AILALink.

Chapter 2

OVERVIEW OF THE APPLICATION PROCESS FOR PERMANENT RESIDENCE

An application for lawful permanent resident (LPR) status for a foreign national usually begins with the filing of Form I-130, Petition for Alien Relative, and supporting documentation with U.S. Citizenship and Immigration Services (USCIS). There may be as many as five steps: filing the petition, a marriage interview (if the petition is marriage based), an application for adjustment of status or an immigrant visa, the adjustment or immigrant visa interview, and inspection and admission by U.S. Customs and Border Protection (CBP). The rules that implement the Intercountry Adoption Act of 2000[1] also apply if the petitioner is applying on behalf of an adopted child.[2]

General Filing Considerations

Applicants for family-based immigration benefits—including employment authorization, advance parole, adjustment of status, and approval of the Petition for Alien Relative—used to face little risk of deportation if the petition or application were denied and they were unlawfully present. On June 28, 2018, USCIS announced a new policy about when the agency would issue a Notice to Appear (NTA) or refer a case to Immigration and Customs Enforcement (ICE) for potential initiation of removal proceedings.[3] According to the memo, if an application or petition is denied and the applicant or beneficiary is not lawfully present, USCIS will issue an NTA. If the applicant is lawfully present but subject to removal, and the application or petition is denied, USCIS will issue an NTA if the applicant falls into a specific enforcement category. Also, USCIS may refer a case to ICE before adjudicating the application or petition if the agency suspects fraud or the applicant has certain criminal history.

Incremental implementation of the policy began in the fall of 2018 and it is currently in effect with respect to the following "status-impacting" applications: I-914/914A, I-918/918A, I-929, I-360, I-485, I-539, and I-730. Because of the major impact of an application denial on persons who are removable, practitioners should conduct a careful case assessment at the initiation of representation and provide the client

1 Pub. L. No. 106-279, 114 Stat. 825 (Oct. 6, 2000).

2 Convention on Protection of Children and Cooperation in Respect of Intercountry Adoption, May 29, 1993, S. Treaty Doc. 105-51 (1998), 32 I.L.M. 1139, was enacted to comply with obligations under the Hague Convention. For in-depth guidance on international adoption issues, see *The International Adoption Sourcebook* (AILA 2008), available at http://agora.aila.org.

3 USCIS Memorandum, *Updated Guidance for the Referral of Cases and Issuance of Notices to Appear (NTAs) in Cases Involving Inadmissible and Deportable Aliens* (June 28, 2018), AILA Doc. No. 18070540.

with information about risks and benefits so that the client can make an informed decision. A sample consent form discussing these possible risks is included as Appendix 3.

The other significant change in the adjudication process was a memo issued by USCIS on July 13, 2018, which expands adjudicators' discretion to deny an immigration application, petition, or request without first issuing a Request for Evidence (RFE) or a Notice of Intent to Deny (NOID) pursuant to 8 CFR §103.2(b)(8).[4] USCIS officials may now issue a denial without sending an RFE or NOID in cases where the evidence initially submitted fails to establish eligibility for the benefit. The memo provides two examples: waiver applications submitted with little or no supporting evidence, and cases in which the statute, regulation, or form instructions require a particular document be submitted at the time of filing, but the document is not included. An example of the latter would be when a family-based adjustment application that requires an I-864, Affidavit of Support under Section 213A of the INA, was filed without one.

However, the memo does note that certain regulations or form instructions may specifically allow filing without all required initial evidence or may limit the authority of USCIS to deny the application based solely on the submission of limited evidence. While the memo does not provide specific examples, one instance might be the instructions for Form I-485, Application to Register Permanent Residence or Adjust Status, which provide that adjustment applicants are not required to submit the Form I-693, Report of Medical Examination and Vaccination Record, at the time of filing due to its time-limited validity.[5]

In addition, USCIS will continue its practice of "statutory denials," i.e., denying a case without an RFE or NOID, when there is no legal basis for the benefit sought or the relevant program has been terminated. The memo cites two examples of justified statutory denials: a waiver application that requires showing extreme hardship to a qualifying relative where the applicant is claiming hardship to a nonqualifying relative; and a family-based visa petition filed for a relative who does not fall into a relationship authorized by statute.

First Step: Filing the Petition for Alien Relative (Form I-130)

Form I-130 and its supporting documentation are used to establish that the petitioner is a U.S. citizen, an LPR, or a U.S. national, and that the claimed relationship to the foreign-national beneficiary is a legally qualifying one.[6] When USCIS adjudicates the petition, it must verify the status of the petitioner and the validity of the

---

4 USCIS Memorandum, Issuance of Certain RFEs and NOIDs; Revisions to Adjudicator's Field Manual (AFM) Chapter 10.5(a), Chapter 10.5(b) (July 13, 2018), AILA Doc. No. 18071377.

5 Form I-485 Instructions, 15 (10/15/19).

6 8 CFR §204.1(a)(1).

relationship. At this stage, the agency is not screening for potential inadmissibility or eligibility for adjustment of status. Inadmissibility is assessed at the second stage of the process, adjustment of status or consular processing. For purposes of completing the Form I-130, the petitioner, or, more precisely, the "you" indicated in the form, is the U.S. citizen, LPR, or U.S. national who is petitioning for the foreign national relative. The intending immigrant is the "beneficiary."

Who May File a Form I-130 Petition?

As was explained in chapter 1, "immediate relatives" are defined as the spouse, parents, and unmarried children (under age 21) of U.S. citizens.[7] All other qualifying relationships fall within the preference categories.[8] These include the siblings, unmarried sons and daughters (over age 21), and married children or sons and daughters of U.S. citizens. They also include the spouses and unmarried children or sons and daughters of an LPR.

Different rules apply for family dependents, or "derivative beneficiaries." These include the spouse and unmarried children under 21 of the principal beneficiary in the preference categories. In these cases, the derivative beneficiaries may immigrate without the need to file a separate Form I-130 petition, provided they have that relationship at the time the principal beneficiary immigrates and at the time that they immigrate.[9] Derivative relationships include the spouses of the principal beneficiary immigrating through the third– and fourth-preference categories. Unmarried children under 21 may immigrate as derivatives of the principal beneficiary in the first–, second–, third–, and fourth-preference categories.

In most cases, the petitioner is not able to file a separate I-130 petition on the derivative's behalf. For example, a U.S. citizen may not file a separate I-130 petition for the spouse and children of a married son or daughter in the third-preference category or the spouse and children of a sibling in the fourth-preference category. Only when an LPR is petitioning for his or her spouse does he or she have the option of including the unmarried children under 21 as derivatives or filing a separate petition on their behalf.

The derivative beneficiaries will need to file separate applications for adjustment of status or an immigrant visa. They will be considered "accompanying" the principal beneficiary if they immigrate or adjust concurrently or within six months; they will be "following-to-join" if they immigrate more than six months later.[10]

Petitioners seeking to sponsor immediate relatives must file a separate I-130 petition for each family member, because immediate relatives cannot immigrate

7 INA §201(b)(2)(A)(i).

8 INA §203(a).

9 8 CFR §204.2(d)(4).

10 22 CFR §40.1(a)(1).

with derivatives.[11] For example, if a U.S. citizen is seeking to sponsor a spouse and stepchild, he or she must file a separate Form I-130 for each person and pay separate filing fees. Similarly, if a U.S. citizen child over age 21 is petitioning for his or her parent, the parent's spouse or unmarried child may not immigrate as derivatives, because the parent is an immediate relative. In that case, the U.S. citizen must file a separate I-130 petition for the stepparent and for the sibling. If the spouse of the parent does not qualify as a stepparent, or the child of the parent as a sibling, they will have to wait until the parent—the principal beneficiary—immigrates. That parent, once an LPR, then may file a second-preference petition for the spouse and child.

Who Files Form I-130A?

If the I-130 petition is based on a spousal relationship, the beneficiary must complete a Form I-130A, Supplemental Information for Spouse Beneficiary. The I-130A is used to collect background information on the beneficiary, such as address and employment history for the last five years, last physical address outside the United States, and parental information. If a spouse is overseas, the Form I-130A must still be completed, but the spouse abroad does not need to sign the form.

Completing the Form I-130

Note: These instructions refer to the version of the form dated February 13, 2019.

Part 1

The form is completed by the U.S. citizen, U.S. national, or LPR. The first questions ask for the petitioner's relationship to the sponsored relative. If the petition is based on a parent-child relationship, the petitioner must select the option that describes the nature of the parent-child relationship. Additional questions relate to adoption including whether the petitioner gained status through adoption. The qualifying relationships, including those for adopted children, are set forth in chapter 1.

Part 2

The next part, Part 2, asks for basic information regarding the petitioner: alien registration number (if any), USCIS online account number (if any), Social Security number, full name, other names used, place and date of birth, gender, mailing and physical address. Include only Social Security numbers obtained lawfully by the petitioner from the Social Security Administration, not fictitious or "borrowed" ones. Type the petitioner's last name in capital letters. Information regarding place and date of birth should be taken from the birth certificate or passport. Be sure to include all other names used by the petitioner, including aliases and maiden names.

---

11 8 CFR §204.2(a)(4).

Give the petitioner's current mailing address and indicate whether it is the same as the physical address. If the petitioner resides abroad, in certain specified countries, he or she may file the petition with the USCIS office abroad.[12] Be aware, however, that the petitioner eventually must complete an affidavit of support, which requires that he or she be domiciled in the United States.[13] Provide the petitioner's physical addresses for the last five years, whether inside or outside the United States, and the dates he or she resided at each.

This part of the form also asks about the petitioner's marital status and history. Indicate how many times the petitioner has been married and current marital status. If the petitioner is currently married, use the marriage certificate to complete the sections on date and place of present marriage. Provide the name of the current spouse and all prior spouses (if any) and the dates on which the marriages ended. Note that if the petitioner is an LPR who obtained such status through marriage, and the petitioner is seeking second-preference classification for a foreign national spouse, certain requirements must be met.[14] Either five years must have elapsed since the date the petitioner acquired LPR status,[15] or the petitioner must establish through clear and convincing evidence that the prior marriage was not entered into for purposes of evading the immigration laws.[16] Alternatively, the prior marriage must have ended through the death of the petitioner's former spouse.[17] If five years have elapsed since the date on which the petitioner acquired legal residency, USCIS cannot use the "clear and convincing" evidence standard to deny a petition filed on behalf of petitioner's new spouse.[18]

In Part 2, the petitioner also must provide information about his or her parents. Provide the full name, date of birth, gender, country of birth, and place of residence for each parent.

The petitioner must select whether he or she is a U.S. citizen or lawful permanent resident and, if a citizen, how citizenship was obtained. For U.S. citizens who have a certificate of naturalization or citizenship, use information from the certificate to complete the information on the certificate: number, place of issuance and date of issuance. If the petitioner is an LPR, indicate the class of admission such as IR1 for spouse of a U.S. citizen or F21 for the spouse of an LPR. The class of admission can be found on the front of the I-551 permanent resident card. The date of admission is the date of adjustment of status or admission to the United States on

12 8 CFR §204.1(e)(2).

13 INA §213A(f)(1)(C).

14 INA §204(a)(2)(A).

15 INA §204(a)(2)(A)(i).

16 INA §204(a)(2)(A)(ii).

17 INA §204(a)(2)(B).

18 *Matter of Pazandeh*, 19 I&N Dec. 884 (BIA 1988).

an immigrant visa issued by a U.S. consulate. The place of admission is the place where adjustment was granted or where entry into the United States occurred.

The final section of Part 2 asks for the petitioner's employment history for the last five years, whether inside or outside the United States. Provide current employment first and include the name of the employer, address, occupation and dates of employment. If unemployed or retired, type or print "Unemployed" or "Retired" in the box for "Name of Employer/Company."

Part 3

Part 3 asks for biographic information on the petitioner. The petitioner must select his or her ethnicity, race, eye and hair color, and provide height and weight. This information will be used when USCIS conducts background checks on the petitioner.

Part 4

Part 4 asks for information regarding the beneficiary: alien registration number (if any), USCIS online account number (if any), Social Security number (if any), full name, other names used, place and date of birth, gender, physical address and contact information. The alien registration number refers to that number assigned to LPRs, persons placed into removal proceedings (including prior deportation or exclusion), and persons who have otherwise been involved in an investigation conducted by USCIS or submitted requests for certain benefits to USCIS. If the person has an "A" number, that may indicate to the Department of Homeland Security (DHS) that the foreign national is in proceedings. Foreign nationals who marry while in deportation, exclusion, or removal proceedings (but not rescission proceedings) are subject to a two-year foreign residency requirement before the I-130 petition may be adjudicated.[19] Alternatively, the petitioner must establish by clear and convincing evidence that the marriage was entered into in good faith and not solely for immigration purposes.[20]

As with petitioners, include only Social Security numbers obtained lawfully from the Social Security Administration, not fictitious or "borrowed" ones. Type the beneficiary's full name and all other names used including maiden names, aliases, and nicknames. Information regarding place and date of birth should be taken from the birth certificate or passport. The beneficiary's country of birth may have significance for a preference-category petition, since the availability of a visa in a particular category may depend on the beneficiary's country of birth.[21]

Provide the beneficiary's physical address, even if it is temporary. If the beneficiary lives outside of the United States and his or her address does not include a specific

19 INA §204(g).

20 INA §245(e)(3).

21 INA §202(e).

street number or name, do not leave those items blank. Put N.A. instead of leaving any questions blank. List the address in the United States where the beneficiary intends to live if different from the beneficiary's physical address already provided. Provide the beneficiary's address outside the United States if different from the beneficiary's physical address already provided. If the address in the United States where the beneficiary intends to live or the address outside the United States is the same as the physical address provided, type or print "SAME" in the section requesting street name and number. If the beneficiary and the petitioner are spouses residing in the United States and not residing together, this will raise suspicions and may result in USCIS conducting an investigation or interview regarding the validity of the marriage. However, the fact that the couple is not currently living together is not, in and of itself, a valid basis for denying the visa petition.[22]

If the beneficiary is currently married, list the date and place of the marriage; that information should be found on the marriage certificate. Provide the name of the current spouse and all prior spouses and the date(s) the prior marriage(s) ended.

Part 4 continues with a question regarding the name, date of birth, and country of birth of the foreign national relative's spouse and children. If the petition is being filed on behalf of a spouse, include the name of the petitioner. Refer to the earlier section on who can file an I-130 petition to determine which relatives require separate Form I-130 applications and which can immigrate as derivatives, or family dependents, with the principal beneficiary.[23]

Indicate whether the beneficiary has ever been in the United States. This information is important in determining eligibility for adjustment of status. It will also be important in determining if the beneficiary has incurred any periods of "unlawful presence," which is defined in chapter 6.[24] If he or she is currently in the United States and arrived as a nonimmigrant, write down the following information, taken from the Form I-94: the class of admission, which is the letter designation of the nonimmigrant status at entry (e.g., B-1/B-2, F-1); the 11-digit I-94 number; date of arrival; the date authorized stay will expire or did expire; and the passport or travel document number, country of issuance and expiration date. If the beneficiary is currently in the United States but entered without being inspected or was paroled into the country, enter that information on the form. This information may also be important in determining eligibility to adjust status.[25]

Provide the name and address of the beneficiary's current employer, as well as the date the beneficiary began employment. This information could be used by USCIS to begin an investigation as to whether the employer violated the statute relating

---

22 *Matter of McKee*, 17 I&N Dec. 332, 334 (BIA 1980).

23 *See* 8 CFR §204.2(a)(4), (d)(4).

24 INA §212(a)(9)(B), (C).

25 INA §245(c), (i).

to employment of foreign nationals who are unauthorized to work.[26] It also could be used to determine if the beneficiary worked without authorization and thus is ineligible for adjustment of status. (That requirement does not apply to immediate relatives who entered the United States with inspection.)[27] If the federal government begins again to enforce civil document fraud under Immigration and Nationality Act (INA) §274C, this information also could be used to commence those actions.

Indicate whether the beneficiary has ever been in exclusion, deportation, removal, rescission, or judicial proceedings. Provide the date and place where the proceedings took place. This information may be important in determining whether the beneficiary married while in immigration proceedings. If the beneficiary has been deported or removed from the United States and has not remained outside the country for the required period of time, he or she may need to file a request for permission to reenter.[28] If a beneficiary in that situation reentered the United States on or after April 1, 1997, he or she may have triggered a more serious bar under INA §212(a)(9)(C), which is described in chapter 6.[29]

Be aware that USCIS is enforcing INA §241(a)(5), which allows the reinstatement of deportation or removal orders, immediate physical removal from the country, and ineligibility for adjustment of status.[30] This occurs if the foreign national left the United States under an order of deportation, exclusion, or removal and subsequently re-entered illegally, regardless of the date of reentry.

In addition, foreign nationals who were ordered deported *in absentia* are inadmissible for five years after their departure[31]; those who were granted voluntary departure but failed to leave on time may be barred from adjusting status, as well as other forms of relief, for up to 10 years.[32]

If the foreign national is currently in proceedings (pending before an immigration judge or the Board of Immigration Appeals), he or she may be eligible to file for adjustment of status with the Executive Office for Immigration Review. If the person was previously in immigration proceedings and received a final order that has not been effected by a subsequent departure, he or she may have to move to reopen the proceedings to apply for adjustment before an immigration judge.[33] The trial attorney may have to consent to this motion to reopen.[34]

---

26 INA §274A.

27 INA §245(c).

28 INA §212(a)(9)(A)(iii).

29 INA §212(a)(9)(C).

30 8 CFR §241.8.

31 INA §212(a)(6)(B).

32 INA §240B(d).

33 INA §240(c)(7)(C).

34 8 CFR §1003.2(c)(3)(iii).

In a spousal petition, list the address where the couple last resided together. If they are currently residing together, that address should be the same as that listed previously on the form. If the parties have never resided together, type or print "Never lived together" on the form. Be aware that suspicions may be raised as to the legitimacy of the marriage, and an investigation and marriage interview may result, so the couple should be prepared.

Indicate on the form if the beneficiary will apply for adjustment of status in the United States. The petitioner must understand the eligibility requirements for adjustment of status.[35] These are set forth in chapter 3. If the foreign national relative cannot meet the adjustment requirements, he or she will go through processing abroad at a U.S. consulate.[36] These eligibility requirements and differences are set forth below. If you know that the intending immigrant will be consular processing, indicate the appropriate consular office. It normally will be in the country of the foreign national's citizenship and in the city of the U.S. consulate closest to the foreign national's place of residence or last residence abroad.[37] Consult the website of the Department of State (DOS) to obtain the locations of the consulates abroad, their geographic jurisdictions, their contact information, and whether they process immigrant visas. Do not designate a consulate other than the appropriate one unless prior arrangements have been made.

Part 5

Part 5 asks for information on other petitions. If the petitioner simultaneously is submitting I-130 petitions for other relatives, indicate their names and relationship. If the petitioner has ever submitted an I-130 petition for this or any other foreign national in the past, include that information as well. If the petition was for the same relative and the petition was denied, do not refile unless the facts have changed or new evidence can be supplied to overcome the reasons for the denial. Indications that the petitioner has filed other I-130 petitions for prior spouses may raise suspicions about the validity of the present marriage.

Part 6

The petitioner, not the sponsored relative, signs the Form I-130.[38] The petitioner must indicate if he or she can read and understand English or if an interpreter was used. If an interpreter was used, that person's name, mailing address, and contact information must be provided. The interpreter must certify and sign the form. Anyone who assists in preparing the Form I-130, even if a separate Form G-28

35 8 CFR §245.1(b), (c).

36 INA §§221, 222.

37 9 FAM 504.4-9 (U).

38 8 CFR §204.1(d)(1).

is filed,[39] also should sign the petition at the end of the form. The preparer must provide his or her name, mailing address and contact information and indicate whether he or she is an attorney or accredited representative.

Supporting Documentation

The petitioner must attach certain supporting documents to establish U.S. citizenship, U.S. national, or LPR status, and familial relationship to the beneficiary.[40] Read the instructions for the Form I-130 for detailed information on the specific documents that are required. The instructions require the petitioner to provide a photocopy of each required document only. If the petitioner submits an original, USCIS may retain it for its records or destroy it. Submit a translation of all documents in a foreign language, along with a certification that the translation is accurate and the translator is competent to translate.[41] The regulations require a translation of the document in its entirety, but some USCIS service centers and district offices accept "summary" translations of common foreign documents.

Primary evidence consists of official government documents that are properly authenticated or certified. Secondary evidence would include records that are made or recorded contemporaneously with the event in question, such as baptismal, hospital, church, school, or employment records. When petitioners have established that primary evidence listed in the *Foreign Affairs Manual* is generally unavailable in that country, or that they are unable to obtain a copy of the official document, they may submit secondary evidence.[42] The rules for establishing this and the types of acceptable secondary evidence are set forth in the regulations.[43] Secondary evidence also could include declarations from persons with personal knowledge of the event.[44]

The standard of proof that the petitioner must satisfy is the "preponderance of the evidence."[45] This means that it is more likely than not that the statements are true and that the relationship is valid.[46] There are three situations, however, in which the petitioner must satisfy a higher standard, that of "clear and convincing evidence," which must be enough to "produce … a firm belief or conviction" that the relationship is valid.[47] If the petitioner is an LPR who obtained that status within five years through a prior marriage to a U.S. citizen or LPR, and the prior marriage

39 8 CFR §292.4.

40 8 CFR §204.1(f)(1).

41 8 CFR §204.1(f)(3).

42 8 CFR §204.1(f)(1).

43 8 CFR §204.1(f), (g).

44 8 CFR §204.1(g)(2)(ii).

45 *Matter of Soo Hoo*, 11 I&N Dec. 151 (BIA 1965).

46 *See U.S. v. Cardoza-Fonseca*, 480 U.S. 421 (1987).

47 *Matter of Carrubba*, 11 I&N Dec. 914 (BIA 1966).

did not end through death of the spouse, the petitioner must establish through clear and convincing evidence that the prior marriage was entered into in good faith.[48] If the foreign national spouse married a U.S. citizen or LPR while in immigration proceedings, and the foreign national has not subsequently resided abroad for two years, the petitioner must also meet that higher burden to establish the bona fides of the marriage.[49] And if the petitioner submitted a previous I-130 petition for the same beneficiary that was denied or withdrawn, USCIS may require additional evidence to establish the relationship.[50]

The following documents must be attached:

- *Petitioner's evidence of U.S. citizenship, U.S. national, or LPR status.* Acceptable primary and secondary evidence of citizenship are listed in the regulations.[51] Primary evidence of U.S. citizenship includes the following: birth certificate if born in the United States; certificate of naturalization; certificate of citizenship; valid unexpired U.S. passport; or Form FS-240, Report of Birth Abroad of a U.S. Citizen.[52] U.S. nationals should submit a copy of a U.S. passport, certificate of identity showing U.S. nationality, or a birth certificate.[53] Primary evidence of LPR status includes a copy of the Form I-551, Permanent Resident Card, or a stamp in the foreign passport indicating temporary evidence of LPR status.[54]
- *Evidence of the family relationship.* The requirements are set forth in the regulations and the instructions for the form.[55] Primary evidence includes birth certificates, marriage certificates, and adoption decrees.

If a marriage certificate is required and either of the parties has been married previously, include documents showing termination of the prior marriage.[56] In all spousal petitions, the petitioner should submit one or more of the following documents to establish good-faith marriage: joint ownership of real property or joint tenancy; joint ownership of personal property or commingling of financial resources; birth certificates of children born from the relationship; or declarations from persons who have known the married couple who can attest that it was bona fide.[57] Other evidence could include photos or other proof of the wedding, insurance forms naming the other spouse as a beneficiary, and joint tax returns.

---

48 INA §204(a)(2)(A).

49 INA §§204(g), 245(e)(3).

50 *Adjudicator's Field Manual* (AFM) ch. 20.4, located in 6 *USCIS Policy Manual* pt. A.

51 8 CFR §204.1(g)(1).

52 8 CFR §204.1(g)(1)(i)–(vi).

53 AFM ch. 21.2(a)(9)(C), located in 6 *USCIS Policy Manual* pt. B.

54 8 CFR §204.1(g)(1)(vii).

55 8 CFR §204.2.

56 8 CFR §204.2(a)(2).

57 8 CFR §204.2(a)(1); Instructions for I-130, Petition for Alien Relative.

For mother-child relationships, primary evidence includes the child's birth certificate bearing the name of the mother. For father-child relationships, it includes the child's birth certificate bearing the father's name, as well as a marriage certificate showing the father's marriage to the child's mother. If the child was born out of wedlock, it must include evidence of legitimation. This could be either a formal court decree of legitimation or proof of a subsequent marriage between the child's father and mother before the child turned 18. In the alternative, the petitioning father may submit evidence of a bona fide parent-child relationship (e.g., custody, provision of support) before the child turned 21.

Primary evidence of a sibling relationship includes the petitioner's and the beneficiary's birth certificates showing at least one parent in common. It may also have to include marriage certificates of the parent(s), prior divorce decrees, and evidence of legitimation for children born out of wedlock.

Other Forms and Documents Included in the Form I-130 Application Packet

The complete I-130 petition packet is made up of the following documents:

- Form I-130, Petition for Alien Relative;
- Form I-130A, Supplemental Information for Spouse Beneficiary (only for spousal petitions);
- Photos of the petitioner and the beneficiary in a spousal petition (if the beneficiary spouse is abroad, only petitioner's photo is required);[58]
- Evidence of petitioner's citizenship (birth certificate, naturalization certificate, certificate of citizenship, U.S. passport, Form FS-240) or LPR status (Form I-551);
- Evidence of family relationship between petitioner and beneficiary (marriage certificate, birth certificate);
- Evidence of termination of prior marriages (if appropriate); and
- Evidence of the bona fides of the marriage (if a spousal petition).

Where to File

If the petitioner is in the United States, he or she will file the petition and supporting documents with either the Dallas or the Phoenix lockbox facility. Those residing in the following states or territories will file the petition at USCIS, Attn: I-130, P.O. Box 21700, Phoenix, AZ 85036: Alaska, American Samoa, Arizona, California, Colorado, Florida, Guam, Hawaii, Idaho, Kansas, Montana, Nebraska, Nevada, New Mexico, North Dakota, Northern Mariana Islands, Oklahoma, Oregon, Puerto Rico, South Dakota, Texas, Utah, Virgin Islands, Washington, Wyoming. Those

[58] 8 CFR §204.2(a)(2).

filing by express mail or courier delivery should send the petition to USCIS, Attn: I-130, 1820 E. Skyharbor Circle S, Suite 100, Phoenix, AZ 85034.

Those residing in the following states or territories will file the petition at USCIS, Attn. I-130, P.O. Box 650264, Dallas, TX 75265: Alabama, Arkansas, Connecticut, Delaware, Georgia, Illinois, Indiana, Iowa, Kentucky, Louisiana, Maine, Maryland, Massachusetts, Michigan, Minnesota, Mississippi, Missouri, New Hampshire, New Jersey, New York, North Carolina, Ohio, Pennsylvania, Rhode Island, South Carolina, Tennessee, Vermont, Virginia, Washington, D.C., West Virginia, and Wisconsin. Those filing by express mail or courier delivery should send the petition to USCIS, Attn: I-130, 2501 S. State Hwy, 121, Business Suite 400, Lewisville, TX 75067.

If the petitioner is filing the Form I-130 concurrently with an application for adjustment of status, he or she should file the whole packet at the following address: USCIS, P.O. Box 805887, Chicago, IL 60680-4120. Those filing the Form I-130 and Form I-485 by express mail or courier delivery should send the packet to USCIS, FBAS, 131 S. Dearborn, 3rd Floor, Chicago, IL 60603-5517.

Petitioners residing overseas can file the petition with the USCIS Dallas lockbox facility or online with the USCIS website. In certain limited circumstances, they may file it with the U.S. embassy or consulate in the country where they are residing.

After approval of the Form I-130, the petition will be retained by USCIS if the parties indicated that they will be adjusting status. If the I-130 petition indicates that the parties will be consular processing, the petition will be forwarded to the National Visa Center (NVC) in Portsmouth, NH, which will in turn transmit it to the appropriate consulate when the priority date is current. The role of the NVC is described in greater detail in chapter 4.

Filing Fee

The filing fee for the I-130 petition is currently $535. Always check the USCIS website for the latest fee schedule.

Second Step: USCIS Marriage Interview

In marriage-based cases, USCIS may schedule an interview with the parties or conduct an independent investigation to determine the validity of the marriage.[59] Circumstances that may raise USCIS's suspicions in a marriage case include vast age differences between the parties; indications that they are not currently residing together or never have resided together; the fact that the couple do not speak a common language; and the fact that they have filed for legal separation.[60]

---

59 8 CFR §103.2(b)(7).

60 AFM ch. 21.3(a)(2)(H), located in 6 *USCIS Policy Manual* pt. B.

There is no requirement that the marriage be viable at the time one spouse is seeking to sponsor the other, provided that the marriage has not been terminated.[61] But evidence that the marriage is not viable puts a greater burden on the parties to establish that it was valid at the time it was entered into. Whenever USCIS schedules a marriage interview, the parties should be prepared to establish the validity of the marriage through documentary evidence, photos, their testimony, and the testimony or declarations of friends and relatives.

The following are some of the documents that should be submitted when the validity of the marriage is questioned: wedding photos and other records of the ceremony; photos, letters, telephone bills, airline tickets, and other evidence of the couple's relationship during courtship; lease or other records showing the couple are residing or resided together; insurance policies; employment records showing marital status and any employment-related benefits paid; joint credit cards, bank accounts, or other contractual relationships; joint tax returns; and birth certificates of children born of the relationship.

At the interview, expect the examiner to inquire into the following areas, either with the couple together or separate:

- *Ancient history*—place and date of birth of spouse; names and addresses of siblings and parents; basic biographical information, such as spouse's residences during the last 10 years, etc.
- *Relationship history*—where did the couple first meet, first go out together, go on trips together, ask the other to get married, get dressed before the marriage ceremony, get married, etc.
- *Recent history*—what was the last movie they saw together; who usually leaves first in the morning; who usually comes home first in the evening; what side of the bed does the spouse prefer; discuss everything they did together on a certain day, etc.
- *Situational history*—describe current living quarters: number of radios or TVs, location of clocks, color of bathroom rug or shower curtain, type of oven or microwave, etc.
- *Private history*—scars or birth marks, favorite perfume, nicknames, spouse's favorite color or food, spouse's best friend, etc.

Third Step: Adjustment of Status or Consular Processing

The next step is to determine whether the foreign national is eligible to adjust status or intends to consular process. The requirements for adjustment of status are set forth in detail in chapter 3. The following are the basic requirements for adjustment of status:

---

61 *Matter of Boromand*, 17 I&N Dec. 450, 454 (BIA 1980).

- Immediate relative relationship:
  - Inspected and admitted or paroled into the United States[62]; or
  - Eligible for adjustment pursuant to INA §245(i), which requires that an I130 petition, I-360 petition, or labor certification have been filed on behalf of the beneficiary on or before April 30, 2001[63]; and
  - Not inadmissible.
  - Preference category:
  - Inspected and admitted or paroled into the United States,[64] and maintained lawful nonimmigrant status since admission, including no unlawful employment; or
  - Eligible under §245(i), and visa currently available[65]; and
  - Not inadmissible.

All those who are not eligible to adjust must consular process. The procedure and requirements for consular processing are set forth in chapter 4.

Fourth Step: Inspection and Admission by CBP

For persons who have gone through consular processing and received an immigrant visa from a U.S. consulate, the last step is presenting themselves for inspection and admission before a CBP or USCIS official at the border.[66] The visa is valid for up to six months, after which it expires.[67] Even though DOS has considered the applicant eligible for admission as an immigrant, CBP also has the right to make a separate determination.[68] If CBP believes the person to be ineligible for an immigrant visa or inadmissible, the agency may deny admission.[69]

The immigrant must be prepared to establish to the satisfaction of the inspector that he or she is not inadmissible. This means that at the time of inspection the inspector may inquire as to eligibility for the immigrant visa (e.g., legitimacy of marriage, proper familial relationship), as well as admissibility, taking into account all the grounds of inadmissibility.

---

62 INA §245(a).

63 INA §245(i)(1).

64 INA §245(a).

65 8 CFR §245.2(a)(5)(ii).

66 INA §221(a)(2).

67 INA §221(c); 22 CFR §42.72.

68 8 CFR §235.1(f).

69 INA §221(h).

The foreign national must remain eligible for admission as an immigrant at the time of presentation to the agent. In other words, a foreign national immigrating based on marriage to a citizen or LPR must be married to that person at the time of inspection; a foreign national immigrating as an unmarried son or daughter must remain unmarried; and a foreign national immigrating as a "child" still must meet that definition.

Because the agent may inquire as to whether any of the grounds of inadmissibility apply, the foreign national must be admissible both at the time of the consular interview and at the time of inspection at the border. Foreign nationals who have committed certain crimes or certain acts after the granting of the visa may be denied admission.

Petition Revocation

- Intending immigrants may lose their ability to immigrate under an approved I-130 petition if circumstances occur that trigger automatic petition revocation. These circumstances include:
- Notice of the withdrawal of the petition by the petitioner;
- Death of the beneficiary;
- Termination of the marriage in an immediate-relative or second-preference spouse petition case;
- Marriage of a second-preference petition beneficiary (child, son, or daughter of an LPR);
- Loss of the petitioner's permanent residency in family-based cases; and
- Death of the petitioner, unless the USCIS in its discretion determines that for humanitarian reasons revocation would be inappropriate.[70]

If the U.S. citizen spouse dies, the noncitizen spouse may qualify for immigration benefits as a widow or widower.[71] Eligibility for that status and the procedures for seeking permanent resident status are explained in chapter 5.

Other surviving family members may qualify for immigration benefits after the petitioner or principal beneficiary has died based on INA §204(*l*).[72] The main requirements are that the beneficiary must have been residing in the United States at the time of the petitioner's death and continue to reside here. The other requirement is that he or she must obtain a substitute sponsor who can file an affidavit of support. Substitute sponsors are covered in greater detail in chapter 8.

---

70 8 CFR §205.1(a)(3)(i).

71 INA §204.2(b)(2)(A)(i).

72 INA §204(*l*); USCIS Memorandum, *Approval of Petitions and Applications after the Death of the Qualifying Relative under New Section 204(l) of the Immigration and Nationality Act* (Dec. 16, 2010), AILA Doc. No. 11011061.

According to USCIS, there are two ways to request section 204(*l*) relief. If the petitioner died while the petition or application was pending, the beneficiary will simply notify USCIS and request that the agency proceed with adjudication of the petition or application. This presumes that the petition or application was filed on or after October 28, 2009, or was pending on that date. If it was filed and adjudicated before that date, and the agency has formally revoked the approved petition based on the petitioner's death, USCIS will allow the affected beneficiary to file an untimely motion to reopen if he or she would otherwise be protected by the provisions of section 204(*l*). The second manner of requesting 204(*l*) relief applies to beneficiaries whose petitioner died after the petition or application was approved. Assuming the beneficiary satisfies the residency requirements, he or she can request reinstatement of the approved petition or application. A sample request to reinstate an I-130 petition based on section 204(*l*), with a list of supporting documents, is attached as Appendix 2.

Beneficiaries who can benefit from this 2009 statutory amendment include immediate-relative children and parents of a U.S. citizen and all preference-category principal and derivative beneficiaries in the family-based categories. If the principal beneficiary meets the residence requirements, but the derivatives do not, they may still qualify for relief. It is not necessary that all the derivative beneficiaries meet the residence requirements. According to USCIS, if "any one beneficiary of a covered petition meets the residence requirements of section 204(*l*) of the Act, then the petition may be approved…"[73] This interpretation helps in cases where the principal beneficiary satisfies the residence requirements, but the spouse and/or children have been residing abroad.

Section 204(*l*) also provides relief in situations where the principal beneficiary—not the petitioner—has died. In the past, when the principal beneficiary had died, either the derivatives were left without a basis for immigrating (e.g., derivative children in first-preference cases or derivative spouses and children in third- or fourth-preference cases), or the petitioner had to file a new petition for the child (second-preference cases). The statute now allows these derivatives "of the qualifying relative" in all the family-based preference categories to proceed unaffected by the principal beneficiary's death.

The Department of Homeland Security (DHS) retains the power to deny relief under section 204(*l*) when it determines that approval of the petition or application "would not be in the public interest." The exercise of this discretion is nonreviewable. According to USCIS, "only truly compelling discretionary factors should be cited as a basis to deny the visa petition under section 204(*l*)."[74] And before making such a determination, the officer must first consult with headquarters.

---

73 USCIS Memorandum, Dec. 16, 2010, *at* 5.

74 *Id.* at 12.

Section 204(*l*) does not allow a surviving family member to apply for adjustment of status if not otherwise eligible. Nor does it require approval of a petition or application if the officer believes the beneficiary or applicant is ineligible. For example, the officer might determine that there was no good-faith marriage in a marriage-based case. This statutory amendment does not waive or excuse the grounds of inadmissibility or deportability; it simply allows the petition or application to be adjudicated notwithstanding the death of the petitioner or principal beneficiary. But the agency interprets the statute as allowing the grant of a waiver of inadmissibility—even though the qualifying relative has died and there is obviously no extreme hardship to be suffered by the decedent—if the beneficiary meets the residence requirements of section 204(*l*). USCIS will note that the qualifying relative has died and the death will be "deemed to be the functional equivalent of a finding of extreme hardship."[75] This does not mean that the waiver will necessarily be approved. USCIS retains the right to exercise its discretion in adjudicating waivers, even if extreme hardship is established.

The affidavit-of-support requirements are not waived for family-based cases involving a deceased petitioner—other than a widow or widower—though the beneficiary may submit one from a substitute sponsor. Substitute sponsors may include a close relative of the beneficiary (spouse, parent, mother-in-law, father-in-law, sibling, child at least 18 years of age, son, daughter, daughter-in-law, son-in-law, sister-in-law, brother-in-law, grandparent, or grandchild) or a legal guardian.

A substitute sponsor must be either a U.S. citizen or LPR and be domiciled in the United States. If the sponsor has insufficient income to satisfy the 125-percent-of-poverty requirement for their household size, he or she may obtain a joint sponsor who does meet it. Beneficiaries residing in the United States whose petitioning family member has died will need to move to reinstate the petition under 204(*l*) and file a substitute affidavit of support as part of the adjustment of status or consular processing procedure. Beneficiaries who cannot secure a substitute sponsor will be unable to reinstate the revoked petition, even if they satisfy the other 204(*l*) requirements or could present humanitarian factors. Alternatively, the affidavit-of-support requirements are satisfied if the intending immigrant has earned or can be credited with 40 qualifying quarters under Social Security law or will be deriving citizenship under INA §320.

In cases involving the death of the petitioner where the beneficiary cannot establish residency in the United States, the regulations contain an exception that may apply if the beneficiary establishes that it would be "inappropriate" to revoke the application based on humanitarian factors.[76] This relief is available when the petitioner died *after* the petition was approved, and it requires a formal motion or request to reinstate the petition.

---

75 *Id.* at 11.

76 8 CFR §205.1(a)(3)(i)(C)(2).

USCIS has indicated that the following factors would be considered in satisfying the test of inappropriateness: impact of revocation on the family unit in the United States, the beneficiary's poor health or advanced age, the beneficiary's long residence in the United States, absence of any ties to the beneficiary's country of origin, and any undue delay by USCIS or the consulate in processing the petition or application.[77]

USCIS internal documents provide some examples of when humanitarian reinstatement should be granted: (1) where "the original petitioner died prior to the person receiving an immigrant visa or adjusting status, especially in preference cases if there was a long wait,"[78] or (2) "if there is one family member (out of many) who has been unable to immigrate because of the petitioner's death."[79]

In order to reinstate the I-130 petition, the beneficiary must file a formal motion or request, attach supporting documentation, and submit the motion to reinstate to the USCIS office that approved the petition. There is no fee for this type of motion. The motion must include the following:

- Death certificate of the petitioner;
- Form I-797, Notice of Approval of I-130 petition;
- Declaration from the beneficiary detailing the humanitarian factors in the case;
- Substitute Form I-864, Affidavit of Support, from family member; and
- Proof of substitute sponsor's relationship to the beneficiary.

Additional documentation establishing the humanitarian factors might include any of the following:

- Proof of the bona fides of the relationship to the deceased petitioner
- Proof of the beneficiary's long residence in the United States
- Proof of relationship to other family members and their immigration/ citizenship status
- Proof of any health-related problems of the beneficiary or the beneficiary's home country
- Proof of attachment to the local community and/or involvement in civic organizations

---

77 AFM ch. 21.2(h)(1)(C), located in 6 *USCIS Policy Manual* pt. D.

78 PowerPoint slide handouts prepared in 2003 by the Department of Homeland Security, USCIS Office of Adjudications, for training presentations in New York, Miami, Chicago, Los Angeles, and San Francisco on "Grounds of Inadmissibility, Affidavit of Support, 212(h) Criminal Waivers, and Unlawful Presence."

79 AFM ch. 21.2(g)(1)(C), located in 6 *USCIS Policy Manual* pt. D.

- Declarations from friends, religious leaders, employers, and others, describing the beneficiary's good moral character and benefit to the community

After implementation of INA §204(*l*), applicants for humanitarian reinstatement will largely consist of those who have never resided in the United States. In those cases, the presence of other family members in the United States who were able to immigrate or adjust should be stressed.

If USCIS reinstates the I-130 petition, either based on section 204(*l*) or humanitarian reasons, it will forward the approved petition either to the office adjudicating the adjustment of status application or to the NVC or appropriate DOS post.

Immigrating Adopted Children Under the Hague Convention Rules

The immigration of a child adopted on or after April 1, 2008, requires compliance with the Intercountry Adoption Act of 2000,[80] which the United States enacted to comply with its obligations under the Hague Convention.[81] U.S. citizens seeking to adopt and emigrate a child from one of the convention member countries must satisfy certain requirements.[82] The Hague Convention rules were intended to provide more centralization and uniformity in the international adoption process. They have now brought more harmony between different countries' laws, more transparency, more communication among agencies established in the member countries, and more assurance that the adoption and emigration is in the best interests of the child. But at the same time, these rules have brought significant changes in the way practitioners approach this area of law.

The first step in advising a client who is considering adopting a noncitizen child is to understand the Hague Convention rules and determine if they apply. If the rules apply, the adoptive parent does not have a choice of proceeding with a family or an orphan petition—the client must follow the Hague procedures. To emphasize the importance of this initial determination, it is helpful to know the major differences between the Hague rules and the other two procedures. The following is a summary:

- Only U.S. citizens—not LPRs—may adopt and immigrate children subject to the Hague rules[83];

---

80 Pub. L. No. 106-279, 114 Stat. 825 (Oct. 6, 2000).

81 Convention on Protection of Children and Cooperation in Respect of Intercountry Adoption, May 29, 1993, S. Treaty Doc. 105-51 (1998), 32 I.L.M. 1139. For in-depth guidance on international adoption issues, see *The International Adoption Sourcebook* (AILA 2008), available at http://agora.aila.org.

82 INA §101(b)(1)(G); 8 CFR §204.300 et seq.; 22 CFR §42.24.

83 8 CFR §204.307.

- DOS coordinates with the equivalent "Central Authority" or designee in the child's home country and this foreign entity is heavily involved in the process[84];
- Adoption cannot serve as the basis for the child's immigration unless it follows certain prescribed steps and sequences;
- The adoptive parents are prohibited from contacting the birth parents unless they fall within narrow exceptions;[85]
- The adopted child must be under 16 when the decree is finalized or the Form I-800 is filed[86]; there is no exception for children between ages 16 and 18 whose siblings have been adopted while under 16; and
- The definition of "adoptable" child is broader than orphan and includes those whose: (1) single birth parent has relinquished control; (2) two living birth parents are incapable of providing care and have released the child for adoption; or (3) unmarried birth father, who can qualify as a "sole parent," releases the child for adoption after the birth mother has abandoned the child.[87]

Hague Convention rules apply to children who are "habitual residents" of one of the approximately 94 countries that have signed on to the international treaty.[88] For a current list of these signatories, check the DOS website at http://adoption.state.gov. Some of the countries that have not ratified the Hague Convention include Russia, Ethiopia, and South Korea. Some of the ones that have include China, India, Mexico, and the Philippines.

The Hague Convention rules apply only to adoptions between two Hague Convention countries. This could be significant for children born in one foreign country but who have been residing in another country, including the United States. If the foreign Central Authority determines that the child is now habitually residing in the United States, for example, the Hague rules would not apply. But children are generally considered to be habitual residents of the country of their citizenship unless their status in the third country is sufficiently stable. Make sure the prospective adoptive parents are habitual residents of a Hague country, e.g., residing in the United States or residing temporarily abroad with the intention of returning before the child turns 18.

USCIS has issued an interim policy memo that provides more flexibility in determining when a child is to be considered a habitual resident.[89] If the child is

---

84 8 CFR §204.301.

85 8 CFR §204.309(b)(2).

86 INA §101(b)(1)(G); 8 CFR §204.313(c)(2).

87 INA §101(b)(1)(G).

88 8 CFR §204.303(b).

89 USCIS Policy Memorandum, *Criteria for Determining Habitual Residence in the United States for Children from Hague Convention Countries* (Dec. 23, 2013), AILA Doc. No. 14010341.

a citizen of a Hague country and residing in the United States, he or she is still presumed to be a habitual resident of that home country. But the presumption can be overcome by showing that the child has been residing in the United states for a "substantial period of time" and that the intending adopting parent has properly notified the Central Authority of the pending adoption proceeding. Children physically present in the United States for two years or more will be presumed to have "compelling ties" in this country and to have demonstrated the necessary period of time here.

Absent such a presumption, USCIS adjudicators can look at a variety of factors showing that the child has compelling ties to the United States. Notification to the Central Authority must be made at least 120 days prior to the adoption in order to allow the Central Authority to object to the proceeding. Evidence of the Central Authority's nonobjection must be incorporated into the language of the adoption decree. A final requirement is that the child must have entered the United States for reasons other than adoption.

Hague rules do not apply to adoptions finalized before April 1, 2008. Adoptions finalized on or after that date may possibly be reopened and granted *nunc pro tunc* to an earlier date. They do not apply to cases where the prospective adoptive parents filed either the Form I-600 or Form I-600A before April 1, 2008. They also do not apply to cases where the adoptive parent has resided for at least two years with legal and physical custody of the adopted child in the child's original country before filing a family petition.

Procedure for Applying

If the Hague Convention rules apply, the following steps must be adhered to in this precise order. First, the prospective adoptive parent(s) obtains an approved home study from an accredited provider, licensed in the adoptive parents' state, and authorized to conduct such studies.[90] The adoptive parent(s) then files Form I-800A, Application for Determination of Suitability to Adopt a Child from a Convention Country, with USCIS, along with the home study. USCIS may need to communicate with the designated adoption service provider.

After approving the Form I-800A and home study, USCIS forwards them to the adoption service provider and the National Visa Center, which in turn forwards them to the Central Authority of the designated foreign country. That Central Authority then identifies a child and refers him or her to the prospective parent(s) along with a report on his or her medical and social background. If the family accepts the referral, they file Form I-800, Petition to Classify Convention Adoptee as an Immediate Relative, with USCIS. USCIS then provisionally approves the petition and forwards it to the appropriate U.S. consulate.

90 22 CFR Part 96.

The consular officer screens the child for admissibility and annotates the visa application with the child's ability to immigrate following adoption. The officer also transmits the "Article Five Letter" to the Central Authority, which basically affirms that the adoptive parents may proceed with the adoption. The family then completes the adoption or guardianship process and submits the official decree to the consulate, which approves the Form I-800 and issues the immigrant visa (IH-3 or IH-4).

Forms I-800A and I-800 are filed at the USCIS Dallas lockbox facility for initial processing using the following address: USCIS, P.O. Box 660087, Dallas, TX 75266. These forms will then be forwarded to the National Benefits Center in Lee's Summit, MO, which processes these petitions.

Chapter 3

ADJUSTMENT OF STATUS

There are two ways to obtain lawful permanent resident (LPR) status through a family-based petition: adjustment of status, which is processed by U.S. Citizenship and Immigration Services (USCIS) in the United States[1]; or consular processing, which is governed by the Department of State and usually takes place in the intending immigrant's country of residence.[2] This chapter discusses the eligibility requirements and procedure for adjusting status. Consular processing is discussed in chapter 4.

Requirements for Adjustment of Status

Historical Background

Prior to mid-1994, the law was quite clear and rigid as to who was eligible to adjust status in the United States: only foreign nationals who had been inspected and admitted or paroled into the United States and met other eligibility requirements.[3] In general, persons who had not entered with inspection were required to return to their home countries and go through consular processing. This caused both economic and other hardships to many applicants, who had to spend money and time outside the United States. Other advantages to adjusting status in the United States include eligibility for employment authorization,[4] advance parole,[5] and access to administrative and judicial appeals in removal proceedings if the application is denied.[6]

To relieve some of the workload at U.S. consulates and raise needed revenue for the Immigration and Naturalization Service, Congress passed a law in 1994, codified in section 245(i) of the Immigration and Nationality Act (INA), that added many classes of noncitizens who were eligible to adjust in the United States if they were willing to pay a penalty fee.[7] This section was created with a three-year sunset clause, and indeed the provision lapsed at the end of 1997, with a brief extension

---

1 INA §245.

2 INA §221(a).

3 INA §245(a) (1994).

4 8 CFR §274a.12(c)(9).

5 8 CFR §212.5(f).

6 8 CFR §245.2(a)(5)(ii).

7 Department of Commerce, Justice, and State Appropriations Act for 1995, Pub. L. No. 103-317, 108 Stat. 1724 (1994).

into early 1998.[8] However, Congress restored section 245(i) to cover beneficiaries of certain petitions filed on or before April 30, 2001.[9] These individuals are considered "grandfathered" beneficiaries of section 245(i).[10] Any foreign nationals who adjust pursuant to section 245(i) must pay a penalty fee of $1,000, in addition to the regular fee for adjustment.[11] There are some exceptions to the penalty fee, such as for minor children.[12] The specific requirements are described in greater detail below.

The 1996 immigration law further complicated the question of who is eligible to adjust by creating many new grounds of inadmissibility and new grounds of ineligibility for adjustment pursuant to INA §245.[13] This chapter will describe eligibility for adjustment of status; the grounds of inadmissibility will be covered in chapter 6.

INA §245(a) and (c): Adjustment Eligibility Without Penalty Fee

Beneficiaries of an approved Form I-130 petition are eligible to adjust status in the United States without paying a $1,000 penalty fee as long as they can show all of the following:

- *They entered the United States legally.* This means they were inspected and admitted or paroled.[14] To be inspected and admitted is to have presented oneself to an immigration officer at the border, or its functional equivalent, for questioning.[15] To be paroled is to be allowed into the United States for a designated period based on humanitarian factors or in the public interest.[16] Most nonimmigrants and parolees receive a Form I-94, Arrival–Departure Record, which indicates their status upon admission.
- *A visa is currently available.* This means they are an immediate relative of a U.S. citizen or in a preference category for which their priority date is

8 Departments of Commerce, Justice, and State, the Judiciary, and Related Agencies Appropriations Act, 1998, Pub. L. No. 105-119, 111 Stat. 2440 (Nov. 26, 1997).

9 The Legal Immigration and Family Equity (LIFE) Act Amendments of 2000, Pub. L. No. 106-554, appx. D, div. B, §§1501–06, 114 Stat. 2763, 2763A–324 to 2763A–328 (Dec. 21, 2000).

10 *See* 8 CFR §245.10(a)(1) (defining "grandfathered alien" for purposes of regulations governing adjustment of status).

11 8 CFR §245.10(b)(6).

12 8 CFR §245.10(c)(3).

13 INA §212(a)(9)(B)(i).

14 INA §245(a).

15 *Matter of Areguillin*, 17 I&N Dec. 308 (BIA 1980). To establish "admission" for purposes of INA §245(a) eligibility, the foreign national need only prove procedural regularity in his or her entry, which does not necessarily require that he or she have been questioned by immigration authorities or admitted in a particular status. *Matter of Quilantan*, 25 I&N Dec. 285 (BIA 2010).

16 INA §212(d)(5).

current.[17] USCIS will rely on Chart A, Application Final Action Dates for Family-Sponsored Preference Cases, in the *Visa Bulletin* to determine if the priority date is current for purposes of application approval.

- *They never worked without USCIS permission*—unless they are immediate relatives. They could not have worked illegally even for a day.[18]
- *They always maintained lawful nonimmigrant or parolee status*—unless they are immediate relatives. They could not have overstayed their period of time allowed on the Form I-94 by even a day.[19] "Technical violations," or those that are not the fault of the applicant, will be excused.[20] Foreign nationals who are granted an extension of stay based on a timely filed extension application, or even an untimely one that is "reasonably excusable," remain eligible for adjustment.
- *They were not a crew member, an alien admitted in transit without a visa, an alien admitted in the S visa category, or an exchange visitor admitted in the J visa category* (unless the J visa holder is exempt or has complied with the two-year foreign residency requirement or obtained a waiver of that requirement).[21]
- *They were not a nonimmigrant admitted without a visa under the visa waiver program*—unless they are an immediate relative.[22]
- *They were not admitted with a K visa*—unless they are adjusting based on marriage (within 90 days of entry) to the U.S. citizen who filed the nonimmigrant visa petition.[23]
- *They are not inadmissible*[24]—unless they qualify for a waiver. The 10 categories constituting the grounds of inadmissibility are discussed in chapter 6. Sample waivers are provided with chapter 7.

Qualifying Under Section 245(i)

Overview

The amendments to the INA in 1994 and at the end of 2000 made many persons who had been unable to adjust under INA §245(a) and (c) eligible to adjust if they

17 8 CFR §245.2(a)(2)(i).

18 INA §245(c); 8 CFR §245.1(b)(4).

19 8 CFR §245.1(b)(6).

20 8 CFR §245.1(d)(2); *Matter of L–K–*, 23 I&N Dec. 677 (BIA 2004).

21 8 CFR §245.1(b)(2).

22 8 CFR §245.1(b)(8).

23 8 CFR §245.1(c)(6).

24 INA §212(a).

paid a $1,000 penalty fee.[25] To be eligible for section 245(i), the applicant must be the beneficiary of one of these petitions, filed on or before April 30, 2001: Form I-130, Petition for Alien Relative; Form I-360, Petition for Amerasian, Widow(er), or Special Immigrant; Form I-140, Immigrant Petition for Alien Worker; Form I-526, Immigrant Petition by Alien Entrepreneur; or Form ETA-750, Application for Alien Employment Certification.[26] That petition or application must have been approvable when filed, which is explained below. If they satisfy that requirement, the following persons, who would otherwise be ineligible to adjust status, are eligible:

- Foreign nationals who entered the United States illegally (without inspection and admission or parole)
- Preference-category applicants who overstayed a period of authorized stay or who violated the terms of their nonimmigrant status
- Preference-category applicants who worked without USCIS employment authorization
- Foreign nationals admitted in the S nonimmigrant category
- Crew members
- Foreign nationals admitted in transit without a visa or admitted under the visa waiver program[27]

Section 245(i) does not waive grounds of inadmissibility, and thus should not be confused with other waivers, such as the waiver required for persons who have acquired "unlawful presence" in the United States and incurred the three– or ten-year bar.[28] However, adjusting through section 245(i) allows the intending immigrant to remain in the United States and thus not trigger the three– or ten-year bar.[29] Section 245(i) also does not prevent application of the bar to adjustment under INA §240B(d) for persons granted voluntary departure who did not leave the United States during the allotted period, nor the application of reinstatement of removal and the bar to adjustment under INA §241(a)(5) for persons deported or removed who reentered illegally.[30] Nor does it waive the five-year bar to admissibility for those who effect an *in absentia* order of removal by their subsequent departure or removal.[31]

---

25 INA §245(i).

26 8 CFR §245.10(a)(1).

27 INA §245(c), (i).

28 *Matter of Torres-Garcia,* 23 I&N Dec. 866 (BIA 2006).

29 Immigration and Naturalization Service (INS), D. Martin, General Counsel Opinion Letter: The Impact of the 1996 Act on Section 245(i) of the Act (Feb. 19, 1997), AILA Doc. No. 97021991.

30 INA §241(a)(5); *Fernandez-Vargas v. Ashcroft*, 548 U.S. 30 (2006).

31 INA §212(a)(6)(B).

Children under 17 years of age and "family unity" recipients or applicants may qualify for section 245(i) relief without having to pay the penalty fee.[32] "Family unity" is a special temporary status for spouses and unmarried children of parents who gained their permanent residency through one of the legalization programs.[33] The spouse or child must have been residing in the United States before either May 5, 1988, or December 1, 1988, depending on the legalization program under which the spouse or parent immigrated.[34] In addition, the child must be under age 21 when filing for adjustment.[35]

Approvable Petition on File by April 30, 2001

Only applicants who had a Form I-130, Form I-360, Form I-526, Form I-140, or a labor certification filed on or before April 30, 2001, are eligible to file for adjustment under INA §245(i). The petition must have been "approvable when filed,"[36] which means that it must have been submitted with the proper filing fee and signature, be a bona fide application, and meet all other substantive requirements.[37] The petition might later be denied, revoked, or withdrawn.[38] However, what is important is whether, based on the facts known at the time of filing, it was approvable by USCIS or the Department of Labor (DOL).

Beneficiaries

All beneficiaries of a designated petition or labor certification filed on or before April 30, 2001, are eligible to take advantage of INA §245(i) through "grandfathering," even if they are seeking adjustment based on a different petition.[39] USCIS has adopted an "alien-based" interpretation, which means the status of being a grandfathered beneficiary stays with the foreign national.[40] There is no time period during which the foreign national must use that section 245(i) adjustment eligibility. Beneficiaries include the unmarried children under 21 and the spouse of the principal beneficiary (derivative beneficiaries) in existence at the time the preference-category petition was filed.[41] The derivative beneficiary does not have to adjust with the principal beneficiary or even be named on the I-130 petition to be considered grandfathered.

---

32 8 CFR §245.10(c).

33 8 CFR §236.10.

34 INA §245(i)(1)(C).

35 *Adjudicator's Field Manual* (AFM), ch. 23.5(c)(3)(C), located in 7 *USCIS Policy Manual* pt. C.

36 8 CFR §245.10(a)(3).

37 8 CFR §245.10(a)(2).

38 8 CFR §245.10(a)(3).

39 *See* 8 CFR §245.10(a)(1) (defining "grandfathered alien" for purposes of regulations governing adjustment of status).

40 INS Memorandum, R. Bach, *Accepting Applications for Adjustment of Status Under Section 245(i) of the Immigration and Nationality Act* (June 10, 1999), AILA Doc. No. 99061940.

41 8 CFR §245.10(a)(1)(ii).

The grandfathering provision also includes derivative beneficiaries in the second-preference visa categories who "age out" before the principal beneficiary immigrates, and on whose behalf separate I-130 petitions may have been filed. Likewise, it includes second-preference derivative beneficiaries who lose preference status when the petitioner naturalizes, and thus require a separate I-130 petition to be filed.

The Board of Immigration Appeals (BIA) has held that in order for a derivative beneficiary to be grandfathered under section 245(i), the principal beneficiary of the qualifying visa petition must satisfy the grandfathering requirements, including the physical presence requirement.[42] The implications of this decision are that as long as the principal beneficiary satisfies the physical presence and other requirements, a derivative beneficiary who is grandfathered, and who qualifies to file independently based on a separate petition, does not have to satisfy the physical presence requirements.

"After-acquired" spouses and children—children born after the cutoff date, and the spouse of a principal beneficiary in the third– or fourth-preference category whose marriage took place after the cutoff date—are allowed to adjust under section 245(i) as long as they acquire their status as spouse or child before the principal adjusts.43 The BIA has clarified the term "after-acquired" to mean that the marriage of the derivative spouse or the birth of the derivative child took place after April 30, 2001.44

There is an important distinction between those who are grandfathered (those on whose behalf the original application was filed) and derivatives, who include the spouse and unmarried child of the principal beneficiary in the preference categories. After-acquired spouses or children who were neither grandfathered nor derivatives on or before April 30, 2001, can still take advantage of section 245(i). These spouses and children do not acquire grandfathered status, but they can apply for adjustment under section 245(i) as derivatives of the principal grandfathered foreign national.[45]

In sum, section 245(i) protects all of the following persons if they were beneficiaries of an approvable petition filed on or before April 30, 2001:

- Derivatives who could have derived status at the time the petition was filed, even if they were not identified on the petition;
- Derivatives who lose derivative status (need to file a new I-130 petition);

---

42 *Matter of Ilic*, 25 I&N Dec. 717 (BIA 2012).

43 INS Memorandum, June 10, 1999.

44 *Matter of Estrada*, 26 I&N Dec. 180 (BIA 2013).

45 USCIS Memorandum, W. Yates, *Clarification of Certain Eligibility Requirements Pertaining to an Application to Adjust Status Under Section 245(i) of the Immigration and Nationality Act* (Mar. 9, 2005), AILA Doc. No. 05031468. *But see Matter of Legaspi*, 25 I&N Dec 328 (BIA 2010) (derivative spouse is not independently grandfathered for section 245(i) by virtue of marriage to a grandfathered alien who adjusted under section 245(a)).

- Beneficiaries who marry and lose second-preference eligibility, but who can still establish immediate-relative or third-preference eligibility (need to file a new I-130 petition);
- Foreign nationals whose LPR or U.S. citizen spouse divorces or dies but who qualify under a new I-130 petition filed by a subsequent spouse or under a widow's Form I-360 self-petition; and
- After-acquired spouses (i.e., the marriage takes place after April 30, 2001) and after-acquired children (i.e., those born after April 30, 2001), as long as they acquire the status of spouse or child before the principal adjusts and they are adjusting as derivatives of the principal beneficiary.

Filing Under Section 245(i)

Adjustment applicants filing under INA §245(i) must include proof of filing the Form I-130, Form I-360, Form I-140, Form I-526, or labor certification application on or before April 30, 2001.[46] In most cases, this will be satisfied by submitting the USCIS or DOL filing receipt indicating a priority date on or before that date. However, applicants can qualify under section 245(i) if the I-130 petition was postmarked by that date. If the USCIS filing receipt indicates that it received the I-130 petition after April 30, 2001, applicants may have to submit other proof that the Form I-130 was filed timely—such as certified-mail receipts or express-mail tracking records.

In addition, if the petition was filed after January 14, 1998, the principal beneficiary who is applying for adjustment of status will have to submit proof of physical presence in the United States on December 21, 2000.[47] To demonstrate physical presence on December 21, 2000, the applicant should submit documentation issued by the Department of Homeland Security (DHS) or other federal, state, or local authorities. The applicant also may submit nongovernment-issued documentation, such as school records, rent receipts, utility bill receipts, employment records, and credit card statements.[48] Spouses and unmarried children who were classified as derivative beneficiaries under section 245(i) are exempt from the physical presence requirement, even if they are now adjusting under section 245(i) as principal beneficiaries.[49]

According to USCIS, until a grandfathered foreign national adjusts status, there is no limit to the number of applications he or she may file for adjustment of status under section 245(i). This reverses the policy of some local district offices, which were allowing those who were grandfathered to use section 245(i) only once.

46 8 CFR §245.10(a)(2).

47 INA §245(i)(1)(C).

48 8 CFR §245.10(n).

49 8 CFR §245.10(a)(1)(B)(ii); *Matter of Ilic*, 25 I&N Dec. 717 (BIA 2012).

Under the clarified policy, foreign nationals who are denied or who withdraw their adjustment application may use their grandfathered status to reapply in the future, should they become eligible.[50]

Discretionary Act

Adjustment of status is a discretionary act on the part of USCIS.[51] This means that even if the applicant satisfies all the statutory requirements, and is not inadmissible, he or she still may be denied because of certain negative factors that the adjudicator believes are significant. In practice, however, USCIS rarely exercises its discretion to deny an applicant unless there are serious adverse factors that outweigh the positive ones. Negative factors that have caused such an exercise of discretion include criminal convictions or fraudulent conduct that does not make the applicant inadmissible.[52]

Process for Adjusting Status

The application for adjustment is made on Form I-485, Application to Register Permanent Residence or Adjust Status. An Alien Relative Petition (Form I-130) may be filed at the same time as the Form I-485 for a person who will be eligible to adjust as soon as the visa petition is approved, such as an immediate relative.[53] Other applicants will have to file their I-485 petition with the I-130 petition approval notice once the priority date is current, or a visa is available, in accordance with Chart B, Dates for Filing Family-Sponsored Visa Application, in the Department of State *Visa Bulletin*, assuming USCIS has confirmed that it is following Chart B for that month.

Completing the Form I-485

Note: These instructions refer to the version of the form dated October 15, 2019.

Part 1

The beneficiary of the approved I-130 petition, or concurrently filed I-130 petition, becomes the applicant on the Form I-485 application. Part 1 of the Form I-485 requires background information on the applicant, including name, other names used, gender, U.S. mailing address, date of birth, country of birth, and country of

---

50 USCIS Memorandum, Mar. 9, 2005. But see *Matter of Legaspi*, 25 I&N Dec 328 (BIA 2010) (derivative spouse is not independently grandfathered for section 245(i) by virtue of marriage to a grandfathered alien who adjusted under section 245(a)).

51 INA §245(a).

52 AFM ch. 23.2(d), located in 7 *USCIS Policy Manual* pt. D.

53 8 CFR §245.2(a)(2)(B).

citizenship. Include only Social Security numbers obtained lawfully by the applicant from the Social Security Administration, not fictitious or "borrowed" ones.

The alien registration number (A-number) refers to the number assigned to LPRs, persons placed in removal proceedings (including prior deportation or exclusion), and persons who have otherwise been involved in an investigation conducted by DHS. Refer to the I-130 petition approval notice or the foreign national's Form I-94 and enter this number here. If no A-Number appears, then enter "none."

The form requires information regarding the applicant's immigration history. If the applicant last entered using a passport or travel document, enter that information in Questions 15–19. When indicating "place of last arrival" on Question 20, indicate the closest city or town, regardless of whether the applicant entered lawfully or not. For example, if the applicant entered illegally, give the approximate place of entry, such as "near El Paso."

When indicating the "date of last arrival" on Question 21, refer to the applicant's Form I-94 (Arrival-Departure Record), passport, or entry document, if any. Otherwise, enter the approximate date on which the applicant entered the United States, either legally or illegally. If the applicant was inspected and admitted, indicate that in Question 22a. Provide the generic term for the immigration status at the time of admission (e.g., visitor, student). If the applicant had no immigration status, but was nevertheless "waived through," then state that. If the applicant was paroled into the country pursuant to INA §212(d)(5), enter that information in Question 22b. If the applicant entered the country without inspection and admission or parole, indicate that in Question 22c.

If the applicant was issued an I-94, put that number in Question 23a. Put the date of expiration in Question 23b, and the status or class of admission Question 23c, such as "B-1/B-2" or "paroled under 212(d)(5)." If the immigration status has changed since arrival, indicate the applicant's current status. For example, the applicant could have formally changed from B-1/B-2 to F-1. Or, more commonly, the applicant could have overstayed the time allowed on the I-94. If the latter, indicate that by writing "overstay."

Part 2

Question 1 in Part 2 asks if the applicant is the principal beneficiary named in the I-130 or is a derivative spouse or child. Question 2a–f provides six options for those adjusting based on a family-based petition: (1) immediate relative (spouse, unmarried child, or parent of U.S. citizen); (2) beneficiary in one of the preference categories (spouses of LPRs, unmarried children or sons and daughters of LPRs, siblings of U.S. citizens, or married or unmarried sons and daughters of U.S. citizens); (3) fiancé(e) of a U.S. citizen in the K-1 visa category who married the citizen petitioner within 90 days of admission,[54] or child of the fiancé(e) who was admitted in the K-2 category; (4) widow or widower; (5) VAWA self-petitioner; and (6) spouse, child, or parent of a deceased U.S. active duty service member.

Questions 12-13 require those who are applying for adjustment based on section 245(i) as a principal beneficiary to provide the receipt number and priority date of the underlying petition that was filed on or before April 30, 2001. Derivative beneficiaries applying for adjustment based on section 245(i) will answer Questions 14–18 and provide information on the principal beneficiary: name, date of birth, A-number (if any), receipt number of the underlying petition, and priority date.

Part 3

This part requires further biographical information relating to the applicant and the applicant's family members. The first question is whether the applicant has ever applied for an immigrant visa at a U.S. consulate or embassy. If so, indicate the city and country of the consular post, date of decision, and whether the application was approved, refused, denied, or withdrawn.

Questions 5–22 ask for the applicant's addresses and employment, as well as dates of residence or employment, for the past five years.

Part 4

This part asks for information regarding the applicant's parents. Enter the applicant's mother's and father's first, middle, and last name. The parents' names should match those on the applicant's birth certificate. Enter their date of birth, city and country of birth, and current residence.

Part 5

This part asks for information regarding the applicant's current marital status and any prior marriages. Enter the current status as either: single, never married; married; divorced; widowed; annulled; or legally separated. If married, indicate whether the spouse is a current member of the U.S. armed forces or Coast Guard. Enter the current spouse's biographical information to Questions 4–10. In response to Question 10, check "yes" only if the spouse is also a derivative beneficiary applying for LPR status at the same time.

Enter the name of any prior spouses and provide the place where the prior marriage took place and ended to Questions 11–16. Make sure that the date the marriage legally ended is *before* the date of the marriage to the current spouse in response to Question 15.

---

54 8 CFR §245.1(c)(6).

Part 6

This section asks for the name, date of birth, country of birth, and "A" number of the applicant's living children, regardless of their age, address, or marital status. It is important to list *all* children, even if they are not living in the United States or immigrating with the applicant. Remember that the definition of "child" includes stepchildren, adopted children, those born in or out of wedlock, those born in or outside of the current marriage, those who have become emancipated, and those over whom the applicant has lost all parental rights. Indicate whether they will be applying for adjustment concurrently with the principal applicant.

Part 7

Enter the requested biographical information to Questions 1–6.

Part 8

This section is the longest and most difficult, since it covers all the possible grounds of inadmissibility.

List all present and past memberships in any organization to which the applicant has belonged to Questions 1–13. Although only membership in a Communist or totalitarian party, or terrorist organization, will be a factor in determining admissibility,[55] list all clubs, parties, societies, associations, and nonpolitical organizations, such as church membership, as well. These could be organizations in the United States or anywhere in the world. List any military service here, too. List the name of the organization, location, dates of membership, and the nature of the organization. If you are not certain whether the organizational affiliation of the applicant may create inadmissibility issues, do not file the application until you can resolve this issue.

Questions 14–80 ask about potential grounds of inadmissibility for fraud, false claims of citizenship, smuggling, unlawful presence and immigration violations, criminal acts, security-related issues, and public charge. Below are tips to bear in mind when answering some of the questions. The grounds of inadmissibility and possible waivers are described in chapters 6 and 7 and will not be repeated here. Public charge and the affidavit of support requirements are covered in chapter 8. It is important to note that a "yes" answer to any of the questions in this section may mean that the applicant is inadmissible. For this reason, you should not file the application unless you are able to evaluate whether the applicant may be found inadmissible and, if so, whether he or she qualifies for a waiver.

General eligibility. Questions 14–24 go to eligibility to apply for adjustment under INA §245(a). For example, applicants who have ever been denied a visa or admission would need to disclose the circumstances, which would likely lead to an

---

55 INA §212(a)(3)(B)(i).

investigation as to whether the applicant was inadmissible at that earlier time and whether that inadmissibility still exists. Questions 16–17 ask if the applicant ever worked in the United States without authorization or violated the terms of his or her nonimmigrant visa. If the applicant is applying for adjustment of status in one of the family preference categories, INA §245(c) prevents eligibility to adjust if the applicant ever worked illegally or failed to maintain lawful immigration status. Immediate relatives and special immigrants are not subject to this preclusion.

Question 18 asks if the applicant has ever been in removal, exclusion, deportation, or rescission proceedings. If so, USCIS may not have jurisdiction over the application.[56] Persons who are still in proceedings (have not been issued a final order) must apply for adjustment of status before the immigration court, which may require moving to recalendar, reopen, or terminate the proceedings. Persons in removal proceedings who are considered "arriving aliens"[57] are generally eligible to apply for adjustment before USCIS.[58]

Question 19 asks if the applicant has ever been issued a final order of exclusion, deportation, or removal, and Question 20 asks if such an order had ever been reinstated. Persons who have been issued a final order of deportation or removal but who have not executed it by departing the country are still considered in proceedings, and therefore USCIS would not have jurisdiction. Note, however, that if an individual has an unexecuted order of exclusion, she or he may still apply for adjustment of status with USCIS.[59] Those who did execute the order by departing and then returned illegally may be subject to inadmissibility under INA §212(a)(9)(C)(i)(II) or reinstatement of removal under INA §241(a)(5). Those who executed the order by departing and subsequently reentered and had that order reinstated under INA §241(a)(5) are ineligible for "any relief under this Act," including adjustment of status.

Question 21 asks if the applicant has ever had LPR status rescinded. This could indicate an underlying ground of inadmissibility. Question 22 asks if the applicant was ever granted voluntary departure but failed to depart within the required period of time. If so, this could make the applicant ineligible for adjustment of status for a 10-year period beginning on the date the applicant failed to depart.[60] Question 23 asks if the applicant ever applied for any relief from removal, exclusion, or deportation, which also opens up whether the applicant is still in proceedings and whether he or she is inadmissible.

---

56 8 CFR §§245.2(a)(1), 1245.2(a)(1).

57 8 CFR §1.1(q).

58 8 CFR §§245.2(a)(1), 1245.2(a)(1).

59 *Matter of C—H—*, 9 I&N Dec. 265, 266 (Reg'l Comm'r 1961).

60 *See* INA §240B(d)(1)(B).

Questions 24a–c ask whether the applicant entered the United States on a J nonimmigrant visa that subjected the person to the two-year foreign residency requirement and, if so, whether the applicant has either complied with the requirement or been granted a waiver. If not, the person is ineligible to apply for adjustment of status under 8 CFR §245.1(c)(2).

Criminal grounds. Questions 25–45 ask about incidents that could trigger one of the criminal grounds of inadmissibility found in INA §212(a)(2). These grounds cover crimes of moral turpitude, multiple criminal convictions, controlled substance violations or traffickers, prostitution and commercialized vice, serious criminal activity where the person asserted immunity, foreign government officials who have committed severe violations of religious freedom, human trafficking, or money laundering. The first one, Question 25, is quite broad and asks if the applicant has ever been arrested, cited, charged, or detained for any reason by any law enforcement official, including immigration officials, U.S. armed forces, or U.S. Coast Guard, in the United States or in another country. Question 26 asks if the applicant ever committed a crime of any kind, "even if you were not arrested, cited, charged with, or tried for that crime." Question 30 asks if the applicant ever violated or attempted or conspired to violate any controlled substance law in the United States or in another foreign country.

Applicants who answer "yes" to any of these questions must provide an explanation that includes why, where, and when he or she was "arrested, cited, detained, or charged" and the outcome or disposition of any proceeding. When listing all arrests and violations of any law or ordinance, one can exclude traffic violations unless they resulted in criminal charges, or involved alcohol, drugs, or injury to a person or property.[61] Given that even minor crimes may affect the applicant's eligibility and perhaps deportability, it is important not to file on behalf of a person with any criminal record until you are able to assess what, if any, immigration consequences may result from the arrest and disposition of the case. Note that any arrest must be listed, even if the conviction was subsequently expunged or vacated, the person was a juvenile at the time, or the records were otherwise sealed or cleared.

Security and related grounds. Questions 46–60 relate to possible security– and terrorist-related grounds of inadmissibility found in INA §212(a)(3)(A) and (B). The security-related grounds cover those who seek to enter the United States "to engage solely, principally, or incidentally in" activity related to espionage, sabotage, or the overthrow of the United States by force. It is unlikely that any of your clients would be subject to this ground, but the terrorist-related ground is more expansive. Terrorist activity and a terrorist organization are both defined in the statute.[62]

---

61 I-485 Instructions at p. 13.

62 INA §212(a)(3)(B)(iii), (iv), (vi).

Question 49 asks if the applicant ever received any type of military, paramilitary, or weapons training. Question 53 asks if the applicant ever worked or served "in any prison, jail, prison camp, detention facility, labor camp, or any other situation that involved detaining persons." And Question 55 asks if the applicant ever served in a military or police unit. These three questions may require an answer in the affirmative if the applicant has ever served in the military. If so, explain in Part 14 what the applicant did or what occurred, including the dates and locations.

Public Charge. Question 61 asks whether the applicant is exempt from the public charge ground of inadmissibility. A complete list of those who are exempt is included in chapter 8 as well as the Form I-485 instructions. The most common adjustment applicants who are exempt from public charge include asylees, refugees, VAWA self-petitioners, U visa grantees, T visa grantees, and those filing under the Cuban Adjustment Act. Those who are subject to public charge will need to complete Form I-944, Declaration of Self-Sufficiency, which is also covered in chapter 8.

Questions 62a–n ask if the applicant is exempt from the affidavit of support requirements. All adjustment applicants who are exempt from the public charge ground of inadmissibility are also exempt from the affidavit of support requirements. In addition, some who are subject to public charge are exempt from the affidavit of support requirements. This is covered in chapter 8. The most common applicants who are exempt from having to file an I-864, Affidavit of Support under Section 213A of the INA, are those who are widow(er)s, are children under 18 of a U.S. citizen parent who will derive citizenship upon becoming an LPR and residing in the United States, or have earned or been credited with 40 qualifying quarters under Social Security law. If any of those exemptions apply, check the box in Question 62a–c. Question 62d–n do not apply to family-based adjustment applicants.

Fraud, false claims of citizenship, in absentia orders, smuggling: *Questions 63–69.* These nine questions are somewhat unrelated and are labeled as "illegal entries and other immigration violations." Questions 63a–c ask if the applicant has been ordered removed *in absentia.* A person subject to an *in absentia* removal order is ineligible for various forms of discretionary relief, including adjustment of status, for a 10-year period if he or she was provided with oral notice of the consequences of failing to appear.[63] In addition, a person with an unexecuted removal order is not eligible to seek adjustment of status with USCIS in any event. In this circumstance, jurisdiction over the adjustment-of-status application is with the immigration court, and the applicant would need to file a motion to reopen to seek this relief.

Questions 64–65 relate to inadmissibility for immigration fraud, which is set forth in INA §212(a)(6)(C). That ground of inadmissibility covers someone who "by fraud or willful misrepresentation of a material fact, ever sought to procure, or procured, a visa, other documentation, entry into the United States, or any other

---

63 INA §240(b)(7).

immigration benefit."[64] This covers applicants who knowingly lied to a consular official or immigration agent at the time of admission concerning a material fact that would have made them inadmissible had they told the truth. It also covers use of false written statements or false documents at the time of admission or application for a visa, an application for employment authorization, or an application for other immigration benefits (e.g., asylum, temporary protected status, or a reentry permit). It does not cover false statements on a Form I-9, Employment Eligibility Verification, or documents used to obtain a job, since the statements are not being made to a government official or to obtain admission, a visa, or other immigration benefit. There is a waiver available for this ground of inadmissibility for some applicants.[65]

Question 66 asks if the applicant ever falsely claimed to be a U.S. citizen. A separate ground of inadmissibility applies to persons who make a false claim to U.S. citizenship on or after September 30, 1996, for any purpose under the INA or any other federal or state law.[66] This would include such activity as claiming to be a U.S. citizen on a driver's license application, a Social Security card, voter registration, U.S. passport, public benefit, or Form I-9 employment verification. Only a small category of applicants is eligible for an exception to this inadmissibility ground, and there is no waiver.

Question 68 asks if the applicant has ever smuggled anyone into the United States, which includes encouraging, assisting, or aiding them in any way.[67] Make sure you ask if the applicant ever entered the United States illegally with a child or other family member. There is a waiver for this ground of inadmissibility for those who smuggled only their spouse, parent, or child.[68]

Question 69 asks if the applicant has received a final order for violating civil document fraud pursuant to INA §274C. Enforcement of this section of the law was enjoined from 1996 until early 2001, and prior orders were rescinded.[69] To date, USCIS has not recommenced enforcement of this provision. After passage of the 1996 legislation, waivers for violating section 274C are available for certain applicants.[70]

Removal, unlawful presence, or illegal return: Questions 70–73. Question 70 asks whether the applicant has received a final order of deportation, exclusion, or removal that was executed by his or her subsequent departure from the United States. If the

64 INA §212(a)(6)(C)(i).

65 INA §212(i).

66 INA §212(a)(6)(C)(ii).

67 INA §212(a)(6)(E).

68 INA §212(d)(11).

69 *Walters v. Reno*, 145 F.3d 1032 (9th Cir. 1998).

70 INA §274C(d)(7).

answer to this question is "yes," the applicant may be subject to multiple obstacles to adjustment eligibility, including:

- Inadmissibility under INA §212(a)(9)(A) for five or ten years, depending on the type of removal order and how long the applicant remained outside the United States following the removal order;
- Inadmissibility under INA §212(a)(9)(C) for triggering the permanent bar if the applicant reentered the United States without inspection and admission after a removal order on or after April 1, 1997; and
- Exposure to reinstatement of removal under INA §241(a)(5), if the applicant returned to the United States unlawfully after a prior order of removal.

Exercise caution in this situation, because the applicant is unlikely to be eligible to adjust status. If an application for adjustment of status is filed, it may lead to the applicant's detention and removal.

Questions 71–72 relate to unlawful presence and the three- or ten-year bar that may have been triggered upon departing the United States.[71] Questions 73a–b relate to the "permanent bar" that may have been triggered upon reentering the United States illegally, or attempting to reenter illegally, after a year or more of unlawful presence or after being deported, excluded, or removed. These grounds of inadmissibility are covered in detail in chapter 6.

Miscellaneous grounds. Questions 74–80 relate to polygamists, child abductors, deserters, draft evaders, U.S. citizens who renounced their citizenship for tax reasons, and other unlikely events. Question 77 asks if the applicant ever voted in a state, federal, or local election. This would trigger a ground of inadmissibility found in INA §212(a)(10)(D), for which there is no waiver and only a limited exception.

Part 9

Indicate if the applicant will be seeking certain accommodations based on being deaf or hard of hearing, blind, or some other disability or impairment.

Parts 10–12

The applicant must sign the form in Part 10 as well as provide contact information. If the applicant is using an interpreter, that person must also sign in Part 11 as well as provide contact information and certify to his or her qualifications. Anyone who assists in preparing the Form I-485, even if a separate Form G-28 is filed, must also sign the application in Part 12 and provide contact information.[72] If you are an attorney or accredited representative, indicate whether you are also filing a Form G-28, Notice of Entry of Appearance. If you are not filing a G-28, you are

---

71 INA §212(a)(9)(B).

72 8 CFR §103.2(a)(2).

still acknowledging that you are representing the applicant in connection with the completion of the adjustment of status application.

Other Forms and Documents Included in Adjustment Application Packet

The complete adjustment packet is made up of the following documents:

- Form I-485, the adjustment application
- Supplement A to Form I-485 for those applicants who are eligible to adjust under INA §245(i),[73] documentary evidence of the principal beneficiary's residence in the United States on December 21, 2000, if necessary, and penalty fee of $1,000, unless the applicant qualifies for an exception
- Filing fee and biometrics fee, plus $1,000 penalty if filing under §245(i).[74] There is no additional filing fee for employment authorization (Form I-765) and advance parole (Form I-131) if these are submitted at the same time. Biometrics is required for persons age 14 to 79. Applicants under 14 years who are filing together with a parent pay a special fee.
- Two identical color passport-style photos of the applicant
- An I-130 petition with supporting documents, or an approval notice of a previously approved relative petition. (If filing an I-130, the applicant must also file a separate fee. If the petition is based on marriage between the petitioner and the beneficiary, also complete a Form I-130A, Supplemental Information for Spouse Beneficiary.)
- Form I-693, Report of Medical Examination and Vaccination Record, completed after a medical examination by a USCIS-approved civil surgeon.[75] This may be submitted: (1) at the time of filing the I-485; (2) by mail, after filing the I-485 in response to receiving an RFE or letter from USCIS asking for it; or (3) in person, at an interview in a USCIS field office. Because a completed I-693 has limited validity, it is recommended that it not be submitted until after receiving an RFE or until an interview. Applicants who entered on a K visa who are applying within one year of submitting their earlier medical examination results need not submit another one, but do need to submit a vaccination supplement.
- Copy of passport page with nonimmigrant visa and/or Form I-94 showing lawful admission or parole, if applying under INA §245(a). Other acceptable proof could include a border crossing card, airline tickets, or affidavits attesting to the lawful entry.

---

73 8 CFR §245.10(b)(5).

74 8 CFR §103.7(b). Always check, as fees may change.

75 8 CFR §245.5.

- Form I-864, Affidavit of Support Under Section 213A of the Act, signed by the sponsor, if the applicant is required to submit one.[76] The Form I-864 must be accompanied by the required supporting documentation detailed in the instructions, including the last federal income tax return.[77]
- Form I-944, Declaration of Self-Sufficiency, if the applicant is subject to the public charge ground of inadmissibility. The form requires the submission of supporting documents, including three years of tax returns, assets and resources, employment history and job skills, education, credit reports, debts and liabilities, health insurance, and education.
- Copy of applicant's birth certificate, with English translation
- Evidence of appropriate family relationship, such as a copy of a birth or marriage certificate, with translation, if applying as derivative[78]
- Form I-765, Application for Employment Authorization (optional)
- Form I-131, Application for Travel Document, if travel is contemplated before the adjustment is granted[79]
- Form G-28, Notice of Entry of Appearance as Attorney or Representative, if applicable

Those applying for adjustment of status through marriage also will have to provide evidence that a marriage is bona fide, such as joint bank accounts, credit accounts, insurance policies with both names, rental agreements with both names, birth certificates of children, and so on. See the list of documents useful in proving bona fide marriage in chapter 2. A sample document checklist for adjustment-of-status applicants is included as Appendix 4.

Adjustment applicants, other than those in H-1B, K-3, K-4, or L-1 nonimmigrant status, who wish to leave the United States while the application is pending must apply for and obtain advance parole. If these applicants leave the United States without obtaining advance parole, they will be viewed as having abandoned their application.[80] Applicants must submit a Form I-131, Application for Travel Document, and provide a basis for granting parole. Lately the USCIS has been requiring applicants to justify their need to travel.

Where to File

In all areas of the country, USCIS now requires the adjustment application and supporting documentation to be filed by postal mail with the USCIS National

---

76 INA §213A.

77 The affidavit of support requirements and procedures are set forth in chapter 8.

78 8 CFR §204.1(f)(1).

79 8 CFR §245.2(a)(4)(ii)(B).

80 8 CFR §245.2(a)(4)(ii).

Benefits Center (NBC) in Missouri via a lockbox in Chicago. The NBC then forwards the application to the appropriate district office if an adjustment interview is required. This policy affects the filings of Form I-485, Application to Register Permanent Residence or Adjust Status; Form I-765, Application for Employment Authorization; and Form I-131, Application for Travel Document.

The lockbox address is U.S. Citizenship and Immigration Services, P.O. Box 805887, Chicago, IL 60680-4120. For non–U.S. Postal Service deliveries (e.g., private couriers), the address is U.S. Citizenship and Immigration Services, Attn. FBAS, 131 South Dearborn, 3rd Floor, Chicago, IL 60603-5517. Widow(er)s will be filing at a different address: USCIS, Vermont Service Center, Attn: CRU, 75 Lower Welden Street, St. Albans, VT 05479-0001.

After filing the application(s) and supporting documents, the applicant will receive a notice from the nearest application support center instructing him or her to appear for the taking of 10-digit fingerprints.

Arriving aliens who are in removal proceedings may apply for adjustment of status using the procedure described above.[81] An arriving alien in removal proceedings may renew an adjustment application filed with USCIS if he or she is returning on advance parole and the district director has denied the adjustment application.[82]

Filing Fees

For the most up-to-date information about filing fees, go to www.uscis.gov and click on the Forms tab. There is no fee waiver eligibility for family-based adjustment applications, nor for the $1,000 penalty fee if applying under §245(i).[83]

Interview Process

The USCIS adjudicator is trained to review the applicant's file, including any approved petitions, and note any potential problems (e.g., the applicant is subject to a possible ground of inadmissibility or has previously been placed in removal proceedings).[84] At the interview, the USCIS officer will go over the information in the adjustment application and confirm that it is accurate.[85] The officer also will resolve any issues that were identified during the preinterview review. The applicant should bring the originals of any document submitted with the adjustment application. Applicants immigrating through marriage should be prepared to answer questions about the validity of their marriage. If necessary—for example, to satisfy any doubts about the bona fides of a marriage—the officer may conduct

---

81 8 CFR §245.2(a)(1).

82 8 CFR §1245.2(a)(1)(i), (ii).

83 8 CFR §103.7(c).

84 AFM ch. 23.2(f), located in 7 *USCIS Policy Manual* pt. D.

85 8 CFR §245.6.

separate interviews of the parties. See chapters 2 and 5 for tips on preparing for such interviews.

For certain family-based petitions, USCIS may decide to waive the adjustment-of-status interview.[86] The decision as to whether an interview can be waived is made on a case-by-case basis in situations where there is enough evidence in the file to make a decision without an interview. Interviews may be waived in the following family cases:

- Unmarried minor children and stepchildren of U.S. citizens when accompanied by original or certified copies of supporting documentation;
- Parents of U.S. citizens when accompanied by original or certified copies of supporting documentation; and
- Children of lawful permanent residents who are unmarried and under 14 years old.[87]

Decision

If the USCIS officer approves the application, the applicant may receive a stamp in his or her passport with temporary evidence of LPR status; practices vary between different USCIS district offices. The applicant will then be mailed the Form I-551, Permanent Resident Alien card.

If the examiner is going to deny the application, he or she will provide the applicant with the reasons.[88] There is no appeal of a denial, but applicants are entitled to reapply before an immigration judge if placed in removal proceedings.[89] The immigration judge will apply a *de novo* review of the application. An applicant may also seek to challenge the denial by filing a motion to reopen or reconsider with USCIS.

---

86 *Id.*

87 AFM ch. 23.2(h), located in 7 *USCIS Policy Manual* pt. D.

88 8 CFR §245.2(a)(5)(ii).

89 *Id.*

CHAPTER 4

CONSULAR PROCESSING

Applicants for a family-based immigrant visa will apply at a U.S. consulate if they are residing abroad or are ineligible, or elect not, to adjust status in this country.[1] This process is controlled mostly by the Department of State (DOS) and is performed by the National Visa Center (NVC) and the immigrant visa sections at U.S. consulates or embassies.[2] Applicants in the United States who are eligible to adjust status under Immigration and Nationality Act (INA) §245(a) or (i) usually elect to do so rather than suffer the inconveniences, expenses, and uncertainties of consular processing. However, many intending immigrants in the United States are ineligible to adjust status and will need to consular process. In addition to the added time and expense, leaving the United States may trigger certain bars to reentry.[3] The grounds of inadmissibility and possible waivers are set forth in chapters 6 and 7. This chapter will describe the process of applying for the immigrant visa at U.S. consulates.

If the U.S. citizen or lawful permanent resident (LPR) relative is residing in the United States, he or she first will petition for the family member by filing a Form I-130 with U.S. Citizenship and Immigration Services (USCIS). If the petitioner is residing abroad, in most cases he or she will also file the I-130 petition with USCIS in the United States. However, in limited circumstances the DOS has authority to adjudicate a relative petition filed by a U.S. citizen residing abroad on behalf of an immediate relative.[4] The I-130 petition process is set forth in chapter 2.

After the I-130 petition is approved, USCIS sends notice of the approval to the petitioner and forwards the approved petition to the NVC. The NVC creates a case by inputting data on the beneficiary listed on the Form I-130 – now the applicant for the immigrant visa – and assigns a case number. Once a case is created, NVC sends out an initial notice on case processing that includes instructions on logging on to the DOS's Consular Electronic Application Center (CEAC). Applicants are instructed to use CEAC to check the status of the case, pay the necessary fees, and continue with the next steps in processing. Once the fees are paid, the applicant must complete the appropriate forms and gather the necessary documents. After the required forms and documentation are submitted, the NVC forwards the file to the appropriate consular post and schedules the visa interview. This process is explained in greater detail below.

---

1 INA §§221, 245.

2 INA §§104(a), 202(a)(1)(B).

3 INA §212(a)(9)(B).

4 6 *USCIS Policy Manual* pt. B, ch. 3.A.

National Visa Center

After USCIS approves the I-130 petition and sends an approval notice to the petitioner, it forwards the approved petition to the NVC if the petitioner indicated on the I-130 that the beneficiary will be consular processing. The NVC, located in Portsmouth, NH, is part of the DOS's Bureau of Consular Affairs and is responsible for centralizing the preappointment processing stage. It advises the intending immigrant on when the priority date is current, the fees that need to be paid, the documents that need to be submitted, and the process of obtaining the immigrant visa through the consulate.[5] The NVC requests and reviews the required forms and documents from the applicant and schedules the visa appointment. After this initial processing is complete, the NVC forwards the approved I-130 petition and the completed forms and documents to the appropriate consulate.

The intending immigrant will apply for an immigrant visa at one of the following U.S. consulates: the consulate in the country where the applicant is residing or last resided; the consulate in the country where the applicant is physically located and intends to remain throughout the processing; or any other consulate that will accept jurisdiction of the case as a matter of discretion.[6] A consulate may accept jurisdiction if the applicant is currently residing in the United States and can establish hardship if he or she were forced to return to the country of last residence.[7] Hardship can be civil unrest or war, but cannot be simply economic factors. Applicants residing in a country with which the United States does not maintain diplomatic relations or where the consular section is closed because of unstable or insecure conditions are called "homeless" visa applicants.[8] These applicants will go through processing at a consulate designated by DOS.[9]

After NVC creates a case, it sends the intending immigrant instructions for the next steps in the process. The Notice of Immigrant Visa Case Creation instructs the applicant to log on to CEAC to check case status, pay fees, submit documents, and read messages. The applicant must use the NVC case number and invoice number provided on the case creation notice to log into CEAC. If the applicant is in a preference category that is not current, the NVC stores the approved I-130 petition until the priority date is current in Chart B, Dates for Filing Family-Sponsored Visa Applications, in the Department of State's *Visa Bulletin.* The NVC will notify the applicant when the case is ready for continued processing. A sample Notice of Immigrant Visa Case Creation is included at Appendix 5A. Notices are generally sent by email unless e-mail addresses have not been provided, in which case correspondence will be sent via regular mail to the petitioner, the applicant, and

---

5 9 *Foreign Affairs Manual* (FAM) 504.4.

6 22 CFR §42.61.

7 9 FAM 504.4-8(D).

8 9 FAM 504.4-8(E).

9 *Id.*

the representative. Notices are sent to the attorney or accredited representative who assisted in filing the Form I-130 and who submitted a G-28, Notice of Entry of Appearance as Attorney or Accredited Representative.

If the petitioner filed the Form I-130 *pro se*, or there is a change in representation, a Form G-28 can be submitted through the "Ask NVC" public inquiry form described below. The applicant may also choose an agent who will receive further communication from the NVC and the consulate. The agent can be a family member, friend, or other trustworthy person. CEAC allows the applicant to provide up to six e-mail addresses, and correspondence on the case will be sent using each address. For cases initiated before the enhanced CEAC portal, to choose an agent, the applicant completes and submits Form DS-261, Choice of Address and Agent.

Payment of Fees

The immigrant-visa and affidavit-of-support fees should be paid electronically from a checking or savings account held at a U.S. financial institution. To pay online, payers are instructed to go to the CEAC Immigrant Visa Invoice Payment Center and follow the fee collection instructions. The payer will need the immigrant visa case number and the invoice identification number found on the initial NVC notice. The payer will also need his or her bank's routing number and checking or savings account number. The online payment system requires separate transactions for the immigrant visa fee and the affidavit of support fee. Once payments are made, the payer can print or have a receipt e-mailed. It can take up to a week for the NVC to process payments. Applicants should log back into CEAC to check the status of the payment. Applicants will not be able to access the DS-260, Online Immigrant Visa and Alien Registration Application, until NVC has processed the payments.

Currently, the fee for the affidavit of support processing is $120 and the immigrant visa application fee is $325. Check the NVC website for the most up-to-date fees. A sample fee receipt is provided in Appendix 5B.

Affidavit of Support

The petitioner must complete and submit the I-864, Affidavit of Support under Section 213A of the INA, and supporting documentation to the NVC for a technical review. A signed form and documentation must be submitted for each family member immigrating with a separate visa petition. If a form is not complete, or documentation is not sufficient, the NVC will send a notice through CEAC explaining what is wrong and requesting correction and resubmission. Immigrant visa applicants should also prepare the DS-5540, Public Charge Questionnaire, and related documents to present at the interview. As of June 2020, the NVC does not play a role in reviewing the DS-5540. Detailed information on public charge and completing the affidavit of support is set forth in chapter 8.

The Immigrant Visa Application

After the necessary fees have been paid, all applicants must complete and submit the DS-260. The form is completed and submitted through the CEAC website. To access the form the applicant or preparer must input the NVC case number and invoice ID number. All of the information entered online is accessible by the NVC and consular posts and the applicant is not required to submit a paper version to the NVC or bring a copy to the visa interview. The DS-260 requests standard biographical data on the visa applicant.

The form includes questions on the applicant's spouse, parents, children, places the applicant has lived for at least six months since the age of 16, previous travel to the United States, previous employment, and educational institutions attended. Applicants must also provide information on each social media platform used within the last five years, including platform names and the usernames or handles used for each. Additionally, the form asks questions related to the applicant's admissibility and whether the applicant has ever been refused admission to the United States. It is important to note that the questions asking for dates of residence in or visits to the United States may reveal periods of "unlawful presence," which could trigger the three– or ten-year bar to admissibility.

Once all of the fields on the DS-260 are completed, the applicant submits the form by clicking on the "Sign and Submit Application" button. Once submitted, there is currently no way for the applicant to make edits or corrections before the consular interview. Applicants should be sure to inform the consular officer if any corrections or changes need to be made. At the time of the interview, the applicant will be required to swear under oath that the information entered into the form is true and correct, and he or she will provide a biometric signature.

Required Documentation

The intending immigrant is required to submit civil documents and police certificates (unless the applicant is from a country where those are not available) to the NVC for prescreening.[10] Most applicants will now upload and submit documents through CEAC. This process is discussed in more detail below. For older cases, photocopies are sent to the NVC. For these cases, it is important to send these documents with the NVC document cover sheet that contains the case number and bar code. In all situations, the applicant must be prepared to present the original documents, plus an additional photocopy of each, at the time of the visa interview.

Documents not in English or not in the native language of the jurisdiction where the consular post is located must be translated into English. The translations should bear a certificate of accuracy in which the translator swears that he or she is familiar

10 22 CFR §42.65(b).

with both languages, has translated the document into English, and that it is a true and complete translation. The documents that are required include the following:

- a photocopy of the biographic data page of the applicant's valid, unexpired passport[11]
- photocopy of applicant's birth certificate
- photocopy of marriage certificate
- evidence of the termination of each prior marriage, such as a final divorce decree, death certificate, or annulment papers
- if a U.S. citizen is petitioning for a parent or sibling, a certified copy of petitioner's birth certificate
- if a petitioning spouse was previously married, a certified copy of a final divorce decree, death certificate, or annulment papers for each prior marriage
- if the applicant has served in the military forces of any country, a copy of his or her military record
- if the applicant has been convicted of a crime, a certified copy of each court disposition
- if the applicant is age 16 or older, he or she must submit a police certificate, if available, from that country

Primary documentation, such as of a birth or marriage, would be a certificate from a government agency that maintains official records. Applicants should consult the U.S. Visa: Reciprocity and Civil Documents by Country page on the www.travel.state.gov website for information on the availability of civil documents in each foreign country. If a document is listed as unavailable, the applicant is not required to submit it. If a document is listed as available, but the applicant is unable to obtain the document, he or she may submit secondary evidence, which may consist of such documents as baptismal or other church records.[12] The applicant must provide an explanation to the NVC as to why the document cannot be obtained and any attempts made to get the document. Applicants should be aware that the consular officer may still require submission of the document at the time of the visa interview.

Document Submission

The NVC has developed a system for the electronic submission of required civil and financial documents. Most immigrant visa applicants will now upload and submit their documents online through CEAC. Applicants can either scan or take a photo of their documents, save the documents on their computers, and then upload them. Applicants will not be able to upload civil documents in CEAC until they have

11 The original passport should not be sent to the NVC.

12 22 CFR §42.65(d).

completed and submitted the DS-260 immigrant visa application. CEAC creates a list of required documents for each applicant based on information provided on the DS-260. Additionally, scanned documents must meet size, type, and quality specifications to be uploaded. In addition to the civil documents, the I-864 and the sponsor's financial documents must also be uploaded through CEAC. If NVC determines a submitted document is incorrect, a notice will be sent to the applicant that the status of his or her case has been updated and instructing him or her to log back into CEAC to review messages. If a new document needs to be submitted, the applicant should delete the rejected document and upload and submit the new one. A sample NVC Notice Regarding your Immigrant Visa Case is included in Appendix 5C.

When applicants submit documents through CEAC, they are not required to mail the forms, civil documents, and other supporting documents to the NVC, but they must be prepared to present the original physical documents, plus a photocopy of each, at the time of the visa interview. Once all of the required documents have been submitted and reviewed by the NVC, the applicant will receive an email that the case is documentarily complete and that the NVC will coordinate with the appropriate embassy or consulate to schedule the immigrant visa appointment. A sample notice that a case is documentarily complete is included in Appendix 5D. Applicants uploading their documents on CEAC also may use the system's enhanced features, which include the ability to check case status, receive feedback on document submission, add or remove derivatives, and add joint sponsors and household members to the affidavit of support. An additional benefit of the system is that logging into CEAC is considered a contact with the NVC to avoid termination of registration for a visa. Termination of registration is discussed in more detail below.

Appointment Letter for Immigrant Visa Applicants

Approximately four to six weeks before the scheduled immigrant visa interview, the applicant will receive an appointment letter that contains the date, time, and location of the visa interview.[13] This letter will be issued by the NVC and instructs applicants to visit the DOS website for interview preparation instructions and to review consulate-specific instructions. A sample appointment letter is included at Appendix 5E.

The website provides information to the visa applicant on preparing for the medical examination and reminds the applicant of all the necessary original documents that must be available at the time of the interview. Additionally, applicants are provided with a number of important notices about the visa interview process. These notices advise the applicant that:

---

13 22 CFR §42.62(b).

- Failure to bring a copy of the appointment letter to the interview may delay the interview;
- He or she should not make any travel arrangements or give up employment or property prior to issuance of the visa;
- It is possible that the applicant will have to spend several hours at the consulate before a decision is made on the application. Should complications arise, the applicant may not receive a visa on the day of the appointment and may have to return to the consulate at a later date; and
- No assurances can be given in advance that a visa will be issued.

In addition to the general notices provided on the website, applicants are advised to look at specific instructions provided by the individual consulate to determine if there are other requirements or documents needed. For example, many embassies and consulates require applicants to register for courier services used to return applicant passports and visas after interviews.

Once the NVC has completed the administrative processing and scheduled the visa interview, it will send the case file along with electronic data to the appropriate U.S. consulate abroad.

Contacting NVC

For information on the status of a case still pending at the NVC, one may call the automated voice center at (603) 334-0700. Telephone operators are available to answer questions Monday through Friday from 7:00 a.m. to midnight (Eastern). The NVC no longer responds to inquiries sent by regular mail. Any case inquiry postmarked on or after June 1, 2020, will not receive a response from NVC and the correspondence will be destroyed. Case inquiries should be made through the Ask NVC Public Inquiry form at https://nvc.state.gov/inquiry. The form asks for the NVC case number or USCIS receipt number, the principal applicant's name and date of birth, the petitioner's name, and an e-mail address. The form requires the inquirer to identify him or herself as the petitioner, principal applicant, attorney of record, or other. The NVC website provides time frames on when to expect a response to an inquiry. Applicants can also log into CEAC to get information on the status of their case and receive messages from NVC.

The Medical Examination

All applicants for an immigrant visa must undergo a medical examination.[14] The examination must be conducted by a designated doctor, called a panel physician, located in the country where the interview takes place.[15] Medical examinations are

---

14 INA §221(d); 22 CFR §42.66(a).

15 22 CFR §42.66(b).

conducted according to regulations published by the Department of Health and Human Services (HHS) and procedures established by the Centers for Disease Control and Prevention, an agency of HHS.[16] The medical examination is not a complete examination, but is designed to screen for certain medical conditions that are relevant to the applicant's admissibility to the United States.

Each consulate website provides a listing of the panel physicians authorized to conduct the medical examination in that location. Applicants are instructed to contact one of the physicians to schedule a medical examination and to obtain information on the cost of the examination and necessary testing. In addition to the list of panel physicians, each consulate provides specific instructions on scheduling the medical examination and the documents needed for the appointment. A sample Medical Examination Instructions from the travel.state.gov website is included as Appendix 5F.

In all cases the applicant must bring the visa appointment letter, his or her passport, and vaccination records, if available. The vaccination requirements constitute an important part of the medical examination. A discussion of the vaccination requirements and other health-related grounds of inadmissibility can be found in chapter 6. Additionally, a discussion of the waivers available for certain health-related grounds can be found in chapter 7.

Following the medical examination, the panel physician either will forward the results directly to the consulate or will provide the applicant with the results in a sealed envelope for the applicant to bring to the interview.

The Consular Interview

During the interview, the consular official will confirm the information contained in the Form DS-260 application, screen for any applicable ground of inadmissibility, review the supporting documents, ensure that the medical examination does not reveal any health-related problem that could prevent approval or require a waiver, and determine whether the applicant is likely to become a public charge.[17] The consular officer has the right to inquire into the validity of the marriage or the relationship that forms the basis of the immigrant petition.[18]

If the applicant is found inadmissible on a ground that is waivable, the applicant will submit the waiver form and supporting documentation by mail to a USCIS lockbox in the United States. The lockbox facility will forward the waiver application to the appropriate service center for adjudication. Once a decision is made on the

---

16 42 CFR §34.3; Centers for Disease Control and Prevention, Technical Instructions for the Medical Examination of Aliens [panel physicians], available at www.cdc.gov/ncidod/dq/panel.htm.

17 The grounds of inadmissibility are described in chapter 6 and the affidavit of support requirements are set forth in chapter 8.

18 22 CFR §42.62(b).

waiver, USCIS will send an electronic notification to the appropriate U.S. embassy or consulate abroad.

When an immigrant visa is issued, it can be valid for up to six months.[19] To obtain permanent residence status, the immigrant visa holder must travel to the United States and be admitted within the visa validity period. Additionally, in order to obtain a visa, the applicant must present a passport that is valid for at least 60 days beyond the validity of the immigrant visa.[20] Immigrant visa holders in the first– and second-preference categories, as well as children in the immediate-relative category, should be warned by consular officials that they are admissible in those categories only if they remain unmarried at the time of application for admission at the port of entry.[21]

If an immigrant visa is refused, the consular officer will inform the applicant of the reasons for the denial, including the provision of law or regulation on which the refusal is based.[22] If the reason for the refusal may be overcome with the submission of additional documents, and the applicant indicates an intention to submit the additional evidence, the file will remain open for up to one year.[23] Once the applicant has obtained the necessary documentation, the interview should be rescheduled. However, if no action is taken on the case for one year after the interview, registration—i.e., eligibility to apply for an immigrant visa—may be terminated.[24] The consular officer at the post should notify the applicant of the termination and the right to have the registration reinstated within one year by demonstrating that the failure to act was due to circumstances beyond his or her control.[25]

If the consular officer is requesting information or documentation that the applicant or representative believes is inappropriate or unnecessary, it is advisable to communicate directly with the consular post by telephone, e-mail, or the public inquiry form on the consulate website. Concerns should be put in writing with cites to the appropriate regulations, a *Foreign Affairs Manual* (FAM) section, or DOS cables that support the applicant's position. If attempts to persuade the consular official who is handling the case are unsuccessful, the applicant or representative may seek a review from the principal consular officer at that post.[26] In most instances, there is no judicial review

19 22 CFR §42.72(a).

20 22 CFR §42.64(b).

21 22 CFR §42.72(d).

22 22 CFR §42.81(b).

23 *Id.*

24 9 FAM 504.13-2(A)(2).

25 22 CFR §42.83(d).

26 22 CFR §42.81(c).

of a visa denial.[27] Representatives also may seek intervention from officials at the DOS Visa Office in Washington, D.C. For such intervention or to request an advisory opinion on a specific legal issue, an e-mail should be sent to legalnet@state.gov.

USCIS Immigrant Fee

Immigrant visa holders are required to pay a USCIS immigrant fee (check https://my.uscis.gov/uscis-immigrant-fee/ for current fee) after they receive the visa packet from the consulate or embassy. This fee is separate from the immigrant visa fee paid to DOS. The fee covers the cost of producing and delivering the permanent resident card once the visa holder is admitted to the United States. The fee must be paid online through the USCIS website with a debit or credit card or a checking account from a U.S. financial institution. Once the fee is paid, the payer should print a confirmation and keep it for his or her records. The fee does not have to be paid by the applicant himself or herself but can be paid by any other person on the applicant's behalf.

If the USCIS immigrant fee is not paid, the visa holder will still be admitted to the United States and will receive a passport stamp valid for one year evidencing LPR status. However, the new resident will not receive a Form I-551, Permanent Resident Card, until the required fee is paid. Adopted children who immigrate under the intercountry adoption programs and K visa holders are exempt from paying this fee. Children under 18, who will be residing in the United States with at least one U.S. citizen parent, may also elect not to pay the fee and instead apply for a U.S. passport or certificate of citizenship, since they will have acquired citizenship upon taking up residence.[28]

Termination of Registration

Under INA §203(g), DOS is authorized to terminate the registration of anyone who fails to apply for an immigrant visa within one year of notification of the availability of the visa. This provision applies if the applicant fails to contact the NVC after being notified of visa availability or if the applicant fails to appear for a scheduled interview and does not contact the consulate within a year of the missed appointment.[29] Registration is also terminated if an applicant fails to submit evidence to overcome the basis for a visa denial within one year after visa refusal.[30]

The regulations require that the consulate notify the registrant of the termination of registration and the right to seek reinstatement within one year of notification by establishing that the failure to apply for an immigrant visa within one year was due to

---

27 *Kleindienst v. Mandel*, 408 U.S. 753 (1972) (judicial review when the government denies a visa if no facially legitimate and bona fide reason).

28 INA §320(a).

29 22 CFR §42.83(a).

30 22 CFR §42.83(b).

circumstances beyond the applicant's control.[31] Such circumstances include illness preventing the applicant from traveling and inability to get travel documents.[32]

31 22 CFR §42.83(c).

32 22 CFR §42.83(e).

CHAPTER 5

IMMIGRATING THROUGH MARRIAGE

The process of immigrating to the United States through marriage to a U.S. citizen or lawful permanent resident (LPR) has so many special rules and procedures that it merits a separate chapter in this book. For example, the Immigration Marriage Fraud Amendments of 1986 (IMFA) imposed special restrictions on foreign nationals who obtain or attempt to obtain permanent residence based on marriage to a U.S. citizen or LPR.[1] The most significant change IMFA made was to create a two-year "conditional residence" status for these foreign national spouses.[2] IMFA also imposed severe penalties on persons found to have entered into a sham, or fraudulent, marriage.[3] A sham marriage is one that the parties enter into not to establish a life together as husband and wife but rather to circumvent immigration laws.[4] IMFA's provisions were successful in making it more difficult to immigrate by way of a fraudulent marriage and less attractive to try. Some of the harshest aspects of IMFA were tempered by later provisions of the Immigration Act of 1990.[5]

There are special civil and criminal penalties for the commission of marriage fraud. One civil penalty, for example, imposes an absolute prohibition from future approval of petitions on behalf of applicants who ever attempted or conspired to commit marriage fraud.[6] Foreign nationals who have ever sought admission into the United States or any "other benefit" under the Immigration and Nationality Act (INA) by fraud or by willfully misrepresenting a material fact are inadmissible.[7] LPRs who file second-preference visa petitions within five years of obtaining permanent resident status must satisfy additional requirements if they obtained that status based on a previous marriage.[8] And harsh criminal penalties are imposed on persons who engage in marriage fraud.[9]

Foreign nationals who marry while they are in exclusion, deportation, or removal proceedings face a tougher standard than others when seeking adjustment of status.[10] To adjust status in these circumstances, the parties must establish through "clear

---

1 Immigration Marriage Fraud Amendments Act of 1986, Pub. L. No. 99-639, §5(b), 100 Stat. 3537, 3543.

2 INA §216.

3 INA §204(c).

4 *Bark v. INS*, 522 F.2d 1200 (9th Cir. 1975).

5 Pub. L. No. 101-649, 104 Stat. 4978.

6 INA §204(c).

7 INA §212(a)(6)(C)(i).

8 INA §204(a)(2)(A).

9 18 USC §1546(a).

10 INA §204(g).

and convincing evidence" that the marriage is legitimate.[11] If they cannot meet that burden, their immigrant visa petition will not be adjudicated until the foreign national spouse has resided outside the United States for two years.

U.S. citizens may petition for their foreign fiancé(e)s to enter the United States on a K-1 nonimmigrant visa if the couple intends to marry within 90 days of entry.[12] If the couple marries within 90 days, the foreign fiancé(e) can file for adjustment of status under INA §245 procedures. In addition, the Legal Immigration and Family Equity Act (LIFE)[13] allows spouses who are married to U.S. citizens to enter the United States on a nonimmigrant K-3 visa rather than having to wait abroad for an immigrant visa.[14] These laws will all be discussed in this chapter.

Conditional Resident Status

Basic Principles

Many foreign national spouses who immigrate through marriage to a U.S. citizen, and possibly even some who immigrate based on marriage to an LPR, must first obtain "conditional" permanent resident status before they achieve the "unconditional" rights of other LPRs. This conditional status is imposed on foreign nationals who obtain LPR status based on a marriage that occurred within two years of their (1) entering the United States as a permanent resident, or (2) adjusting to permanent resident status within the United States.[15] Conditional status also is imposed on the foreign national spouse's children if they obtained immigrant status based on the parent's marriage, assuming the parent also acquired immigrant status based on that marriage.

During the two-year conditional residence period, these foreign nationals have the same rights, privileges, and responsibilities as other permanent residents.[16] However, conditional permanent residents must take additional steps at the end of the second year to preserve permanent resident status.[17]

A conditional resident will be issued a permanent resident card (Form I-551) that appears similar to the "green cards" issued to other permanent residents. However, the cards differ in two important respects. First, to indicate the bearer's conditional resident status, the classification code on the front, or photo side, of the conditional

---

11 INA §§204(g), 245(e).

12 INA §214(d).

13 Pub. L. No. 106-553, §1(a)(2) (appx. B, H.R. 5548, §§1101–04), 114 Stat. 2762, 2762A–142 to 2762A–149 (Dec. 21, 2000).

14 INA §101(a)(15)(K)(ii).

15 INA §216.

16 8 CFR §216.1.

17 INA §216(d)(2).

resident's card is marked "CR" rather than "IR." Second, the card expires two years after the date of admission or adjustment.

At the end of the two-year period, the couple must file a joint petition to have the conditions removed.[18] If U.S. Citizenship and Immigration Services (USCIS) grants this petition and removes the conditional status, the conditional resident spouse is accorded unconditional LPR status. USCIS, however, can terminate the conditional status at any time during the two-year period if it discovers that the marriage was dissolved or annulled, or if it determines that the marriage was entered into fraudulently.[19] If USCIS terminates the conditional status during the two-year period or denies the couple's joint petition to remove the condition, the conditional resident loses lawful immigration status and becomes subject to removal.

Foreign National Spouses Affected

The conditional residence provision affects only foreign national spouses whose marriage occurred less than two years before they either were admitted to the United States as LPRs or adjusted status here. The law applies only to those spouses who are the direct beneficiaries of an immigrant petition.[20] In other words, it affects beneficiaries of immediate-relative or second-preference petitions that are based on marriage to a U.S. citizen or LPR. It does not affect foreign nationals who enter the United States through derivative means, such as those who are accompanying or following to join a family member who has been granted an employment-based immigrant visa. Similarly, it does not apply to the foreign national spouse of a third-preference immigrant (a person immigrating as a married son or daughter of a U.S. citizen), nor to the spouse of a fourth-preference foreign national (a person immigrating as a brother or sister of a U.S. citizen).

Only foreign nationals who either adjust their status or are admitted to the United States as immigrants within two years of the date they were married will be subject to the conditional residence requirements. It is important to keep this time frame in mind when advising clients who have delayed filing for an immigrant visa or adjustment of status. Because visas issued by U.S. consulates are valid for up to six months,[21] it might be possible for a person who has been granted an immigrant visa within two years of the marriage date to time his or her entry into the United States so that the admission occurs at least two years after the marriage date. When being admitted, the foreign national should inform the inspector that he or she is entering as a permanent resident without conditions. Alternatively, if the foreign national will be adjusting status in the United States and USCIS schedules the adjustment

[18] 8 CFR §216.4(a).

[19] INA §216(b).

[20] INA §216(h).

[21] INA §221(c).

interview within two years of the marriage that qualifies him or her for adjustment, the person may request that it be rescheduled.

Children Affected

The law also affects foreign national children who immigrate legally to the United States within two years of their parent's marriage, assuming the parent also immigrated based on that marriage.[22] Like their immigrating parent, these children enter the country as conditional residents and will need to petition at the end of two years for the conditions to be removed.

If the foreign national parent is married to a U.S. citizen or LPR, that person's children can immigrate in one of three possible ways. First, the U.S. citizen or LPR spouse can adopt the children if they are under 16 and have resided with the adopting parent for at least two years.[23] If the adopting parent is a U.S. citizen, and the child is from one of the Hague Convention member countries, certain requirements must be met and procedures followed.[24] An adopted child would be entering with no conditions, because the relationship with the citizen petitioner is independent of the marriage of the child's parent. Second, the citizen or LPR spouse can file a stepparent petition on behalf of his or her stepchildren.[25] Stepchildren who obtain LPR status within two years of the marriage are granted conditional status. A third alternative is that after the foreign national parent becomes a conditional resident, the parent can file second-preference visa petitions on behalf of his or her children.[26]

Moreover, some dependent children who acquire immigrant status through their parent's marriage are not subject to the conditional residence requirements because their parent is not an "alien spouse" as defined in the statute.[27] For example, if the foreign national parent marries a U.S. citizen but acquires LPR status by means other than the marriage (e.g., he or she immigrates on an employment-based visa), the foreign national parent does not fall within the category of "alien spouse" and is therefore not subject to conditional residency. The U.S. citizen spouse in such a marriage could file a stepparent petition for the foreign national spouse's children. Even though the children would be gaining immigrant status based on the parent's marriage to a citizen that took place within two years of the foreign national's entry

22 INA §216(h)(2).

23 INA §101(b)(1)(E).

24 INA §101(b)(1)(G).

25 INA §101(b)(1)(B).

26 INA §203(a)(2).

27 INA §216(h)(1); Immigration and Naturalization Service (INS) Memorandum, W. Cook to J. Puleo, *Legal Opinion: Your CO 216-C Memorandum of May 23, 1989: Interpreting the definition of son/daughter and qualifying marriage under the Immigration Fraud Marriage Act* (Jan. 12, 1990), *reported and reprinted in* 67 *Interpreter Releases* 159, 166 (Feb. 5, 1990).

to the United States, the children would not be considered "alien sons or daughters" because the parent does not meet the definition of an "alien spouse."

Children who enter as conditional residents will have to follow requirements similar to those their foreign national parents must follow to remove the conditional status after the two-year period.[28] If the foreign national parent's status is terminated during these two years based on divorce, annulment, or a determination by USCIS that the marriage is fraudulent, the conditional resident status of the children will be terminated also.

Termination of Conditional Status by USCIS

USCIS may terminate a person's conditional status at any time during the two-year period if it determines that: (1) the person entered the qualifying marriage to procure an immigrant visa; (2) the qualifying marriage has been judicially annulled, dissolved, or terminated, other than through the death of a spouse; or (3) a fee or other consideration was given for filing the immigrant visa petition, other than fees to an attorney for preparing the petition.[29]

Before making such a finding, USCIS must send a formal written notice to the conditional resident notifying him or her of the agency's intention to terminate the status.[30] Before issuing a notice of termination, USCIS must provide the conditional resident with an opportunity to review and rebut the evidence on which it is relying.[31] After providing the foreign national an opportunity to challenge this finding, USCIS may issue a notice of termination.

When USCIS issues the notice of termination, the foreign national immediately loses all rights and privileges that accompany LPR status—e.g., permission to reside and work in the United States. In most cases USCIS will issue a notice to appear (NTA), which initiates removal proceedings, at the same time it issues the termination notice.[32] No special procedure exists for administratively appealing a decision to terminate conditional resident status, but the foreign national may ask an immigration judge to review the decision in a removal hearing.[33]

At the removal hearing, the agency has the burden of proving by a preponderance of the evidence that the foreign national is not entitled to conditional resident status.[34] This is a lower burden of proof than in other removal proceedings, in which the trial attorney must prove that a deportable foreign national is subject to removal by clear

---

28 INA §216(a)(1).

29 INA §216(b).

30 8 CFR §216.3(a).

31 *Id.*

32 INA §216(b)(2); 8 CFR §216.3(a).

33 INA §216(b)(2); 8 CFR §216.3(a).

34 INA §216(b)(2); 8 CFR §216.3(a).

and convincing evidence. This creates the anomaly that conditional residents can be ordered removed on weaker evidence than deportable foreign nationals who may never have established lawful entry or status in the United States.

Upon receiving the notice of termination, the conditional resident may file a waiver application (Form I-751, Petition to Remove Conditions on Residence).[35] These waiver applications can be filed at any time, either before or after the two-year conditional residence period has expired. If USCIS grants the waiver, the condition on the foreign national's permanent resident status will be removed effective the second anniversary of the alien's admission for permanent residence.

Most terminations will occur after the two-year conditional period has ended because, as a practical matter, USCIS rarely will initiate an investigation before then or discover through other means that the marriage has ended or that it was entered into fraudulently.

If a conditional resident fails to comply with the requirements for removing the condition at the end of the two-year period, USCIS can terminate the status at that time.[36] In the ensuing removal proceedings, the burden of proof will be on the foreign national to establish that he or she has complied with the removal-of-condition requirements.[37]

Even if the person has satisfied the requirements for removing the condition, the agency can still bring proceedings to rescind his or her adjustment to permanent residence and any subsequent naturalization. However, the only valid basis for such an action would be that the agency determined that the foreign national obtained LPR status through a marriage that he or she entered into to evade the immigration laws.[38]

Removing Conditional Status

Unless conditional residents take certain steps to remove the condition, they lose their lawful status. Within 90 days before the second anniversary of the date on which the foreign national obtained permanent residence, he or she must file a Form I-751, Petition to Remove the Conditions on Residence.[39] The two-year period is not tolled by any time spent by the foreign national outside the United States. In other words, the amount of time the conditional resident has spent outside the United States during the two years since acquiring conditional residence does not affect the requirement that he or she file the petition within the specified time period.

---

35 8 CFR §216.5(a).

36 INA §216(c)(2)(A).

37 INA §216(c)(2)(B).

38 8 CFR §216.3(b).

39 8 CFR §216.4.

Failure to file the petition or failure to comply with the interview requirements will lead to automatic termination of conditional resident status and the initiation of removal proceedings.[40] As noted above, in removal proceedings, the foreign national will bear the burden of proof to establish that he or she has complied with the prerequisites for having the condition removed.

Filing the Joint Petition

If the conditional resident is still lawfully married to the spouse through whom he or she obtained immigrant status, and if that spouse agrees to cooperate in completing the petition, then the couple will be filing a joint petition.[41] On the form, both spouses must declare under penalty of perjury that they were married in accordance with the laws in the jurisdiction where the marriage took place, and that they did not enter into the marriage to procure an immigration benefit. If the marriage has ended because of divorce, or annulment, then the conditional resident must seek a waiver of the joint petition requirement.

If the conditional resident has filed a joint petition but at the time of the interview is legally separated or is in divorce or annulment proceedings, USCIS will want the petitioner to submit the final decree and request that the joint petition be treated as a waiver petition. The service center adjudicating the petition has been instructed to issue a request for evidence (RFE) granting the petitioner 87 days to submit the final decree of divorce or annulment. If the divorce or annulment is finalized within that period and the conditional permanent resident submits the decree, the Form I-751 will be amended from a joint petition to a waiver application without requiring the petitioner to refile.[42]

Filing for a Waiver of the Joint Petition Requirement

In lieu of the couple's completing the joint petition, the conditional resident can request that this joint filing requirement be waived, based on any of three grounds:

- The marriage was entered into in good faith, but the marriage has been terminated by divorce or annulment;[43]
- The marriage was entered into in good faith, but the conditional resident has been battered or subjected to extreme cruelty by the U.S. citizen or LPR spouse;[44] or

---

40 INA §216(c)(2).

41 8 CFR §216.4(a)(1).

42 USCIS Memorandum, D. Neufeld, *I-751 Filed Prior to Termination of Marriage* (Apr. 3, 2009), AILA Doc. No. 09072166.

43 INA §216(c)(4)(B).

44 INA §216(c)(4)(C).

- Termination of permanent residency and deportation would result in extreme hardship.[45]

The conditional resident may apply for a waiver based on one or more of the grounds. For example, the conditional resident may claim both the battered spouse and the extreme hardship grounds.

Two of the possible waiver grounds include the requirement that the applicant prove that the marriage was entered into in good faith. The regulations state that USCIS will consider evidence concerning the amount of commitment each party has shown to the marital relationship.[46]

To prove good faith, USCIS suggests submitting evidence showing the following:

- a sharing of financial assets and liabilities;
- the length of time the parties cohabited;
- birth certificates of children born of the marriage; and
- any other pertinent evidence.[47]

This is essentially the same type of proof a foreign national spouse seeking conditional residency has to provide to establish a bona fide marriage .

Divorce/Annulment Waiver. The joint petition requirement can be waived if the conditional resident demonstrates that the marriage has ended in either divorce or annulment and that it was entered into in good faith. The divorce/annulment waiver is available to all conditional residents whose marriage has failed, regardless of who was at fault for the breakup and who initiated the divorce or annulment proceedings.[48]

Under current USCIS policy, conditional residents may apply for this waiver if the parties have separated and one has filed for dissolution or annulment but the decree has not yet been finalized. The service center has been instructed to issue a Request for Evidence (RFE) granting the petitioner 87 days to produce the final decree. If the divorce or annulment is finalized within that period, the waiver will be adjudicated based on the merits. If the divorce or annulment is not finalized within that period, USCIS will deny the waiver, terminate the conditional residency, and refer the case through the proper chain of command for issuance of removal proceedings.[49]

Foreign nationals who have filed for divorce or annulment and who are nearing the end of their two-year conditional residency must therefore make a decision.

---

45 INA §216(c)(4)(A).

46 8 CFR §216.5(e)(2).

47 8 CFR §216.5(e)(2)(i)–(iv).

48 *Adjudicator's Field Manual* (AFM), ch. 25.1(h)(2), located in 6 *USCIS Policy Manual* pt. I.

49 USCIS Memorandum, D. Neufeld, *I-751 Filed Prior to Termination of Marriage* (Apr. 3, 2009), AILA Doc. No. 09072166.

If they suspect that the divorce or annulment will not be finalized within 87 days of receiving the RFE, they can file under one of the other two waivers—battered spouse or extreme hardship—if applicable and then amend the application, or file under this waiver once the divorce is final.

Battered Spouse Waiver. The conditional resident may request a waiver of the joint petition requirement based on being a victim of battery or other forms of spousal or parental abuse. The statute allows this waiver if "during the marriage the alien spouse or child was battered by or was the subject of extreme cruelty perpetuated by his or her spouse or citizen or permanent resident parent…."[50] In other words, the conditional resident spouse may request this waiver if either the conditional resident or the conditional resident's child has been abused by the other spouse.

Regulations implementing the battered spouse waiver further define the statutory terms and set forth the requirements for being granted the waiver. The regulations clarify that the waiver is available to conditional residents, regardless of their current marital status.[51] They may be married and living with the abusing spouse, be separated, be divorced, or be in the process of seeking a divorce. As a practical matter, the battered spouse waiver is often sought by foreign nationals who are not seeking divorce. Spouses who are divorced often request the "divorce/annulment" waiver because of its more relaxed proof requirements. Also, to be eligible for the waiver, the foreign national must not have departed the United States after his or her conditional resident status has terminated.

Acts that constitute battery or extreme cruelty include, but are not limited to, "any act or threatened act of violence, including any forceful detention, which results or threatens to result in physical or mental injury."[52] Acts of violence include "psychological or sexual abuse or exploitation, including rape, molestation, incest (if the victim is a minor), or forced prostitution."[53]

If the foreign national is alleging physical abuse, he or she can submit any credible evidence. This "may include, but is not limited to, expert testimony in the form of reports and affidavits from police, judges, medical personnel, school officials and social service agency personnel."[54] The applicant should also include a detailed statement explaining the abuse suffered and the other relevant facts to establish eligibility for the waiver.

In the regulations, USCIS limits "extreme cruelty" to that which qualifies as "extreme mental cruelty." Although the regulations require waiver applicants

50 INA §216(c)(4)(B).

51 8 CFR §216.5(e)(3)(ii).

52 8 CFR §216.5(e)(3)(i).

53 *Id.*

54 8 CFR §216.5(e)(3)(iii).

alleging extreme cruelty to furnish independent evidence from "a professional recognized by [USCIS] as an expert in the field,"[55] statutory changes under the Violence Against Women (VAWA)[56] supersede the regulations and prohibit this requirement.[57] Under the amended statute, USCIS must consider "any credible evidence" in deciding a waiver based on physical abuse or extreme cruelty.[58] USCIS does have discretion to determine what evidence is credible and the proper weight to be given to the evidence.[59]

The statute and regulations also require that USCIS keep information contained in the waiver petition or supporting documents in strict confidence.[60] It may not release the information to any party without a court order or the written consent of the applicant. Information may be released only to the applicant, his or her authorized representative, an officer of USCIS, or any state or federal law enforcement agency.[61]

Extreme Hardship Waiver. The conditional resident spouse may request a waiver of the joint petition requirement based on "extreme hardship." Although the statute is silent about whom the extreme hardship must affect, USCIS has stated that the conditional resident may file for this waiver based on hardship either to himself or herself, to children of the marriage, or to a new spouse. The statute and regulations state that USCIS will take into account only factors that arose after the foreign national's entry as a conditional resident.[62] For example, USCIS presumably will not consider a preexisting medical problem that requires care and treatment in the United States. But medical problems that developed after the conditional resident entered the United States would be relevant, as would adverse political, social, or economic conditions that have developed recently in his or her home country.

USCIS recognizes that any removal is likely to result in a certain degree of hardship; but only when the hardship is "extreme" will it grant the waiver. Case law developed in the context of applications for the former relief of suspension of deportation will be relevant in defining what "extreme" means in the context of joint petition waivers. According to those cases, extreme hardship consists of something more than the hardship that persons ordinarily would experience upon being deported—e.g., the emotional strain that accompanies relocating, separation from family and friends, and economic loss.

---

55 8 CFR §216.5(e)(3)(iv).

56 Violence Against Women Act of 1994, Pub. L. No. 103-322, tit. IV, 108 Stat. 1796, 1902–55.

57 INS Memorandum, T. Aleinikoff, *Implementation of Crime Bill Self-Petitioning for Abused or Battered Spouses and Children of U.S. Citizens or Lawful Permanent Residents* (Apr. 16, 1996), AILA Doc. No. 96041690.

58 INA §216(c)(4).

59 *Id.*

60 INA §216(c)(4); 8 CFR §216.5(e)(3)(viii).

61 8 CFR §216.5(e)(3)(viii).

62 INA §216(c)(4); 8 CFR §216.5(e)(1).

The Board of Immigration Appeals (BIA) has listed 10 criteria that it considers relevant in determining whether the hardship a foreign national would suffer is extreme enough to meet the standard for granting suspension of deportation:

- The alien's age;
- The alien's ties to family in the United States and abroad;
- How long the alien has resided in the United States;
- The alien's health;
- Economic and political conditions in the alien's home country;
- The alien's occupation and work skills;
- His or her immigration history;
- His or her position in the community;
- Whether the alien is of special assistance to the United States or to the community; and
- Whether the alien could adjust status by alternate means[63]

Foreign nationals with health problems that would not receive adequate treatment in their home country have been particularly successful in establishing that extreme hardship makes them eligible for suspension of deportation or cancellation of removal. By itself, the probability that a foreign national will suffer economic detriment is usually not enough to meet the standard for establishing extreme hardship, unless the person can show that it will be impossible for him or her to find work in the home country. But when economic hardship is combined with advanced age, illness, or family ties in the United States, USCIS is more likely to find that the person faces extreme hardship. The practitioner thus should consider carefully all possible equities in a case, especially those that demonstrate a special hardship. An unusually strong equitable factor, together with more typical hardships such as psychological suffering, loss of ties in the community, and separation from family, will be very helpful in meeting the test for extreme hardship.

Death of the Spouse. The conditions also may be removed if the marriage was entered into in good faith, but the petitioner spouse is deceased. If filing the I-751 due to death of the spouse, the conditional resident should submit a copy of the death certificate with evidence of the bona fide marriage.

Procedures for Filing the Petition

The Form I-751 and supporting documentation must be filed by mail with either the Phoenix or Dallas lockbox depending on the petitioner's state of residence. Always check the USCIS website for the most up-to-date filing addresses.

---

63 *Matter of Anderson*, 16 I&N Dec. 596 (BIA 1978).

If the conditional resident is in removal proceedings at the end of the two-year period, the petition nevertheless should be filed with USCIS rather than with the immigration judge. In the removal proceedings, however, the immigration judge has authority to review USCIS's decision regarding the joint petition or the waiver application.[64]

The Form I-751 filing fee is currently $595, plus the $85 cost of biometrics. Each conditional resident dependent included on the principal petitioner's Form I-751 is required to submit the additional biometrics fee of $85. Always check the USCIS website for the most up-to-date filing fees.

Documentary Evidence

When filing a joint petition, the regulations require the submission of certain documentary evidence to show that the marriage was entered into in good faith. The following types of documents may be submitted: mortgage contract or lease showing joint ownership or joint occupancy of a common residence; financial records showing joint ownership of assets and/or responsibility for liabilities; birth certificates of children born of the marriage; affidavits from third parties having knowledge of the marriage; or "other documentation" establishing that the marriage is legitimate.[65]

The best type of evidence shows that the parties have made a true commitment to live together. In addition to the documents suggested in the regulations, other evidence may include: joint tax returns, insurance policies, health care plans, evidence that the couple has jointly purchased land or personal property (such as a car or appliances) and of other joint holdings. Other persuasive evidence could include photographs taken together at family and social events and evidence of vacationing or traveling together.

When filing for a waiver of the joint petition requirement, documentation must be submitted to prove eligibility for the particular waiver. If requesting a waiver based on multiple grounds, documentation should be submitted to establish each ground.

Travel Abroad

The regulations do not require that either spouse be physically present in the United States when the joint petition is filed,[66] although the conditional resident must be willing to return to the United States with his or her spouse and any dependent children to appear for a scheduled interview. Conditional residents outside the United States can file the petition by sending it to the appropriate USCIS lockbox address in the United States.

---

64 INA §216(c)(3)(D).

65 8 CFR §216.4(a)(5).

66 8 CFR §216.4(a)(4).

After it receives the joint petition or waiver application, USCIS will send the conditional resident a fee receipt. While USCIS is adjudicating the petition, the conditional resident can travel abroad even if his or her permanent resident visa has expired. The person may reenter the United States within six months after the two-year conditional residence period has ended by presenting the expired Form I-551 in lieu of a visa, plus the joint petition or waiver application filing receipt.[67]

The conditional resident must be returning to an "unrelinquished lawful permanent residence" in the United States from a temporary absence abroad that did not exceed one year. The expired Form I-551, together with the fee receipt, also can be used to satisfy Form I-9 employment eligibility verification requirements.

Should USCIS terminate the foreign national's conditional residence, he or she may travel outside the United States and reenter only if the local USCIS district director grants the foreign national advance parole (i.e., advance permission to reenter the United States). If USCIS already has begun removal proceedings against the foreign national, it cannot grant advance parole.

Late Petitions

If a petitioner can show that he or she has good cause for filing a late petition to remove conditional status, USCIS will allow it.[68] The conditional resident must state in writing the specific reasons why the petition was not filed before the end of the two-year period. Some examples of what constitutes good cause have been provided by USCIS and include hospitalization, long-term illness, death of a family member, the recent birth of a child, and having a family member on active duty with the U.S. military.[69] If a petitioner fails to provide a written explanation of good cause for not filing on time, the petition will be automatically denied.[70] USCIS will not issue a request of evidence but will send a denial notice based on the untimely filing.

USCIS customarily accepts late petitions with good-cause explanations that are submitted within a few days or weeks after the deadline. When a joint petition or waiver is filed several months late, however, USCIS will scrutinize the reasons for the delay more carefully.

Because the petitioner files for a waiver as an alternative to filing the petition jointly, usually the Form I-751 requesting a waiver should be filed within the 90 days preceding the end of the two-year conditional residence period. Sometimes,

---

67 8 CFR §211.1(a)(5).

68 8 CFR §216.4(a)(6).

69 USCIS Memorandum, D. Neufeld, *Adjudication of Form I-751, Petition to Remove Conditions on Residence Where the CPR Has a Final Order of Removal, Is in Removal Proceedings, or Has Filed an Unexcused Untimely Petition or Multiple Petitions* (Oct. 9, 2009), AILA Doc. No. 09110667.

70 *Id.*

however, it may be appropriate to file for the waiver before or after the 90-day period. For example, if the parties' divorce becomes final or the conditional resident is experiencing battery or extreme cruelty by the U.S. citizen or LPR spouse, USCIS will adjudicate a waiver request filed early and, if it approves the waiver, remove the conditional status at that time. On the other hand, the petitioner may file for a waiver after the 90-day period if the parties initially filed a timely joint petition, but the citizen spouse subsequently refuses to cooperate or the parties divorce. Moreover, if USCIS denies the joint petition, the conditional resident then can resubmit a Form I-751 with a waiver request.

Failing Marriages

USCIS cannot deny or refuse to accept a Form I-751 joint petition based solely on the current viability of the parties' marriage.[71] In other words, if the marriage is failing at the end of the two-year period—even if the parties have separated or filed for divorce—USCIS still must accept a timely filed joint petition or waiver application. If the petition or waiver application establishes that the marriage was bona fide at the time it was entered into, USCIS cannot deny either on the grounds that the marriage is no longer viable. The parties' conduct after they enter the marriage should affect USCIS's decision only if it bears on the parties' state of mind at the time they were married.

Petitions and Waivers Filed for Children

Dependent children of a conditional resident who acquire their legal status concurrently with their parent may be included in the parent's Form I-751, whether filed as a joint petition or with a request for waiver of the joint petition requirement.[72] It does not matter how old the "child" is at the time the petition is filed. USCIS regulations use the term "children" when referring to the procedures for removing the condition, but the statute refers to "sons and daughters," a term without a statutory age limitation.[73]

However, to be included on the petition, the child must have been granted conditional resident status within 90 days of the parent's being granted the status, because otherwise the child's eligibility to file for removal of the condition would not begin until after the parent's eligibility period had expired. A child who entered the United States more than 90 days after the conditional resident parent entered, and who thus cannot be included in the petition filed by the parent, must file an independent petition. The child would have to establish only that the parent's marriage was entered into in good faith and has not been terminated. The child's

---

71 USCIS Memorandum, D. Neufeld, *I-751 Filed Prior to Termination of Marriage* (Apr. 3, 2009), AILA Doc. No. 09072166.

72 8 CFR §216.4(a)(2).

73 INA §216(c)(1).

representative can do this by checking the appropriate box on Form I751 and stating in the cover letter why the child could not be included on the parent's petition. If the parent's I-751 has been approved, submit a copy of the parent's approval notice. The outcome of the child's I-751 petition usually will follow that of the parent's.

If the child is not included in the parent's Form I-751 application, or if the parent does not file a joint petition because of death, disability, or health reasons, the child must file his or her own I-751 petition.[74] In those circumstances, the child should submit the parent's death certificate or evidence showing why the parent cannot file the petition, together with some evidence that the marriage was bona fide.[75] The child need not submit evidence of extreme hardship unless USCIS requests it. In other situations in which the parent did not file an I-751 petition, the child would need to submit a waiver request based on any of the permissible grounds. When a conditional permanent resident child applies separately, based on abuse by the U.S. citizen stepparent or extreme hardship upon removal, USCIS will adjudicate the child's I-751 petition independently of the parent's case.

USCIS Interview

After the conditional resident has submitted the I-751 petition, either as a joint petition to remove the condition or with an application to waive the joint petition requirement, he or she will receive a filing receipt. When the conditional permanent residence card expires at the end of two years, this receipt serves as evidence of the person's continued lawful status.[76]

USCIS must schedule or waive an interview and adjudicate the joint petition within 90 days of receiving it.[77] The statute does not state what will happen when USCIS fails to schedule an interview or adjudicate the joint petition by this deadline. Although it could be argued that in such a situation the petition should be treated as automatically approved, the Immigration and Naturalization Service rejected that argument and took the position that it is not bound to issue a decision within the 90-day period.[78] The statute does not impose a corresponding limitation on the time USCIS has to schedule an interview if the conditional resident files a waiver request.[79]

---

74 8 CFR §216.4(a)(2).

75 *See* 8 CFR §216.5(a)(1) (requirements when conditional resident alien is unable to meet the requirements for a joint petition).

76 8 CFR §216.4(a)(1).

77 8 CFR §216.4(b).

78 INS Legal Opinion, W. Cook, *INS' ability to deny petition for change in permanent resident status after expiration of the statutory time limit* (June 21, 1990), *reported and reprinted in* 67 *Interpreter Releases* 979, 991 (Aug. 31, 1990).

79 INA §216(c)(3).

USCIS has discretion to schedule or waive interviews for foreign nationals who file an I-751 petition. Under guidance issued by USCIS on November 30, 2018, a waiver of the interview is appropriate where:

- The record contains sufficient evidence about the bona fides of the marriage and that the marriage was not entered into in order to evade U.S. immigration laws;
- For I-751 petitions received on or after December 10, 2018, USCIS has previously interviewed the principal petitioner, for example for an I-485 or I-130;
- There is no indication of fraud or misrepresentation in the I-751 or the supporting documentation; and
- There are no complex facts or issues that require an interview to resolve questions or concerns.[80]

If USCIS decides to require an interview before adjudicating the petition, the service center will forward the file to the USCIS district office that has jurisdiction over the couple's residence.

A conditional resident who receives an interview notice should take additional affidavits or documents to the interview attesting to the validity of the marriage or, if he or she requested a waiver, showing that the waiver grounds have been met.

Waiver of the Interview Requirement

If one of the petitioning parties cannot attend the interview, the agency may, in some cases, waive the attendance requirement. For example, if the U.S. citizen spouse is overseas in the military, USCIS could interview the conditional resident without requiring that the citizen spouse be present. But USCIS still would have to be satisfied, based on all the evidence, that the marriage was legitimate and that the reasons given for the spouse not appearing for the interview were valid.

Consequences of Failure to Appear

Usually, if the conditional resident—or in the case of a joint petition, either spouse—fails to appear for the interview, USCIS will deny the petition or waiver application, terminate conditional resident status, and start removal proceedings.[81] USCIS must provide the conditional resident with written notification of and specific reasons for the termination. In most cases, an NTA will accompany the termination notice. The conditional resident can ask USCIS to reconsider the decision to terminate, but he or she bears the burden of showing valid reasons for having failed to comply with

---

80 USCIS Policy Memorandum, *Revised Interview Waiver Guidance for Form I-751, Petition to Remove Conditions on Residence* (Nov. 30, 2018). AILA Doc. No. 18121035.

81 8 CFR §216.4(b)(3).

the interview requirements.[82] The conditional resident can submit a written request that the interview be rescheduled or waived.[83] The USCIS district director may grant the request if he or she believes there is good cause to do so.[84] In such cases, the notice to terminate and the NTA will be rescinded.

Approval of the I-751 Petition

If USCIS approves the I-751 petition, the conditional status will be removed.[85] USCIS will send a written notice of the decision to the conditional resident and USCIS will produce a new permanent resident card valid for 10 years. In the same way as any other permanent resident, the conditional resident will be eligible to file for naturalization three years after his or her date of adjustment of status or entry as a conditional resident if the foreign national is still married to the U.S. citizen. USCIS will not approve the naturalization application, however, until it has approved the I-751 petition. Conditional resident spouses granted a waiver of the joint petition requirement because of having been battered or subjected to extreme cruelty by their U.S. citizen spouse or parent are also eligible to adjust after three years without meeting the marital union requirement.[86]

Denial and Review in Removal Proceedings

If USCIS denies the I-751 petition, it must provide written notice of the decision stating the reasons for the denial. USCIS will instruct the conditional resident to surrender any I-551 card in his or her possession. The foreign national's lawful immigration status will terminate, and he or she will be served with an NTA starting removal proceedings.[87]

There is no appeal available from USCIS's denial of an I-751 petition, but once the foreign national is in removal proceedings, he or she can ask the immigration judge to review the denial. In these proceedings, the agency bears the burden of proving by a preponderance of the evidence that the information contained in the petition is false and that its denial of the petition was proper.[88] Denial of the I-751 petition can be reviewed by an immigration judge only if the foreign national previously filed it with USCIS; the I-751 petition cannot be filed for the first time with the immigration judge.

---

82 *Id.*

83 *See id.*

84 *Id.*

85 8 CFR §216.4(d)(1).

86 USCIS Memorandum, W. Yates, *Clarification of Classes of Applicants Eligible for Naturalization under Section 319(a) of the Immigration and Nationality Act (INA), as amended by the Victims of Trafficking and Violence Protection Act of 2000 (VTVPA), Pub. L. 106-386* (Jan. 27, 2005), AILA Doc. No. 05020760.

87 8 CFR §216.4(d)(2).

88 INA §216(c)(3)(D).

Assuming the immigration judge has jurisdiction to review USCIS's denial of the I-751 petition, the standard of review is de novo. In other words, the judge should accept all relevant evidence and make an independent determination about whether the joint petition or waiver request should be approved. If the immigration judge is reviewing the agency's denial of a waiver petition, the foreign national bears the burden of proving that the waiver should be approved. Although the agency bears the initial burden of proving that the foreign national is subject to removal, the foreign national bears the burden of proving eligibility for any form of discretionary relief from removal for which he or she applies, and that he or she merits a favorable exercise of discretion.

If the conditional resident has failed to file a timely joint petition or waiver application, he or she still may attempt to file it late with USCIS, even if an NTA has been issued. USCIS can accept a late filing if it finds that there is good cause to do so. If jurisdiction already has vested with the immigration judge (which occurs when the NTA is filed with the immigration court), the alien can ask the judge to continue the proceedings until USCIS makes a decision.[89] If USCIS approves the joint petition or waiver application, the immigration judge can terminate the proceedings upon a joint motion filed by the foreign national and U.S. Immigration and Customs Enforcement (ICE).

Final Removal Orders

USCIS will automatically deny an I-751 joint petition or waiver filed by a conditional permanent resident who is subject to a final order of removal. The denial will indicate that it is based on a final removal order and the case may be sent to ICE's Enforcement and Removal Operations.[90]

Multiple I-751 Filings

Because there are no limits on how many times a conditional permanent resident may file a Form I-751, a second joint petition or waiver may be filed subsequent to the denial of a previous joint petition or waiver. This may happen when a joint petition is filed but then the conditional resident and his or her spouse divorce or domestic violence occurs. The subsequent joint petition or waiver will also be denied if no different or additional evidence is submitted with the new petition. The new denial will incorporate by reference the basis for denial of the earlier petition and unless the petitioner is already in proceedings, the adjudicator will send the file to the appropriate unit for issuance of an NTA.[91]

---

89 *See Matter of Mendes*, 20 I&N Dec. 833 (BIA 1994).

90 USCIS Policy Memorandum, *Approval of Petitions and Applications after the Death of the Qualifying Relative under New Section 204(l) of the Immigration and Nationality Act* (Dec. 16, 2010), AILA Doc. No. 11011061.

91 *Id.*

Reapplication for an Immigrant Visa After Conditional Residence Terminates

As noted, a conditional resident's status may terminate at the end of the two-year period because he or she failed to file a petition, filed late, or the petition was denied by USCIS. In all these situations, there is limited opportunity for appeal or review. Nevertheless, couples in this situation may have another alternative. After the conditional residence has terminated, the couple can file a second I-130 petition and have the spouse receive the immigrant visa abroad through consular processing. Because this time the marriage will have taken place more than two years before the foreign national enters the United States on the second immigrant visa, the spouse will enter as a permanent resident without conditions.

Alternatively, the spouse may qualify for adjustment of status. For example, if the marriage creating the conditional residency ends through divorce or annulment within two years, the conditional resident could file a timely application for a waiver of the joint petition requirement. If USCIS denies the waiver application and terminates the conditional residency, the foreign national can request the waiver before an immigration judge. Alternatively, if the foreign national remarries another U.S. citizen, he or she could apply for adjustment of status.[92] The couple first would have to file an I-130 petition with USCIS. But after that is approved, the foreign national spouse could request adjustment either with USCIS or before an immigration judge.

USCIS had originally interpreted INA §245(d) as forever barring adjustment of status to foreign nationals who were granted conditional residency. But the agency's own regulation implies that this statutory bar only applies to conditional residents while they are in conditional resident status.[93] The BIA confirmed that once the conditional residency status has been terminated, the foreign national is not ineligible for adjustment of status pursuant to INA §245(a).[94] Additionally, USCIS guidance has been updated to confirm that conditional residence "terminates" when the agency issues a notice of termination, and it is not necessary for an immigration judge to make a finding of termination before a new adjustment application can be filed.[95]

USCIS Notice Requirements

USCIS is required to provide notice to affected persons concerning the conditional status–related requirements.[96] Although the statute contains two separate notice

---

92 *Matter of Stockwell*, 20 I&N Dec. 309 (BIA 1991).

93 8 CFR §245.1(c)(5).

94 *Matter of Stockwell*, 20 I&N Dec. 309.

95 7 *USCIS Policy Manual* pt. B, ch. 7.

96 INA §216(a)(2).

provisions,[97] USCIS nevertheless can terminate a conditional resident's status and start removal proceedings against him or her even if the foreign national never receives the required USCIS notices.

First, at the time the foreign national obtains conditional resident status, USCIS must provide notice "respecting the provisions of this section," including what the foreign national must do to have the conditional status removed.[98] Then, USCIS is required to provide similar notice approximately 90 days before the end of the two-year conditional residence period.[99] However, failure by USCIS to provide notice will not affect its power to enforce the statute.[100] Nor does such failure relieve the foreign national of the requirement to file the I-751 petition.[101]

Other Provisions Related to Preventing Marriage Fraud

Marriage in Removal Proceedings

Foreign nationals seeking to immigrate based on a spousal petition face tougher standards if the marriage to a U.S. citizen or LPR took place while that person was in removal proceedings. In that case, the INA prohibits approval of a relative petition and adjustment of status until that person has resided outside the United States for two years after the marriage.[102] However, petitioners may request a "bona fide marriage" exemption from this requirement by presenting "clear and convincing evidence" that the marriage is legally valid and was entered into in good faith and not for the purpose of immigrating the beneficiary spouse.[103] The "clear and convincing evidence" burden of proof is a higher standard than the "preponderance of the evidence" standard that applies in the adjudication of other petitions. The petitioner must request the exemption in writing when filing the I-130 and I-130A petitions. The written request should explain the reasons for the exemption and be accompanied by documentation establishing eligibility for the exemption.[104]

Since this prohibition applies only to those who marry while in removal proceeding, it is critical for the foreign national to know when removal proceedings commence and when they terminate. Under the current structure of removal proceedings, in effect since April 1, 1997, removal proceedings commence when the Form I-862,

---

97 INA §216(a)(2)(A), (B).

98 INA §216(a)(2)(A).

99 INA §216(a)(2)(B).

100 INA §216(a)(2)(C).

101 8 CFR §216.2(c).

102 INA§§204(g), 245(e)

103 INA §245(e).

104 8 CFR §204.2(a)(1)(iii).

Notice to Appear (NTA), is filed with the immigration court, not when the NTA is served on the foreign national.[105]

Second-Preference Petitions

Persons who obtain LPR status through marriage to a U.S. citizen or LPR cannot remarry and then file a second-preference visa petition on behalf of their new spouse unless five years have elapsed since the date the foreign national acquired LPR status.[106] In the alternative, the person must establish that he or she did not enter the previous marriage to gain immigration benefits.[107]

This prohibition on the granting of "second generation" petitions does not apply if the first marriage ended in the death of the previous spouse.[108] It also does not apply if the foreign national has become a naturalized citizen and files an immediate-relative petition based on a subsequent marriage that occurred within five years of the foreign national's immigrating to the United States. Moreover, the prohibition does not apply if the person originally obtained immigrant status through a means other than marriage to a U.S. citizen or LPR. For example, the applicant could have gained derivative status through marriage to a person immigrating through an employment-based visa category. Finally, the provision only applies to spouses, so a petition for a child would not be subject to the five-year bar.

The burden is on the applicant to prove through clear and convincing evidence that the previous marriage was legitimate.[109] In these circumstances, the petitioner should submit the same type of evidence used to support an I-751 petition to remove conditional status. In fact, if USCIS has previously removed the conditions on the applicant's residency, that determination should be given substantial weight. USCIS will take into consideration such factors as the length of time the foreign national and the previous spouse lived together, whether any children were born of that marriage, joint ownership of assets and assumption of liabilities, and the reasons why the marriage was terminated.[110] If possible, the petitioner should try to obtain the cooperation of the previous spouse and submit a statement from him or her regarding the bona fides of that marriage.

If the foreign national fails to meet this burden and USCIS denies the second-preference visa petition, he or she can reapply after acquiring five years of permanent residence.[111] The denial does not prejudice any subsequent petition, although the

---

105 8 CFR §§1003.13, 1003.14(a), 245.1(c)(8)(i).

106 INA §204(a)(2)(A)(i).

107 INA §204(a)(2)(A)(ii).

108 INA §204(a)(2)(B).

109 8 CFR §204.2(a)(1)(i)(A)(1).

110 8 CFR §204.2(a)(1)(i)(B).

111 8 CFR §204.2(a)(1)(i)(C).

applicant will not be able to use the previous filing as a priority date for the later petition.

If USCIS gains information indicating that the applicant entered the previous marriage fraudulently, it can elect to initiate removal proceedings.[112] However, if USCIS chooses not to initiate proceedings, that decision will not establish that the previous marriage was legitimate. This presents a strategic problem for persons who may have difficulty proving the legitimate nature of the earlier marriage. Based on an applicant's petition, supporting documentation, and other evidence, USCIS might conclude that the previous marriage was fraudulent and initiate removal proceedings, which could result in the petitioner's losing his or her LPR status. However, if the applicant waits until the five-year period has ended, he or she is not required to submit these documents or meet this additional burden.

The Fiancé(e) Visa—K-1 and K-2: Intending Spouses of U.S. Citizens and Their Children

Initiating the Process

The process of obtaining a nonimmigrant fiancé(e) visa begins when the citizen fiancé(e) files a petition with USCIS.[113] Form I-129F, Petition for Alien Fiancé(e), requests basic information regarding both parties, such as their addresses, whether either has been married previously, and the names of any children of the foreign-national fiancé(e). The petitioner must submit proof that he or she is a U.S. citizen and that each party is free to contract a valid marriage with the other. The petitioner must swear that each party intends to marry the other within 90 days of the foreign national fiancé(e)'s entry into the United States.

If, based on the evidence submitted, USCIS is satisfied that the parties have the legal capacity and the intention to marry, it will approve the petition and forward the file to the appropriate consular office.[114] Upon receiving the approved K-1 visa petition, a consular officer will notify the fiancé(e) of the documents he or she needs to submit. The consulate will interview the intended beneficiary after he or she has obtained security clearances and collected necessary documents. If it finds the applicant to be admissible and eligible as a fiancé(e), the consulate will issue a K-1 visa.

Previous Meeting Requirement

As a result of Congress's attempt to deter cases involving "mail-order brides," a couple must have "met in person" within two years preceding the filing of the

---

112 *Id.*

113 INA §214(d)(1).

114 9 *Foreign Affairs Manual* (FAM) 502.7-3(C)(1).

fiancé(e) petition.[115] However, Congress also was aware that in some countries it is still common practice for persons to enter prearranged marriages. In those countries, strict and long-established customs may prevent couples from meeting between the time the marriage is arranged and the wedding day. To accommodate these situations, the law allows the attorney general to waive the "previous meeting" requirement "in his discretion." USCIS regulations permit this exemption (1) for persons who can show that they are following strict cultural or social practices; and (2) for those who would experience extreme hardship if forced to comply with this requirement.[116]

Established-Custom Exemption

To satisfy requirements for the first exemption, the petition must show both that the personal meeting would violate established customs and that all other aspects of the traditional marriage arrangements will be followed. If the couple is following cultural or social practices, they should submit affidavits from religious or other appropriate officials attesting to the details of those traditional arrangements. Letters from family members also might help prove that the parties are complying with requirements that they not meet before the marriage.

Extreme-Hardship Exception

If the petitioner is claiming extreme hardship, he or she should submit all possible supporting evidence. This might include evidence of the couple's having met before the two-year period; of political conditions preventing travel to the fiancé(e)'s country; of problems preventing the fiancé(e) from leaving the home country and traveling to the United States; of financial barriers; or of medical problems that have affected the mobility of either party. The regulation offers no guidance for defining the term "extreme hardship" under the second waiver option.

In fact, the statute, regulations, and legislative history provide little guidance as to what factors USCIS should consider in granting exemptions under either of the two grounds. As a result, petitioners should provide as much documentation as possible to show a bona fide intent to marry and eligibility for the requested exemption. Many situations that could give rise to a legitimate claim by the parties that hardship prevented their being able to see each other during the preceding two years are conceivable. Cases are common in which couples have met and carried on a long-distance relationship, but because of financial, political, or medical reasons have been unable to meet during the preceding two years.

---

115 8 CFR §214.2(k)(2).

116 *Id.*

Filing the Form I-129F and Documenting the Petition

The fiancé(e) petition and all supporting documents should be filed by the U.S. citizen fiancé(e) at the USCIS Dallas lockbox facility. Always check the USCIS website for the most up-to-date filing address. The current filing fee is $535. Always check the USCIS website for the most up-to-date filing fee.

Fiancé(e) petitioners must document instances in which the couple have met over the course of the preceding two years.[117] Such evidence could include copies of airline tickets, passport stamps, photos of the couple together, and affidavits from third parties who have knowledge of the meeting(s). Evidence of a couple's bona fide intention to marry could include copies of correspondence or long-distance telephone charges. The practitioner should err on the side of overdocumenting these cases, because some USCIS and consular officials are demanding significant evidence for K visa applicants.

Adjustment of Status for Fiancé(e)s

The foreign national fiancé(e) is required to marry the citizen petitioner within 90 days of entry or lose his or her lawful status and be subject to deportation.[118] If the parties marry within 90 days, the person who received the fiancé(e) visa must follow the INA §245 adjustment procedures. If he or she adjusts within two years of marriage, he or she will be subject to the two-year conditional residence requirement.[119] If they adjust more than two years after the marriage, they will not be subject to those requirements.[120]

A K-1 visa holder must marry the fiancé(e) petitioner to be able to file for adjustment.[121] In other words, if the parties did not marry but instead broke their relationship, and the foreign national fiancé(e) subsequently married another U.S. citizen, the applicant could not adjust status in the United States. Rather, he or she would have to go through consular processing abroad and reenter the United States as a conditional resident. However, the BIA has ruled that a fiancé(e) may still adjust status even if the underlying marriage has been terminated, provided the parties did enter into a bona fide marriage within the 90-day period.[122] In that case, the adjustment application was adjudicated more than two years after the marriage and the conditional residency requirements did not apply. USCIS is still requiring, however, that the I-129F petitioner submit an affidavit of support on behalf of the spouse.

---

117 INA §214(d)(1).

118 8 CFR §212.2(k)(5).

119 8 CFR §214.2(k)(6).

120 *Matter of Sesay*, 25 I&N Dec. 431 (BIA 2011).

121 INA §245(d).

122 *Matter of Sesay*, 25 I&N Dec. 431.

Unmarried children of a foreign national granted a K-1 visa may obtain a K-2 visa to accompany or follow-to-join the fiancé(e).[123] After the parent has married the U.S. citizen, the children may adjust status in the same way as the parent, although they might have been over 18 at the time the marriage took place and otherwise would not satisfy the definition of stepchildren. In addition, a K-2 visa holder who entered the United States before age 21 may adjust status even if he or she turned 21 before the adjustment application was adjudicated.[124]

The K-3 and K-4 for Spouses of U.S. Citizens and Their Children

The Legal Immigration and Family Equity (LIFE) Act[125] and LIFE Act Amendments of 2000[126] expanded eligibility for a K visa to spouses of U.S. citizens and their dependents who are residing outside the United States.[127] These categories of nonimmigrant fiancé(e) visas are called K-3 (spouses) and K-4 (dependents). The requirements include the following:[128]

- The alien entered into a valid marriage with the U.S. citizen petitioner, is the beneficiary of an alien relative visa petition filed by the petitioner, and seeks to enter the United States to await approval of the I-130 petition and availability of immigrant visa, or
- The alien is a child of a parent described above and is accompanying or following to join the principal beneficiary.
- If married to a U.S. citizen, the consular officer must have received a Form I-129F petition filed in the United States by the U.S. citizen spouse and approved by the USCIS service center.
- If the marriage took place outside the United States, the alien spouse must receive the K-3 visa from the consulate in the country where the marriage took place.

Applicants must submit the Form I-129F and proof of filing the I-130 petition.[129] Although the I-130 petition is filed with the appropriate service center, the I-129F petition is filed with the USCIS Dallas lockbox. Always check the USCIS website for the most up-to-date filing address.

---

123 8 CFR §214.2(k)(3).

124 *Matter of Le*, 25 I&N Dec. 541 (BIA 2011).

125 Pub. L. No. 106-553, §1(a)(2) (appx. B, H.R. 5548, §§1101–04), 114 Stat. 2762, 2762A–142 to 2762A–149 (Dec. 21, 2000).

126 Pub. L. No. 106-554, appx. D, div. B, §§1501–06, 114 Stat. 2763, 2763A–324 to 2763A–328 (Dec. 21, 2000).

127 INA §101(a)(15)(K)(ii).

128 8 CFR §214.2(k)(7).

129 *Id.*

Foreign nationals who enter the United States with K-3 and K-4 visas are eligible for employment authorization.[130] Their period of authorized admission terminates 30 days after denial of the underlying I-130 petition, application for immigrant visa, or application for adjustment of status.

Spouses with K-3 visas and K-4 derivatives may only adjust status based on the Form I-130, Petition for Alien Relative, filed by the visa petitioner.[131] The U.S. citizen spouse must file a separate Form I-130 for the K-4 derivative beneficiary to immigrate; if the derivative beneficiary is over 18 at the time the marriage to the K-3 spouse takes place, he or she does not qualify as a stepchild and will not be eligible to adjust status.[132]

This expansion of the K visa took place on December 21, 2000. The law applies to any foreign national who is a beneficiary of an I-130 petition filed under INA §204 before, on, or after that date. The premise of the K-3 visa is that consular processing in K-3 status is faster than entering as an immigrant. But with the acceleration of the processing of I-130 petitions by the service centers and the comparable amount of time for processing the I-129F petition, the K-3 option has lost most of its rationale.

In addition, the Department of State (DOS) provided guidance on cases where both the I-130 petition and the Form I-129F have been approved and forwarded to the NVC.[133] In those circumstances the NVC and consulates will stop processing of the K-3 visa and administratively close the case. DOS will proceed only with the immigrant visa application. If the NVC has received only an approved Form I-129F and the I-130 petition is still pending, the agency will proceed with nonimmigrant visa processing and will forward the petition to the appropriate U.S. consulate.

Widow/Widower Petitions

Certain widows and widowers may be able to obtain permanent residence after their spouse has died. Immigration law provides that they may immigrate if they meet the following requirements: (1) they were married to a U.S. citizen; (2) the deceased spouse was a citizen at the time of his or her death (not necessarily during the whole period of the marriage); (3) they were not legally separated at the time of the death; (4) they file a Form I-360, Petition for Amerasian, Widow(er), or Special Immigrant petition within two years of the death; and (5) they are not inadmissible.[134] In addition, they must not have remarried before acquiring the immigrant visa.[135] A

---

130 8 CFR §214.2(k)(9).

131 INA §245(d); *Matter of Valenzuela*, 25 I&N Dec. 867 (BIA 2012).

132 *Matter of Akram*, 25 I&N Dec. 874 (BIA 2012).

133 DOS Changes to Procedures for Certain I-129F Petitions, AILA Doc. No. 10021965.

134 INA §201(b)(2)(A)(i), as amended by FY2010 Department of Homeland Security Appropriations Act, Pub. L. No. 111-83, 123 Stat. 2142, §568(c)(1), (Oct. 28, 2009).

135 8 CFR §204.2(b)(1).

2009 law eliminated the prior requirement that the couple have been married for at least two years.

These widows and widowers are considered immediate relatives, and thus immigrate outside the numerical quota restrictions and the long waiting period that exists in many of the preference categories. They may either adjust status or consular process. But unlike other immediate relatives, their unmarried children under age 21 will be considered derivative beneficiaries and may accompany or follow to join the parent.[136]

Widows and widowers file a Form I-360, Petition for Amerasian, Widow(er), or Special Immigrant. The filing fee is currently $435. Always check the USCIS website for the most up-to-date filing fee.

If the widow/widower last entered the United States with a nonimmigrant visa, he or she is eligible to adjust status, even though the person may have overstayed the permitted time or worked illegally. Alternatively, if the Form I-360 was filed on or before April 30, 2001, the applicant may be able to adjust in the United States pursuant to INA §245(i). Widows and widowers should list any and all unmarried children under 21 years of age on the Form I-360 so they may immigrate with or follow to join the principal beneficiary.

If the citizen spouse had filed an I-130 petition on behalf of the foreign national spouse, that petition will automatically convert to an I-360 petition upon the petitioner's death.[137] This automatic conversion will occur to I-130 petitions that are pending or approved at the time of the petitioner's death. It applies to I-130 petitions that are pending on or approved before, on, or after October 28, 2009.

Documents that should accompany the Form I-360 application include:

- Proof of the deceased spouse's citizenship at the time of the death (through either birth in the United States or naturalization);
- Proof of the deceased spouse's death;
- Proof of marriage to the deceased spouse;
- Proof of termination of any prior marriage of either party; and
- Proof of the relationship of any unmarried children under 21 years of age.[138]

If the widow or widower is residing in the United States and otherwise eligible to adjust status (based on lawful entry or section 245(i)), he or she may file the Form I-360 along with a Form I-485 with the Chicago lockbox.

---

136 8 CFR §204.2(b)(4).

137 8 CFR § 204.2(i)(1)(iv).

138 8 CFR §204.2(b)(2).

If the person is ineligible for adjustment of status, he or she will file the I-360 petition at the Phoenix or Dallas lockbox. Always check the USCIS website for the most up-to-date filing address.

Applicants for either adjustment of status or an immigrant visa are exempt from the affidavit of support (Form I-864) requirements. Widows and widowers will indicate on the Form I-485 that they qualify for the exemption. The applicant will have to submit proof that he or she is not likely to become a public charge, which may include Forms I-944 or DS-5540.

If the widow or widower is ineligible for adjustment of status, determine whether she or he will trigger the ground of inadmissibility for unlawful presence on leaving the country to consular process. If a widow or widower was physically present in the United States when the citizen spouse dies and remains here until departing for the consular interview, the foreign national spouse will be able to file the waiver notwithstanding the death of the citizen spouse/qualifying relative. This applies to cases where the citizen spouse died while the I-130 petition was pending or after it was approved; it would not apply in cases where no petition was filed. Similarly, the agency will presume extreme hardship.[139]

Widows/widowers who had a pending I-130 petition on October 28, 2009, will not be deemed to have accrued any unlawful presence.[140] But those who have acquired more than 180 days of unlawful presence in the United States will trigger the three– or ten-year bar to lawful reentry. Although there is a waiver under INA §212(a)(9)(B)(v), the applicant must demonstrate extreme hardship to a U.S. citizen or LPR spouse or parent. Most widows/widowers will lack that qualifying relative.

---

139 USCIS Policy Memorandum, *Approval of Petitions and Applications after the Death of the Qualifying Relative under New Section 204(l) of the Immigration and Nationality Act* (Dec. 16, 2010), AILA Doc. No. 11011061.

140 USCIS Memorandum, D. Neufeld, *Additional Guidance Regarding Surviving Spouses of Deceased U.S. Citizens and their Children (REVISED)* (Dec. 2, 2009), AILA Doc. No. 09121430.

CHAPTER 6

GROUNDS OF INADMISSIBILITY

The grounds of inadmissibility specified in section 212(a) of the Immigration and Nationality Act (INA) affect those seeking admission to the United States, those present in the United States without having been inspected and admitted, and those seeking adjustment of status or certain other benefits under the INA. The 10 inadmissibility categories are:

- health-related grounds
- criminal-related grounds
- national security grounds
- public charge
- labor protection grounds
- fraud or other immigration violations
- documentation requirements
- grounds relating to military service in the United States
- prior removals or unlawful presence in the United States
- miscellaneous grounds

The grounds of inadmissibility overlap with many, but not all, of the grounds of deportation found in INA §237. Although the grounds of inadmissibility, especially criminal and security grounds, often coincide with grounds of deportation, there are several grounds of inadmissibility that are unique. Prostitutes,[1] uncertified health care workers,[2] practicing polygamists,[3] and others are inadmissible but not deportable from the United States. Similarly, there are unique grounds of deportation not found in the grounds of inadmissibility. For example, those convicted of violation of a protection order[4] or certain firearm offenses[5] are deportable but not inadmissible...

Each inadmissibility category comprises several grounds. This chapter will focus on the most common grounds of inadmissibility, particularly those affecting persons immigrating through family-based petitions.

---

1 INA §212(a)(2)(D).

2 INA §212(a)(5)(C).

3 INA §212(a)(10)(A)(E)(ii).

4 INA §237(a)(2).

5 INA §237(a)(2)(C).

Health-Related Grounds

There are four health-related grounds of inadmissibility. The first excludes foreign nationals who have "a communicable disease of public health significance."[6] The second excludes foreign nationals who are seeking admission as permanent residents and who were not vaccinated against certain diseases. The third relates to physical or mental disorders with associated behavior that poses a threat to the property, safety, or welfare of the foreign national or others. The fourth ground excludes drug abusers and addicts.[7]

Communicable Diseases

The first health-related ground makes inadmissible any foreign national who is determined to have "a communicable disease of public health significance,"[8] as determined by the secretary of the Department of Health and Human Services (HHS). Communicable diseases of public health significance include both specific diseases and categories of diseases that lead to inadmissibility. HHS currently considers the following diseases to be communicable and of public health significance: active tuberculosis, infectious Hansen's disease, and two venereal diseases (gonorrhea and the infectious stage of syphilis).[9] Several of these diseases may be treated, whereupon the individual may be admissible to the United States. Note that HIV infection, infectious leprosy, chancroid, granuloma inguinale, and lymphogranuloma venerum are no longer listed diseases, therefore, they no longer lead to inadmissibility.[10] Also included in the definition of communicable diseases of public health significance are quarantinable diseases that are designated by Presidential Executive Order and diseases that meet the criteria of a public health emergency of international concern, which require notification to the World Health Organization (WHO).[11]

Lack of Vaccination

Intending immigrants must present evidence that they were vaccinated against the following: mumps, measles, rubella, polio, tetanus and diphtheria toxoids, pertussis, influenza type B, hepatitis A, hepatitis B, rotavirus, meningococcal, varicella, pneumococcal, and any other vaccinations recommended by the Advisory

---

6 INA §212(a)(1)(A)(i).

7 INA §212(a)(1).

8 INA §212(a)(1)(A)(i).

9 42 CFR §34.2.

10 74 Fed. Reg. 56547 (Nov. 2, 2009); 81 Fed. Reg. 4191 (Jan. 26, 2016).

11 8 CFR § 34.2(b) . Currently designated quarantinable diseases include cholera, diphtheria, infectious tuberculosis, plague, smallpox, yellow fever, viral hemorrhagic fevers, severe acute respiratory syndromes, and influenza caused by novel or re-emergent influenza (pandemic flu).

Commission for Immunization Practices (ACIP).[12] Whenever the ACIP recommends new vaccinations for the general U.S. population, the Centers for Disease Control and Prevention (CDC) will determine which vaccinations are required for individuals immigrating to the United States.[13] The human papillomavirus and zoster vaccines, though recommended by the ACIP for the general U.S. population, are no longer required for intending immigrants.

Physical or Mental Disorders

Foreign nationals are inadmissible under the physical or mental disorder inadmissibility ground if they have or had a condition that has an associated behavior that poses a threat to the property, safety, or welfare of themselves or others.[14] If the foreign national no longer has the condition, it does not constitute an inadmissibility ground unless the behavior is likely to recur or the condition is likely to lead to other harmful behavior.[15]

The current HHS/CDC regulations do not identify specific diseases that would make a foreign national inadmissible under the physical or mental disorder inadmissibility ground, but instead refer to conditions that are currently accepted medical diagnoses. Physical or mental disorders are respectively defined by the most recent editions of the *Manual of the International Classification of Diseases, Injuries, and Causes of Death* (ICD) published by the WHO, or the *Diagnostic and Statistical Manual* (DSM) published by the American Psychiatric Association; or in another authoritative resource approved by the Director.[16]

The CDC Technical Instructions for both civil surgeons and panel physicians list the major diagnostic categories of mental disorders.[17] The CDC Technical Instructions also list mental disorders for which harmful behavior is commonly associated with the diagnosis.[18] Note, however, that some of the disorders listed (such as mood disorders) do *not* always have associated harmful behavior; a doctor would have to make a specific finding of associated harmful behavior for a person to be inadmissible for some of these disorders. Alcohol dependence and abuse are disorders that trigger inadmissibility only where there is evidence of current or past harmful behavior as part of the diagnosis.[19]

---

12 INA §212(a)(1)(A)(ii).

13 Centers for Disease Control and Prevention (CDC), Vaccination Technical Instructions for Civil Surgeons, www.cdc.gov/immigrantrefugeehealth/exams/ti/civil/vaccination-civil-technical-instructions.html; CDC, Vaccination Technical Instructions for Panel Physicians, www.cdc.gov/immigrantrefugeehealth/exams/ti/panel/vaccination-panel-technical-instructions.html.

14 INA §212(a)(1)(A)(iii)(I).

15 INA §212(a)(1)(A)(iii)(II).

16 81 Fed. Reg. 4194 (Jan. 26, 2016).

17 This list is reproduced as Appendix 6A.

18 Appendix 6B reproduces the table that lists these conditions and their associated harmful behaviors.

19 9 *Foreign Affairs Manual* (FAM) 302.2-7(B)(3).

If the doctor examining a foreign national uncovers a history of physical or mental disorder and an associated history of harmful behavior, the condition may be considered in remission—and, therefore, not likely to recur—if no pattern of the behavioral element has manifested in the previous 12 months. Panel physicians are instructed to use their clinical judgment to determine if 12 months is an acceptable period of time for the individual applicant to demonstrate full remission. This judgment is to be made based an assessment of the history of associated harmful behavior and its likelihood of recurrence.[20]

Consular officers are required to refer visa applicants to a doctor if they have either a single alcohol-related arrest or conviction within the last five years; two or more alcohol-related arrests or convictions within the last 10 years; or if there is any other evidence to suggest an alcohol problem.[21] The doctor will determine whether the applicant suffers from alcohol abuse or dependence.

Drug Abusers or Addicts

Foreign nationals who are determined to be "drug abusers" or "addicts" based on dependence or abuse of any of the substances listed in section 202 of the Controlled Substances Act (21 USC §802) are inadmissible. This Act lists hundreds of controlled drugs arranged into five "schedules," which determine the degree of a criminal offense involving a particular drug. For example, marijuana is included on the list in schedule I, the most severely penalized category.

The current CDC Technical Instructions for Physical or Mental Disorders with Associated Harmful Behaviors and Substance Related Disorders detail the standard required to show substance abuse or addiction. In order to make a substance- (either alcohol- or drug-) related diagnosis, the panel physician must document the pattern or use of the substance and behavioral, physical, and psychological effects associated with the use or cessation of use of that substance.[22] Substance use disorder is present when a number of symptoms or criteria are diagnosed. The symptoms evaluated fit within general groupings related to impaired control, social impairment, risky use, and pharmacological criteria (including tolerance and withdrawal). A diagnosis that two to three symptoms are present meets the criteria for mild substance use disorder and will lead to a Class A finding for drug abuse/addiction.[23]

---

20 9 FAM 302.2-7(B)(2).

21 9 FAM 302.2-7(B)(3).

22 CDC, Technical Instructions for Physical or Mental Disorders with Associated Harmful Behaviors and Substance-Related Disorders for Panel Physicians, www.cdc.gov/immigrantrefugeehealth/exams/ti/panel/mental-panel-technical-instructions.html; Technical Instructions for Physical or Mental Disorders with Associated Harmful Behaviors and Substance-Related Disorders for Civil Surgeons, www.cdc.gov/immigrantrefugeehealth/exams/ti/civil/mental-civil-technical-instructions.html.

23 CDC, Technical Instructions for Physical or Mental Disorders with Associated Harmful Behaviors and Substance-Related Disorders for Panel Physicians, www.cdc.gov/immigrantrefugeehealth/exams/ti/panel/mental-panel-technical-instructions.html.

It's important to note that while recreational marijuana is legal in many states, it is not legal under federal law. Noncitizen clients should be cautioned that recreational marijuana use may trigger both health-based inadmissibility as a drug abuser and, in some circumstances, crime-based inadmissibility for admission of a controlled substance violation.

In addition to substance-use disorders, the DSM-5 has a separate category of substance-induced disorders that includes but is not limited to intoxication, withdrawal, and other substance/medication-induced disorders.[24]

As is the case for general mental disorders, sustained, full remission of substance-related disorders is a period of 12 months during which no substance use has occurred. Panel physicians are instructed to use their discretion to determine whether 12 months is an acceptable period of time for an individual applicant to demonstrate full remission. Full remission can be shown through evidence such as completion of a drug treatment program.[25] Therefore, people who stopped using drugs more than 12 months before their medical examination may be able to show that they are not inadmissible.

Chronic alcoholism per se is not included as an inadmissibility ground, nor is it subsumed under the definitions of drug user or drug abuser.[26] HHS has equated "drugs" with "controlled substances" as defined in section 202 of the Controlled Substances Act, and this definition specifically excludes alcoholic beverages and tobacco from its coverage. However, the CDC Technical Instructions instruct physicians to look for alcohol abuse as part of the evaluation for mental and physical disorders with associated harmful behavior.

The same criteria apply for evaluation of alcohol dependence or abuse as are found in the DSM for other substances. The diagnosis of a substance-related disorder alone does not make an applicant ineligible to receive a visa unless there is evidence of current or past harmful behavior.[27] The CDC Technical Instructions on Mental Health note that with alcohol dependence or abuse, there is often associated harmful behavior during periods of intoxication and withdrawal.[28]

Note that there are waivers available for foreign nationals who are inadmissible under the physical or mental disorders bar, unlike the drug abuse or addiction bar.

---

24 9 FAM 302.2-7(B)(3).

25 9 FAM 302.2-8(B)(2)(4).

26 9 FAM 302.2-7(B)(3).

27 9 FAM 302.2-9(B)(3).

28 CDC, Technical Instructions for Physical or Mental Disorders with Associated Harmful Behaviors and Substance-Related Disorders for Panel Physicians, www.cdc.gov/immigrantrefugeehealth/exams/ti/panel/mental-panel-technical-instructions.html; Technical Instructions for Physical or Mental Disorders with Associated Harmful Behaviors and Substance-Related Disorders for Civil Surgeons, www.cdc.gov/immigrantrefugeehealth/exams/ti/civil/mental-civil-technical-instructions.html.

Waivers

U.S. Citizenship and Immigration Services (USCIS) may waive the "communicable diseases" inadmissibility ground for those who are spouses, unmarried sons or daughters, unmarried lawfully adopted children, or parents of U.S. citizens, lawful permanent residents (LPRs), or foreign nationals who have been issued immigrant visas.[29] This ground of inadmissibility may also be waived for VAWA self-petitioners.[30]The "vaccination" ground may be waived for immigrants (1) who subsequently are vaccinated; (2) who obtain a certificate from a civil surgeon or medical officer showing that such vaccination would not be medically appropriate; or (3) for whom USCIS waives the requirement because of the foreign national's religious beliefs or moral convictions.[31]

USCIS does not require those who are subsequently vaccinated, or for whom vaccinations are not medically appropriate, to submit a waiver application and fee. A waiver application and fee are required only for an immigrant seeking a waiver of the vaccination requirements based on religious or moral beliefs. The "physical or mental disorder" inadmissibility ground may be waived for any foreign national; no family relationship is required.[32] INA §212(g) waivers[33] are not available for the "drug abuser or addict" inadmissibility ground.

Criminal Grounds

Foreign nationals are inadmissible for the following criminal-related activity: [34]

- controlled substance violations;
- crimes involving moral turpitude;
- multiple convictions resulting in an aggregate confinement sentence of five years or more;
- controlled-substance trafficking;
- prostitution and commercialized vice;
- assertion of diplomatic immunity from prosecution for serious crimes;
- being responsible for or carrying out any particularly severe violations of religious freedom while serving as a foreign government official, or being the spouse or child of such a person;
- money laundering; and

---

29 INA §212(g)(1).

30 *Id.*

31 INA §212(g)(2).

32 INA §212(g)(3).

33 For more information on waivers of this inadmissibility ground, see chapter 7.

34 INA §212(a)(2).

- trafficking in persons.

A limited waiver is available for some of these "criminal" inadmissibility grounds,[35] and some forms of postconviction relief also may cure inadmissibility.

Several of the criminal grounds of inadmissibility require a "conviction," which is specifically defined in the INA.[36] Under that definition, a person is considered to have been convicted if a court has adjudicated him or her guilty or has entered a formal judgment of guilt against him or her.[37] In addition, even if the court has withheld such an adjudication, a person is considered to have been convicted for immigration purposes if: (1) the person was found guilty or entered a plea of guilty or nolo contendere or has admitted sufficient facts to warrant a finding of guilt, and (2) the judge ordered some form of punishment or restraint on the person's liberty.[38] The imposition of administrative costs alone may constitute punishment under the statute.[39]

Certain "pre-plea" or "diversionary" programs, which exist in many states and counties, are not convictions under state law but may be considered convictions based on the INA definition. The exact conditions of these programs differ, but are generally predicated on an agreement to dismiss the charges if the defendant successfully fulfills certain rehabilitation or community service requirements, which qualify as a form of "punishment" under the INA. Accordingly, whether these programs will result in convictions for immigration purposes often hinges on whether the defendant was required to enter a guilty plea or admit to sufficient facts. For that reason, advocates should always review the exact terms of these programs in the relevant jurisdiction and/or as applied to the client's case.

Additionally, state offenses that do not require proof of guilt beyond a reasonable doubt or do not otherwise comport with standard criminal proceedings may not be convictions for immigration purposes.[40] A *nolle prosequi*, or "nol pros" by the prosecutor, which means that the person was arrested and charged but that the prosecutor dismissed the charges before a determination, will also generally not be considered a conviction for immigration purposes. Finally, charges that are

---

35 INA §212(h).

36 INA §101(a)(48)(A).

37 INA §101(a)(48)(A)(ii).

38 INA §101(a)(48)(A)(i).

39 *Matter of Cabrera,* 24 I&N Dec. 459 (BIA 2008) (holding that the imposition of costs and surcharges following a guilty plea in respondent's Florida criminal case is a penalty or punishment under the INA); *but see Gonzalez v. Sessions*, 894 F.3d 131 (4th Cir. 2018) (determining that because the costs ordered in respondent's North Carolina case were purely administrative in nature with no discretionary or punitive component, they did not constitute a penalty or punishment as contemplated in INA §101(a)(48)(A)).

40 *Matter of Eslamizar,* 23 I&N Dec. 684 (BIA 2004); *but see Matter of Cuellar-Gomez,* 25 I&N Dec. 850 (BIA 2012) (municipal ordinance violation may constitute conviction where formal entry of guilty is entered and the proceedings are genuine criminal proceedings).

dismissed due to insufficient evidence or because the victim failed to cooperate will often not rise to the level of a conviction when no plea was entered and no sentence was imposed.

Beyond the existence of the conviction itself, some grounds of inadmissibility and deportability apply only to convictions for which there was a certain term of imprisonment imposed. The INA specifically defines a "term of imprisonment" as including the period of incarceration or confinement ordered by the court, regardless of any suspension of the imposition or execution of the sentence.[41]

Once a foreign national has been convicted of and sentenced for a crime, there may be state-based postconviction relief mechanisms available to vacate or expunge the conviction or to alter the sentence. Whether that postconviction relief will effectively ameliorate the attendant immigration consequences, however, depends on the basis upon which such relief was pursued.

For example, in *Matter of Roldan*, the BIA held that following the 1996 INA amendments, which included an added definition of "conviction," any state action that purports to expunge, dismiss, cancel, vacate, discharge, or otherwise remove a guilty plea or other record of guilt or conviction by operation of a state rehabilitative statute, such as the one under which Roldan's conviction was expunged, will be given no effect for immigration purposes.[42] Four years later, however, the Board clarified in *Matter of Pickering* that while rehabilitative statutes cannot serve as vehicles to ameliorate the immigration consequences of criminal convictions, orders to vacate that are based on an underlying legal defect in the original conviction can.[43]

In three additional cases, the Board analyzed the effects of postconviction relief related specifically to sentencing and concluded that a state court's order *modifying* an individual's sentence should be given "full… faith and credit"[44] in subsequent immigration matters but that an order *clarifying* a sentence must be evaluated on a case-by-case basis to determine if it would be given effect for immigration purposes.[45]

Recently, however, in *Matter of Thomas*, the attorney general eliminated the BIA's prior distinctions between different conviction and sentencing-related relief mechanisms, and concluded instead that under the entire umbrella of postconviction relief the only relevant inquiry for immigration purposes is whether the relief is or is not based on an underlying legal defect.[46] Accordingly, the test articulated in

41 INA §101(a)(48)(B).

42 22 I&N Dec. 512, 527–28 (BIA 1999).

43 *Matter of Pickering,* 23 I&N Dec. 621, 624 (BIA 2003).

44 *Matter of Cota-Vargas*, 23 I&N Dec. 849, 850–52 (BIA 2005); *see also Matter of Song*, 23 I&N Dec. 173 (BIA 2001).

45 *Matter of Estrada*, 26 I&N Dec. 749, 755–56 (BIA 2016).

46 *Matter of Thomas*, 27 I&N Dec. 674, 680 (A.G. 2019).

Matter of Pickering now provides the applicable legal rule, even when evaluating "state-court orders that modify, clarify, or otherwise alter the term of imprisonment or sentence associated with a state-court conviction."[47]

Although this new framework curtails the legal avenues available to foreign nationals for ameliorating the immigration consequences of their criminal history, some uncertainty still remains about the impact of *Thomas* moving forward. Such uncertainty exists because (1) advocates intend to appeal the attorney general's ruling to the circuit court, and (2) the attorney general made no comment on the retroactivity considerations of his opinion. Accordingly, foreign nationals whose postconviction relief predated *Matter of Thomas* and relied on the broader legal frameworks available at that time for sentencing orders should still set forth arguments that the new rule should not be applied retroactively to his or her case. For foreign nationals seeking postconviction relief moving forward, however, the safest approach is to ensure that any such relief is predicated on a legal defect as outlined in *Matter of Pickering*, unless or until *Matter of Thomas* is overturned.

Another consideration for whether a conviction will trigger grounds of inadmissibility is whether it is considered final. Before the Illegal Immigration Reform and Immigrant Responsibility Act of 1996 (IIRAIRA), the rule was that a conviction should not be considered final until the direct appeal had been either waived or exhausted.[48] After IIRAIRA, however, a circuit court split emerged regarding whether Congress had eliminated the finality requirement when it added a definition of "conviction" to the INA.[49] More recently, the BIA issued a decision in *Matter of J.M. Acosta* holding that a conviction "does not attain a sufficient degree of finality for immigration purposes until the right to direct appellate review on the merits of the conviction has been exhausted or waived."[50] Accordingly, in circuits with no case law to the contrary, *Acosta* should apply.

Still, direct appeals and collateral attacks that are unrelated to the merits of the conviction—such as seeking a reduction in sentencing or pursuing rehabilitative relief—do not impact the finality determination.[51]

---

47 *Id.*

48 *Pino v. Landon*, 349 U.S. 901 (1955).

49 *Planes v. Holder*, 652 F.3d 991 (9th Cir. 2011) (concluding that the INA's definition of conviction does not include any requirement that direct appeal rights be waived or exhausted); *U.S. v Saenz-Gomez*, 472 F.3d 791 (10th Cir. 2007) (same); *Montenegro v. Ashcroft*, 355 F.3d 1035 (7th Cir. 2004) (same); *Moosa v. INS*, 171 F.3d 994 (5th Cir. 1999) (same); *see also Griffiths v. INS*, 243 F.3d 45 (1st Cir. 2001) (deferring to the BIA's interpretation that finality is not required under the deferred-adjudication portion of INA §101(a)(48)(A)); *but see Orabi v. Att'y Gen.*, 738 F.3d 535 (3d Cir. 2014) (determining that a conviction does not attain a sufficient degree of finality until direct appeal is waived or exhausted).

50 *Matter of J.M. Acosta*, 27 I&N Dec. 420 (BIA 2018).

51 *Id.* at 433.

A conviction by a court in a foreign country may trigger inadmissibility in the same manner as a conviction inside the United States if it is for conduct that would also be considered criminal in the United States.[52]

Additionally, the general rule is that findings of delinquency by a juvenile court are not convictions for immigration purposes.[53] However, if the minor is convicted by a court as if he or she were an adult, it will be considered a conviction for immigration purposes.[54] Within the United States, such a conviction may occur if a state court forgoes the option of treating the minor as a juvenile.

Inadmissibility for commission of a crime of moral turpitude or a controlled substance offense also may be established without a conviction where a foreign national admits commission of the crime or the essential elements of the crime. For an admission to be valid, the consular officer or USCIS officer must establish all of the following:

- the act is considered criminal under the law in force where the act was alleged to have been committed;
- the alien was advised in a clear manner of the essential elements of the alleged crime;
- the alien has clearly admitted conduct constituting the essential elements of the crime; and
- the admission was made in a free and voluntary manner.[55]

Although a guilty plea is generally considered an admission for immigration purposes, it cannot be used as an admission if it "results in something less than a conviction."[56] Additionally, admissions made either as an adult or a minor about the commission of offenses that would constitute juvenile delinquency findings rather than crimes should not trigger the admissions-based grounds of inadmissibility.[57]

Crimes Involving Moral Turpitude

A foreign national is inadmissible if he or she has been convicted of a crime involving moral turpitude (CIMT) or admits having committed a CIMT.[58]

---

52 *See Matter of McNaughton*, 16 I&N Dec. 569 (BIA 1978).

53 INA §212(a)(2)(A)(ii)(I); *Matter of Devison*, 22 I&N Dec. 1362 (BIA 2000).

54 *See, e.g., Vieira Garcia v. INS*, 239 F.3d 409, 414 (1st Cir. 2001) (concluding that federal courts are bound by a local court's decision to charge a juvenile as an adult and that such an adjudication is a conviction for immigration purposes); *Vargas-Hernandez v. Gonzales*, 497 F.3d 919, 923 (9th Cir. 2007) (same).

55 *Matter of K*, 7 I&N Dec. 594 (BIA 1957).

56 *Matter of Seda*, 17 I&N Dec. 550, 554 (BIA 1980).

57 *Matter of M–U–*, 2 I&N Dec. 92 (BIA 1944).

58 INA §212(a)(2)(A).

What Is a CIMT?

The INA does not define a "crime involving moral turpitude," though the term "moral turpitude" has been held as referring "generally to conduct which is inherently base, vile, or depraved, and contrary to the accepted rules of morality and the duties owed between persons or to society in general."[59]

In evaluating whether a particular crime involves moral turpitude, USCIS does not look at the underlying conduct of the applicant, but at the elements of the relevant criminal statute.[60] If the statute is broad or multisectional (a "divisible statute," in the parlance of the law), the courts will look at the record of conviction—i.e., the "charge (indictment), plea, verdict, and sentence"—to determine whether the crime for which the person was convicted involved moral turpitude.[61] In April 2015, the U.S. attorney general resolved a split in the circuit courts of appeal and upheld this traditional framework for analyzing whether a conviction is for a CIMT.[62]

Although an attorney must always analyze the specific statute involved in a client's case, there are some basic concepts that apply to the analysis of whether a crime involves moral turpitude. For example, crimes that have fraud as an element are considered to involve moral turpitude.[63] Crimes of violence involving specific intent, such as murder, voluntary manslaughter, or rape, also involve moral turpitude.[64] Other physical assault-related offenses may or may not be CIMTs, however, depending on the level of intent and the level of harm contemplated in the statute. For example, the BIA has indicated that involuntary manslaughter is not a crime of moral turpitude unless the statute requires reckless conduct involving the conscious disregard of a substantial and unjustifiable risk,[65] and that menacing can be a CIMT when it requires a specific intent to cause fear of imminent serious physical injury.[66] Generally, however, simple assault and simple battery convictions do not involve moral turpitude.[67] Still, the BIA has held that assault statutes with an aggravating

---

59 *Matter of Franklin*, 20 I&N Dec. 867, 868 (BIA 1994), *aff'd*, 72 F.3d 571 (8th Cir. 1995).

60 *Matter of L-V-C-*, 22 I&N Dec. 594, 597 (BIA 1999).

61 *See, e.g.*, *U.S. v. Corsi*, 63 F.2d 757 (2d Cir. 1933).

62 *Matter of Silva-Trevino*, 26 I&N Dec. 550 (A.G. 2015) (vacating the AG's prior decision in *Matter of Silva-Trevino*, 24 I&N Dec. 687 (A.G. 2008), which allowed for evidence outside the record of conviction to be considered in certain circumstances).

63 *Matter of Adetiba*, 20 I&N Dec. 506 (BIA 1992).

64 *Matter of Awaijane*, 14 I&N Dec. 117 (BIA 1972) (attempted murder); *Carter v. INS*, 90 F.3d 14 (1st Cir. 1996) (manslaughter); *Matter of Beato*, 10 I&N Dec. 730 (BIA 1964) (attempted rape).

65 *See Matter of Franklin*, 20 I&N Dec. 867 (BIA 1994); *Matter of Lopez*, 13 I&N Dec. 725 (BIA 1971).

66 *Matter of J–G–P–*, 27 I&N Dec. 642 (BIA 2019).

67 *See, e.g.*, *Matter of Fualaau*, 21 I&N Dec.475 (BIA 1996) (Hawaii's third-degree assault is not a CIMT); *Matter of Garcia-Hernandez*, 23 I&N Dec. 590 (BIA 2003) (simple battery under California's Penal Code §242 is not a CIMT).

factor, such as the willful infliction of bodily injury to a spouse or child, may give rise to a CIMT finding.[68]

Some sexual crimes, such as prostitution, [69] and certain sexual offenses against minors[70] will be considered CIMTs, as will some crimes against property, such as certain robbery offenses, [71] and theft offenses that involve an intent to deprive the owner of his or her property either permanently or under circumstances where the owner's property rights are substantially eroded.[72] A conviction for simple driving under the influence (DUI) or driving while intoxicated (DWI) ordinarily does not involve moral turpitude, although certain aggravated DUI offenses may be CIMTs.[73]

Exceptions

The law contains two exceptions for certain foreign nationals who have been convicted of CIMTs or who have made valid admissions regarding such crimes. Foreign nationals who have committed more than one CIMT, however, cannot claim either of the exemptions.

The first exception provides that if the crime was committed while the foreign national was under age 18 and the foreign national both committed the crime and was released from prison more than five years before he or she applied for a visa, for other documentation, or for admission to the United States, then the foreign national is not inadmissible.[74] This provision is different from the rule that juvenile delinquency findings are not considered convictions for purposes of immigration law.

In such a case, the foreign national would not have been convicted of any crime and would not be inadmissible. However, if the minor was convicted as if he or she were an adult, or, in the case of foreign convictions, if the minor's conviction does not fall within the type of proceedings that federal law considers necessarily as juvenile proceedings, then this exception comes into play.

---

68 *Compare Matter of Tran*, 21 I&N Dec. 291 (BIA 1996) (finding moral turpitude) *with Matter of Sejas*, 24 I&N Dec. 236 (BIA 2007) (no moral turpitude).

69 *Matter of Lambert*, 11 I&N Dec. 340 (BIA 1965).

70 *See, e.g.*, *Matter of Jimenez-Cedillo*, 27 I.&N. Dec. 782 (BIA 2020) (holding that Maryland's Criminal Code § 3-324(b) (sexual solicitation of a minor), is categorically a CIMT).

71 *Compare Mendoza v. Holder*, 623 F.3d 1299, 1303–04 (9th Cir. 2010) (concluding that California's Penal Code §211 is categorically a CIMT), *with Barbosa v. Barr*, 926 F.3d 1053, 1059 (9th Cir. 2019) (holding that because Oregon's ORS §164.395 requires a minimal use of force, it is not categorically a CIMT).

72 *Matter of Diaz-Lizarraga*, 26 I&N Dec. 847 (BIA 2016).

73 *Matter of Lopez-Meza*, 22 I&N Dec. 1188 (BIA 1992).

74 INA §212(a)(2)(A)(ii)(I).

The second exception, known as the "petty offense" exception, has two requirements. First, the CIMT under which he or she was convicted, or to which he or she admitted, must have had a maximum possible imprisonment penalty of one year.[75] Second, the applicant must establish that he or she was not sentenced to a term of imprisonment exceeding six months, regardless of how much time he or she actually served.[76] If both of these elements are met, the foreign national is not inadmissible under INA §212(a)(2)(A)(i)(I).

Multiple Criminal Convictions

To be inadmissible under the multiple criminal convictions provision, (1) a foreign national must have been convicted of two or more crimes (other than purely political offenses), and (2) the aggregate sentences to confinement must have been five years or more.[77] Under this ground, it is irrelevant whether the convictions occurred in a single trial, whether the offenses arose from a single scheme of misconduct, or whether they involved moral turpitude.[78]

Controlled-Substance Violations

There are two grounds of inadmissibility relating to drug crimes. The first ground is triggered when a foreign national has been convicted of or made valid admissions about the commission of controlled-substance offenses.[79] Specifically, this inadmissibility ground applies to a violation of, or conspiracy to violate, "any law or regulation of a State, the United States, or a foreign country relating to a controlled substance (as defined in section 802 of [the Controlled Substances Act])."[80] Furthermore, the use of the words "any law or regulation ... relating to a controlled substance" has been interpreted broadly to encompass convictions for being under the influence of drugs,[81] or facilitating the unlawful sale of cocaine.[82]

Traffickers in Controlled Substances

The second drug-related ground of inadmissibility does not require a conviction or even a valid admission and instead applies to "[a]ny alien who the consular or immigration officer knows or has reason to believe is or has been an illicit trafficker

---

75 INA §212(a)(2)(A)(iii)(II).

76 *Id.*

77 INA §212(a)(2)(B).

78 *Id.*

79 INA §212(a)(2)(A)(i)(II).

80 *Id.*

81 *Matter of Esqueda*, 20 I&N Dec. 850 (BIA 1994).

82 *Matter of Del Risco*, 20 I&N Dec. 109 (BIA 1989); *Cf. Mellouli v. Lynch*, 575 U.S. 798 (2015) (concluding that a Kansas conviction for possession of drug paraphernalia triggers removal under INA §237 only if it is connected to a drug defined in the Controlled Substances Act).

in any such controlled substance."[83] It also applies to persons who knowingly assist in illicit drug trafficking, and to abettors, conspirators, and those who collude with others in furtherance of such acts.[84] Spouses and children who knowingly obtained a financial or other benefit from the illicit activity within the previous five years are also inadmissible.[85]

An "illicit trafficker" is "a knowing and conscious participant or conduit in an attempt to smuggle" a controlled substance.[86] This broad definition applies not only to persons who smuggle or attempt to smuggle drugs into the United States, but also to people who serve as conduits for the drug trade within the United States.[87] Although a person can be an illicit trafficker even if he or she has committed only one transgression,[88] the finding must still be supported by reasonable, substantial, and probative evidence.[89]

This ground may also apply to lawful permanent residents under two theories, including that: (1) a person is removable under INA §237(a)(1)(A) for having been inadmissible at the time of entry or adjustment of status pursuant to INA §212(a)(2)(C) as an illicit trafficker in controlled substances where an immigration official knows or has reason to believe that the foreign national was a trafficker in controlled substances at the time of admission,[90]and (2) if an LPR travels abroad, he or she could be regarded as seeking admission if this ground of inadmissibility applies.[91]

Prostitution and Commercialized Vice

Unlike the other grounds included under INA §212(a)(2), prostitution and commercialized vice are not technically "criminal" inadmissibility grounds. They apply even to persons who come from countries where prostitution is legal and presumably also to those who reside in states where prostitution is legal.[92] This ground's three subsections make inadmissible the following:

- people who are coming to the United States to engage in prostitution or who have engaged in prostitution within 10 years of the date of application for a visa, adjustment of status, or entry into the United States;

---

83 INA §212(a)(2)(C).

84 INA §212(a)(2)(C)(i).

85 INA §212(a)(2)(C)(ii).

86 *Matter of Rico*, 16 I&N Dec. 181, 186 (BIA 1977).

87 *Matter of R H*, 7 I&N Dec. 675 (BIA 1958).

88 *Matter of Rico*, 16 I&N Dec. at 186.

89 *Id.* at 185.

90 *Matter of Casillas-Topete*, 25 I&N Dec. 317 (BIA 2010).

91 *See* INA §101(a)(13)(C)(v).

92 22 CFR §40.24(c).

- people who are procurers of prostitutes, or who attempt to procure, or who receive the proceeds of prostitution, or people who have done any of these activities within 10 years of applying for a visa, adjustment of status, or entry into the United States; and
- people who are coming to the United States to engage in unlawful commercialized vice, whether or not it is related to prostitution.[93]

The phrase "engage in prostitution" requires a regular pattern of behavior or conduct.[94] Additionally, the BIA has held that it does not apply to a single act of soliciting prostitution on one's own behalf.[95] However, foreign nationals falling into any of these three subsections are inadmissible even if there is no conviction for an offense involving prostitution.

Foreign Government Officials Who Have Engaged in Particularly Severe Violations of Religious Freedom

Foreign nationals who were responsible for or carried out particularly severe violations of religious freedom at any time while serving as a foreign government official, and the spouse and children of such persons, are inadmissible.[96]

Particularly severe violations of religious freedom are defined as "systematic, ongoing, egregious violations of religious freedom, including violations such as—

(A) torture or cruel, inhuman, or degrading treatment or punishment;

(B) prolonged detention without charges;

(C) causing the disappearance of persons by the abduction or clandestine detention of those persons; or

(D) other flagrant denial of the right to life, liberty, or the security of persons."[97]

Significant Traffickers in Persons

Any foreign national who commits or conspires to commit human trafficking offenses in the United States, or who certain governmental officials have reason to believe, is or has been a knowing aider, abettor, assister, conspirator, or colluder with such a trafficker in severe forms of trafficking in persons, is inadmissible.[98] Spouses, sons, and daughters (except unmarried children under 21) of traffickers

93 INA §212(a)(2)(D).

94 *See Matter of T*, 6 I&N Dec. 474 (BIA 1955).

95 *Matter of Gonzales-Zoquiapan*, 24 I&N Dec. 549 (BIA 2008).

96 INA §212(a)(2)(G).

97 22 USC §6402(13).

98 INA §212(a)(2)(H)(i).

who have, within the previous five years, knowingly obtained any financial or other benefit from the trafficker's illicit activity are also inadmissible.[99]

The term "severe forms of trafficking in persons" is defined as either (1) sex trafficking in which a commercial sex act is induced by force, fraud, or coercion, or in which the person induced to perform the commercial sex act is under 18 years of age, or (2) the recruitment, harboring, transportation, provision, or obtaining of a person for labor or services, through the use of force, fraud, or coercion, for the purpose of subjection to involuntary servitude, peonage, debt bondage, or slavery.[100]

Resources for Evaluating Immigration Consequences of Crimes

Practitioners should consult *Immigration Consequences of Criminal Activity: A Guide to Representing Foreign-Born Defendants* by Mary E. Kramer.

Also, there are many online resources that may help you evaluate the immigration consequences of criminal activity. These websites include:

- National Immigration Project of the National Lawyers Guild:
- www.nationalimmigrationproject.org
- Law Offices of Norton Tooby
- www.criminalandimmigrationlaw.com
- Immigrant Defense Project
- www.nysda.org/idp/index.htm
- National Defending Immigrants Partnership, through the National Legal Aid and Defender Association
- www.nlada.org/Defender/Defender_Immigrants

National Security Grounds

Foreign nationals inadmissible under the political/national security grounds are divided into five categories:

- Persons seeking to enter the United States to engage in prejudicial and unlawful activities, including espionage, sabotage, "any unlawful activity," or the violation or evasion of "any law prohibiting the export from the United States of goods, technology or sensitive information";[101]
- Persons "engaging in" "terrorist activities";[102]

---

99 INA §212(a)(2)(H)(ii), (iii).

100 22 USC §7102(9).

101 INA §212(a)(3)(A).

102 INA §212(a)(3)(B).

- Persons whose admission into the United States would bring about serious foreign policy consequences;[103]
- Members of the Communist or any totalitarian party;[104] and
- Participants in Nazi persecution or genocide.[105]

Under the foreign-policy inadmissibility ground, foreign nationals can be found inadmissible for purely ideological reasons. That is, the U.S. secretary of state may exclude a foreign national "because of the alien's past, current, or expected beliefs, statements, or associations" if the person's admission would "compromise a compelling U.S. foreign policy interest." Mere membership in a Communist party is also a bar to entry, but only for foreigners seeking lawful permanent residence.[106]

Espionage, Sabotage, Export Control Violations, and Other Unlawful Activities

Any foreign national is inadmissible if a consular officer or the U.S. attorney general has reason to believe that the person will: (1) engage in espionage or sabotage; (2) attempt to violate or evade export control laws; (3) engage in activities with a view to overthrowing the U.S. government by unlawful means; or (4) engage in any other unlawful activity.[107]

For such a person to be barred from admission, it is sufficient for the consular officer or USCIS to have reasonable grounds to believe that the person intends to engage in the proscribed activities. The applicant is inadmissible even if he or she intends to engage only incidentally in the described activities.

The provision barring entry to those who seek to "violate or evade any law prohibiting the export from the United States of goods, technology, or sensitive information"[108] was intended by Congress to forbid the entry not only of those whom the consular officer has reason to believe seek to violate the export control laws, but also of those who have the intention to *evade* those laws. Thus, the ground covers activity not expressly forbidden by the export control laws. However, the legislative history indicates that this provision should be applied only to those cases in which such evasion would harm the national security.

103 INA §212(a)(3)(C).

104 INA §212(a)(3)(D).

105 INA §212(a)(3)(E).

106 INA §212(a)(3)(D)(i).

107 INA §212(a)(3)(A).

108 INA §212(a)(3)(A)(i)(II).

Terrorist Activity

This ground of inadmissibility, which was greatly expanded by the USA PATRIOT Act of 2001[109] and the REAL ID Act of 2005,[110] has three essential, interrelated prongs: "engaging in" "terrorist activity," and belonging to or working on behalf of a "terrorist organization." INA §212(a)(3)(B) makes inadmissible any foreign national who has "engaged in a terrorist activity;" whom a consular officer or the Department of Homeland Security (DHS) knows or reasonably believes is engaging in or will after entry engage in "terrorist activity;" who has incited "terrorist activity" with an intent to cause death or serious bodily harm; who is a representative or member of a "terrorist organization"; who endorses or espouses terrorist activity; who has received military-type training from a terrorist organization; or who is the spouse or child of such a foreign national if the activity occurred within the last five years.[111]

"Terrorist activity" includes hijacking and sabotaging conveyances; kidnapping someone and threatening her or him with death or injury in order to compel actions from a third party as a condition of release; violent attacks on internationally protected persons; assassination; use of biological, chemical, or nuclear weapons; use of explosives, firearms, or other weapons to endanger people or substantially damage property; or a threat or conspiracy to do any of the foregoing.[112]

"Engaging" in terrorist activity under the statute encompasses more than directly performing any of the acts above. It also includes preparing and planning a terrorist activity; gathering information for potential targets of terrorist activity; soliciting funds either for terrorist activity or terrorist organizations; soliciting individuals to engage in terrorist activity or to join a terrorist organization; giving "material support" (including a safe house, transportation, communications, funds [in any amount], false documents, weapons, explosives, or training) for the commission of a terrorist activity or to a terrorist organization.[113] Note that officers, official representatives, and spokesmen of the Palestine Liberation Organization are considered under the statute to be "engaged in terrorist activity."[114]

The INA sets out three different tiers of "terrorist organizations." The groups in the first two tiers are specifically designated by the Department of State (DOS) as terrorist organizations.[115] Groups in the third tier are not specifically named

---

109 Uniting and Strengthening America by Providing Appropriate Tools Required to Intercept and Obstruct Terrorism (USA PATRIOT) Act of 2001, Pub. L. No. 107-56, 115 Stat. 272 (Oct. 26, 2001).

110 Pub. L. No. 109-13, div. B, 119 Stat. 231, 302–23 (Jan. 4, 2005).

111 INA §212(a)(3)(B)(i).

112 INA §212(a)(3)(B)(iii).

113 INA §212(a)(3)(B)(iv).

114 INA §212(a)(3)(B)(i).

115 *See* DOS Bureau of Counterterrorism, Foreign Terrorist Organizations, www.state.gov/j/ct/rls/other/des/123085.htm; DOS, Terrorist Exclusion List, www.state.gov/j/ct/rls/other/des/123086.htm.

anywhere; the third tier comprises any "group[s] of two or more individuals, whether organized or not," which engage in, or have subgroups that engage in, terrorist activities.[116] Anyone who is a *representative* of a terrorist organization from any of the three tiers is inadmissible. *Members* of Tier I and II organizations are inadmissible, while a member of a Tier III organization is inadmissible unless he or she can show that he or she did not know, and reasonably should not have known, that the organization was a terrorist organization.[117]

The statute as originally passed contained few specific exemptions from these bars. There is an exception to inadmissibility for the spouse or child of a foreign national who had engaged in terrorist activity within the last five years. To be eligible for this exception, the spouse or child must show that he or she reasonably should not have known about the activity that made his or her parent or spouse inadmissible under this section; or whom the consular officer or DHS officer has reason to believe has renounced this activity.[118] There is also an exception for individuals who provided "material support" to terrorists or terrorist organizations if they can show, by clear and convincing evidence, that they did not know that the organization in question was a terrorist organization.[119]

Legislation passed at the end of 2007 gave DHS and DOS explicit authority to exempt many more individuals from some of the terrorism-related bars to admission.[120] These exemptions are often referred to as "waivers," although technically speaking, they are not waivers, and one does not use a waiver application to request these exemptions. The following persons may be exempted from the terrorism-related bars: members and representatives of Tier III groups; people who knowingly and voluntarily engaged in terrorist activity as long as it was not on behalf of a Tier I or Tier II group; people who engaged in terrorist activity on behalf of a Tier I or Tier II group, but did not do so knowingly or willingly; and spouses and children of people inadmissible under INA §212(a)(3)(B) who are not covered by the exception at INA §212(a)(3)(B)(i)(IX).[121]

Exemptions may be available to individuals with associations to certain groups[122] or who are otherwise inadmissible under the following situations: those who under duress provided material support to, solicited funds for, or received military training from or on behalf of a terrorist organizations; individuals who have

---

116 INA §212(a)(3)(B)(vi)(III).

117 INA §212(a)(3)(B)(i)(VI).

118 INA §212(a)(3)(B)(ii).

119 INA §212(a)(3)(B)(iv)(VI)(dd).

120 Consolidated Appropriations Act, 2008, Pub. L. No. 110-161, §6, div. J, sec. 691, 121 Stat. 1844, 2364–66 (Dec. 26, 2007).

121 INA §212(d)(3)(B)(i).

122 USCIS, Terrorism-Related Inadmissibility Grounds (TRIG), www.uscis.gov/legal-resources/terrorism-related-inadmissibility-grounds-trig.

provided medical care to members of a terrorist organization; individuals who provided certain limited material support (including routine commercial or social transactions, certain humanitarian assistance, and material support provided under substantial pressure); or insignificant material support to terrorist organizations or their members; and certain applicants with existing immigration benefits who have engaged in select voluntary and nonviolent associations or activities.[123] To date, DHS has not exercised the full scope of its exemption authority.

On October 19, 2017, USCIS issued a policy memorandum revising the agency "hold policy" regarding certain persons subject to terrorism-related inadmissibility grounds (TRIG).[124] Under prior policy, USCIS was holding cases for adjudication for certain applicants inadmissible for TRIG who were not applicants for asylum, refugee status, suspension of removal or cancellation of removal under the Nicaraguan Adjustment and Central American Relief Act (NACARA). Now, cases for which no exemption is currently available should not remain on or be placed on hold absent a specific USCIS Headquarters directive.

Potential for Serious Adverse Consequences for Foreign Policy

Another ground bars the entry of a foreign national if the secretary of state has reasonable ground to believe that the foreign national's entry or proposed activities would have serious adverse foreign policy consequences.[125]

Beliefs, Statements, and Associations Exception

Beliefs, statements, or associations that would be lawful within the United States do not make foreign nationals inadmissible on the foreign policy ground. However, the secretary of state may override this exception if she or he "personally determines that the foreign national's admission would compromise a compelling United States foreign policy interest."[126] The law provides that if the secretary of state makes such a determination, he or she must notify the chairs of the Judiciary and Foreign Affairs Committees of the House of Representatives and of the Judiciary and Foreign Relations Committees of the Senate regarding the foreign national's identity and the reasons for the determination.[127]

---

123 *Id.*

124 USCIS Policy Memorandum, *Revised Guidance for Processing Cases Subject to Terrorism-Related Inadmissibility Grounds and the Rescission of the Prior Policy Hold for Such Cases*, (Oct. 19, 2017), AILA Doc. No. 17103131.

125 INA §212(a)(3)(C).

126 INA §212(a)(3)(C)(iii).

127 INA §212(a)(3)(C)(iv).

Exception for Foreign Politicians

Another exception to the adverse foreign-policy effect inadmissibility ground specifically protects foreign politicians. No official of a foreign government or purported government, and no candidate in a foreign election during the period immediately preceding the election, may be excluded on the basis of beliefs, statements, or associations, if such beliefs, statements, or associations would be lawful in the United States. The secretary of state has no authority to override this exception.[128]

Membership in the Communist or a Totalitarian Party

The INA bars the admission of members or former members of the Communist party or of any totalitarian party.[129] Speech-related conduct, such as "advocating or teaching totalitarian doctrine, or writing, publishing, distributing, printing, or possessing totalitarian materials," no longer constitutes a ground of inadmissibility. And foreign nationals are no longer inadmissible, as they once were, for being members of organizations proscribed by the Subversive Activities Control Act of 1950.

Meaning of Membership in a Totalitarian or Communist Party

Giving, loaning, or promising support or money for any purpose to any organization is presumed, according to the INA, to constitute "affiliation" with the organization.[130] The term "totalitarian party" refers to an organization that advocates the establishment in the United States of a one-party system and that forcibly suppresses opposition.

The *Foreign Affairs Manual* says that "intellectual interest in, sympathy for, or favoring the ideologies of the Communist or other totalitarian party does not constitute affiliation ... unless accompanied by some positive and voluntary action which provides support, money, or another thing of value."[131] DOS regulations also provide that voluntary service in the armed forces of a Communist country is not by itself considered voluntary membership or affiliation with the Communist party.[132] Voluntary service in a political capacity, on the other hand, is considered affiliation with or membership in the party.[133]

Membership must be a "meaningful association" to be the basis of inadmissibility. In 1957, the U.S. Supreme Court held that membership is not present when the

---

128 INA §212(a)(3)(C)(ii).

129 INA §212(a)(3)(D).

130 22 CFR §40.34(a).

131 9 FAM 302.5-6(B)(1).

132 22 CFR §40.34(b).

133 22 CFR §40.34(c).

motivating impulse to the affiliation was devoid of political implications.[134] In that case, the foreign national had joined the Communist party of the United States in the 1930s because he considered it the only way to fight for food and shelter, and he seemed unaware of such Communist aims as the overthrow of the state.

In a 1963 decision, the U.S. Supreme Court stated that membership is not meaningful if it is temporary and if the person does not know of the party's international relationships, but believes it to be a group solely trying to remedy unsatisfactory social or economic conditions, carry out trade union objectives, eliminate racial discrimination, combat unemployment, or alleviate distress and poverty.[135] The BIA has held that membership is absent if the foreign national joined an affiliate of the Communist party when the foreign national had no knowledge of the affiliate's relationship with the Communist party.[136]

Consular officers seeking to determine whether a foreign national's membership in a Communist or totalitarian party was meaningful may (and in some cases must) request an advisory opinion from DOS's Visa Office.

Membership in the Communist Party and Foreign Policy Considerations

Historically, courts have held that the executive power should not circumvent limitations on its power to exclude foreign nationals who are members of the Communist party by resorting to the foreign policy inadmissibility ground. To exclude a Communist party member under this ground, the government was required to have a foreign policy reason independent from the foreign national's organizational membership.

Involuntary Membership Exception

The law exempts from the Communist party membership ground of inadmissibility foreign nationals whose membership in or affiliation with the Communist party (1) is or was involuntary; (2) was solely when the person was under 16 years of age; (3) arose solely by operation of law; or (4) was for the purpose of obtaining employment, food rations, or other essentials of living.[137]

Past Membership Limitations

Former membership in a Communist or totalitarian party will not bar the former member's entry into the United States if the consular officer determines that (1) such membership or affiliation terminated two years before the date the former member applied for a visa (or five years before in the case of a member of a totalitarian party

---

134 *Rowoldt v. Perfetto*, 355 U.S. 115 (1957).

135 *Gastelum-Quinones v. Kennedy*, 374 U.S. 469 (1963).

136 *Matter of Rusin*, 20 I&N Dec. 128 (BIA 1989).

137 INA §212(a)(3)(D)(ii).

that still controls the government of the foreign state at the time of application for the visa); and (2) the foreign national is not a threat to the security of the United States.[138]

Participant in Genocide or Nazi Persecution

The INA bars admission of individuals who, as members of the Nazi government or its allies, participated in the persecution of others on account of race, religion, national origin, or political opinion.[139] Another inadmissibility ground excludes foreign nationals who have engaged in genocidal conduct as defined by the International Convention on the Prevention and Punishment of Genocide.[140] The convention defines genocide as the commission of any of a number of specified acts with intent to destroy, in whole or in part, a national, ethnic, racial, or religious group as such.[141] The acts specified are:

- killing members of the group
- causing serious bodily or mental harm to the members of the group
- deliberately inflicting on the group conditions of life calculated to bring about its physical destruction
- imposing measures intended to prevent births within the group
- forcibly transferring children of the group to another group.[142]

Waivers

INA §212(a)(3) specifically provides for only one type of waiver applicable to persons inadmissible because of membership in Communist or totalitarian parties. Only parents, spouses, sons, or daughters of U.S. citizens or LPRs and brothers or sisters of U.S. citizens are eligible for this waiver.[143] USCIS is authorized to grant these waivers for humanitarian purposes, to ensure family unity, or when it is in the public interest, provided the person is not a threat to the security of the United States.

Public Charge

The public charge inadmissibility ground is discussed in Chapter 8.

---

138 INA §212(a)(3)(D)(iii).

139 INA §212(a)(3)(E)(i).

140 INA §212(a)(3)(E)(ii).

141 18 USC §1091(a).

142 *Id.*

143 INA §212(a)(3)(D)(iv).

Labor Protection Grounds

The law singles out two groups—U.S. workers and U.S. physicians and health care workers—as deserving of special protection from possible erosion of living standards due to foreign competition. The inadmissibility ground that provides general protection to U.S. workers, INA §212(a)(5)(A), prohibits the entry of those coming to the United States to perform skilled or unskilled labor without having first obtained a "labor certification."[144] A labor certification is a process involving the state employment agency and the Department of Labor (DOL) whereby the employer demonstrates to the satisfaction of both the state and federal departments of labor that there are no available or qualified U.S. workers to do the job.

DOL must "certify" that there are no U.S. workers able, willing, qualified, and available to accept the job at the prevailing wage for that occupation in the geographic area, and that the employment of the immigrant will not adversely affect the wages and working conditions of similarly employed U.S. workers.[145] Labor certification decisions by DOL may be appealed to the Board of Alien Labor Certification Appeals.

The protection extended to U.S. physicians and health care workers under INA §212(a)(5)(B) prevents graduates of foreign medical schools and health care workers who have not received a certificate from the Commission on Graduates of Foreign Nursing Schools, or an equivalent credential, from entering the United States.[146]

Labor protection grounds apply only to foreign nationals seeking admission under the second and third employment-based preference categories. They do not apply to foreign nationals seeking permanent residence through family-based immigrant categories or under other non–employment-based immigrant categories.[147]

Previous Immigration Violations

INA §212(a)(6) covers certain immigration-related misconduct. These grounds of inadmissibility apply to numerous categories of foreign nationals, including:

- those present in the United States without being lawfully admitted or paroled
- those who fail to attend removal proceedings
- those who engage in fraud or misrepresentation
- those who falsely claim U.S. citizenship
- stowaways

---

144 INA §212(a)(5)(A)(i).

145 20 CFR §656.1.

146 INA §212(a)(5)(B), (C).

147 INA §212(a)(5).

- smugglers
- those who have been found to have committed civil document fraud
- foreign students who study at public institutions

Foreign Nationals Present Without Permission or Parole

This ground of inadmissibility applies to foreign nationals who are present in the United States without being admitted or paroled, or who arrive at a place other than a designated port of entry.[148]

This ground does not apply to foreign nationals who leave the United States for consular processing, as they will not then be present in the United States. This ground also does not bar foreign nationals who entered the United States without inspection from adjusting status to permanent residence under the special provisions of INA §245(i).[149]

There is an exception to this ground of inadmissibility for foreign nationals who qualify for immigrant status under the INA's provisions for battered spouses and children.[150] For foreign nationals who first arrive in the United States after April 1, 1997, there are further restrictions on this exception. They must show that the spouse or child was battered or subjected to extreme cruelty by a spouse or parent, or a member of the spouse or parent's family in the household, and that there was a substantial connection between the battery or cruelty and the foreign national's unlawful entry to the United States.[151]

Failure to Attend Removal Proceedings

Another bar to admissibility applies to foreign nationals who, without reasonable cause, fail to attend their removal proceedings.[152] Reasonable cause is defined as "something that is not within the reasonable control of the alien."[153] Those who are subject to this bar are inadmissible for a period of five years following their subsequent departure or removal from the United States. This ground applies only to foreign nationals who failed to attend removal proceedings; it does not apply to foreign nationals who failed to attend deportation or exclusion proceedings.

In other words, the ground applies only to foreign nationals who fail to attend proceedings that were initiated on or after April 1, 1997, and who were served with Form I-862, Notice to Appear.[154] Moreover, this ground applies only to foreign

148 INA §212(a)(6)(A).

149 *Adjudicator's Field Manual* (AFM) §40.6.2(a)(4)(i), located in 8 *USCIS Policy Manual* pt. I.

150 INA §212(a)(6)(A)(ii).

151 INA §212(a)(6)(A)(ii)(III).

152 INA §212(a)(6)(B).

153 9 FAM 302.9-3(B)(1).

154 AFM §40.6.2(b)(2)(iv), located in 8 *USCIS Policy Manual* pt. I.

nationals who departed the United States after failing to attend a removal hearing. Those who did not leave the United States and are seeking to adjust status would need to reopen the removal proceedings.

It should also be noted that foreign nationals who fail to attend removal proceedings after receiving notice may be ordered removed *in absentia*.[155] Moreover, in situations in which a foreign national: (1) has received oral notice of the time and place of proceedings and the consequences of failing to appear; (2) fails to appear for less than "exceptional circumstances"; and (3) an in absentia order results, the foreign national is ineligible to apply for 10 years for cancellation of removal, voluntary departure, adjustment of status, change of status, or registry.[156] This 10-year period could be satisfied through residence in the United States or abroad.

Fraud or Willful Misrepresentation

A foreign national is inadmissible if he or she commits willful misrepresentation or fraud in attempting to obtain, or in obtaining, a visa, other documentation, admission into the United States, or other benefit.[157] "Other documentation" refers to documents required at the time of the foreign national's admission to the United States, such as re-entry permits, border crossing cards, refugee travel documents, advance parole, or U.S. passports. "Other benefit" is understood to include, among other things, adjustment of status, extension of stay, asylum, naturalization, change of nonimmigrant classification, parole, employment authorization, and voluntary departure.[158]

All such misrepresentations that are material create a permanent bar to admission. The BIA has held that "fraud" and "misrepresentation" are the same, except that in cases of "willful misrepresentation" it is unnecessary to prove that the "person to whom the misrepresentation was made was motivated to action because of the misrepresentation."[159]

Under this ground, only misrepresentations to U.S. officials (generally a consular officer or a USCIS officer) are the basis of inadmissibility. Therefore, buying documents from a private individual does not make a foreign national inadmissible under the ground of procuring a document by fraud or misrepresentation, nor does using false documents to procure an entry into the United States make a foreign national inadmissible, unless they are presented to a U.S. official.[160] However, foreign nationals are inadmissible if they are subject to a final order under the civil

155 INA §240(b)(5)(A).

156 INA §240(b)(7).

157 INA §212(a)(6)(C)(i).

158 8 *USCIS Policy Manual* pt. J, ch. 3.

159 *Matter of G G*, 7 I&N Dec. 161 (BIA 1956).

160 *Matter of D–L– & A–M–*, 20 I&N Dec. 409 (BIA 1991).

document fraud provisions of INA §274C.[161] Presenting false documents to an airline or transportation company constitutes a violation of section 274C.[162]

The visa fraud inadmissibility ground does not apply if the statements made by the foreign national were not untrue at the time they were uttered. Thus, the foreign national's activities after entering the United States do not necessarily indicate that the foreign national misrepresented his or her intentions at the time of applying for a visa or for admission. For example, if a foreign national applies for adjustment of status to permanent residence after entering the United States with a tourist visa, this does not mean necessarily that the foreign national misrepresented his or her intentions at the time he or she obtained the visa. A person may have valid reasons for changing his or her plans after admission.

For many years, DOS consular officers employed a "30/60" day rule to evaluate whether a visa applicant may be inadmissible for material misrepresentation or fraud. Under this rule, a nonimmigrant who was in the United States and engaged in conduct inconsistent with his or her nonimmigrant status within 30 days of arrival was subject to a presumption that he or she misrepresented intentions in applying for the nonimmigrant visa. Violations of status occurring more than 30 days but less than 60 days after entry did not give rise to a presumption of misrepresentation but could be the basis for a reasonable belief that the visa applicant misrepresented his or her intent. The same rule provided that where the inconsistent conduct took place after 60 days, no such presumption applied.

In September 2017, DOS replaced this rule with a new standard that provides that an individual who engages in conduct inconsistent with his or her nonimmigrant visa within 90 days of entry is subject to a presumption that he or she made a willful material misrepresentation in applying for the nonimmigrant visa or at the time of admission.[163] Examples of inconsistent conduct include working without authorization, enrolling in school without being in a nonimmigrant status authorizing study, and marrying a U.S. citizen or lawful permanent resident while in B or F status and taking up residence in the United States.

USCIS followed with updated instructions acknowledging that the State Department's 90-day rule is an analytic tool for consular officers—not a mandatory principle—and that the rule is not binding on USCIS. Nevertheless, it advised adjudicators "to evaluate cases for potential fraud indicators and, when appropriate, refer cases to Fraud Detection and National Security according to existing procedures."[164]

For the misrepresentation to be willful, intent to deceive is not necessary.[165] It is sufficient that the false statement be made in a deliberate and voluntary manner or

---

161 INA §212(a)(6)(F)(i).

162 INA §274C(a)(6).

163 9 FAM 302.9-4(B)(3).

164 8 *USCIS Policy Manual* pt. J, ch. 3.

165 *Matter of Kai Hing Hui*, 15 I&N Dec. 288 (BIA 1975).

that the applicant has knowledge of the falsity of the documentation he or she is employing.[166]

A timely retraction of a misrepresentation can prevent it from being considered a basis for inadmissibility.[167] In general, a retraction should be made at the first opportunity.[168]

Only misrepresentations of material facts may make a person inadmissible. In this context, a misrepresentation can be fairly characterized as material: (1) if the foreign national was inadmissible on the true facts, or (2) if the misrepresentation tended to shut off a line of inquiry that was relevant to the foreign national's eligibility and that line of inquiry might have resulted in a proper determination that the foreign national not be admitted.[169]

When the true facts would not have made the foreign national inadmissible, but it has been established that the misrepresentation tended to cut off a relevant line of inquiry, the foreign national has the burden of persuasion and production to show that the inquiry would not have resulted in a proper determination that he or she was inadmissible.[170] This burden is higher than just showing that the foreign national is eligible for a visa, because passage of time may have deprived the government of the possibility of making an adequate investigation.

Consequently, when available facts indicate the existence of a substantial question as to the foreign national's eligibility for admission to the United States, a holding that the foreign national's misrepresentation was material may be warranted. On the contrary, if the record does not contain indications of inadmissibility, the misrepresentation will not be considered material. This holds even when applicants misrepresented their identity, if nothing in the record suggests that by disclosing their true name and identity, they would have revealed an inadmissibility ground.

Misrepresentations on behalf of others do not make an applicant inadmissible under this section. They may, however, lead to inadmissibility due to foreign national smuggling under INA § 212(a)(6)(E).[171]

There is no exception in the INA for misrepresentations made by minors. Under current USCIS policy, however, material misrepresentations made by a person under age 18 may not lead to a finding of inadmissibility if the adjudicator concludes that the individual, due to young age or mental incompetence, was unable to independently form an intent to make a misrepresentation.[172] DOS policy

166 *Falaja v. Gonzales*, 418 F.3d 889 (8th Cir. 2005).

167 *Matter of M*, 9 I&N Dec. 118 (BIA 1960).

168 8 *USCIS Policy Manual* pt. J, ch. 3.

169 *Kungys v. U.S.*, 485 U.S. 759 (1988).

170 *Matter of S & B C*, 9 I&N Dec. 436 (BIA 1961).

171 AFM §40.6.2(c)(1)(B)(v), located in 8 *USCIS Policy Manual* pt. I.

172 8 *USCIS Policy Manual* pt. J, ch. 3.

on this issue, as previously set forth in the *Foreign Affairs Manual* (FAM), has been that noncitizens under the age of 15 are not capable of acting willfully, those aged 15–16 may be capable of acting willfully or may be acting at the direction of an adult, and those aged 17 and over are presumed to be acting willfully unless they establish they lacked knowledge or capacity. The most recent version of the FAM, however, does not include this text. It remains to be clarified whether this is due to an omission or a change in policy.

A waiver for this ground of inadmissibility is available for an individual who can establish that his or her U.S. citizen or lawful permanent resident parent or spouse will suffer extreme hardship if the foreign national is denied admission. This waiver is discussed further in chapter 7.

False Claim of U.S. Citizenship

Any foreign national who, on or after September 30, 1996, falsely represents himself or herself to be a citizen of the United States for any purpose or benefit under the INA or any other federal or state law is inadmissible.[173] This could include false claims of citizenship to a USCIS agent for purposes of gaining admission to the United States, as well as false claims of citizenship to a state employee for purposes of obtaining a driver's license or public benefit, or voting.

Unlike inadmissibility for fraud or misrepresentation, a foreign national can be inadmissible for making a false claim to citizenship to an individual who is not a government official. In particular, a number of circuit courts of appeals, as well as the BIA, have held that inadmissibility for false claim to citizenship is triggered by claiming to be a citizen on a Form I-9 for the purpose of obtaining employment.[174] Note, however, that while the current Form I-9 asks the prospective employee to mark whether he or she is a U.S. citizen, the earlier version of the form, in use until April 3, 2009, required the employee to indicate whether he or she was a U.S. citizen or national. Because an affirmative answer to this question does not, by itself, establish a false claim to citizenship, a person who completed an I-9 before April 3, 2009, may be able to demonstrate that she or he is not inadmissible on this basis.[175]

Falsely claiming to be a U.S. citizen in the course of an arrest by local police has been held not to constitute a false claim under this section.[176] The court reasoned that even if the respondent had lied to the local police about his immigration status

173 INA §212(a)(6)(C)(ii).

174 *See, e.g., Diaz-Jimenez v. Sessions,* No. 15-73603 (9th Cir. 2018); *Dakura v. Holder,* 772 F.3d 994 (4th Cir. 2014); *Crocock v. Holder,* 670 F. 3d 200 (2d Cir. 2012); *Rodriguez v. Mukasey*, 519 F.3d 773 (8th Cir. 2008); *Matter of Bett,* 26 I& N Dec. 437 (BIA 2014).

175 8 *USCIS Policy Manual* pt. K, ch. 2, stating that a noncitizen who falsely claims to be a U.S. national but not a U.S. citizen is not inadmissible for false claim to U.S. citizenship.

176 *Castro v. Att'y Gen.*, 671 F.3d 356 (3d Cir. 2012).

and falsely claimed birth in Puerto Rico, he would only have done so to minimize the risk that the police would report him to DHS. This, the court found, is not a legal benefit, certainly not the kind of "purpose or benefit" under state or federal law that must be sought to trigger inadmissibility under §212(a)(6)(C)(ii).

In April 2020, USCIS changed its policy manual to delete the requirement that a false claim to citizenship must be made knowingly in order to trigger inadmissibility.[177] The change was made to conform to the analysis in a 2019 BIA decision holding that the false claim to citizenship deportability ground, which uses the same statutory language as the inadmissibility ground, does not require that a false claim be knowingly made.[178] In addition to making this change, the *USCIS Policy Manual* also removed prior text providing that a person who made a false claim while under the age of 18 may overcome inadmissibility by showing this she or he lacked the capacity to understand the nature and consequence of the false claim. DOS policy guidance in the *Foreign Affairs Manual* still references an affirmative defense for minors who make false claims,[179] but this is likely to change to conform with *USCIS Policy Manual* text.

An exception for certain persons was included in section 201(b)(2) of the Child Citizenship Act of 2000.[180] Under that exception, the inadmissibility ground does not apply if each natural or adoptive parent of the foreign national is or was a U.S. citizen, by birth or naturalization, the foreign national permanently resided in the United States prior to reaching age 16, and the foreign national reasonably believed at the time of making the representation that he or she was a citizen.[181] The exception applies to representations made on or after September 30, 1996.[182]

Timely retraction of a false claim to U.S. citizenship may be used as a defense to this section. As with timely retractions of general fraud and misrepresentation, the retraction must be both voluntary and without delay in order to be effective.[183]

Stowaways

Stowaways are persons who obtain transportation without the consent of the owner or person in command of the vessel or aircraft on which they are traveling.[184] A passenger who travels with a valid ticket is not a stowaway. Stowaways are inadmissible and there is no specific waiver available for this ground of inadmissibility.[185]

---

177 8 *USCIS Policy Manual* pt. K, ch. 2, at fn 1.

178 *Matter of Zhang,* 27 I&N Dec. 569 (BIA 2019).

179 9 FAM 302.9-5(B)(1)(c).

180 Pub. L. No. 106-395, §201(b)(2), 114 Stat. 1631, 1634 (Oct. 30, 2000).

181 INA §212(a)(6)(C)(ii)(II).

182 Pub. L. No. 106-395, §201(b)(3), 114 Stat. 1631, 1634 (Oct. 30, 2000).

183 AFM §40.6.2(c)(2)(C)(viii), located in 8 *USCIS Policy Manual* pt. I.

184 INA §101(a)(49).

185 INA §212(a)(6)(D).

Smugglers and Encouragers of Unlawful Entry

Immigrants and nonimmigrants are inadmissible to the United States if they have at any time knowingly encouraged, induced, assisted, abetted, or aided any other foreign national to enter the United States illegally.[186] There is no requirement that the smuggling have been for gain.[187] One federal circuit court has found that mere presence in a vehicle with knowledge that an undocumented person was hiding in the vehicle does not constitute alien smuggling without there being an affirmative act to aid or abet the smuggling.[188] The mistaken belief that the smuggled foreign national was legally entitled to enter the United States may be used as a defense to this ground.[189] Individuals who qualified for Family Unity[190] and who are applying for either Family Unity or an immigrant visa under the immediate-relative or the second-preference family visa provisions of the INA are not subject to this ground.[191]

Some consulates have tightened their screening for this ground of inadmissibility, particularly where a parent and child illegally entered the United States together. In those situations, expect further inquiry as to what form of support the parent provided. Inquiries could also extend to situations where the applicant illegally entered the country in the company of others, including a paid "coyote." The legal standard in this context should be whether the applicant's support to the co-travelers was material to their being able to enter. Where a group of individuals is traveling together and they would have entered illegally regardless of the assistance of the visa applicant, this should not support a smuggling finding.[192]

Congress created a waiver to ameliorate the smuggling inadmissibility ground's possibly harsh results. However, only two groups of foreign nationals can take advantage of this waiver: (1) LPRs who are returning from a visit abroad, and (2) foreign nationals seeking permanent residence as immediate relatives of U.S. citizens or under the first three family-preference categories.[193] In other words, those seeking to immigrate as siblings of U.S. citizens do not qualify for the waiver. Even for those individuals who do qualify to apply, the waiver is available only if

---

186 INA §212(a)(6)(E).

187 AFM 40.6.2(e)(3)(iii), located in 8 *USCIS Policy Manual* pt. I.

188 *Altamirano v. Gonzales*, 427 F.3d 586 (9th Cir. 2005). *See also Sanchez v Holder*, 704 F.3d 1107 (9th Cir. 2012) (affirmative knowing acts by passenger in vehicle to aid unlawful entry of another constitutes smuggling).

189 AFM 40.6.2(e)(2)(i), located in 8 *USCIS Policy Manual*, pt. I.

190 *See* Immigration Act of 1990, Pub. L. No. 101-649, 104 Stat. 4978.

191 INA §212(a)(6)(E)(ii).

192 Minutes from meeting with the author and the Chief, Immigrant Visa Section, U.S. Consulate, Ciudad Juarez, Nov. 15, 2012.

193 INA §212(d)(11).

the foreign national they encouraged or assisted to enter illegally was, at the time of the smuggling, their "spouse, parent, son or daughter (and no other individual)."[194]

The attorney general is authorized to grant these waivers for humanitarian purposes, to ensure family unity, and when it is in the public interest. It should also be noted that any conviction for smuggling is now an "aggravated felony," unless the smuggling was done only to assist a spouse, parent, son, or daughter.[195]

Final Civil Document Fraud Order

Any foreign national who is subject to a final order for violation of INA §274C, which authorizes civil penalties for making or using false documents, or using documents issued to other persons, for purposes of satisfying any requirement imposed by the INA, is inadmissible.[196]

Many of these activities also are prohibited under a criminal statute and may be punished criminally. However, to impose civil penalties under INA §274C, an administrative law judge (ALJ) only needs to determine by a preponderance of evidence that the violations have been committed. There is no administrative appeal from an order by an ALJ under this section, and the order becomes final unless the attorney general vacates or modifies it within 30 days of the decision. Once the order becomes final, the affected person has 45 days to file a petition for review of the order with a court of appeals.

However, the document fraud procedures the government establishes to implement INA §274C must comport with due process. The government was enjoined from implementing confusing and misleading document fraud procedures that violated immigrants' due process rights.[197]

There is a waiver for this ground of inadmissibility.[198] The waiver is available only to the following: (1) LPRs who temporarily left the country voluntarily and are otherwise admissible, and (2) foreign nationals seeking admission or adjustment based on immediate-relative or family-preference petitions who have not previously been fined under section 274C and whose offense was committed "solely to assist, aid, or support the foreign national's spouse or child (and not another individual)."[199]

---

194 *Matter of Farias-Mendoza*, 21 I&N Dec. 269 (BIA 1997).

195 INA §101(a)(43)(N).

196 INA §212(a)(6)(F).

197 *Walters v. Reno*, 145 F.3d 1032 (9th Cir. 1998).

198 INA §212(a)(6)(F)(ii).

199 INA §212(d)(12).

Documentary Requirements

Immigrants are prohibited from being admitted to the United States unless they are "in possession of a valid unexpired immigrant visa, reentry permit, border crossing identification card, or other valid entry document," as well as a passport or other suitable travel document, or document of identity or nationality, as required by regulation.[200] Immigrants also are inadmissible if their visas were not issued according to the INA's numerical selection system governing allocation of visas according to family-based preferences.[201] These two grounds do not apply if the applicant for admission otherwise is admissible under a specific provision of the INA.[202]

The INA's documentary requirements are subject to many waivers and exemptions. Immigrants who are inadmissible for failure to comply with the INA's documentary requirements may be admitted to the United States if they can prove that their inadmissibility was not known to them or they could not have reasonably discovered it before arriving in the United States.[203] The foreign national applies for this waiver at the port of entry on Form I-193 (Application for Waiver of Passport or Visa). If USCIS denies the waiver, the foreign national may renew the request before an immigration judge in removal proceedings. If USCIS fails to act on the waiver application before the hearing, the immigration judge may adjudicate the application without waiting for USCIS's decision.

In July 2019, the Department of Homeland Security announced the expansion of expedited removal to apply to noncitizens present in the United States who are inadmissible for lack of valid documents, material misrepresentation or false claim to citizenship.[204] A preliminary injunction issued in September 2019 has prevented the expansion from being implemented.[205]

Ineligible for Citizenship

Foreign nationals are inadmissible if they are "ineligible to citizenship" or are draft evaders.[206] By "ineligible to citizenship," the INA refers only to foreign nationals who are permanently barred from becoming U.S. citizens because of laws relating to military service.[207] For this ground of inadmissibility to apply, the primary

200 INA §212(a)(7)(A)(i)(I).

201 INA §212(a)(7)(A)(i)(II).

202 INA §212(a)(7).

203 INA §212(k); *Matter of Aurelio*, 19 I&N Dec. 458 (BIA 1987).

204 84 Fed Reg.35409 (July 23, 2019).

205 *Make the Road New York v. McAleenan*, Case 1:19-cv-02369, (D.D.C. 2019).

206 INA §212(a)(8).

207 *Matter of Kanga*, 22 I&N Dec. 1206 (BIA 2000).

purpose of the departure or remaining abroad must be to avoid military service.[208] These foreign nationals also are barred from entry into the United States, but only as immigrants.[209]

A foreign national may be barred permanently from citizenship if he or she has deserted the U.S. armed forces or if he or she has been excused from having to serve because he or she is a foreign national. Though somewhat redundant of the inadmissibility ground that bars admission of deserters and draft evaders, INA §314 specifically makes ineligible for citizenship any foreign nationals who have been convicted by a martial court or by a court of pertinent jurisdiction. INA §315, on the other hand, relates to persons who applied for exemption or discharge from military training or service based on alienage. Since World War I, Congress has enacted various statutes exempting certain foreign nationals in the United States from military service with the condition that those taking advantage of the exemption would be ineligible for citizenship.

For a foreign national to be permanently barred from citizenship under INA §315, all the following elements must be present:

- The applicant must apply for exemption or discharge;
- The exemption or discharge must be from training or service in the U.S. armed forces or the U.S. National Security Training Corps;
- The basis for the request for exemption or discharge must be the fact that the applicant is an alien; and
- The applicant must have been relieved or discharged from such training or service based on alienage.

This inadmissibility ground is applicable only if the person sought and obtained a permanent exemption. Subsequent voluntary availability for service does not remove the bar to citizenship. Foreign nationals automatically exempted from service are not subject to these provisions.

Though at present there is no draft, young men are required to be registered for the draft. Because the Military Selective Service Act[210] automatically exempts nonimmigrants from U.S. military service, nonimmigrants will not be required to exchange the right to become U.S. citizens for exemption from military service if a draft is instituted. Foreign nationals who take advantage of treaties mutually exempting nationals of their country and of the United States from service in the other's military will not become ineligible for citizenship if, before exercising their treaty rights, they have served in the armed forces of their country of nationality.

208 9 FAM 302.10-2(B).

209 22 CFR §40.82(b); 9 FAM 302.10-2(B)(1).

210 50 USC App. §451 *et seq.*

Foreign nationals are inadmissible if they left the United States during time of proclaimed national emergency or war to escape military service. Foreign nationals who deserted after induction or who remained outside the United States to evade military service also are inadmissible.[211]

Nonimmigrants are exempt from this ground. However, foreign nationals who were LPRs at the time of the evasion or desertion are barred from even temporary visits to the United States. The general rule is that a foreign national not subject to the draft at the time of departure is not inadmissible upon return. But foreign nationals who depart the country to avoid future military service are inadmissible. In these cases, though, exclusion is required only when the primary motive for departing or remaining outside the United States was to avoid military conscription.

There are no specific waivers for military-related inadmissibility grounds. However, a deserter who has been unconditionally pardoned by the president of the United States is relieved from the penalties imposed by law, including ineligibility for citizenship. When President Jimmy Carter granted a blanket pardon to Vietnam-era draft evaders and deserters, he declared that draft evaders "shall be permitted as any other alien to enter the United States."[212] DOS interprets the wording of this pardon as being conditional. It regards the pardon as being effective against the draft evader inadmissibility ground, but not in removing the inadmissibility ground based on "ineligibility to citizenship" because of a conviction by court martial for evasion or desertion.

Prior Removal Orders or Periods of Unlawful Presence

INA §212(a)(9) includes grounds of inadmissibility for foreign nationals who have committed specified immigration violations. It applies to those who:

- Were previously excluded;
- Were previously deported;
- Were unlawfully present in the United States for specified periods of time and now seek admission;
- Enter or attempt to enter the United States after having previously been unlawfully present in the United States for one year; and
- Enter or attempt to enter the United States after having been previously ordered removed.

211 *Espinoza-Castro v. INS*, 242 F.3d 1181 (9th Cir. 2001).

212 Proclamation 4483, Executive Order 11967 (Jan. 24, 1977).

Having Previously Been Removed

Foreign nationals who have been ordered removed under expedited removal, or ordered removed after proceedings initiated upon arrival in the United States (in other words, the equivalent of exclusion proceedings under pre-1996 law), are inadmissible for a period of five years after the date of their removal.[213] Other foreign nationals who have been ordered removed, deported, or excluded are inadmissible for 10 years.[214] They are inadmissible for 20 years after a second removal, and forever if they have been convicted of an aggravated felony.[215]

These inadmissibility bars do not apply if the attorney general has consented to the foreign national's reapplying for admission.[216] The inadmissibility periods set in the current statutory provisions went into effect on April 1, 1997, and apply retroactively; for example, foreign nationals who were subject to the prior five-year bar based on a deportation must now wait 10 years.[217] However, a 1998 DOS memorandum indicated that the Immigration and Naturalization Service (INS) would extend "sympathetic consideration" on a case-by-case basis to requests for reentry if the foreign national served the required period of time outside the United States pursuant to the prior law.[218]

Not every person who has been apprehended by USCIS will be subject to this inadmissibility ground. A foreign national who (1) was granted voluntary departure—either administratively by USCIS or in deportation proceedings by an immigration judge—and (2) left the United States on his or her own within the period specified in the voluntary departure order is not subject to this inadmissibility ground. However, foreign nationals who leave the United States at their own expense after an immigration judge has entered a deportation or removal order against them are considered to have self-deported or self-removed and are thus also subject to this ground.

Unlawful Presence Bars

Foreign Nationals "Unlawfully Present" Who Depart the United States

Another ground of inadmissibility applies to foreign nationals who are "unlawfully present" in the United States for certain periods of time, leave the country, and then seek admission.[219] These provisions are prospective, and time spent in the United

213 INA §212(a)(9)(A)(i).

214 22 CFR §40.91(b).

215 INA §212(a)(9)(A)(ii).

216 INA §212(a)(9)(A)(iii).

217 Pub. L. No. 104-208 Update No. 36: 212(a)(9)(A)–(C), 212(a)(6)(A) and (B), 98 State 060539 (Apr. 4, 1998), AILA Doc. No. 98040490.

218 *Id.*

219 INA §212(a)(9)(B).

States "unlawfully" prior to April 1, 1997, does not count toward this bar. Foreign nationals who are unlawfully present in the United States for a period of more than 180 days (but less than one year) after April 1, 1997, who voluntarily depart the United States prior to the commencement of removal proceedings, and who then seek admission to the United States, are inadmissible for a period of three years from the time they departed.[220] Foreign nationals who are unlawfully present in the United States for one year or more after April 1, 1997, and who depart and then seek admission, are inadmissible for a period of 10 years from the date they departed.[221]

The three-year bar provisions apply only to foreign nationals who voluntarily depart the United States before the commencement of removal proceedings.[222] If removal proceedings have commenced, the foreign national may not be subject to the three-year bar, but may be subject to the 10-year bar. This means that foreign nationals who leave the United States under voluntary departure granted by an immigration judge will not be subject to the three-year bar and will be subject to the 10-year bar only if they accumulated a year or more of unlawful presence in the United States prior to departure. Further, by the terms of the statute, the 10-year bar may be triggered by a departure or removal that is not voluntary.

Under this ground, periods of "unlawful presence" in the United States are not counted in the aggregate, but rather each period is counted separately. Thus, this bar does not apply to a foreign national with multiple periods of "unlawful presence" if no single period exceeded 180 days.[223]

Leaving the United States with Advance Parole Does Not Trigger the Three– or Ten-Year Bars

Prior to April 2012, foreign nationals who had applied for and been granted an advance parole document, and then left the United States after having accrued more than 180 days of "unlawful presence," were generally paroled back into the United States—but then at the time of adjustment, they were found inadmissible under INA §212(a)(9)(B). This changed on April 17, 2012, when the BIA published a decision, *Matter of Arrabally and Yerrabelly*, which held that leaving the United States temporarily pursuant to a grant of advance parole does not constitute a "departure" for purposes of section 212(a)(9)(B).[224] The case dealt with an adjustment of status applicant who obtained advance parole pursuant to his adjustment application, but USCIS extended the *Arrabally* holding to others who travel on advance parole, including those with DACA and Temporary Status.

---

220 INA §212(a)(9)(B)(i)(I).

221 INA §212(a)(9)(B)(i)(II).

222 INA §212(a)(9)(B)(ii).

223 AFM §40.9.2(a)(4)(A).

224 *Matter of Arrabally and Yerrabelly*, 25 I&N Dec. 771 (BIA 2012).

On November 2014, U.S. Department of Homeland Security Secretary Jeh Johnson directed the Department's general counsel to issue written legal guidance clarifying that *Arrabally* applies in all cases in which an individual travels on advance parole.[225] To date, however, no such guidance has been issued.

Definition of "Lawfully Present" and "Unlawfully Present"

There are no regulations interpreting the meaning of unlawful presence. The statute lists certain categories of individuals who are not subject to accruing unlawful presence,[226] and all other guidance on this topic comes from the *Adjudicator's Field Manual* (AFM), section 40.9.[227] The statute says that "unlawfully present" means that the foreign national is present after overstaying an authorized period of stay, or without being admitted or paroled.[228]

Nonimmigrants who are admitted without receiving a specific period of authorized stay—such as Canadian citizens and some Mexicans who enter with border crossing cards—do not accrue unlawful presence on a date designated at the time of admission. This was also true for those students (F nonimmigrant), exchange visitors (J nonimmigrant), and vocational students (M nonimmigrant) who were admitted for "duration of status" or "D/S." For these nonimmigrants who subsequently violate the terms of their visa or status—such as by working without authorization—unlawful presence begins only after a determination by USCIS or an immigration judge that the foreign national violated status.[229]

On August 9, 2018, USCIS issued a new policy on unlawful presence determinations as they related to individuals in F, M, or J status who are admitted for "duration of status" without a specified expiration date. Under this policy, a J, F, or M nonimmigrant who fails to maintain his or her nonimmigrant status will begin to accrue unlawful status on the day after the noncompliance occurs, which includes actions such as withdrawing from a course of study or working without authorization.[230] A determination from USCIS or an immigration judge that the nonimmigrant violated his or her status is not required. Note, however, that no unlawful presence will accrue if the individual successfully applies for reinstatement of status. This policy is currently not in effect because it is subject to a nationwide permanent injunction.[231]

---

225 DHS Memorandum, Jeh Johnson, *Directive to Provide Consistency Regarding Advance Parole* (Nov. 20, 2014), AILA Doc. No. 14112014 .

226 INA §212(a)(9)(B)(iii).

227 This section of the AFM is now located in 8 *USCIS Policy Manual* pt. I.

228 INA §212(a)(9)(B)(ii).

229 AFM §40.9.2(b)(1)(E)(i), located in 8 USCIS Policy Manual pt. I.

230 USCIS Policy Memorandum, *Accrual of Unlawful Presence and F, J, and M Nonimmigrants* (Aug. 9, 2018), AILA Doc. No. 18081003; *see also* AFM, ch. 40.9.2(b)(1)(E).

231 *Guilford College et al v. Chad Wolf et al,* 1:18CV891 (M.D.N.C. Feb. 20, 2020).

As noted in the AFM,[232] unlawful presence and unlawful status are related but distinct concepts. In many instances, an individual may be present in the United States without lawful status but is nevertheless protected from accruing unlawful presence based on statutory or policy-based exceptions, as summarized below.

The statute recognizes six categories of individuals who do not accrue unlawful presence.[233] They are:

- Those under 18 years of age
- Applicants for asylum during the pendency of the application, provided the alien did not work without employment authorization
- Those who have been granted Family Unity during the authorized period
- Battered spouses and children, provided there is a substantial connection between the abuse and the unlawful presence
- Victims of a severe form of trafficking in persons if the trafficking was at least one central reason for the unlawful presence
- Nonimmigrants who have made a timely, non-frivolous application for an extension of stay or change of status during the 120-day period after filing the application[234]

Section 40.9 of the AFM, now located in 8 USCIS Policy Manual pt. I, lists additional classes of aliens whom USCIS regards as being present in the United States pursuant to a period of authorized stay:

- Persons with properly filed applications for adjustment of status under INA §245(a) or 245(i), including persons who in removal proceedings renew adjustment applications that were denied by USCIS, but not including persons who first apply for adjustment when in removal proceedings[235]
- Persons admitted to the United States as refugees under INA §207 or granted asylum under INA §208[236]
- Persons granted withholding of removal under INA §241(b)(3)[237]

232 AFM §40.9.2(a)(2), located in 8 USCIS Policy Manual pt. I.

233 INA §212(a)(9)(B)(iii), (iv).

234 This period may extend to include all the time such an application is pending, beyond the 120-day period stated in the statute. INS Memorandum, M. Pearson, *Period of Stay Authorized by the Attorney General After 120-Day Tolling Period for Purposes of section 212(a)(9)(B) of the Immigration and Nationality Act (the Act)* (Mar. 3, 2000), AILA Doc. No. 00030774; *see also* AFM, ch. 30.1(d).

235 AFM §40.9.2(b)(3)(A), located in 8 *USCIS Policy Manual* pt. I.

236 AFM §40.9.2(b)(1)(F)(i) and (ii), located in USCIS Policy Manual Vol 8, Part I This group includes derivative asylees and refugees, from the date a bona fide Form I-730, Asylee/Refugee Relative Petition, is filed with USCIS.

237 AFM §40.9.2(b)(3)(K), located in 8 *USCIS Policy Manual* pt. I.

- Persons granted withholding or deferral of removal under the Convention Against Torture[238]
- Persons with legalization and special agricultural worker applications for lawful temporary residence pending through an administrative appeal[239]
- Persons granted deferred enforced departure[240]
- Applicants for adjustment of status under the Nicaraguan Adjustment and Central American Relief Act and the Haitian Refugee and Immigrant Fairness Act[241]
- Cuban/Haitian entrants as defined under Pub. L. No. 99-603, §202(b)[242]
- Persons granted voluntary departure, during the period allowed[243]
- Persons granted suspension of deportation or cancellation of removal[244]
- Persons granted deferred action status[245]
- Persons under a current grant of temporary protected status (TPS), including applicants for TPS, provided the application was granted[246]
- Conditional residents who timely file a petition to remove the conditions on residence, or whose late filing is accepted by USCIS or an immigration judge[247]
- Parolees, during the allowed parole period[248] and
- Persons granted a stay of removal, during the authorized stay period[249]

Foreign nationals not considered to be in a period of authorized stay under this ground include:

- Persons under an order of supervision (pending removal)[250]
- Persons with pending applications for cancellation of removal[251]

---

238 AFM §40.9.2(b)(3)(L), located in 8 *USCIS Policy Manual* pt. I.

239 AFM §40.9.2(b)(3)(E), located in 8 *USCIS Policy Manual* pt. I.

240 AFM §40.9.2(b)(3)(M), located in 8 *USCIS Policy Manual* pt. I.

241 AFM §40.9.2(b)(3)(A), located in 8 *USCIS Policy Manual* pt. I.

242 *Id.*

243 AFM §40.9.2(b)(3)(H), located in 8 *USCIS Policy Manual* pt. I.

244 AFM §40.9.2(b)(1)(D), located in 8 *USCIS Policy Manual* pt. I.

245 AFM §40.9.2(b)(3)(J), located in 8 *USCIS Policy Manual* pt. I.

246 AFM §40.9.2(b)(1)(F)(iii), located in 8 *USCIS Policy Manual* pt. I.

247 AFM §40.9.2(b)(1)(C), located in 8 *USCIS Policy Manual* pt. I.

248 AFM §40.9.2(b)(1)(G), located in 8 *USCIS Policy Manual* pt. I.

249 AFM §40.9.2(b)(3)(I), located in 8 *USCIS Policy Manual* pt. I.

250 AFM §40.9.2(b)(6), located in 8 *USCIS Policy Manual* pt. I.

251 *See* AFM §40.9.2(b)(1)(D), located in 8 *USCIS Policy Manual* pt. I.

- Persons with pending applications for withholding of removal[252]
- Asylum applicants who have worked without employment authorization[253]
- Persons present pursuant to pending federal court litigation[254]

Period of Inadmissibility

USCIS has generally taken the position that the unlawful presence period must be spent outside the United States in order to overcome inadmissibility through the passage of time. A foreign national who triggers the three-year bar by departure and then returns to the United States without inspection six months later can expect USCIS to consider that he or she is still inadmissible even after the passage of three years. Note, however, that a 2012 BIA decision holds open the possibility that the unlawful presence bar could run while the foreign national was present in the United States, and other unreported BIA decisions have accepted this argument as well.[255]

In the case of foreign nationals who trigger the unlawful presence bar and return to the United States with parole, USCIS has clarified that the inadmissibility period can be overcome by passage of time in the United States.[256] This means that if a foreign national triggered a three-year bar period of inadmissibility by leaving the United States, subsequently returning under a grant of parole, the foreign national would no longer be inadmissible three years after the departure date, even if the foreign national had been in the United States during the inadmissibility period. The USCIS Administrative Appeals Office has issued at least three unreported decisions with the same analysis of this issue.

Waiver of Inadmissibility

The three– and ten-year bars may be waived by the attorney general in the case of an immigrant who is the spouse, son, or daughter of a U.S. citizen or LPR who will experience extreme hardship if his or her family member is refused admission to the United States.[257] Note that an immigrant is not eligible for a waiver based on showing extreme hardship to a U.S. citizen or LPR child.

---

252 *See* AFM §40.9.2(b)(3)(K) and (L), located in 8 *USCIS Policy Manual* pt. I.

253 *See* AFM §40.9.2(b)(2), located in 8 *USCIS Policy Manual* pt. I.

254 *See* AFM §40.9.2(b)(5)(B), located in 8 *USCIS Policy Manual* pt. I.

255 *Matter of Lemus-Losa*, 25 I&N Dec. 734 (BIA 2012),

256 Letter from R. Divine, USCIS Chief Counsel, to D. Berry & R. Wada (July 14, 2006), AILA Doc. No. 08082930.

257 INA §212(a)(9)(B)(v).

Note that INA §245(i) does not waive inadmissibility under §212(a)(9)(B)(i)(II). A foreign national subject to the ten-year bar may not use section 245(i) to waive the bar but must seek a waiver under section 212(a)(9)(B)(v).[258]

Reentering the United States Without Authorization

A more severe ground of inadmissibility applies to a foreign national "who has been unlawfully present in the United States for an aggregate period of more than one year"," and then enters or attempts to enter the United States without being admitted.[259] Because this provision applies only to unlawful presence accruing after April 1, 1997, it applies to persons who enter or attempt to enter illegally on or after April 1, 1998. The same definition of the term unlawful presence applies here.[260] However, the period of unlawful presence requires only an "aggregate period" of more than one year. This means that a foreign national may trigger inadmissibility under this section with repeated periods of unlawful presence that may each have been too short to trigger the three-year unlawful presence bar, but cumulatively add up to more than one year. While a foreign national may seek relief from this ground of inadmissibility after remaining outside the United States for 10 years, the bar has no set expiration date, unlike the three– and ten-year unlawful presence bars. For this reason, the bar is termed "permanent."

A similar ground of inadmissibility applies to a foreign national who has been ordered removed under any provision of law and who then enters or attempts to enter the United States without being admitted on or after April 1, 1997.[261] This covers persons who were ordered removed, deported, or excluded at any time. Such foreign nationals are permanently inadmissible, although they may seek permission to reapply for admission to the United States 10 years after their last departure.

In the one policy guidance memorandum addressing this issue, the INS stated that the statutory exceptions to unlawful presence listed in INA §212(a)(9)(B) do not apply to the inadmissibility under (a)(9)(C).[262] This means, for example, that a minor who does not accrue unlawful presence for purposes of the three– and ten-bars prior to age 18 is nevertheless subject to the permanent bar if he or she enters the United States without admission after accruing more than one year of unlawful presence.

---

258 *Matter of Lemus-Losa*, 25 I&N Dec. 734 (BIA 2012).

259 INA §212(a)(9)(C)(i).

260 INS Memorandum, P. Virtue, Implementation of Section 212(a)(6)(A) and 212(a)(9) Grounds of Inadmissibility (Mar. 31, 1997), ILA Doc. No. 97033190; INS Memorandum, P. Virtue, Additional Guidance for Implementing Sections 212(a)(6) and 212(a)(9) of the Immigration and Nationality Act (June 17, 1997), AILA Doc. No. 97061790.

261 INA §212(a)(9)(C)(i)(II).

262 INS Memorandum, AILA Doc. No. 97033190; *see* AFM §40.9.2(b)(i).

Per the BIA's decision in *Matter of Torres-Garcia*,[263] approval of a Form I-212 (Application for Permission to Reapply for Admission into the United States After Deportation or Removal) cannot cure inadmissibility under the permanent bar until the person has remained outside the United States for 10 years after the date of last departure. Consequently, such a foreign national is ineligible to adjust status. Following the BIA's decision, USCIS issued policy guidance conforming to this analysis.[264] As a result of the *Torres-Garcia* decision, the Ninth Circuit overruled a prior circuit decision that had allowed for adjustment eligibility under INA §245(i) for persons subject to inadmissibility under INA §212(a)(9)(C)(i)(II).[265]

In addition, the BIA has ruled that a person subject to the permanent bar for entering the United States without admission after accruing unlawful presence in the aggregate of one year or more is not eligible to adjust status under INA §245(i).[266] The two circuit courts of appeals that had previously ruled otherwise on this issue have since revisited this conclusion in light of the BIA's decision and both the Ninth and Tenth Circuits now follow the BIA's decision.[267]

Under the statute, only VAWA self-petitioners are eligible to seek a waiver of permanent bar inadmissibility immediately. The statute provides that a waiver is available when a self-petitioner can establish a connection between his or her removal, departure from the United States, reentry, or attempted reentry and the battery or extreme cruelty to which he or she was subjected.[268] To date, there is no USCIS guidance on this point to interpret the statutory language.

---

263 23 I&N Dec. 866 (BIA 2006).

264 USCIS Memorandum, M. Aytes & D. Carpenter, *Effect of Perez-Gonzalez v. Ashcroft on Adjudication of Form I-212 Applications Filed by Aliens Who Are Subject to Reinstated Removal Orders Under INA §241(a)(5)* (Mar. 31, 2006), AILA Doc. No. 06080967.

265 *Duran Gonzalez v. DHS,* 508 F.3d 1227 (9th Cir. 2007), overruling *Perez-Gonzalez v. Ashcroft,* 379 F.3d 783 (9th Cir. 2004); based on a final settlement in this case certain individuals in the Ninth Circuit who filed an application for adjustment of status and an I-212 application on or after August 13, 2004, and on or before November 30, 2007, may be eligible to proceed with their applications for adjustment or have denied applications reopened. A similar case holding that a foreign national who had triggered the 212(a)(9)(C) bar due to reentry after unlawful presence could nevertheless file an I-212 and adjust under 245(i), *Padilla-Caldera v. Gonzalez*, 453 F.3d 1237 (10th Cir. 2006), was overturned after the BIA decision in *Matter of Briones*, 24 I&N Dec. 355 (BIA 2007). *Padilla-Caldera v. Holder*, 637 F.3d 1140 (10th Cir. 2011).

266 *Matter of Diaz and Lopez,* 25 I&N Dec. 188 (BIA 2010), *reaffirmed Matter of Briones,* 24 I&N Dec. 355 (BIA 2007); *see also Matter of Lemus-Losa,* 24 I&N Dec. 373 (BIA 2007).

267 *Padilla-Caldera v. Holder*, 637 F.3d 1140 (10th Cir. 2011); *Garfias-Rodriguez v. Holder*, No. 09-72603, (9th Cir. 2012).

268 INA §212(a)(9)(C)(iii).

Miscellaneous Grounds

The "miscellaneous" inadmissibility grounds concern "unlawful voters," practicing polygamists, guardians required to accompany an inadmissible person, former citizens who renounced their citizenship in order to avoid taxation, and international child abductors.[269] Unlawful voters are individuals who voted in a U.S. election in violation of federal, state, or local law.[270] According to the Board, an individual may be deportable for unlawful voting even without knowledge that his or her voting was unlawful.[271] However, unlawful voters will not be considered inadmissible if their natural parents are or were citizens of the United States.[272]

The inadmissibility ground including practicing polygamists applies only to persons coming to the United States to practice polygamy.[273] Until 1990, the law barred persons who are polygamists, practice polygamy, or advocate the practice of polygamy. Since 1990, only those practicing polygamy are inadmissible under the statute.[274]

An international child abductor is a person who detains, retains, or withholds a U.S. citizen child outside the United States from the person granted custody of such child.[275] Persons who are abductors or who assist, support, or provide safe haven to abductors, including the spouse, child, parent, sibling, or agent of the abductor, are inadmissible.[276]

Former citizens of the United States who renounced citizenship to avoid taxation are inadmissible.[277] This provision is applicable to persons who renounced U.S. citizenship for taxation purposes after September 30, 1996.[278]

A guardian required to accompany an inadmissible person is also inadmissible.[279] A medical officer may certify that the person being accompanied is helpless from sickness, mental or physical disability, or infancy, and that the guardianship is required to assist the disabled person.[280]

Reinstatement of Removal

Reinstatement of removal under INA §241(a)(5) is not a ground of inadmissibility but is frequently an additional consequence faced by an individual who is potentially

---

269 INA §212(a)(10).

270 INA §212(a)(10)(D).

271 *Matter of Fitzpatrick*, 26 I&N Dec.559 (BIA 2015).

272 22 CFR §40.104.

273 INA §212(a)(10)(A).

274 *Ali v. Reno*, 829 F. Supp. 1415 (S.D.N.Y. 1993).

275 INA §212(a)(10)(C)(i).

276 INA §212(a)(10)(C)(ii).

277 INA §212(a)(10)(E).

278 22 CFR §40.105.

279 INA §212(a)(10)(B).

280 9 FAM 302.10-3(A).

inadmissible under INA §212(a)(9)(A) and (C)(i)(II). Foreign nationals subject to this removal provision may be removed from the United States through the "reinstatement" of the prior order of removal and are not eligible for, and may not apply for, any relief. As implemented by regulation, the term "prior removal orders" includes all prior expulsion orders, including orders of deportation and exclusion.[281]

The INS also implemented reinstatement as a summary proceeding with no right to a hearing before an immigration judge. The proceedings begin with issuance of a notice of intent to reinstate the prior removal, deportation, or exclusion order, on Form I-871. The individual may check a box on the form indicating that he or she wishes to contest the determination. If this box is checked, the individual may make a written or oral statement before the U.S. Immigration and Customs Enforcement (ICE) or other immigration agent adjudicating the reinstatement. The agent is authorized to consider only three issues: (1) whether the individual is the subject of a prior removal or deportation order; (2) whether the individual is in fact the person who was previously removed; and (3) whether the foreign national unlawfully reentered the United States.[282]

Two courts of appeal decisions have held that the unlawful reentry requirement of section 241(a)(5) is not limited to entry without inspection and includes situations where an individual has a "procedurally regular" entry that is unlawful due to fraud.[283]

There are limited exceptions allowing a foreign national subject to reinstatement to apply for relief. A foreign national subject to reinstatement who fears return to the country of designated in the removal order may seek withholding of removal and relief under the Convention Against Torture.[284] In addition, reinstatement of removal does not apply to persons eligible for relief under the Haitian Refugee and Immigrant Fairness Act (HRIFA) and the Nicaraguan Adjustment and Central American Relief Act (NACARA),[285] and for legalization under the Legal Immigration and Family Equity Act (LIFE Act).[286]

Retroactive Application

The U.S. Supreme Court has ruled that reinstatement of removal may be applied to a person who illegally re-entered the United States before the statute's effective date.[287] Four circuit courts of appeals, however, recognized exceptions to the

---

281 8 CFR §241.8(a).

282 *Id.*

283 *Tamayo-Tamayo v. Holder,* No. 08-74005 (9th Cir. 2013) (unlawful entry by presentation of invalid alien registration card meets illegal reentry requirement of 241(a)(5)); *Cordova Soto v Holder,* 659 F.3d 1029 (10th Cir. 2011) (procedurally regular entry may be illegal reentry for purposes of 241(a)(5)).

284 8 CFR §§208.31, 241.9(e).

285 8 CFR §241.9(d).

286 8 CFR §245.18(c).

287 *Fernandez-Vargas v. Ashcroft*, 548 U.S. 30 (2006).

retroactive application of reinstatement when the individual had applied for discretionary relief[288] or took affirmative steps to legalize his or her status prior to April 1, 1997.[289] The issue of whether reinstatement may be applied retroactively in these situations was expressly not decided in the Supreme Court's decision.[290]

Appeals to Federal Court

All circuits have found that a reinstatement order is appealable through a petition for review[291] to the U.S. court of appeals having jurisdiction over the place where the reinstatement order was entered. The INA provides that venue for review of final removal orders is proper with "the court of appeals for the judicial circuit in which the immigration judge completed proceedings."[292] However, the majority of circuits have concluded that such language constitutes a "non-jurisdictional venue provision," meaning that it does not strip other circuits from having subject matter jurisdiction over final orders of removal.[293] Accordingly, while venue is likely proper where the reinstatement order was issued, there may be circumstances in which another circuit court exercises its jurisdiction over review of that order in the interests of justice.[294]

In order to obtain judicial review through a petition for review to the circuit court of appeals, the petition for review must be filed within 30 days of the date the reinstatement order was issued.[295] This deadline is jurisdictional and cannot be extended, so it is crucial to file the petition for review within the deadline. As a practical matter, practitioners should be ready to file the petition for review immediately upon issuance of the reinstatement order and to request a stay of removal.

---

288 *Arevalo v. Ashcroft,* 344 F.3d 1 (1st Cir. 2003); *Faiz-Mohammed v. Ashcroft,* 395 F.3d 799 (7th Cir. 2005); *Sarmiento-Cisneros v. Ashcroft,* 381 F.3d 1277 (11th Cir. 2004).

289 *Valdez-Sanchez v. Gonzales,* 485 F.3d 1084 (10th Cir. 2007).

290 *Fernandez-Vargas v. Ashcroft,* 548 U.S. 30 (2006).

291 *Arevalo v. Ashcroft,* 344 F.3d 1, 9 (1st Cir. 2003); *Garcia-Villeda v. Mukasey*, 531 F.3d 141, 144 (2d Cir. 2008); *Avila-Macias v. Ashcroft*, 328 F.3d 108 (3d Cir. 2003); *Velasquez-Gabriel v. Crocetti*, 263 F.3d 102, 105 (4th Cir. 2001); *Ojeda-Terrazas v. Ashcroft*, 290 F.3d 292 (5th Cir. 2001); *Warner v. Ashcroft*, 381 F.3d 534, 536 (6th Cir 2004); *Gomez-Chavez v. Perryman*, 308 F.3d 796, 800 (7th Cir. 2002); *Briones-Sanchez v. Heinauer*, 319 F.3d 324, 326 (8th Cir. 2003); *Ixcot v. Holder*, 646 F.3d 1202, 1206 (9th Cir. 2011); *Duran-Hernandez v. Ashcroft*, 348 F.3d 1158, 1162 n.3 (10th Cir. 2003); *Sarmiento-Cisneros v. Att'y Gen.*, 381 F.3d 1277, 1278 (11th Cir. 2004).

292 INA §242(b)(2).

293 *See Yang You Lee v. Lynch*, 791 F.3d 1261, 1263–64 (10th Cir. 2015); *Thiam v. Holder*, 677 F.3d 299, 301–02 (6th Cir. 2012); *Avila v. U.S. Att'y Gen.*, 560 F.3d 1281, 1284–85 (11th Cir. 2009) (per curiam); *Khouzam v. Att'y Gen.*, 549 F.3d 235, 249 (3d Cir. 2008); *Moreno–Bravo v. Gonzales*, 463 F.3d at 258–62 (2d Cir. 2006); *Georcely v. Ashcroft*, 375 F.3d 45, 49 (1st Cir. 2004).

294 *See, e.g., Bibiano v. Lynch*, 834 F.3d 966, 973 (9th Cir. 2016) (concluding that even though venue was proper with the Eleventh Circuit, where the underlying reasonable fear proceedings occurred, the Ninth Circuit still retained subject matter jurisdiction and the interests of justice weighed against transfer).

295 INA §242(b)(1).

Several circuits, however, have determined that when an individual with a reinstatement order expresses a fear of persecution in his or her home country, the 30-day window does not commence until the fear-based claim has been resolved (either because an IJ has affirmed the negative reasonable fear determination or because the withholding only proceedings are administratively final).[296] Furthermore, it may be possible to argue that the 30-day window is not triggered until the reinstatement order has been properly served.[297]

Even though circuit court review of a reinstatement order may be available, the extent of that review may vary based on the pertinent circuit court case law. Depending on that precedent, potential claims may include: (1) arguing that reinstatement under INA §241(a)(5) does not apply retroactively to individuals who both reentered and took affirmative steps to obtain lawful status before April 1, 1997;[298] (2) challenging the factual findings underlying the order (i.e., that the individual was ordered removed, that he/she departed under a removal order, or that he/she reentered the country illegally);[299] (3) raising regulatory claims[300] or due process considerations;[301] and (4) raising claims of U.S. nationality.[302]

Additionally, although the INA indicates that reinstatement orders are "not subject to being reopened or reviewed,"[303] certain administrative mechanisms may still be

---

296 *See, e.g.*, *Luna-Garcia v. Holder*, 777 F.3d 1182, 1184–87 (10th Cir. 2015); *Jimenez-Morales v. Att'y Gen.*, 821 F.3d 1307, 1308 (11th Cir. 2016).

297 *See, e.g.*, *Villegas de la Paz v. Holder*, 640 F.3d 650, 654–55 (6th Cir. 2010) (concluding that respondent's petition for review, filed more than seven months after the reinstatement order was issued but only 16 days after she obtained the order, was timely); *but see Lemos v. Holder*, 636 F.3d 365, 366–67 (7th Cir. 2011) (indicating without deciding that the statutory language likely requires the 30-day filing window to commence on the date it was entered, not on the date it was served).

298 *See, e.g.*, *Ixcot v. Holder*, 646 F.3d 1202, 1213 (9th Cir. 2011) (holding that post IIRARA reinstatement is impermissibly retroactive when applied to an immigrant who applied for immigration relief prior to IIRARA's effective date); *Arevalo v. Ashcroft*, 344 F.3d 1, 4 (1st Cir. 2003) (same); *Sarmiento-Cisneros v. Ashcroft*, 381 F.3d 1277, 1278 (11th Cir. 2004) (same); *Valdez-Sanchez v. Gonzales*, 485 F.3d 1084, 1091 (10th Cir. 2007) (same); *but see Molina Jerez v. Holder*, 625 F.3d 1058, 1070 (8th Cir. 2010) (concluding that reinstatement was not impermissibly retroactive as applied to respondent who had filed for asylum pre IIRARA); *Silva Rosa v. Gonzales*, 490 F.3d 403, 410 (5th Cir. 2007) (holding that reinstatement was not impermissibly retroactive as applied to respondent who had an approved visa petition pre- IIRARA but did not apply for adjustment of status until after the new reinstatement provisions went into effect).

299 The circuit court's review of these claims will be limited to the administrative record, and it will be required to treat DHS's factual findings as "conclusive unless any reasonable adjudicator would be compelled to conclude to the contrary." *See* INA §242(b)(4)(A), (B).

300 DHS's reinstatement regulations can be found at 8 CFR §241.8.

301 Due process claims related to reinstatement that do not demonstrate actual prejudice have been consistently rejected across circuit courts. *See, e.g.*, *Lattab v. Ashcroft*, 384 F.3d 8 (1st Cir. 2004); *Garcia-Villeda v. Mukasey*, 531 F.3d 141 (2nd Cir. 2008).

302 *See* INA §242(b)(5).

303 INA §241(a)(5).

available, including filing a motion to reconsider (which is not explicitly barred by the statutory language).

Finally, collateral attacks against the prior removal order may be possible, as some circuit courts have held that the Real ID Act of 2005 conferred jurisdiction for them to review legal and constitutional challenges to those orders, even for individuals subject to reinstatement.[304]

What Practitioners Can Do Now

The most important preventive action a practitioner can take is to determine whether the client is subject to reinstatement before filing for adjustment of status. File a Freedom of Information Act (FOIA) request in all cases in which your client has been in immigration proceedings or has had prior contact with the immigration authorities. In addition, ask the client to describe in detail his or her experiences with the immigration authorities.

In examining the response to the FOIA request, also be aware of who is not subject to reinstatement. First, reinstatement applies only to persons who have left the United States under an order of removal, deportation, or exclusion. If a client has such an order, but has never left the United States, he or she may be arrested and removed, but will not be subject to reinstatement. Thus, the prohibition on applying for any relief under the INA does not attach, and it may be possible to reopen the proceedings to apply for relief. Second, reinstatement applies only to persons who have reentered the United States unlawfully. Remember that an order of voluntary departure converts automatically into an order of deportation if the individual does not leave the country by the voluntary departure date.

If ICE has instituted reinstatement proceedings, the respondent should check the box indicating that he or she wishes to contest the determination. Practitioners should make all possible legal and factual arguments in opposition to reinstatement. These arguments should be made in writing to preserve the record. If ICE orders reinstatement and there are grounds for review, the respondent or counsel should file a petition for review in the federal circuit court immediately, because of the 30-day jurisdictional deadline, and also should file an application for stay of removal with the court.

Practitioners also should investigate the validity of the underlying removal order and, if there are grounds for showing that it was erroneous, consider seeking review in federal district court through a petition for habeas corpus.

304 *See, e.g.*, *Debeato v. Att'y Gen.*, 505 F.3d 231, 234–35 (3d Cir. 2007); *Villegas de la Paz,* 640 F.3d 650, 656 (6th Cir. 2010).

Chapter 7

WAIVERS OF INADMISSIBILITY

This chapter explains the eligibility requirements for waivers of certain inadmissibility grounds, sets forth the legal standards used for adjudicating them, and provides practice pointers for completing waiver applications. Sample waivers and accompanying documents are provided in the appendices. The grounds of inadmissibility are described in chapter 6.

The chapter focuses on four specific waivers allowed by the Immigration and Nationality Act (INA): (1) the section 212(g) waiver for certain health-related grounds; (2) the section 212(h) waiver for criminal conduct; (3) the section 212(i) waiver for fraud or misrepresentation; and (4) the section 212(a)(9)(B)(v) waiver for unlawful presence. Although it is not technically a waiver, this chapter will also cover the request for permission to reenter after a formal deportation or removal order has been entered against the foreign national, which is filed on Form I-212, Application for Permission to Reapply for Admission into the United States After Deportation or Removal. The chapter concludes with a discussion of waivers of inadmissibility grounds for asylees and refugees seeking to adjust status.

Extreme Hardship

Three of the four waiver applications described in this chapter require a showing of "extreme hardship" to a family member who is a U.S. citizen or lawful permanent resident (LPR). Although U.S. Citizenship and Immigration Services (USCIS) has not promulgated a regulation defining extreme hardship, except to articulate a higher standard in the context of waiving criminal grounds of inadmissibility involving violent or dangerous crimes,[1] it has issued guidance defining how that standard should be applied.[2] That guidance is summarized below. USCIS also has created guidance in the form of a standard operations procedures manual for overseas adjudications officers.[3]

The extreme hardship standard did not originate in the context of inadmissibility waivers. For many years it has been a requirement in establishing eligibility for suspension of deportation before an immigration judge.[4] Although immigration judges differed in how they interpreted that requirement, most applied a rather high

1 8 CFR §212.7(d).

2 USCIS Policy Alert, *Determining Extreme Hardship* (Oct. 21, 2016), AILA Doc. No. 16102107, codified in 9 *USCIS Policy Manual* pt. B.

3 USCIS, *Immigrant Waivers: Procedures for Adjudication of Form I-601 for Overseas Adjudication Officers* (Apr. 28, 2009), AILA Doc. No. 09061772.

4 *Matter of B*, 6 I&N Dec. 713 (BIA; A.G. 1955).

standard.[5] Extreme hardship in the suspension context was more than the ordinary hardship that one would suffer in being separated from a spouse, children, and other loved ones, or from a country and lifestyle to which one had become accustomed. Successful suspension applicants usually needed to demonstrate something out of the ordinary, such as a specific medical hardship, loss of special educational opportunities, or inability to provide for oneself in the home country.[6] The percentage of applicants who were successful in winning suspension of deportation also varied throughout the country.

The factors set forth in the seminal Board of Immigration Appeals (BIA) case defining extreme hardship for suspension applicants include the following:

- The foreign national's age;
- Length of residence in the United States;
- Family members in the United States and abroad, and their citizenship or immigration status;
- Health factors and the availability of medical care in the home country;
- Financial impact of departure from the United States;
- Possibility of other means of immigrating;
- History of immigration violations;
- Position in the community; and
- Economic and political factors in the home country.[7]

The BIA also has stated that the following factors, taken alone, do not qualify as extreme hardship: birth of citizen children, significant reduction in standard of living of the person who remains in the United States, difficulty in readjusting to life in the native country, and lower-quality medical or educational facilities in the native country.[8] Nevertheless, these factors may be considered in combination and together might satisfy the standard.[9] Additionally, case law in this area has shown that the more educated, wealthy, or employable the applicant, the less the likelihood of extreme hardship.[10] The factors listed above are not exhaustive, so in attempting to show extreme hardship, the practitioner should include all factors that are relevant to the particular case.

There are additional extreme hardship factors for battered spouses and children seeking relief under the Violence Against Women Act (VAWA), according to a

---

5 *INS v. Jong Ha Wang*, 450 U.S. 139 (1981).

6 *Matter of Gibson*, 16 I&N Dec. 58 (BIA 1976).

7 *Matter of Anderson*, 16 I&N Dec. 596 (BIA 1978).

8 *Matter of Ige*, 20 I&N Dec. 880 (BIA 1994).

9 *Ravancho v. INS*, 658 F.2d 169 (3d Cir. 1981).

10 *Matter of L–O–G–*, 21 I&N Dec. 413 (BIA 1996).

1998 Immigration and Naturalization Service (INS) memorandum.[11] Some of the factors mentioned in the memorandum include:

- Whether the foreign country has laws protecting victims of domestic violence or laws or practices that legitimize it
- The loss of access to the U.S. courts and criminal justice system, including the ability to obtain and enforce orders of protection
- The need for social, medical, and psychological or other support services that are unavailable in the home country
- Linguistic or cultural factors that make securing employment in the home country difficult
- Any other economic factors in the United States or abroad

Three of the waivers—for fraud, crimes, and unlawful presence—require that the extreme hardship be to the U.S. citizen or LPR family member ("qualifying relative"), who will be either remaining in the United States or joining the waiver applicant in the foreign country.[12] Therefore, the hardship will be based either on separation from the foreign national after his or her departure from the United States or on relocation if the qualifying relative will be accompanying the waiver applicant to the home country.[13]

In addition, the applicant could allege hardship in both situations. Although hardship to the foreign national's children may not be considered for two of the three waivers—fraud and unlawful presence—it will be an indirect factor, because the citizen or LPR spouse or parent who is remaining in the United States may be raising them without the financial and other support of the foreign national. Or in the alternative, if the children and the qualifying relative will be accompanying the waiver applicant, the relocation hardship to the children will also be experienced through the qualifying relative. Hardship to the waiver applicant will not be considered.

The 2016 USCIS final guidance on extreme hardship changed in significant ways how the standard is to be interpreted and implemented.[14] Adjudicators had been requiring waiver applicants to demonstrate that the qualifying relative would suffer extreme hardship in two scenarios: if he or she were to relocate to the applicant's country, *and* if he or she were to remain in the United States separated from the applicant. This requirement was set forth in the adjudicator's training manual (Standard Operating Procedures, or SOP) and was boilerplate language

---

11 INS Memorandum, P. Virtue, *"Extreme Hardship" and Documentary Requirements Involving Battered Spouses and Children* (Oct. 16, 1998), *reprinted in* 76 *Interpreter Releases* 162 (Jan. 25, 1999).

12 *INS v. Hector*, 479 U.S. 85 (1986); *Matter of Cervantes-Gonzalez*, 22 I&N Dec. 560 (BIA 1999).

13 *See Matter of Recinas*, 23 I&N Dec. 467 (BIA 2002).

14 USCIS Policy Alert, *Determining Extreme Hardship* (Oct. 21, 2016), AILA Doc. No. 16102107, codified in 9 *USCIS Policy Manual* pt. B.

in every written decision, even though it was not explained to the applicant in the instructions to the Form I-601 or I-601A. One of the most significant changes is the reduction in this burden of demonstrating extreme hardship to the qualifying relative. The final guidance allows the applicant to decide whether the qualifying relative would *either* relocate or remain in the United States. The applicant now only must establish extreme hardship in one of those scenarios rather than both. The guidance still allows the qualifying relative to show that extreme hardship would result from both separation and relocation.

The qualifying relative is required to submit a statement certifying under penalty of perjury the decision either to relocate with or to separate from the waiver applicant in the event the waiver is denied. The statement should be "sufficiently detailed" and "credible," and should explain the reasons for the decision. The qualifying relative is encouraged to submit any documentation that would support the basis for the decision, although due to its subjective nature, the statement itself may be the best available evidence. In most cases, "in the absence of inconsistent evidence, a credible, sworn statement from the qualifying relative of his or her intent to relocate or separate would generally suffice to demonstrate what the qualifying relative plans to do."[15]

Written decisions on unlawful presence waivers reveal that it is easier to establish that the qualifying relative would suffer extreme hardship due to relocating to the applicant's country. Decisions often cite the qualifying relative's lack of foreign language skills, unfamiliarity with the foreign country, inability to find comparable employment, the stress in relocating to a different culture, and any health-related factors that would be exacerbated by such a move. In most cases, it is more difficult to establish that the qualifying relative would suffer extreme hardship due to separation from the waiver applicant. The final guidance may encourage applicants to show why it is reasonably foreseeable that the qualifying relative would accompany them to the foreign country in order to maintain family unity and why such a move would result in extreme hardship.

The qualifying relative for the waiver for certain criminal grounds of inadmissibility under INA §212(h) can include the applicant's spouse, parent, child, son, or daughter. Where the qualifying relative is a child, note that there is a general presumption that the child would relocate with the parents. For this reason, the parent would bear the burden of overcoming that presumption if claiming that the child would be left behind in the United States and suffer separation hardship. In that case, the waiver applicant would need to provide a credible plan for the care and support for the child. This affirmative statement and evidence would not apply if the child will be left behind in the care of the other parent.

15 9 *USCIS Policy Manual* pt. B, ch. 4.B.

Adjudicators are reminded in the final guidance that the hardship factors must be considered in the aggregate and that no single hardship, taken in isolation, needs to rise to the level of extreme. This principle was already set forth in administrative appeal decisions and is codified in the SOP. But accentuating it in the guidance may encourage applicants to set forth all possible hardship factors if, taken together, they add up to extreme hardship.

Similarly, the final guidance also underscores that extreme hardship means "more than the usual level of hardship that commonly results from family separation or relocation."[16] Common consequences of separation or relocation include the following: family separation, economic detriment, difficulties of readjusting to life in the foreign country, quality and availability of educational opportunities abroad, inferior quality of medical services and facilities, and the ability to pursue a chosen employment abroad. While none of these "common" results taken alone would be enough to satisfy the extreme hardship standard, their combination may be sufficient.

While the applicant needs to demonstrate extreme hardship only to one qualifying relative, in some cases two qualifying relatives—for example, a spouse and a parent—may be present. The applicant can combine the hardships that both qualifying relatives might experience. This may be helpful if neither qualifying relative alone would be able to establish extreme hardship, but taken together the aggregate of their hardships would meet that standard. For example, the qualifying relatives may each experience the common results of separation or relocation that when taken alone do not rise to the level of extreme hardship, yet the combination of these hardships, or their cumulative impact, may meet the necessary standard.

The guidance also explains that widow(er)s whose U.S. citizen spouse had filed an I-130 petition before dying qualify to file a waiver if they were residing in the United States at the time of the death and continue to reside here. The same is true under INA §204(*l*) for other family members where the petitioner or principal beneficiary has died after the I-130 was filed and where they meet the residency requirements. In cases where the deceased relative would have been the qualifying relative for a waiver of inadmissibility, the agency will presume extreme hardship and will allow eligibility for the waiver even though the qualifying relative has died.[17]

Children cannot be qualifying relatives under the requirements for waivers for fraud or unlawful presence, nor can hardship to the waiver applicant be considered. Nevertheless, "the hardship experienced by non-qualifying relatives can be considered as part of the extreme hardship determination, but only to the extent that such hardship affects one or more qualifying relatives."[18] For this reason, the

16 9 *USCIS Policy Manual* pt. B, ch. 2.A.

17 9 *USCIS Policy Manual* pt. B, ch. 4.C.

18 9 *USCIS Policy Manual* pt. B, ch. 4.D.

guidance encourages applicants to describe the emotional or other hardship that the qualifying relative parent would experience due to the suffering of a child who must either relocate to a foreign country or remain separated from the applicant. This "derivative hardship" is one of the factors that adjudicators must consider in weighing the totality of the circumstances.

The guidance points out that any factor that the applicant presents should be considered. It sets forth the five most common factors and their impact: (1) family ties; (2) social and cultural issues; (3) economic issues; (4) health conditions and care; and (5) country conditions.

It then spells out examples of what hardships might fall within each of the five categories. For example, social and cultural impact could be evidenced by loss of access to U.S. courts, our criminal justice system, and the protection of family law proceedings (protection orders, child support, or visitation). It could also be demonstrated by fear of persecution or social ostracism and lack of access to social institutions and support networks. Other examples include the more obvious: lack of language skills, quality of educational opportunities, assimilation into U.S. culture, and community ties here versus in the foreign country. The country conditions category could include the designation of TPS, civil unrest or generalized level of crime and violence, and State Department Travel Warnings or Alerts.

The final guidance also identifies five factors that "often weigh heavily in support of a finding of extreme hardship."[19] While the existence at the time of adjudication of one or more of these "particularly significant factors" would not create a presumption of extreme hardship, they are "often likely to support findings" of it. The five particularly significant factors are:

- Qualifying relative was granted Iraqi or Afghan Special Immigrant Status, T nonimmigrant status, or asylee or refugee status from the waiver's applicant's country of relocation;
- The qualifying relative is on active duty with any branch of the U.S. Armed Forces;
- Either the qualifying relative or a member of the household who is dependent on the qualifying relative's care is disabled or suffers from a medical/ physical condition that makes travel to or residence in the foreign country detrimental to his or her health or safety;
- The Department of State has issued either a country-wide travel warning or one for a region of the country where the applicant or the qualifying relative would likely relocate; or

19 9 *USCIS Policy Manual* pt. B, ch. 5.E.

- Separation would result in the qualifying relative becoming the primary caretaker—and possibly income-earner—for the couple's children or otherwise taking on significant parental or other caregiving responsibilities.20

The first two factors do not need further elaboration. The third circumstance would apply if the qualifying relative is disabled and is going to either separate from the applicant or relocate to a foreign country where services are unavailable or significantly inferior to those in the United States. It would also apply if the disabled person is another household member who is going to relocate or remain in the United States. Regardless of whether the disabled person is the qualifying relative or another household member, if separation is alleged, he or she needs to establish the need for the applicant's assistance due to the disability.

The fourth circumstance is particularly significant for applicants from Mexico, Honduras, Nicaragua, Guatemala, and El Salvador where the State Department has issued country-wide or region-specific travel warnings. To check the current status and level of travel warnings, go to https://travel.state.gov/content/travel/en/traveladvisories/traveladvisories.html/.

The fifth circumstance would apply in situations where the separation would result in a substantial shift in caregiving responsibilities from the applicant to the qualifying relative. It assumes that the qualifying relative is responsible for the welfare of a child. The applicant needs to establish a bona fide relationship between the child and either the applicant or the qualifying relative. For purposes of this hardship factor, the immigration status of dependent children is irrelevant—they may be U.S. citizens, LPRs, or undocumented.

Sample questions to ask the qualifying relative to elicit potential hardship factors are included as Appendix 7.

INA §212(g) Waivers for Health-Related Grounds

Communicable Disease, Physical, or Mental Disorder

A prospective immigrant who is determined to have a communicable disease of public health significance, or to have a Class A mental or physical condition, may obtain a waiver under INA §212(g).[21] The communicable disease waiver is available to a foreign national who is the spouse, unmarried son or daughter (including minor lawfully adopted child), or parent of a U.S. citizen, an LPR, or a foreign national who has been issued an immigrant visa.[22] Self-petitioners and derivative beneficiaries who are filing under VAWA are also eligible, and do not

20 *Id.*

21 Immigration and Nationality Act (INA) §212(g)(1).

22 INA §§212(g)(1)(A), (B).

need qualifying relatives.[23] The waiver for mental and physical conditions also does not require a qualifying relative.[24]

The statute does not spell out any requirements for the communicable disease waiver beyond the requirement of the qualifying relative, and the requirement that the applicant comply with the regulations. The regulations specify that applicants who are inadmissible because of active tuberculosis must fill out Statement A on the Form I-601, Application for Waiver of Grounds of Inadmissibility (supplement).[25] Furthermore, the health facility or physician who will be treating the foreign national in the United States must complete Statement B and agree to supply treatment or necessary observation for the proper management of the tuberculosis.[26] If the treating physician is in private practice or it is a private facility, the supplement also must be endorsed by the local or state health officer.[27]

Section 212(g) waivers are also available to foreign nationals who have been found inadmissible because they have a physical or mental disorder along with behavior associated with the disorder that may pose, or has posed in the past, a threat to others.[28] There is no requirement of a qualifying relative; the statute merely refers to complying with the "terms, conditions, or controls, if any, including the giving of bond" as the attorney general may by regulation prescribe after consultation with the secretary of health and human services. The regulations require that an applicant (or her or his "sponsoring family member") submit a medical report containing the foreign national's complete medical history, details of any hospitalization or institutional care or treatment for the condition at issue, and findings on his or her current health and mental condition.[29]

The regulations further require, for foreign nationals with a history of mental illness, information on which the U.S. Public Health Service may base a determination as to whether the foreign national has been free of the disease long enough to demonstrate recovery.[30] They further require that the foreign national or his or her family have made financial arrangements for any treatment in the United States, and that he or she will comply with such treatment.[31]

Practically speaking, it appears that to grant a waiver, USCIS wants to see that a foreign national found inadmissible based on a physical or mental disorder with

23 INA §212(g)(1)(C).

24 INA §212(g)(3).

25 8 CFR §212.7(b)(3).

26 *Id.*

27 *Id.*

28 INA §212(g)(3).

29 8 CFR §212.7(b)(4)(i).

30 *Id.*

31 8 CFR §212.7(b)(4)(ii).

associated harmful behavior is either no longer ill or is receiving treatment that keeps the illness and harmful behavior in check. This is tantamount to contesting the Class A finding—in other words, to get a waiver, you need to show that you should not need a waiver. Although there is, theoretically, a procedure to contest a physician's Class A finding through the Centers for Disease Control (CDC), it is cumbersome and unclear. For many applicants, it will be easier to seek a section 212(g) waiver and submit evidence that they are in treatment or the disease is in remission than to seek a reconsideration of the Class A determination.

If an intending immigrant is found inadmissible, application for the waiver is made on Form I-601, Application for Waiver of Grounds of Inadmissibility.

Vaccination Requirement

Three waivers are available for persons deemed inadmissible because they cannot present proof of vaccinations.[32] The vaccination requirement may be waived if: (1) the immigrant is subsequently vaccinated against a disease for which he or she failed to present documentation of previous vaccination; (2) a civil surgeon or panel physician certifies that the vaccination would not be medically appropriate; or (3) the vaccination would be contrary to the foreign national's religious or moral beliefs.[33] The first two waivers are straightforward, and USCIS and DOS have implemented them liberally. The third waiver is slightly more complicated, but the agencies still appear to be implementing the waiver in a flexible manner.

A "blanket" waiver can be granted by USCIS in adjustment of status cases to persons who are ineligible on the first two grounds, and authority has been delegated to DOS's consular officers to grant such blanket waivers to immigrant visa applicants abroad. In these cases, no waiver application form is required, and the applicant does not have to pay an application fee.[34]

The first vaccination waiver provision is a departure from usual procedures for determinations on inadmissibility grounds and submission of waivers. This waiver addresses situations in which the vaccination requirement has been met through the person's receiving the required vaccination(s). Under other provisions of the INA, when a foreign national is found inadmissible and subsequently meets the requirements for admissibility, the refusal is deemed to be overcome. The applicant is no longer ineligible and a waiver, therefore, is not required. The first vaccination waiver provision, however, is different. The language at INA §212(g)(2)(A) indicates that a waiver for ineligibility is required notwithstanding the fact that

32 INA §212(g)(2).

33 INA §212(g)(2)(A), (B), (C).

34 INS Memorandum, P. Virtue, *New Vaccination Requirements* (Apr. 10, 1997), AILA Doc. No. 97041091.

the applicant subsequently presents documentation showing that all immunizations have been obtained.

The second waiver of the vaccination requirements is available when a vaccine would not be medically appropriate, as determined by the Department of Health and Human Services.[35] The CDC provides guidance to civil surgeons and panel physicians performing medical examinations and assessing the vaccination status of adjustment of status and immigrant visa applicants.[36]

The CDC guidelines state that a vaccination is "not medically appropriate" under the following circumstances:

- The vaccine is not age appropriate, because it is not recommended for the applicant's age group;
- There is a contraindication to the vaccine (for example, allergies to eggs, yeast, hypersensitivity to prior vaccines, and pregnancy, among other medical reasons);
- The foreign national has taken the initial vaccine, but is unable to complete the entire series within a reasonable period (for example, the recommended series of hepatitis vaccines may take as long as six months to complete); or
- The medical examination is not being performed during the flu season (this will only apply to the influenza vaccine, as it is generally given only during the fall season).

For immigrant visa applicants abroad, a fifth category where it is not medically appropriate to require a particular vaccine exists. This is when the required vaccine is not licensed or not routinely available in the country where the medical exam is performed.[37]

When the civil surgeon's report serves as the basis of determining blanket waiver eligibility, the foreign national's medical examination report (Form I-693) must be properly endorsed by the civil surgeon. For medical examinations conducted abroad, the panel physician completes and endorses the U.S. Department of State (DOS) Vaccination Documentation Worksheet (Form DS-3025).

The third waiver of the vaccination ground—for persons for whom complying with the vaccination requirement would be contrary to their moral or religious beliefs—is more complicated.[38] In these cases, there is no "blanket" waiver, and USCIS must adjudicate each waiver request on a case-by-case basis. This means

35 INA §212(g)(2)(B).

36 Centers for Disease Control (CDC), *Vaccination Technical Instructions for Civil Surgeons*, available at www.cdc.gov/immigrantrefugeehealth/exams/ti/civil/vaccination-civil-technical-instructions.html.

37 CDC, *Vaccination Technical Instructions for Panel Physicians*, available at www.cdc.gov/immigrantrefugeehealth/exams/ti/panel/vaccination-panel-technical-instructions.html.

38 INA §212(g)(2)(C).

that the applicant must file the standard waiver form (Form I-601) and pay the corresponding fee.

To qualify for the moral/religious waiver, the applicant must show that:

- He or she is opposed to vaccinations in any form;
- The objection is based on religious belief or moral convictions (whether or not as a member of a recognized religion); and
- The religious belief or moral conviction (whether or not as part of a "mainstream" religion) is sincere.[39]

Thus, an individual does not have to be an active member of any denomination to qualify for the waiver. This means, for example, that if an individual is a vegetarian for moral reasons, and those same reasons preclude him or her from receiving some vaccinations, he or she should be eligible for the waiver, if the above factors apply. When the waiver application is for a child, the child's parent must satisfy these three requirements.[40]

As part of their application for a waiver, individuals should provide written evidence that they meet the three requirements. If the applicant is a member of a religious denomination that opposes vaccinations in any form, it is recommended that he or she obtain a letter from a leader or authority on that religion explaining the belief.

It is important to note that this waiver is intended for those with religious or moral objections to vaccinations. Concerns about medical dangers of vaccinations (such as the fear that autism is caused by vaccines) would *not* qualify one for this waiver.

INA §212(h) Waivers for Criminal Conduct

INA §212(h) provides for waivers of some of the criminal inadmissibility grounds. A waiver is available for foreign nationals who are inadmissible for the following reasons:

- Crimes of moral turpitude;
- Multiple criminal convictions;
- Prostitution and commercialized vice;
- Assertion of immunity from prosecution for serious criminal misconduct; and
- A single offense of simple possession of 30 grams or less of marijuana.[41]

---

39 *See* Instructions for Application for Waiver of Grounds of Inadmissibility [Form I-690], www.uscis.gov/files/form/i-690instr.pdf, item 2.

40 *Id.*

41 INA §212(h).

Most substance abuse offenses, trafficking in controlled substances or persons, money laundering, and engaging in particularly severe forms of religious freedom cannot be waived.

Three categories of foreign nationals may benefit from a section 212(h) waiver:

- Applicants who are inadmissible only under the prostitution or commercialized vice grounds of inadmissibility or because of activities occurring more than 15 years before the foreign national applies for a visa, admission, or adjustment of status, if the foreign national's admission would not be contrary to the U.S. welfare or security, and if the foreign national has been rehabilitated[42]
- Applicants who are the spouse, parent, son, or daughter of a U.S. citizen or LPR, if it is established that refusing admission to the foreign national would result in extreme hardship to the U.S. citizen or LPR relative[43]
- Applicants who qualify as a self-petitioning abused spouse or child of a U.S. citizen or LPR, under VAWA[44]

Foreign nationals who have been convicted of, or who have made a valid admission of committing, criminal acts involving murder or torture are specifically barred from obtaining any of these waivers.[45] Additionally, foreign nationals "previously admitted" to the United States as LPRs are not eligible for a section 212(h) waiver if they have been convicted of an aggravated felony, or if they have not resided lawfully and continuously in the United States for seven years prior to the initiation of removal proceedings.[46]

As with other waivers under the INA, section 212(h) waivers are granted in the exercise of discretion. In addition to the requirements mentioned above, the applicant must present evidence showing that the positive factors in his or her case outweigh the negative factors.[47] The regulations governing section 212(h) limit the exercise of discretion in cases involving violent or dangerous crimes. Applicants who committed violent or dangerous crimes must demonstrate "extraordinary

---

42 INA §212(h)(1)(A).

43 INA §212(h)(1)(B).

44 INA §212(h)(1)(C).

45 INA §212(h)(2).

46 *Id.* Four federal circuits have held that these limitations do not apply to LPRs who adjusted status in the United States. *Hanif v. Att'y General*, No. 11-2643 (3rd Cir. Sept. 14, 2012); *Bracamontes v. Holder*, 675 F.3d 380 (4th Cir. 2012); *Lanier v. Att'y General*, 631 F.3d 1363 (11th Cir. 2011); *Martinez v. Mukasey*, 519 F.3d 532 (5th Cir. 2008). Outside these circuits, these 212(h) limitations on LPR eligibility apply without regard to the manner in which LPR status was acquired. *Matter of E.W. Rodriguez*, 25 I&N Dec 784 (BIA 2012), reaffirming *Matter of Koljenovic*, 25 I&N Dec 219 (BIA 2010).

47 *Matter of Mendez-Moralez*, 21 I&N Dec. 296 (BIA 1996).

circumstances," such as national security or foreign policy considerations, or that the denial of admission would result in "exceptional or extremely unusual hardship."[48]

The statute provides that no court has jurisdiction to review an administrative decision to grant or deny a section 212(h) waiver.[49]

The waiver application is filed on Form I-601 and may be used in removal proceedings to cure deportability for having been inadmissible at time of entry. In that case, the waiver is granted as if it had been requested before entry.[50] This waiver is also available in the context of adjustment of status applications in removal proceedings, and can be submitted as a stand-alone form of relief in removal proceedings for an LPR who is being charged with making an admission.[51] However, this waiver will not serve to cure ineligibility for lack of good moral character.[52] Thus, even if the applicant is granted a section 212(h) waiver, he or she will not be eligible for any relief from removal that requires proof of good moral character. Such forms of relief include cancellation of removal for non-LPRs, registry, and voluntary departure.

INA §212(i) Waivers for Fraud or Misrepresentation

INA §212(i) provides for a discretionary waiver of the fraud or misrepresentation inadmissibility ground. To qualify for the waiver, the foreign national must establish that his or her U.S. citizen or LPR spouse or parent would suffer extreme hardship if the foreign national were denied admission.[53] The waiver is not available based on extreme hardship to a child who is a U.S. citizen or LPR. In addition to the equities presented and the extreme hardship to the family member, USCIS may consider the nature of the fraud or misrepresentation. The statute prohibits judicial review of an administrative decision of a fraud waiver.[54]

In *Matter of Cervantes-Gonzalez*, the BIA identified the factors to be considered in determining whether a qualifying relative would suffer extreme hardship if the foreign national were denied admission.[55] Those factors include: the presence of LPR or U.S. citizen family ties both within and outside the United States; the conditions in the country to which the qualifying relative would relocate and the extent of the qualifying relative's ties to that country; the financial impact of departure from the United States; and significant conditions of health, particularly when tied to an unavailability of suitable medical care in the country to which the

---

48 8 CFR §212.7(d).

49 INA §212(h)(2).

50 *See Matter of Millard*, 11 I&N Dec. 175 (BIA 1965).

51 *Matter of Abosi*, 24 I&N Dec. 204 (BIA 2007).

52 *Miller v. U.S.*, 762 F.2d 21 (3d Cir. 1985).

53 INA §212(i)(1).

54 INA §212(i)(2).

55 *Matter of Cervantes-Gonzalez*, 22 I&N Dec. 560 (BIA 1999), *aff'd, Cervantes-Gonzalez v. INS*, 244 F.3d 1001 (9th Cir. 2001).

qualifying relative would relocate. A more detailed discussion of hardship factors is discussed earlier in this chapter.

It is important to note that the section 212(i) waiver only covers fraud or misrepresentation under INA §212(a)(6)(C)(i) (with respect to procuring a visa, other documentation, or admission into the United States, or other benefit provided under the INA). The section 212(i) waiver will not waive inadmissibility under INA §212(a)(6)(C)(ii) for a false claim of U.S. citizenship made after September 30, 1996, for any purpose or benefit under the INA, or any other federal or state law. There is no waiver available for a false claim to U.S. citizenship, only a limited exception. Under the exception, the inadmissibility ground does not apply if each natural or adoptive parent of the foreign national is or was a U.S. citizen by birth or naturalization, the foreign national permanently resided in the United States prior to reaching age 16, and the foreign national reasonably believed at the time of making the representation that he or she was a U.S. citizen.[56]

INA §212(a)(9)(B)(v) Waiver for Unlawful Presence

The statute provides for a waiver for the unlawful presence three– and ten-year bars of INA §212(a)(9)(B)(i) if USCIS determines that refusing admission to the foreign national would result in extreme hardship to a U.S. citizen spouse or parent or LPR spouse or parent.[57] The waiver is not available based on extreme hardship to a U.S. citizen child or LPR child. As with the crimes and fraud waivers, no court may review the discretionary decision whether to grant the unlawful presence waiver.[58] Some applicants qualify to file a provisional waiver if they are consular processing and will be inadmissible only based on unlawful presence. Eligibility for and the procedure for filing a provisional waiver application are explained below.

Strategy and Procedure for Filing

The key to winning a waiver application is establishing extreme hardship, which is best accomplished through a well-organized and thoroughly documented case. Each case has a unique set of facts, and it is critical to highlight those that will support a finding of extreme hardship to the qualifying relative. When preparing waiver applications, it is important to explain the requirements to the applicant and family members and emphasize their essential role in providing declarations and gathering documentation. The goal is to allow the adjudicator to become very familiar with the applicant and his or her family and recognize their distinctiveness and worthiness for the waiver.

A waiver application should include the following:

---

56 INA §212(a)(6)(C)(ii)(II).

57 INA §212(a)(9)(B)(v).

58 *Id.*

- Form I-601
- Check or money order for the fee (currently $585)
- Cover letter and/or index or table of contents to the application. The cover letter or index should contain headings for each of the elements of the waiver, such as qualifying relationship, extreme hardship (subheadings for health issues, financial, educational, etc.), and discretionary factors. The application should be paginated consecutively and the documentation should be tabbed for easy access.
- Documents to establish the relationship with the qualifying U.S. citizen or LPR relative(s). The relationship should be documented by birth certificates and marriage certificates to show the relevant relationship. These must be accompanied by a translation into English if they are in a foreign language. The LPR or U.S. citizen status of the qualifying relative must be established by birth certificates showing birth in the United States or by copies of the relative's permanent resident card or naturalization certificate.
- Documents to establish extreme hardship. Each case must be analyzed individually to determine what hardship factors exits and how to document them. A list of examples of documents can be found in the discussion below.
- Documents to support a favorable exercise of discretion by the adjudicator. The more serious the fraud, immigration violation, or crime necessitating the waiver, the more positive factors will be required to balance out the negative factors and support a favorable exercise of discretion. Positive factors can include the applicant's rehabilitation, positive attributes, service to the community, and dedication to his or her family. These can be demonstrated by declarations and letters from persons having knowledge about the applicant.

As mentioned above, establishing extreme hardship to a qualifying relative is central to getting a waiver granted. The following list provides examples of documents to submit in support of a waiver application. This list is not exhaustive, and each case must be analyzed individually to determine the relevant hardship factors and to decide the best way to document those factors.

- *Declarations from the applicant,* the affected family members, and others who are familiar with the family and its circumstances. The most successful waiver applications contain a thorough declaration in the applicant's words describing the daily life of the applicant and his or her family and explaining how that would change if the waiver is not granted. The declarations should include a description of the likely psychological, medical, educational, financial, and other effects on the family if the applicant is denied the waiver. Others who can provide useful declarations or letters include friends, neighbors, landlords, employers, coworkers, church officials, teachers, therapists, counselors, and other community members.

- *Evidence of any health-related issues,* such as current or anticipated treatment for physical, emotional, or psychological problems of the applicant or family members. Evidence should include medical reports and letters from treating physicians, psychologists, or other health care professionals. The evidence should include documents on the availability and quality of treatment for the condition in the home county. This can include statements from physicians or other medical experts who are knowledgeable about the health care system in the applicant's home country or reports from governmental and nongovernmental organizations. Proof of health insurance in the United States purchased by the applicant or the qualifying family member should also be included.
- *Evidence of the financial status of the applicant* and his or her family in the United States and the financial impact on the family should the waiver not be granted. The evidence can include employment letters, pay stubs, income tax returns, bank account statements, titles, deeds, or other proof of ownership of real or personal property in the United States by the applicant or anchor relative. Other evidence might include reports or articles on the economic situation in the native country and the likely employment prospects. Additional evidence may include financial loss caused by the need to sell a home or business in the United States, and the cost of care for children or elderly parents or relatives in the absence of the applicant or qualifying relative.
- *Evidence of children's educational levels*, achievements, and challenges, and the quality of the education they would receive in the applicant's country, including information on the availability of programs for gifted or special needs children. Include report cards, letters from teachers and guidance counselors, and reports or articles comparing the educational system in the applicant's county with that of the United States. Other evidence could include a professional evaluation indicating the potential impact of relocation to another country on the children's academic progress and overall development.
- *Evidence of the applicant's and/or qualifying relatives' close family ties* in the United States and lack of family ties abroad. Submit evidence of the relationships, such as birth certificates and marriage certificates, and if the relatives are U.S. citizens or LPRs, submit evidence of their status in the United States. These documents can include U.S. birth certificates, naturalization certificates, passports, or resident alien cards. Statements from the applicant and family members should describe the closeness of the family relationship, including how frequently they see each other, the

types of things they do together, how much they rely on each other and for what, and other indications of a close relationship. If any family member is in the armed services, submit evidence of this. Include photographs of the applicant, the qualifying relative, and family members together during holidays or special occasions, or just spending time with one another.

- *If the applicant, qualifying relatives, or children do not speak the language* of the home country, include declarations or letters so stating. If there are any religious, ethnic, or social obstacles or concerns for the applicant, qualifying relative, or children in the home country, submit evidence addressing these concerns. The evidence could be the applicant's and/or relatives' declarations describing the concerns, or governmental or nongovernmental reports or news articles substantiating these issues.
- *Evidence of civil unrest or war,* gang violence, natural disaster, drought, famine, or extreme environmental factors in the applicant's home country. If the applicant is fearful of returning to his or her home country, this should be explained in the applicant's declaration. Submit reports and articles concerning the conditions in the country, produced by DOS or others, as well as DOS travel warnings for that country or province.

When deciding an application for a waiver, the adjudicator must consider all the hardship factors cumulatively.[59] It is therefore very important to document all the hardship factors in a client's case.

Applicants for adjustment of status will file the Form I-601 with the adjustment of status application. If the adjustment application is pending, the applicant will file the I-601 with the Chicago Lockbox. Applicants seeking an immigrant visa at a U.S. consulate and who have been found inadmissible will file the I-601 at the Phoenix lockbox, which will forward it to the appropriate service center for adjudication.

If USCIS approves the waiver, the consulate will schedule another interview for final adjudication of the visa application. In an adjustment case, USCIS would approve the adjustment application. If USCIS denies a waiver application, the applicant can file an appeal to the USCIS Administrative Appeals Office (AAO) within 30 days of the decision.[60] If an applicant is in removal proceedings, he or she should file the waiver directly with the immigration court.

Provisional Waivers for Unlawful Presence

On January 3, 2013, the USCIS finalized its regulation regarding the adjudication of waivers for those who are consular processing and would be triggering the

---

59 *Matter of L–O–G–*, 21 I&N Dec. 413 (BIA 1996); *Matter of Ige*, 20 I&N Dec. 880 (BIA 1994).

60 8 CFR §103.3(a)(2).

unlawful presence ground of inadmissibility.[61] On July 29, 2016, the agency expanded and modified the provisional waiver program.[62] The program provides a process by which the agency will adjudicate these waivers *before* the applicants leave for their immigrant visa interview. The procedure would be available only to immediate relatives who are inadmissible based on unlawful presence—and no other grounds—and who can establish extreme hardship to a qualifying U.S. citizen spouse or parent.[63] To be eligible, the applicant would need to have an approved I-130 or I-360 petition and have paid the immigrant visa fee bill.

USCIS began receiving and adjudicating the provisional waivers on March 4, 2013. Applicants must use Form I-601A, Application for Provisional Unlawful Presence Waiver. The filing fee for the waiver application is currently $585; there is no filing fee waiver available for the provisional waiver or the biometrics that are required as part of the process.

While only immediate relatives were originally eligible to file for the provisional waiver, it has been expanded to cover all beneficiaries in the family-based categories, as well as those in the employment-based categories and the Diversity Visa program.[64] Therefore, the qualifying relative could be an LPR or U.S. citizen spouse or parent.

USCIS may issue Requests for Evidence (RFEs) to address applications that are missing critical information related to extreme hardship or to whether the applicant merits a favorable exercise of discretion. But the agency will not necessarily issue an RFE or Notice of Intent to Deny.[65] Also, bear in mind that on July 13, 2018, USCIS expanded adjudicators' discretion to deny an immigration application, petition, or request without first issuing an RFE or a NOID pursuant to 8 CFR §103.2(b)(8).[66] USCIS officials may issue a denial without sending an RFE in cases filed without sufficient initial evidence. USCIS provides two examples, one of which is when a waiver application is submitted with little or no supporting evidence.[67]

USCIS is retaining its authority to reopen or reconsider a decision based on its own motion if it finds that the decision was issued in error or approval is no longer warranted. While there are no appeals if the provisional waiver is denied, the agency allows for the refiling of a new waiver application.[68] Those who are denied, as well

61 78 Fed. Reg. 536–78 (Jan. 3, 2013).

62 81 Fed. Reg. 50244 (July 29, 2016).

63 8 CFR §212.7(e).

64 81 Fed. Reg. 50244 (July 29, 2016).

65 8 CFR §212.7(e)(8).

66 USCIS *Adjudicator's Field Manual* (AFM) ch. 10.5(a), (b), located in 1 *USCIS Policy Manual* pt. E.

67 AFM ch. 10.5(a)(2), located in 1 *USCIS Policy Manual* pt. E.

68 8 CFR §212.7(e)(9).

as those not eligible for the program, may file a waiver on Form I-601 after they are found inadmissible by the consulate.

The 2016 regulation broadened eligibility to include some persons who have received a final order of removal or deportation. When the person departs the United States while a final order is outstanding, he or she affects or executes that order.[69] And execution of the order would then make the person inadmissible for a period of five or 10 years (20 years in some situations).[70]

The 2016 regulation allows persons who have been ordered removed and who have not executed the order to apply for a waiver of this ground of inadmissibility before they leave. This is done by filing the Form I-212 with the USCIS office in the jurisdiction where the person was ordered removed.[71] If the I-212 is approved, the individual's order of removal, deportation, or exclusion would no longer bar him or her from obtaining an immigrant visa abroad. After obtaining such consent, the person would then be eligible to apply for the provisional waiver. Otherwise, persons subject to a final order of deportation or removal who have not been granted a Form I-212 would be ineligible to file for the provisional waiver.[72]

Persons in removal proceedings in which no final order has been entered are ineligible to file the provisional waiver unless the proceedings are administratively closed.[73] The 2016 regulations also allowed for potential applicants in proceedings who have not yet been ordered deported or removed to move to administratively close the case.[74] But a subsequent decision by the Attorney General, *Matter of Castro-Tum*,[75] revoked immigration judges' and the Board of Immigration Appeals' authority to administratively close cases except in limited situations. Seeking termination without prejudice to be able to pursue the provisional waiver is one option, albeit an unlikely one. Taking voluntary departure and pursuing an I-601 unlawful presence waiver from abroad remains another option. Some practitioners have challenged the denial of administrative closure, arguing that *Castro-Tum* was wrongly decided and that given the provisional waiver regulations, IJs have authority to administratively close. Two courts of appeal have already held that the BIA violated established regulatory authority.[76] Those courts held that 8 CFR §§1003.10(b) and 1003.1(d)(1)(ii) conferred upon immigration judges and the BIA the authority to administratively close cases.

---

69 INA §101(g); 8 CFR §241.7.

70 INA §212(a)(9)(A).

71 8 CFR §212.2(j).

72 8 CFR §212.7(e)(4)(iv).

73 *Id.*

74 8 CFR §212.7(e)(4)(v).

75 27 I&N Dec. 271 (AG 2018). DOJ later issued a fact sheet with background information, key excerpts from the opinion, and additional information. AILA Doc. No. 18052560.

76 *Morales v. Barr*, No. 19-1999 (7th Cir. 2020); *Romero v. Barr*, No. 18-1850 (4th Cir. 2019).

Persons who were able to administratively close their cases before the Attorney General's decision and whose provisional waiver was granted are then advised to move to terminate the proceedings before departing the country. Individuals who have been granted administrative closure by an immigration judge are still considered to be in removal proceedings.[77]

Since unlawful presence does not begin to run for purposes of INA §212(a)(9)(B) until a noncitizen turns 18, applicants must be at least 17 years old to apply for the provisional waiver. Only persons residing in the United States qualify to apply. An individual who otherwise meets the eligibility requirements for filing a provisional waiver may do so regardless of his or her current immigration status. For example, a person having TPS status may apply for the provisional waiver.

The NVC has indicated that it will halt consular processing only after it receives official notice from the USCIS that the applicant has filed an I-601A. The NVC will schedule the interview within an estimated two to three months after USCIS has approved the I-601A and the applicant has submitted all other required documents. Failure to inform the NVC before filing the I-601A might result in the agency's scheduling the consular interview. In cases where the interview has been scheduled on or after January 3, 2013, and the applicant wishes to file for the provisional waiver, he or she should notify the U.S. consulate or embassy and request that it be continued until after the waiver is adjudicated.

The provisional waiver program does not change the extreme hardship standard. It only affects the timing of the adjudication. Those who are approved will be notified that they may proceed with consular processing. At the immigrant visa interview, the consulate will not "second guess" the waiver approval. However, the consulate reserves the right to question the immigrant visa applicant, review current data bases, and investigate for any other possible grounds of inadmissibility that were not previously identified. If it discovers that the applicant was not eligible to apply based on a separate ground of inadmissibility, the provisional waiver approval will automatically be revoked.[78]

If the waiver is denied by the USCIS service center, the applicant will be subject to the current USCIS policy on issuance of a Notice to Appear (NTA), which commences removal proceedings. On June 28, 2018, USCIS issued a policy memorandum, according to which USCIS will issue NTAs when a waiver application is denied and the applicant is not lawfully present.[79] If the applicant is lawfully present but removable and the waiver is denied, USCIS will issue an NTA if he or she falls into

---

77 USCIS, Questions and Answers, USCIS—American Immigration Lawyers Association (AILA) Meeting (Apr. 11, 2013), AILA Doc. No. 13041143.

78 8 CFR §212.7(e)(14).

79 USCIS Policy Memorandum, *Updated Guidance for the Referral of Cases and Issuance of Notices to Appear (NTAs) in Cases Involving Inadmissible and Deportable Aliens* (June 28, 2018), AILA Doc. No. 18070539.

a specific enforcement category. USCIS may refer a case to ICE before adjudicating the waiver if there is suspected fraud or the applicant has a certain criminal history.

Form I-212, Consent to Reapply for Admission

Eligibility

Foreign nationals who have departed or been removed from the United States subsequent to a deportation or removal order are inadmissible.[80] This ground of inadmissibility does not apply to persons who received a final order but who have not subsequently left the United States. A foreign national with a final order may be able to adjust status before the immigration judge if he or she is successful in reopening his or her proceedings.

To ameliorate the harshness of the inadmissibility ground for prior deportation or removal orders, Congress authorized USCIS to waive inadmissibility by granting not a waiver but a "consent [for the applicant] to reapply" for admission.81 In adjudicating an I-212, Application for Permission to Reapply for Admission into the United States After Deportation or Removal, USCIS will not require a showing of extreme hardship to any specific family member. Rather, USCIS will consider the following factors:

- The applicant's moral character;
- The need for the applicant's services in the United States;
- Whether the applicant was ignorant of the fact that he or she was deported;
- The length of time the applicant had been in the United States;
- The reason the applicant originally was deported;
- Hardships resulting from the deportation;
- Recency of the deportation or removal order;
- Evidence of reformation and rehabilitation;
- The applicant's family responsibilities and ties in the United States; and
- The existence of an approved immigrant visa petition for the applicant.[82]

USCIS will balance the positive and negative factors. The following negative factors will also be considered:

- Repeated and significant immigration violations; and
- The fact that the applicant is inadmissible based on other grounds for which there is no waiver.[83]

80 INA §212(a)(9)(A).

81 INA §212(a)(9)(A)(iii).

82 *Matter of Lee*, 17 I&N Dec. 275 (Comm'r 1978).

83 *Id.*

Strategy and Procedure

Application for consent to reapply is made on Form I-212. For an immigrant visa applicant, the form and supporting documentation are filed with the USCIS service center that has jurisdiction over the USCIS district where the deportation or removal proceedings were held.[84] The Form I-212 may be filed before the interview so that this ground of inadmissibility is not an issue at the time of the visa interview.[85] If the I212 application is approved, USCIS will send the approval notice to the consulate.

If the applicant will be consular processing and filing waiver applications (such as a waiver application for unlawful presence), the Form I-212 must be submitted with the Form I-601. Both forms will be filed with USCIS through the Phoenix lockbox and forwarded to the appropriate service center.

A person seeking permanent residence through adjustment of status must file the application with the USCIS office having jurisdiction over the place where the applicant resides.[86] However, a Form I-212 waiver filed before the completion of 10 years of foreign residency does not permit a person to apply for adjustment of status.[87] See chapter 6 for a more detailed explanation of this issue.

A denial of a Form I-212 application is appealable to the AAO, unless it was filed in conjunction with an adjustment application in removal proceedings; in that situation the denial is appealable to the BIA.[88]

The applicant should include the following supporting documents:

- Immigrant visa approval notice;
- Proof of U.S. citizen or LPR family members in the United States;
- A copy of the final deportation or removal order;
- Proof of current and prior employment;
- Proof of filing federal and state taxes;
- Medical records or doctor's statement indicating health-related problems;
- Results of FBI fingerprint check indicating criminal record; and
- Declarations from the applicant, the applicant's family members, and any other person who can vouch for the foreign national's good moral character and hardship that would be suffered if the application is denied.

The fee for filing the Form I-212 is currently $585.

---

84 8 CFR §212.2(d).

85 8 CFR §212.2(j).

86 8 CFR §212.2(e)

87 *Duran Gonzales v. DHS*, 508 F.3d 1227 (9th Cir. 2007); *Matter of Torres-Garcia*, 23 I&N Dec. 866 (BIA 2006).

88 8 CFR §212.2(h).

CHAPTER 8

PUBLIC CHARGE AND THE AFFIDAVIT OF SUPPORT

Public Charge Ground of Inadmissibility

The public charge inadmissibility ground bars any foreign national who, "in the opinion of the consular officer at the time of application for a visa, or in the opinion of the Attorney General at the time of application for admission or adjustment of status, is likely at any time to become a public charge."[1] This ground of inadmissibility has become a more serious challenge for low-income applicants after the Department of Homeland Security (DHS) and Department of State (DOS) started implementing their final rules reinterpreting this ground of inadmissibility.

In 1996 Congress amended the ground of inadmissibility for individuals likely to become a public charge.[2] The ground requires that consular officers and DHS officials consider five factors relating to the applicants for admission, a visa, or adjustment of status:

- Age
- Health
- Family status
- Assets, resources, and financial status
- Education and skills
- An affidavit of support[3]

Prior to the change in the 1996 law, the focus had been on the applicant's ability to establish that he or she would be self-sufficient through anticipated income or support from a family member. The 1996 law codified the five factors that the agencies had already been applying but added the requirement that a sponsor—the family member petitioning for the noncitizen—submit a legally enforceable affidavit of support. The effect of the law was to shift the focus away from the intending immigrant and place it on the sponsor. A properly filed, nonfraudulent Form I-864, Affidavit of Support Under Section 213A of the INA, would normally have been considered sufficient to overcome the public charge ground of inadmissibility and satisfy the "totality of the circumstances" analysis. Only where the immigrant visa applicant evidenced significant public charge concerns—advanced age, physical or

1 INA §212(a)(4).

2 Illegal Immigration Reform and Immigrant Responsibility Act of 1996 (IIRAIRA), Pub. L. No. 104-208, 110 Stat. 3009, §531(a), amending INA §212(a)(4).

3 INA §212(a)(4).

mental disabilities, or serious health problems—would the DHS or consular agent look beyond the affidavit of support.

In an effort to further define the public charge, the Immigration and Naturalization Service (INS) promulgated a memorandum,[4] field guidance,[5] and a proposed rule[6] in the *Federal Register* in 1999 that clarified the meaning of the term. The DOS issued a cable to its consulates providing similar instruction. That cumulative guidance was helpful in clarifying the relationship between public charge and the receipt of certain public benefits.

According to this formal agency interpretation, a noncitizen is a public charge for inadmissibility purposes if he or she has become "primarily dependent on the government for subsistence, as demonstrated by either the receipt of public cash assistance for income maintenance or institutionalization for long-term care at government expense."[7] The Service defined the term "public cash assistance for income maintenance" as including only three forms of benefits: (1) Supplemental Security Income (SSI) for the aged, blind, and disabled; (2) Temporary Assistance for Needy Families (TANF) cash assistance; and (3) state and local cash assistance programs, usually known as general relief or general assistance.[8]

2019 Regulatory Changes

In a sign of things to come, the DOS amended the *Foreign Affairs Manual* (FAM) in January 2018 to increase the burden of satisfying the public charge ground of inadmissibility for immigrant visa applicants. The amended language required the consular officers "in every case" to examine the visa applicant's "age, health, family status, assets, resources, financial status, education, and skills." While the Form I-864 affidavit of support alone used to be sufficient proof of satisfying the public charge test in most cases, it was changed to being merely "a positive factor." Another change in the FAM was the addition of language encouraging the consular officer to consider the likelihood that the sponsor will support the visa applicant. The effect of all of this was to relegate the Form I-864 to a supporting rather than a lead role in the public charge analysis.[9]

This FAM change was followed by the DOS's publication of an interim final rule on October 11, 2019,[10] and its further amending the FAM on February 21, 2020, to

---

4 INS Memorandum, M. Pearson, *Public Charge: INA Sections 212(a)(4) and 237(a)(5)* (May 20, 1999), reproduced in 64 Fed. Reg. 28689 (May 26, 1999).

5 64 Fed. Reg. 28689 (May 26, 1999).

6 64 Fed. Reg. 28676 (May 26, 1999).

7 *Id.* at 28677.

8 *Id.* at 28682.

9 Former (pre-2020) 9 FAM 302.8-2.

10 84 Fed. Reg. 54996 (Oct. 11, 2019).

align it with the new regulatory change.[11] The DHS published a similar final rule on August 14, 2019.[12] The DHS rule was enjoined, but the Supreme Court lifted those injunctions and the agencies' new public charge interpretations took effect on February 24, 2020.

The DOS began implementing its rule immediately and applied it to all immigrant visa applications adjudicated on or after that date. In the discretion of the consular official, applicants may be required to submit a new Form DS-5540, Public Charge Questionnaire, along with supporting documentation. The DHS final public charge rule was also implemented as of February 24, 2020, but applied to adjustment of status applications filed on or after that date. Applicants are now required to include a Form I-944, Declaration of Self-Sufficiency, along with supporting documentation.

Under the new DOS and DHS regulations, the term "likely at any time to become a public charge" has been redefined in four important ways. First, instead of being applied to those who might become "primarily dependent" on a designated list of state and federal programs, it applies to those who are more likely than not to receive any of nine benefit programs for more than 12 months in the aggregate within any 36-month period.

Second, the agencies expanded the list of identified programs that can be considered when applying the public charge "totality of the circumstances" test. In addition to those identified in the 1999 INS memorandum, the final regulations add five new programs. The first four programs will be considered if the applicant is currently receiving or has received them in the past; the last five would be considered if received by the applicant starting on February 24, 2020. The following nine benefit programs are:

- SSI
- TANF
- State general relief or general assistance
- Benefits provided for institutionalization for long-term care
- Medicaid (except for "emergency Medicaid," certain disability services related to education, school-based services, or benefits to children below the oldest age set for secondary school education; benefits received while under age 21; and pregnancy benefits including 60 days post-pregnancy)
- Supplemental Nutrition Assistance Program (SNAP, formerly food stamps)
- Section 8 Housing Choice Voucher Program
- Section 8 Project-Based Rental Assistance, and
- Public housing.[13]

---

11 9 FAM 302.8.

12 84 Fed. Reg. 41292 (Aug. 14, 2019).

13 8 CFR §212.21(b).

The final rule does not include receipt or potential receipt of the following benefit programs:

- Emergency medical assistance
- Disaster relief
- National school lunch or school breakfast programs
- Foster care and adoption
- Head Start
- Child Health Insurance Program
- Earned Income Tax Credit or Child Tax Credit.

Benefits received by the applicant's U.S. citizens children or other family members are not considered in determining whether the applicant is likely to become a public charge. Benefits received by an individual who was in an immigration status not subject to the public charge ground of inadmissibility when the benefits were received would also not be considered.

Third, in determining public charge inadmissibility, the regulation shifts attention away from the petitioning sponsor's income as reported on the affidavit of support and redirects it to the five statutory factors: the applicant's age, health, family status, assets/resources/financial status, and education/skills. Adjudicators will assign weight—negative and positive, as well as heavily negative and heavily positive—to these five factors to determine whether the applicant passes the public charge test.

Finally, the DHS regulations allow for the posting of a public charge bond for applicants who, in the opinion of the USCIS or DOS, might otherwise fail the public charge test. The rule details the procedure for the posting and canceling such bonds. Applicants who are initially determined likely to become a public charge by USCIS may be offered the opportunity to post a public charge bond of at least $8,100. The bond may be canceled only upon the immigrant's death, permanent departure, five years as a lawful permanent resident, or naturalization. The bond will be considered breached if the immigrant receives any of the nine cash or noncash programs identified above for more than 12 months in the aggregate within any 36-month period.

Five Statutory Factors Defined

Pursuant to the final regulations, USCIS and consular officers scrutinize applicants' income and assets relative to their household size, current employment and job history, job skills, health status and enrollment in health insurance, education, and current or history of public benefits receipt.[14] The following is a summary of how the agencies define these five statutory factors:

---

14 *See* 8 CFR §212.22; 22 CFR §40.41.

(1) Age: applicants younger than 18 or older than 61 will need to demonstrate why their age will not impact their ability to work.

(2) Health: applicants who have any medical condition will need to show whether it affects their ability to work, attend school, or care for themselves. In making this determination, USCIS and DOS will generally defer to the civil surgeon or panel physician report. Current enrollment in health insurance is a positive factor, as is evidence that the applicant will enroll within 30 days of becoming an LPR.

(3) Family status: the adjudicators will determine the applicant's household size based on the new household definitions. Under this definition, the household includes dependents and persons providing the applicant with more than 50 percent of their support.

(4) Assets, resources, and financial status: DHS and DOS will consider whether the annual household income of the applicant is at least 125 percent of the Federal Poverty Guideline (FPG) using the new household definition. Assets may be considered to make up an income shortfall. If the applicant is the spouse or child of a U.S. citizen, assets must equal three times the income shortfall; for most others, the value of assets must equal five times the difference between required household income and actual household income. Their financial status will also be measured by considering any civil liabilities; past application for, certification for, or receipt of public benefits; receipt or application for a fee waiver for an immigration benefit; bankruptcies; and credit history and credit score.

(5) Education and skills: DHS and DOS will consider whether the applicant has adequate education and skills to either obtain or maintain lawful employment with an income sufficient to avoid becoming a public charge. Factors include: employment history; education level (high school diploma or GED, or higher education degree); occupational skills and licenses; English proficiency; and status of the applicant as a primary caregiver to another individual in the household.

In addition to these five statutory factors, the agencies would also consider the applicant's prospective immigration status and expected period of admission, i.e., whether the applicant is seeking admission as an immigrant or nonimmigrant. Where an affidavit of support is required, DHS will consider the likelihood that the sponsor will actually provide the statutorily required amount of financial support

Any of the following would be considered a "heavily weighted negative factor":

- The applicant is not a full-time student and is authorized to work, but currently unemployed
- The applicant is currently receiving, or certified or approved to receive one or more of the designated public benefits
- The applicant has been diagnosed with a medical condition that is likely to require extensive medical treatment or institutionalization or will interfere

with the ability to work, attend school, or care for himself or herself, and the applicant is uninsured and has no prospect of obtaining private health insurance or financial resources to pay for reasonably foreseeable medical costs

- The applicant has previously been found inadmissible or deportable based on the public charge ground

Any of the following will be considered a "heavily weighted positive factor":

- The applicant's household has income of at least 250 percent of the FPG for the household size
- The applicant is authorized to work, is gainfully employed, and has an income of at least 250 percent of the FPG
- The applicant has private health insurance, not including insurance for which the applicant received subsidies in the form of premium tax credits under the Patient Protection and Affordable Care Act

Receipt of SSI, TANF, state general relief, or long-term institutionalization benefits before February 24, 2020, will be considered a negative factor, but not a heavily weighted one. The agencies will not consider receipt of any of the other five public benefits before February 24, 2020, as a negative factor.

Applicants Not Subject to Public Charge

Certain categories of noncitizens are not subject to the public charge ground of inadmissibility and thus are not subject to the affidavit of support requirements, which will be explained below. These include the following:

- Refugees and asylees
- Amerasians
- Persons adjusting under the Cuban Adjustment Act
- Persons adjusting under the Nicaraguan Adjustment and Central American Relief Act (NACARA)
- Persons adjusting under the Haitian Refugee Immigration Fairness Act (HRIFA)
- Special immigrant juveniles applying for adjustment of status
- Persons adjusting as self-petitioners under the Violence Against Women Act (VAWA)
- Applicants for U nonimmigrant status
- Applicants for T nonimmigrant status
- Applicants for cancellation of removal
- Lautenberg parolees seeking adjustment of status

- Applicants for registry

Do not confuse the category of persons not subject to public charge with those who are subject to public charge but are exempt from filing a binding Form I-864. For example, the affidavit of support requirements are not applicable to widows or widowers applying for LPR status based on a prior marriage to a U.S. citizen or to applicants who have earned or been credited with 40 qualifying Social Security quarters. However, the public charge ground of inadmissibility still applies. Other persons exempt from the I-864 requirements but still subject to public charge would include fiancé(e) applicants, diversity visa lottery winners, parolees, and returning LPRs who have been absent for more than 180 days.

Tips on Completing and Documenting the Form I-944

The instructions for the Form I-944 provide details on how to complete and file it, and those instructions are not discussed here. The Form I-944 itself has some ambiguous questions that could benefit from suggestions on how to answer them, which this section attempts to do. These instructions are based on the version dated October 15, 2019.

Every adjustment of status applicant must file a separate Form I-944. Any supporting documents that are written in a foreign language must be translated into English.

Part 2. Family Status (Your Household)

Input the biographical information of each household member into boxes A through D of Part 2 Question 1, starting with the applicant in #1A. Answer "yes" to the two questions asking whether the household member resides with the applicant and is also filing an application for an immigration benefit, even though the questions don't really apply. Follow the instructions in calculating the total household size. This number is used determine whether the household income and assets are at or above 125 percent of the Federal Poverty Guidelines (FPG) or if applicants who are employment authorized have income at or above 250 percent of FPG.

Part 3. Your and Your Household Members' Assets, Resources, and Financial Status

USCIS requests proof of the applicant's and other household members' income through prior tax return transcripts, since the agency considers them the "primary evidence of income."[15] It is not clear at this time whether the agency will also accept copies of prior tax returns. Part 3 Question 1 asks for the "total income from the … tax returns." This is annual gross, unadjusted income before any taxes or deductions—line 7b of the 2019 Internal Revenue Service (IRS) Form 1040. For 2018, it is line 6 of Form 1040. For 2017 and earlier years, it is line 22.

15 8 *USCIS Policy Manual* pt. G, ch. 9.C.1.

Part 3 Question 9 asks the applicant to list any assets and resources that are available to him or her or to any household member that can be converted into cash within 12 months. If the applicant's total household income is below 125 percent of FPG, he or she can include household assets and resources to make up the shortfall. In addition, total household income and assets that equal or exceed 250 percent of FPG are a heavily weighted positive factor. Therefore, though it is not required, applicants whose income is at or above 125 percent of FPG but below 250 percent may want to include proof of assets in order to satisfy this higher standard.

USCIS requires applicants to submit a copy of their credit history and score, assuming they have one. A Social Security number (SSN) is commonly relied on because it is a unique identifier assigned to only one individual, but it is not the only identifier used. If an SSN is not reported, credit reporting agencies may rely on other identification elements to compile a credit history. However, the lack of an SSN may make it very difficult to obtain a credit report; an individual taxpayer identification number (ITIN) is not a substitute for an SSN. In many cases, only applicants who have opened a bank account or have a credit card will have a credit report. Applicants who have been residing and working abroad likely will not have a U.S. credit report.

The USCIS officer must not draw any negative inferences if the applicant does not have any credit history or cannot submit a report. If the applicant does not have a credit report, he or she can submit documentary evidence of financial responsibility through proof of regular and continued payments of rent, utilities, or other bills.

Part 3 Question 15A–C asks if the applicant has health insurance. Adjustment of status applicants may purchase private insurance through an employer or directly from a private insurance provider, regardless of their immigration status. Those without access through an employer may be eligible through a parent's or spouse's employer, if they are included on the plan as a dependent. The federal and state health insurance exchanges are platforms that allow individuals to compare numerous health insurance plans and purchase coverage from a private insurer. To be eligible to purchase insurance through the exchange, an individual must reside in one of the states in the United States and be considered "lawfully present" for purposes of the ACA. Applicants for adjustment of status are considered lawfully present and may purchase insurance coverage through the health marketplace if they have a pending Form I-485.

Part 3 Question 16 asks if the applicant has *ever* received one of the nine designated programs. It also asks if he or she is certified to receive one of them in the future. Question 17 asks if the applicant has disenrolled, withdrawn from, or requested to be disenrolled from one of the benefit programs. If so, provide the expected date of disenrollment.

Benefit receipt of Medicaid, SNAP, or the three housing programs does not count against the applicant unless it was received on or after February 24, 2020. Only SSI, TANF, and state general assistance received before that date is considered. And it is considered a negative factor, as opposed to a heavily weighed negative factor. Therefore, do not report in Question 16 SNAP, Medicaid, or any of the three housing programs received or applied for prior to February 24, 2020. Subsidized housing programs may be received by the family unit, but the applicant is not considered a recipient unless his or her name is listed as a beneficiary. Most adjustment applicants are not eligible for federal housing programs.

USCIS considers it a positive factor if the applicant shows that he or she does not qualify for one of the designated public benefits due to his or her income or LPR status. To demonstrate this, USCIS suggests submitting evidence from each federal, state, local, or tribal agency that administers one of the designated public benefit programs. In lieu of trying to gather such evidence, the Catholic Legal Immigration Network, Inc. (CLINIC) has developed documentation for the states with the highest immigrant populations that identifies the income ceilings for the appropriate programs and immigration status requirements. In contains a sample letter describing why the applicant would not be financially eligible for the programs based on his or her income and that of the sponsor, and it explains the federal bars to LPR eligibility.

Part 4. Your Education and Skills

USCIS looks at employment history reported on the Form I-140, Immigrant Petition for Alien Workers, Form I-130, Petition for Alien Relative, and the Form I-485, Application to Register Permanent Residence or Adjust Status. Given that any employment history, even if it is without USCIS employment authorization, is a positive factor, it is important that the officer has a full record of current and prior jobs. Therefore, include proof of current employment through pay stubs, wage receipts, or employer letters, and evidence of any past employment not included in the other forms. Applicants who submitted their Form I-944 many months before being scheduled for the interview need to bring updated information and current evidence of income and job status.

USCIS also may consider valid tentative job offers as a positive factor in the totality of the circumstances. It does not require that these job offers take any particular form, but at a minimum they should be printed on the employer's letterhead, state the job position or title, the wage, the number of hours/week, the start date, and be signed by the potential employer.

Part 4 Question 2 asks if the applicant graduated from high school. If so, submit a copy of the diploma. Question 3A–D asks the applicant to list his or her full educational history, including the school name, degree or certificate, field of study, dates of attendance, and credit hours. The Form I-944 instructions and the *USCIS*

Policy Manual state that if the applicant is including foreign education, he or she "should" include an equivalency report. In some cases, it may seem obvious that the applicant has graduated from the equivalent of high school or college. However, it is unclear if USCIS will reject or deny applications that are submitted without an equivalency evaluation. Practitioners should consider this, along with the time and expense involved in obtaining an evaluation, when determining what to include in the adjustment application.

The most difficult and time-consuming part of the preparation is not the form completion but rather gathering all the necessary documents. These could include: three years of tax transcripts from the applicant and one year for all household members; birth certificates or other proof of relationship to the household members; health insurance policies; treating physician's medical report; proof of current income; prior employment history; job offers; proof of assets and resources; letters signed by a senior bank officer detailing deposits and withdrawals over the last 12 months; credit reports and scores or proof of no report; proof of debts and liabilities; school diplomas and degrees; equivalency evaluations for foreign degrees; job licenses and certifications; proof of English-language proficiency; and documentation establishing that the applicant will not qualify for any of the designated public benefit programs after becoming an LPR.

Tips on Completing the Form DS-5540

In contrast to USCIS and the Form I-944, DOS has not prepared any formal instructions for completing the DS-5540. The only information the agency has provided regarding its interpretation of the interim final public charge regulation is contained in the FAM and on the agency's website. While Form I-944 must be submitted with the application for adjustment of status, the DS-5540 should be prepared and ready to submit at the time of the interview, if it is requested. At the present time, while DOS is in a transitionary period, the DS-5540 is considered "optional." Only one DS-5540 is required per family applying together; it should be completed by the "principal applicant."[16]

In many questions, like "What is your current yearly compensation," it is not obvious if "your" refers to the applicant or the applicant plus his or her household members. One approach is to treat the questions as though they pertain to all members of the family that are applying for an immigrant visa, as well as other household members, where relevant. Another is to define "your" as referring only to the applicant completing the form. In that case, the applicant lists his or her income, but not those of other family members. Without further clarification, there does not seem to be a definitive answer. It is recommended that practitioners be

---

[16] Supporting Statement for Paperwork Reduction Act Submission, Public Charge Questionnaire, OMB Number 1045-XXXX, DS-5540, at 16, reginfo.gov/public/do/PRAViewDocument?ref_nbr=202002-1405-002.

consistent within the form and consider annotating it to clarify if they are limiting the scope of each question to the principal applicant or including other household members.

Part 4. Your Assets, Resources, and Financial Status

Question 6 asks the applicant to list the reported gross income for each of the last three U.S. tax returns that he or she filed. While USCIS and Form I-944 insist on the submission of tax return transcripts, DOS and the DS-5540 allow the submission of tax transcripts or a copy of the complete tax return filed with the IRS.

Since total household income is considered when determining if the applicant meets the threshold of 125 percent of FPG, the DS-5540 should ask for all household members' combined reported income on the last three tax returns. One way to read Question 6 is to interpret "you" to include all the household members. In that case, include the combined gross income for every household member who filed a tax return and attach copies of those returns or transcripts.

Question 8 deals with income. Question 8A asks what the applicant's "yearly compensation" is in U.S. dollars from employment either in the United States or in some other country. Compensation—as opposed to salary—includes nonsalaried income from self-employment. While the FAM instructs the consular officer to only consider "income that will continue to be received after admission to the United States plus any potential income based on expected employment,"[17] that is not what Question 8A asks for. Applicants should, therefore, list yearly compensation without regard to whether it will continue after he or she is admitted to the United States as an LPR.

Part 5. Your Education and Skills

The DS-5540 does not ask about English language skills as Form I-944 does. But the FAM instructs the consular officer to consider "any language proficiency."[18] Therefore, if the applicant can speak and understand basic English, this should be communicated to the consulate in any cover letter, as well as during the consular interview. Using an interpreter to complete the DS-5540 does not mean that the applicant cannot communicate in English.

The form only requires immigrant visa applicants to include two documents: income tax transcripts and proof of health insurance, assuming they exist. But if the consular officer determines that additional documentary evidence is necessary, he or she may request that an applicant submit "evidence of bank deposits, ownership

17 9 FAM 302.8-2(B)(2)(e)(2)(a)(i).

18 9 FAM 302.8-2(B)(2)(f)(1)(a).

of property or real estate, ownership of stocks and bonds, insurance policies, or income from business investments, as well as those of any household members."[19]

Overview of Affidavit of Support

The affidavit-of-support requirements became an integral part of adjustment of status and immigrant visa processing after the change brought on by the 1996 immigration law.[20] The requirements affect all family-based visa applicants, and some employment-based applicants, by imposing burdensome paperwork requirements and other obligations. The law imposes four requirements to establish that an individual is not inadmissible as a public charge:

- The petitioner in all family-based immigrant visa petitions must submit an affidavit of support on Form I-864 or Form I-864EZ;
- The definition of a sponsor excludes anyone who is not a U.S. citizen, national, or lawful permanent resident (LPR), at least 18 years of age, and domiciled in the United States or a U.S. territory or possession;
- The sponsor must evidence "the means to maintain an annual income equal to at least 125 percent of the Federal poverty line"[21]; and
- The sponsor must agree to "provide support to maintain the sponsored alien at an annual income that is not less than 125 percent of the Federal poverty income line," reimburse any federal or state agency that provides a means-tested benefit to the sponsored foreign national, agree "to submit to the jurisdiction of any Federal or State court" for enforcement of the affidavit, and inform U.S. Citizenship and Immigration Services (USCIS) of any change of address.[22]

The affidavit-of-support requirements attempt to simplify the process of establishing financial eligibility by establishing an alternate three-step process for satisfying the income requirements. The first step is for the Form I-130 petitioner (who automatically becomes a sponsor) to demonstrate that he or she has sufficient household income, using the standards set forth below. If the sponsor is unable to satisfy the financial requirement through proof of income, he or she may proceed to steps two or three. Step two allows the sponsor to satisfy the financial requirement by counting certain assets belonging to the sponsor, the sponsored immigrant, or other household members. If the sponsor cannot demonstrate sufficient income or assets, the third step is securing a joint sponsor (cosponsor) who can satisfy the financial requirements.

---

19 9 FAM 302.8-2(B)(2)(e)(3)(a).

20 Illegal Immigration Reform and Immigrant Responsibility Act of 1996 (IIRAIRA), Pub. L. No. 104-208, div. C, 110 Stat. 3009–675 to 3009–680, §551, codified in INA §§212(a)(4), 213A.

21 INA §213A(f)(1)(E).

22 INA §213A(a)(1).

Form I-864EZ, Affidavit of Support Under Section 213A of the Act, may be used in lieu of the longer Form I-864 when the sponsor is petitioning for only one family member, is employed (not self-employed), will satisfy the financial requirements with income (not assets), and will be using only his or her income (not using other household members' or joint sponsors' income) to satisfy the financial requirements. Every reference to the Form I-864 in this chapter should be considered to include the alternative Form I-864EZ where appropriate.

Mandatory Filing Requirement

Who Is Affected

The statute requires almost all family-based visa applicants to submit the Form I-864 affidavit of support as a condition of admissibility.[23] Employment-based immigrant visa applicants are required to submit an affidavit if the applicant's relative either filed the Form I-140, Immigrant Petition for Alien Worker, or has a significant (five percent) ownership interest in the business entity that filed the petition.[24]

For family-based petitions, the affidavit requirement affects intending immigrants who "seek admission or adjustment of status under a visa number issued under section 201(b)(2) or 203(a)" of the INA. These two sections define eligibility for a family-based visa by categorizing the applicant as either an "immediate relative" of the petitioner or as fitting within one of the four "preference" categories.

The process for immigrating a family member is initiated by the U.S. citizen's or LPR's completing and filing of a Form I-130, Petition for Alien Relative. At the time the intending immigrant files for either adjustment of status or an immigrant visa, the petitioner named on the Form I-130 must execute and file an affidavit of support. The term "intending immigrant" is defined as "any beneficiary of an immigrant visa petition filed under section 204 of the [INA], including any alien who will accompany or follow-to-join the principal beneficiary."[25]

In other words, the petitioner must submit an affidavit of support for the principal beneficiary designated on the I-130 petition, as well as for the beneficiary's family members who will be immigrating under the same immigrant visa category. If the principal beneficiary is immigrating through one of the preference categories, his or her spouse and children may be granted an immigrant visa also. That derivative family member could be applying at the same time or within six months of the principal beneficiary (accompanying), or more than six months later (following-to-join).

---

23 INA §212(a)(4)(C)(ii).

24 INA §§212(a)(4)(D), 213A(f)(4)(A).

25 8 CFR §213a.1.

If the petitioner cannot demonstrate sufficient income or assets, as described below, then the petitioner has the right to obtain a joint sponsor who does satisfy the income requirements and agrees to be jointly and severally liable with the petitioner.

Who Is Not Affected

The affidavit of support is only required for persons seeking a family-based (and in limited circumstances an employment-based) immigrant visa. Therefore, the following immigrant visa applicants are *not* affected by the affidavit of support requirement:

- Applicants under the Cuban Adjustment Act
- Applicants under the Nicaraguan Adjustment and Central American Relief Act
- Applicants under the Haitian Refugee Immigration Fairness Act
- Special immigrant juveniles
- Diversity visa lottery applicants
- Persons granted asylum or refugee status
- Registry applicants
- Persons adjusting based on being granted cancellation of removal, or suspension of deportation

The regulations also specify that the affidavit of support requirement does not apply to widows and widowers applying for immigrant status based on prior marriage to a U.S. citizen.[26] The affidavit of support requirement does not apply to nonimmigrant visa applicants, such as those seeking a K or V visa. Fiancé(e)s who enter the United States on a K-1 visa and then marry the U.S. citizen petitioner within 90 days are allowed to file directly for adjustment of status.[27] They must submit an I-864 at the time they file for LPR status.[28]

There is an important exemption for intending immigrants who already have acquired 40 "qualifying quarters."[29] A qualifying quarter is a legal term relating to a unit of wage that, if earned in most types of employment, counts toward coverage for Social Security benefits. One *earns* up to four qualifying quarters in a calendar year. But the spouse and child may also be *credited* with the quarters earned by the spouse or parent: spouses may be credited with all the quarters earned by the other spouse during marriage, assuming the marriage did not end in divorce; children may be credited with all quarters earned by either or both parents until the

26 8 CFR §213a.2(a)(2)(ii)(A).

27 INA §245(d).

28 8 CFR §213a.2(a)(2)(i)(A), (b)(1).

29 INA §213A(a)(3)(B).

child turns 18. Because the affidavit of support requirements terminate when the sponsored immigrant earns or is credited with 40 qualifying quarters, intending immigrants who demonstrate through Social Security earnings statements that they have already satisfied that requirement do not have to submit an affidavit of support. Instead, they indicate eligibility for this exemption on the Form I-485, Application to Register Permanent Residence or Adjust Status and include a copy of the wage earner's Social Security earnings record.

Another exemption applies for children who will be deriving citizenship status pursuant to the Child Citizenship Act of 2000 immediately upon immigrating or adjusting status because they are under 18 and residing with at least one U.S. citizen parent.[30] These children will also indicate eligibility for the exemption on the Form I-485.

When the Affidavit Must be Filed

The affidavit must be filed at the time an intending immigrant is applying for an immigrant visa or adjustment of status.[31] Because all family-based adjustment applications are now filed with the National Benefits Center (NBC) via the Chicago lockbox, the Form I-864 must be submitted together with the Form I-485 and accompanying documents.[32] The affidavit of support must be sufficient both at the time of filing and at the time the adjustment application is adjudicated.[33] If processing at a U.S. consular office, the applicant must submit the Form I-864 to the National Visa Center (NVC) as part of the instruction package processing.

Definition of Sponsor

According to the statute, to qualify as a sponsor, one must satisfy three basic eligibility requirements. A sponsor must be:

- A U.S. citizen, national, or LPR;
- At least 18 years of age; and
- Domiciled within the United States or in any U.S. territory or possession.[34]

There are no exceptions to these requirements. Although a petitioner who is unable to satisfy the income requirements can obtain a joint sponsor who can satisfy them, this is not true for the citizenship/immigration status, age, and domicile requirements. Every sponsor and joint sponsor must satisfy these basic prerequisites.

---

30 8 CFR §213a.2(a)(2)(ii)(E).

31 8 CFR §213a.2(a)(1)(ii).

32 USCIS Memorandum, M. Aytes, *USCIS Policy Regarding Form I-864, Affidavit of Support* (Nov. 23, 2005), AILA I Doc. No. 05120210.

33 USCIS Memorandum, M. Aytes, *Consolidation of Policy Regarding USCIS Form I-864, Affidavit of Support (AFM Update AD06-20)* (June 27, 2006), AILA Doc. No. 06063013.

34 INA §213A(f)(1).

Citizen, National, or Lawful Permanent Resident

Because the sponsor must be a citizen, national, or LPR, the sponsor must be a natural person, and cannot be a corporation or other entity. Joint sponsors or relatives in employment-based petitions who are LPRs must submit proof of that status with the I-864 form.

The citizen/LPR requirement will not affect those family-based petitioners who can satisfy the income requirements; to sponsor a family member for immigration, the petitioner must be a citizen or LPR. However, for those petitioners who must obtain a joint sponsor, this requirement may serve to reduce the potential pool further. For example, nonimmigrants cannot serve as joint sponsors.

Domiciled in the United States

The sponsor must be domiciled in "any of the several States of the United States, the District of Columbia, or any territory or possession of the United States."[35] This requirement could prevent some U.S. citizens or LPRs residing outside the United States from filing a visa petition on behalf of another family member. To overcome this hurdle, it is important to read closely the definition of "domicile" and "residence," as well as the exceptions set forth in the interim regulation.

A domicile is defined as "the place where a sponsor has his or her principal residence, as defined in section 101(a)(33) of the [INA], with the intention to maintain that residence for the foreseeable future."[36] Residence, in turn, is defined as the person's "place of general abode," or the "principal, actual dwelling place in fact, without regard to intent."[37] Taken together, this means that sponsors residing temporarily outside the United States can still qualify to submit an I-864, provided they have a residence in the United States that they use as their "principal, actual dwelling place."

The term "United States" includes Puerto Rico, Guam, and the U.S. Virgin Islands.[38] The terms "territory" or "possession" are not specifically defined in the INA, but the term "outlying possession" is defined to include only American Samoa and the Swains Island.[39] In addition, the Northern Mariana Islands should be considered a territory or possession.

LPRs living abroad temporarily will be considered domiciled in the United States if they apply for and obtain the "preservation of residence" benefit set forth in INA

35 INA §213A(f)(1)(C).

36 8 CFR §213a.1.

37 INA §101(a)(33).

38 INA §101(a)(38).

39 INA §101(a)(29).

§316(b) or 317.[40] Section 316(b) relates to LPRs who have been present in the United States for at least one year after being admitted for permanent residence, but who contemplate being outside the United States for more than one year. To qualify for this benefit, the LPR must be employed or under contract with any of the following:

- The U.S. government;
- An American institution of research recognized by the U.S. attorney general;
- An American firm or corporation engaged in whole or in part in the development of foreign trade and commerce of the United States;
- A subsidiary of the above firm or corporation, more than 50 percent of whose stock is owned by an American firm or corporation; or
- A public international organization of which the United States is a member by treaty or statute and by which the person was not employed until after being an LPR.

In addition, the LPR must establish that the absence from the United States is on behalf of the employer and for the purpose set forth in the employment.

INA §317 relates to persons who are authorized to perform the ministerial or priestly functions of a religious denomination having a bona fide organization within the United States. Alternatively, they could be engaged as a missionary, brother, nun, or sister by a religious denomination or by an interdenominational mission organization having a bona fide organization within the United States. To qualify for this exception, the LPR must have been physically present and residing in the United States for at least one year prior to engaging in the above activities abroad, and their absence must have been for the purpose of performing these activities.

A citizen living abroad temporarily also may be considered domiciled in the United States if the person's employment meets requirements similar to those set forth above.[41] To qualify, the employment must be with one of the following:[42]

- The U.S. government;
- An American institution of research recognized by the U.S. attorney general;
- An American firm or corporation engaged in whole or in part in the development of foreign trade and commerce of the United States;
- A subsidiary of the above firm or corporation; or
- A public international organization of which the United States participates by treaty or statute.

---

40 8 CFR §213a.2(c)(1)(ii)(A).

41 *Id.*

42 INA §319(b)(1).

Alternatively, the citizen may be:[43]

- Authorized to perform the ministerial or priestly functions of a religious denomination having a bona fide organization within the United States; or
- Engaged solely as a missionary by a religious denomination or by an interdenominational mission organization having a bona fide organization within the United States.

If the citizen's or LPR's employment does not fall within the above exceptions, he or she will have to return to the United States and establish a domicile in this country before being able to qualify as a sponsor. Sponsors who are domiciled abroad nevertheless may submit an affidavit of support if they convince USCIS or the consular official that they will reestablish domicile in the United States on or before the date the intending immigrant obtains LPR status.[44] Sponsors who are U.S. citizens and who are accompanying the intending immigrant to the port of entry will be deemed to have established domicile in the United States; sponsors who are LPRs will also be so deemed unless the LPR is denied admission to the country.[45]

Consequences of Petitioner's Dying

Legislation enacted at the end of 2009 allows certain surviving family members who were residing in the United States at the time the petitioner died and who continue to reside here to have their pending I-130 petition or adjustment application adjudicated as if the petitioner were still alive.[46] If the petition had already been approved before the petitioner died, this section of the law also allows the beneficiary to request reinstatement of the petition, which was automatically revoked upon the death of the petitioner.

In addition, regulations pre-dating this statutory change provide relief for those who do not meet these residency requirements but whose petitioner died after the petition was approved. The beneficiary may request that USCIS reinstate a petition that was automatically revoked if such revocation would be "inappropriate" based on humanitarian grounds.[47] This form of relief, referred to as humanitarian reinstatement, would be available to those beneficiaries residing abroad at the time the petitioner died or who subsequently left the United States.

In both situations, however, the beneficiary must submit a substitute affidavit of support from another close relative. Family members of the intending immigrant

43 *Id.*

44 8 CFR §213a.2(c)(1)(ii)(B).

45 *Id.*

46 FY10 DHS Appropriations Act, Pub. L. No. 111-83, 123 Stat. 2142, §568(d) (2009), adding INA §204(*l*).

47 8 CFR §205.1(a)(3)(i)(C).

who can act as substitute sponsors include the following: spouse, parent, mother-in-law, father-in-law, sibling, child (at least 18 years old), son, daughter, son-in-law, daughter-in-law, sister-in-law, brother-in-law, grandparent, grandchild, or legal guardian.[48] Someone who is filing as a substitute sponsor should the check box 1f in Part 1 of the Form I-864 and submit proof of the relationship to the intending immigrant.

Legally Enforceable Contract

The statute provides that the affidavit will be legally enforceable against the sponsor in actions brought by either the sponsored immigrant or a federal, state, or "other entity" that provides a means-tested benefit to the sponsored immigrant.[49] In other words, the sponsored immigrant can sue the sponsor to enforce the maintenance agreement. In addition, should the immigrant ever obtain a means-tested benefit, the agency or entity that provided it can also seek reimbursement from the sponsor.

Enforceable by the Sponsored Immigrant

After adjustment of status or admission to the United States as an LPR, the sponsored immigrant can require the sponsor to maintain him or her at "an annual income that is not less than 125 percent of the Federal poverty guideline."[50] Even persons on active duty in the U.S. armed forces, who must only demonstrate the means to maintain an annual income equal to 100 percent of the poverty line,[51] must agree to maintain the sponsored immigrant at this level. It has been interpreted to mean that the sponsor must provide support equivalent to 125 percent of the poverty line for a family of one.[52] Based on the 2020 federal poverty guidelines, this amounts to $15,950.

Where the sponsor executed affidavits of support for other family members who accompanied the principal beneficiary, it is also unclear whether the sponsor must maintain each immigrant at the $15,950 level (based on the 2020 guidelines) or whether he or she can add them together and apply the household formula. In other words, where the person sponsored a total of four immigrants, must the sponsor maintain each immigrant at the $15,950 level (for a total of $63,800) or may the sponsor satisfy the requirement by maintaining them collectively at the 125 percent level for a household of four ($32,750, based on 2020 guidelines)? Until the courts or USCIS provides clarification, we should assume that the sponsor is obligated to maintain each sponsored immigrant at the $15,950 level.

48 INA §213A(f)(5)(B).

49 INA §213A(e).

50 INA §213A(a)(1)(A).

51 INA §213A(f)(3).

52 *Stump v. Stump*, 2005 U.S. Dist. LEXIS 26022 (N.D. Ind. Oct. 25, 2005).

The sponsor should be able to provide either cash or in-kind benefits, such as housing, food, or clothes. Also, the sponsor should be able to reduce the amount of support by any income or benefits the sponsored immigrant is receiving from other sources. For example, if the sponsored immigrant is working and earning an annual income of $5,000, the sponsor must only provide, based on the 2020 guidelines, maintenance equivalent to $10,950.

It appears that the sponsored immigrant bears no affirmative duty to mitigate damages, although only two courts have addressed this issue. The first case found that the sponsored immigrant had sought employment to mitigate damages, though the court failed to hold that the plaintiff had a duty to do so.[53] The second case held that the sponsored immigrant has no burden to mitigate damages.[54] The court refused to read into the law a requirement that the sponsored immigrant be actively seeking employment. The court found that the goal of the statute was to prevent the admission of immigrants who might become public charges in the future. This goal was best served, according to the court, by not imposing additional burdens on the sponsored immigrant. Instead, by making the obligation air-tight, it might force sponsors to be more prudent before entering into these contracts.

When there is a sponsor and a joint sponsor, they each accept joint and several liability to maintain the sponsored immigrant at the 125 percent of poverty level.[55] For example, in 2020 the sponsor and joint sponsor must collectively ensure that the sponsored immigrant is receiving a minimum of $15,950. The sponsored immigrant can elect to enforce the affidavit agreement against either the sponsor or the joint sponsor. However, he or she can collect a judgment only up to 125 percent of the poverty line.

Enforceable by a Federal, State, or Other Entity

If the sponsored immigrant receives a means-tested benefit, the agency or entity that provided it may seek reimbursement from the sponsor. This means that should the immigrant suffer a debilitating injury or illness, the sponsor could be required to reimburse the full amount of any means-tested medical, cash, or in-kind benefits paid by the government agency or entity.

The term "federal means-tested program" has been defined to include only five programs: Supplemental Security Income (SSI), Medicaid, Temporary Assistance to Needy Families (TANF), Supplemental Nutrition Assistance Program (SNAP) (formerly food stamps), and the State Children's Health Insurance Program

---

53 *Id.*

54 *Liu v. Mund*, No. 11-1453 (7th Cir. July 12, 2012).

55 8 CFR §213a.1.

(SCHIP).[56] Each state is encouraged to identify all state programs that satisfy the definition of means-tested, and to issue public notices of those determinations.[57]

Enforcement in General

The affidavit of support is a contract between the sponsor and the federal government. The intended beneficiaries are the sponsored immigrant and any federal, state, or local government agency or private entity that provides a means-tested benefit to the sponsored immigrant. Any of the intended beneficiaries may bring a civil action to enforce the contract in the appropriate court.[58] By signing the Form I-864, the sponsor also agrees to submit to the personal jurisdiction of any federal or state court in a suit brought by such agency or entity.[59]

Any agency or entity seeking reimbursement for a means-tested benefit provided to the sponsored immigrant must notify the sponsor of the amount owed,[60] which can be the "unreimbursed costs" of such a benefit.[61] For example, if the sponsored immigrant has received SSI benefits, based on age or disability, the federal government can request that the sponsor reimburse the full amount of the monthly benefit. If Medicaid covered a sponsored immigrant's hospital or physician's indebtedness, both the state and the federal government can seek reimbursement for their respective share of the costs.

Legally Enforceable

Although Congress has stated that the affidavit of support form is legally enforceable, that does not make it so. At least three courts held that INS's long-standing affidavit of support, Form I-134, was unenforceable against the sponsor in actions brought by the sponsored immigrant or the states to recover benefits paid to the sponsored immigrant.[62]

Even though the sponsor who executed the I-134 affidavit promised to be "willing and able to receive, maintain and support" the sponsored immigrant, and to "guarantee that [the sponsored immigrant] will not become a public charge," the courts held that the affidavit of support did not form a legal contract, but represented only a moral obligation. They based this on the wording of the affidavit, the lack of intention by the affiant to be contractually bound, and the fact that the affidavit

56 64 Fed. Reg. 28675, 28679–80 (May 26, 1999).

57 8 CFR §213a.4(b).

58 INA §213A(e).

59 Form I-864, pt. 8, Sponsor's Declaration and Certification, para. C (version dated Oct. 15, 2019).

60 8 CFR §213a.4(a)(1).

61 INA §213A(b)(1)(A).

62 *See, e.g.*, *Dept. of Mental Hygiene v. Renal*, 6 N.Y.2d 791 (1959); *State v. Binder*, 356 Mich. 73 (1959); *County of San Diego v. Viloria*, 276 Cal. App. 2d 350, 80 Cal. Rptr. 869 (1969).

was only one form of evidence consular and INS agents considered in determining whether an immigrant was likely to become a public charge.

Several lower courts have upheld the enforceability of the Form I-864,[63] but it is still possible that it could be found to be unenforceable, since so many of the key contractual terms are undefined. These terms include the duration of the liability, which could extend into perpetuity; the amount of any potential financial liability; and the factors that could cause liability, which will largely be determined by future events beyond the control of the affiant.

All household members who are party to the Form I-864A, Contract Between Sponsor and Household Member, must agree to be jointly and severally liable for any reimbursement obligation that the sponsor may incur. They are also jointly and severally liable on a claim brought by either the sponsored immigrant or any agency or entity that provides a means-tested program to the sponsored immigrant. They must submit to the personal jurisdiction of any court hearing the matter. The sponsor may commence a legal action against any of the household members to enforce the I-864A, as may the sponsored immigrant and any agency or entity that provides a means-test benefit program to the sponsored immigrant.[64]

Signing the Form I-864A does not make the person a "sponsor" in the legal sense of that word. In other words, these other household members should not have to meet the domicile or citizenship/permanent residency requirements, nor do they have to file change of address forms with USCIS.[65]

Statutory Requirements for Completing the Form

Satisfying the Minimum Income Requirement

The statute mandates that the sponsor demonstrate the means to maintain an annual income equal to at least 125 percent of the federal poverty income line.[66] Petitioners who are active duty members of the U.S. armed forces and who are petitioning for their spouse or child must only demonstrate that they have an annual income equal to at least 100 percent of the poverty line.[67]

---

63 *Cheshire v. Cheshire*, No. 3:05-cv-00453-TJC-MCR, 2006 U.S. Dist. LEXIS 26602 (M.D. Fla. 2006); *Stump v. Stump*, 2005 U.S. Dist. LEXIS 26022 (N.D. Ind. Oct. 25, 2005); *Schwartz v. Schwartz*, No. CIV-04-770-M, 2005 WL 1242171 (W.D. Okla. 2005); *Tornheim v. Kohn*, No. 00 CV 5084 (SJ), 2002 WL 482534 (E.D.N.Y. 2002); *Davis v. Davis*, No. WD-04-020, 2004 WL 2924344 (Ohio Ct. App. 2004).

64 8 CFR §213a.2(c)(2)(i)(C)(2); Form I-864A, p. 3.

65 8 CFR §213a.2(c)(2)(i)(C)(1).

66 INA §213A(f)(1)(E).

67 INA §213A(f)(3).

Determining Federal Poverty Line

The federal poverty income line is established by the Office of Management and Budget and is published in guidelines updated each year by the Department of Health and Human Services.[68] The amount of income necessary to be above the poverty income line depends on where the sponsor resides (either in any of the 48 contiguous states, in Alaska, or in Hawaii) and the size of the sponsor's family. The poverty income guidelines for 2020, for example, were published on January 17, 2020, and became effective for immigration purposes on March 1, 2020.[69] Those guidelines, and the corresponding levels for 125 percent of the poverty line, are included as Appendix 8.

Determining Family Unit Size

The key to applying the federal poverty income guidelines and satisfying the 125 percent rule is knowing which household members or dependents must be counted in determining family unit size and whose income can be included. Obviously, the more household members who must be counted, the higher the income that must be demonstrated; the more household members' income that can be included, the easier to satisfy the financial means requirement.

The statute offers basic guidance in determining the size of the family unit. It defines family unit to include the sponsor, the sponsor's household members (both family and nonfamily dependents), and "other dependents and aliens sponsored by that sponsor" who may not be part of the household.[70]

The regulations clarify that the family unit size includes the following persons, regardless of their residence:

- Sponsor
- Sponsor's spouse
- Sponsor's unmarried children under 21, unless they are emancipated
- Persons whom the sponsor has claimed as a dependent on the most recent federal income tax return
- The intending immigrant and all accompanying, derivative family members
- Immigrants who have obtained LPR status based on the sponsor's filing of an I-864, assuming the contractual obligations have not terminated.[71]

In addition, the sponsor *may* include other "relatives" residing with the sponsor if it is advantageous to include their income, as explained below. The term "relative"

---

68 *See* INA §213A(h); 42 USC §9902(2); 8 CFR §213a.1 (definition of federal poverty line).

69 85 Fed. Reg. 3060 (Jan. 17, 2018).

70 INA §213A(f)(6)(A)(iii).

71 8 CFR §213a.1 (definition of household size).

is defined to include only the sponsor's spouse, child, adult son/daughter, parent, or sibling.[72]

Counting Income

In determining the amount of household income that can be considered in satisfying the 125 percent requirement, the regulation allows the inclusion of income from the sponsor's spouse and of any other person included in determining the sponsor's household size.[73] In order to count the income of any of these household members, the person must be at least 18 years old and, except for the intending immigrant, execute a Form I-864A.[74] If the household member is not the intending immigrant but is the sponsor's parent, sibling, or son/daughter (other than claimed dependent), he or she must submit proof of that relationship and current residence with the sponsor.[75]

None of these household members, however, need to have been residing with the sponsor for any specific period of time. If the household member is the intending immigrant, other than the sponsor's spouse or claimed dependent, and signs a Form I-864A, that person also must submit proof of current residence. If the household member is the sponsor's spouse, there is no requirement that he or she be residing with the sponsor or submit proof of relationship.

Household members who execute Form I-864A do not have to be U.S. citizens, nationals, or LPRs.[76] Nor is there any specific requirement that they be residing in the United States with lawful immigration status, even though USCIS often tries to impose such a requirement. The Form I-864A only requires that the household member provide a Social Security number if he or she has one. However, he or she must provide the prior year's tax return.

The regulations clarify that the intending immigrant does not need to execute a Form I-864A unless he or she has a derivative spouse or child who will be immigrating "with the intending immigrant."[77] In that situation, the intending immigrant needs to execute an I-864A affidavit to ensure that his or her income may be relied upon to support the derivative family member(s).

To count the intending immigrant's income, he or she must either be residing with the sponsor or be the sponsor's spouse or claimed dependent. But in all circumstances the intending immigrant's income must be derived from "lawful employment in the United States or from some other lawful source that will continue to be available to

72 8 CFR §213a.1 (definition of relative).

73 8 CFR §213a.2(c)(2)(i)(C)(1).

74 8 CFR §213a.2(c)(2)(i)(C)(1), (3).

75 8 CFR §§213a.1 (definition of household size), 213a.2(c)(2)(i)(C)(5).

76 8 CFR §213a.2(c)(2)(i)(C)(1).

77 8 CFR §213a.2(c)(2)(i)(C)(3)..

the intending immigrant after he or she acquires permanent resident status."[78] The latest USCIS memorandum clarifies that it means "authorized employment," or that performed while the worker had an employment authorization document.[79]

This means that most intending immigrants who are residing abroad will be precluded from counting their income as part of the sponsor's total household income, because they will likely be changing employment once they immigrate. The regulation specifies that offers of employment are not sufficient to meet the intending immigrant's burden of showing continuing employment.[80]

Applying the Income Test

The regulation and form place emphasis on *current* income versus that reported on prior tax returns. The step-by-step instructions to the Form I-864 explain that the sponsor is to enter his or her "current individual, earned or retirement, annual income."[81] In most cases, this will be "expected income for the current year."[82] If the sponsor will be relying on the income of the intending immigrant or other household members, it is their current income that will be listed on the Form I-864 and I-864A. The final rule stresses that it is this "reasonably expected household income" that shall be given the "greatest evidentiary weight."[83] Tax returns or other documentation merely will serve as evidence of the likelihood that the sponsor will be able to maintain this income in the future.

The sponsor does not have to be employed. The Form I-864 requires the sponsor to state whether he or she is employed, self-employed, retired, or unemployed.[84] Income could come from almost any source, including interest income and dividends, alimony, or child support.

Question 23a in Part 6 on the Form I-864 (version dated Oct. 15, 2019) requires the sponsor to check a box indicating whether he or she has filed a tax return for each of the three most recent tax years and is attaching a photocopy or transcript of the most recent return. There is an optional box indicating that he or she is voluntarily attaching photocopies of the tax returns for the second and third most recent tax years. Question 25 allows the sponsor to check a box indicating if he or she did not have a tax liability for any of those three years. If the reason is due to insufficient

78 8 CFR §213a.1 (definition of household income).

79 INS Memorandum, M. Cronin, *Clarification of Service Policy Concerning I-864 Affidavit of Support* (Mar. 7, 2000), AILA Doc. No. 00032704.

80 8 CFR §213a.1 (definition of household income).

81 Form I-864, Instructions, p. 7 (version dated Oct. 15, 2019).

82 *Id.*

83 8 CFR §213a.2(c)(2)(ii)(C).

84 Form I-864, pt. 6, q. 1–7 (version dated Oct, 15, 2019).

income, the instructions tell the sponsor to "attach a typed or printed explanation,"[85] so presumably he or she would qualify to check the first box.

If the sponsor is exempt from tax filing because of some other reason, he or she must "attach a typed or printed explanation including evidence of the exemption and how [he or she is] subject to it."[86] The sponsor in that case still may submit other evidence of annual income. The sponsor or household member must establish by a preponderance of the evidence that he or she had no duty to file the tax return.[87] Being exempt from the income tax filing requirement does not exempt the sponsor from the affidavit of support filing requirement.[88]

The sponsor must list on the Form I-864 the total income for the last three tax years as reported on those tax returns, since the returns will be used as an indication of the sponsor's ability to maintain that income over time. If estimated current annual income appears significantly higher than past reported income, or if the income varies widely from year to year, it will likely raise suspicions with an adjudicator. In those cases, expect USCIS or consular official to request additional proof, such as pay stubs or an employer's letter. Otherwise, those employment records need not be submitted with the affidavit of support.

The instructions also specify which line from the tax return should be used when reporting "total" income—either gross or adjusted gross—and explain that it is only the federal tax return that must be submitted.[89] The sponsor or household member should not submit a foreign income-tax return unless the person had no federal tax liability and wants to use the return to verify current income.[90] The sponsor may submit either a plain (uncertified) Internal Revenue Service transcript or a photocopy of the tax return from his or her own records.[91] Include the W-2, Form 1099, and all other attachments and schedules that were submitted with the federal return.[92]

The sponsor may not count any means-tested benefits (SSI, Medicaid, TANF, SNAP, or CHIP) as income, but he or she may include retirement benefits, unemployment compensation, workers' compensation, or other similar benefits.[93] Earlier policy memos explained that sponsors are able to include both taxable and nontaxable income, such as disability and child support payments, as part of the

85 *Id.* at p. 9.

86 *Id. See also* 8 CFR §213a.2(c)(2)(i)(B).

87 8 CFR §213a.2(c)(2)(i)(D).

88 8 CFR §213a.2(c)(2)(i)(B).

89 *Id.*

90 *Id.*

91 *Id.*

92 8 CFR §213a.2(c)(2)(i)(A).

93 71 Fed. Reg. 35731, 35738 (June 21, 2006).

total household income.[94] Until USCIS or DOS issues further guidance, proceed as if those interpretations are still in effect.

Every sponsor who executes a Form I-864 and every household member who executes a Form I-864A must submit a copy of their most recent tax return.[95] Many intending immigrants, however, do not need to submit a Form I-864A. It does not appear that the sponsor has to submit the tax return of the intending immigrant if his or her income is being included and he or she did not execute a Form I-864A. In those cases, the sponsor simply includes the intending immigrant's income in Part 6 of the I-864, checks box #22, and enters the total household income on line #20. But given that the intending immigrant must either be the sponsor's spouse or be residing with the sponsor, in most situations the intending immigrant either will have filed a joint tax return or be listed as a dependent on the sponsor's return. Bear in mind that the intending immigrant still must submit proof that the "lawful" employment will continue from the same source after he or she obtains LPR status.

What happens when the affidavit of support isn't examined for sufficiency until months or even years after it was submitted? The regulation clarifies that the adjudicating official must consider the sufficiency of the affidavit of support based on the income reported for the year the Form I-864 or Form I-864A was submitted, not on the sponsor's income on the date the application for adjustment of status or an immigrant visa is adjudicated.[96] Similarly, adjudicators must use the federal poverty guidelines in effect at the time the affidavit of support is submitted, not at the time it is considered for sufficiency.[97]

If more than one year has passed from the date of submission to the date of adjudication, USCIS or DOS officials may, in the exercise of discretion, request additional evidence, such as income tax returns for the most recent tax year.[98] In those cases, it will be the sponsor's income and poverty guidelines in effect for the year the adjustment or immigrant visa application is adjudicated that will control, not those for the year the affidavit of support was originally submitted.[99]

All derivative beneficiaries who will accompany (i.e., immigrate at the same time as or within six months of) the principal beneficiary must be included on the Form I-864.[100] Each principal and derivative beneficiary must have a separate affidavit of support filed in his or her case, but accompanying derivatives may submit a

---

94 DOS Cable, *I-864 Affidavit of Support—Update No. 17: More Q's and A's*, State 133584 (July 1998), AILA Doc. No. 98081190; INS Memorandum, *Additional Guidance #1—Affidavit of Support* (Mar. 12, 1998).

95 8 CFR §213a.2(c)(2)(i)(A), (C)(4).

96 8 CFR §213a.2(a)(1)(v)(A).

97 *Id.*

98 8 CFR §213a.2(a)(1)(v)(B).

99 *Id.*

100 8 CFR §213a.2(a)(1)(iv).

photocopy of the one submitted for the principal.[101] They do not need to submit a photocopy of the supporting documentation. The photocopy of the Form I-864 does not need to contain an original signature. Each principal beneficiary (e.g., petitioner's mother and father) must submit a separate affidavit of support bearing an original signature.[102]

The I-864, I-864EZ, and I-864A forms do not have to be signed in front of a notary or consular official. The sponsor or household member merely swears under penalty of perjury that the information provided is correct.

Counting Assets

The statute's "flexibility" provision allows for the disclosure of "significant" assets that are "available for the support of the sponsored alien."[103] If the sponsor is unable to show income at or greater than 125 percent of poverty, the sponsor can satisfy the financial means requirement by submitting proof of significant assets.[104] These assets can be owned by either the sponsor, other household members who executed Form I-864A, or the intending immigrant.[105] It is not necessary for the intending immigrant to execute a Form I-864A to count his or her assets.

If the sponsor is a U.S. citizen and the intending immigrant is the sponsor's spouse or child age 18 years or over, the value of these assets must be at least three times the shortfall between the sponsor's household income and the federal poverty line for the sponsor's household size.[106] If the intending immigrant is an orphan to be formally adopted in the United States, the value of the assets must equal only the shortfall between the sponsor's household income and the federal poverty line for the sponsor's household size.[107] In all other situations, the assets must be at least five times the shortfall.[108]

To qualify as "available," the assets must be "readily converted into cash within one year."[109] Examples of such assets include savings in a bank or other financial institution; stocks, bonds, and certificates of deposit; real estate; and personal property.[110] The sponsor must submit the appropriate proof of ownership, which could include bank statements, stock certificates, deeds, titles to vehicles, and

---

101 8 CFR §213a.2(g)(1).

102 8 CFR §213a.2(a)(1)(iii).

103 INA §213A(f)(6)(A)(ii).

104 8 CFR §213a.2(c)(2)(iii)(A).

105 8 CFR §213a.2(c)(2)(iii)(B).

106 8 CFR §213a.2(c)(2)(iii)(B)(1).

107 8 CFR §213a.2(c)(2)(iii)(B)(2).

108 8 CFR §213a.2(c)(2)(iii)(B)(3).

109 9 *Foreign Affairs Manual* (FAM) 302.8-2(B)(1).

110 8 CFR §213a.2(c)(2)(iii)(B).

sales receipts or other proof of purchase.[111] The sponsor must include any liens and liabilities relating to the property, and a statement indicating date of acquisition, where the property is located, and the value of each asset.[112]

If the sponsor is counting a vehicle as an asset, he or she must own more than one, and at least one vehicle is not included as an asset.[113] In estimating the current worth of a vehicle, the "blue book" value should be the standard measurement.

Use of Joint Sponsors

If the petitioner is unable to satisfy the minimum income requirements, through proof of household income or assets, the last option is to obtain a joint sponsor. Failure to satisfy the income test and securement of a joint sponsor does not relieve the petitioner of the obligation of filing a Form I-864. Both the petitioner and the joint sponsor will be executing a Form I-864, and each will be fully liable for maintaining the sponsored immigrant and for means-tested benefits he or she obtains.

Every intending immigrant—whether a principal beneficiary or derivative—may have only one joint sponsor.[114] But in family-based preference category cases comprised of a principal beneficiary and at least one accompanying derivative, the sponsor may use up to two joint sponsors.[115] The sponsor may apportion the financial burden between the two joint sponsors, so that, for example, one joint sponsor bears responsibility for the principal beneficiary and the second joint sponsor bears responsibility for the derivative. In that situation, the first joint sponsor would include the principal beneficiary as a household member and would bear the financial responsibility for that person, while the second joint sponsor would include the derivative.[116] Each joint sponsor would identify on the Form I-864 the intending immigrant(s) that he or she is sponsoring.

Each joint sponsor must execute a separate Form I-864 and satisfy the income requirements independently. In other words, the petitioner and/or cosponsor(s) may not pool their income to arrive at a total that satisfies the 125 percent of poverty requirement.

The statutory "flexibility" provision also applies to joint sponsors, allowing them to submit proof of significant assets if their income is insufficient. The joint sponsor may combine his or her assets with that of the intending immigrant and combine his or her income and assets to that of household members who execute the I-864A.[117]

---

111 *See* 9 FAM 302.8-2(B)(3).

112 *Id.*

113 Form I-864 Instructions, p. 9 (version dated Oct. 15, 2019).

114 8 CFR §213a.2(c)(2)(iii)(C).

115 *Id.*

116 *Id.*

117 *Id.*

USCIS and State Department Discretion

USCIS and consular officials maintain a fair amount of discretion in determining whether the affidavit will be sufficient. The most important factors will be current job status and earnings from current and past employment, as reflected on the three most recent tax returns. INS stated that "in most instances, sponsors will be found eligible if they are employed and demonstrate the ability, along with household members who sign a contract on Form I-864A, to earn income at or above 125 percent of the poverty line for the number of persons who will be supported."[118] In most cases the sponsor will need to be employed, unless the sponsor's income from sources other than employment, the sponsor's assets, or the income/assets from other household members who execute the Form I-864A are sufficient. USCIS's final regulation on public charge added a provision allowing the agency to consider the likelihood that the sponsor will provide financial support in the future.[119] As a result, USCIS has indicated in the *Policy Manual* that it looks at additional factors, including the sponsor's relationship to the adjustment applicant, whether the sponsor has filed for bankruptcy, received public benefits or fee waivers, and whether the sponsor has filed an affidavit of support on behalf of anyone else.[120]

The regulations include a provision that seems to give USCIS and consular officials the power to determine that a sponsor has not satisfied the financial requirements, even if he or she appears to pass the income or assets tests.

Consular and USCIS officials may reject an affidavit of support whose projected income meets the financial requirements, but only if, based on specific facts, it is "reasonable to infer that the sponsor will not be able to maintain his or her household income" at the necessary level.[121] In addition, even when the affidavit of support is found to be sufficient, the intending immigrant may be found inadmissible under INA §212(a)(4) as likely to become a public charge if "specific facts" support such a "reasonable inference."[122]

Termination of the Contract

The liability of the sponsor executing the affidavit of support form terminates only when the sponsored immigrant:

- Becomes a U.S. citizen;
- Earns or is credited with a total of 40 qualifying quarters, as defined by Social Security law;
- Dies;

---

118 INS Fact Sheet, "Affidavit of Support, Form I-864" (Oct. 20, 1997).

119 8 CFR §212.22(b)(7).

120 8 *USCIS Policy Manual* pt. G, ch. 13.D.

121 8 CFR §213a.2(c)(2)(ii)(C).

122 8 CFR §213a.2(c)(2)(iv).

- Loses or abandons LPR status and departs from the United States; or
- Is ordered removed but readjusts status in immigration proceedings through submission of a new Form I-864.[123]

The statute allows termination of the contract on the sponsor's death.[124] However, future liability of the sponsor's estate for actions brought by the sponsored immigrant or agencies seeking reimbursement likely will be a matter of state law interpretation. In any event, the regulations provide that the sponsor's estate is not relieved from liability for any reimbursement obligation that accrued before the sponsor's death.[125]

Abandonment or loss of LPR status can occur through affirmative misconduct or departure from the United States. Misconduct could include the commission of crimes, fraud, or other miscellaneous acts. Abandonment through departure depends on the length of time the LPR has been absent from the United States and his or her intention as to whether the absence is temporary.

Note that a divorce will not nullify the sponsorship agreement. Thus, a spouse who sponsors an immigrant will remain liable under the affidavit until one of the conditions listed above occurs. This may result in a particular hardship for battered spouses, who might otherwise be inclined to divorce the abusing spouse. Divorce cuts off the ability of the sponsor to credit his or her qualifying quarters to the sponsored immigrant and thus terminate the contract sooner.

There is at least one other possible way for the sponsor to be relieved of further liability, and that is through discharge in bankruptcy. The general rule is that all debts, unless specifically exempted by federal statute, are dischargeable in bankruptcy. The exceptions provision of the bankruptcy code does not appear to prohibit the discharge of the types of debts envisioned by the affidavit of support process.

It is significant to note that there is no requirement that the sponsored immigrant, or any federal agency, notify the sponsor when any of the above conditions have been satisfied. In other words, there appears to be no easy way for the sponsor to learn when his or her obligations or liability under the Form I-864 have ended. Information regarding the sponsored immigrant's, or his or her spouse's or parent's, earnings record on file with the Social Security Administration is protected by the federal Privacy Act.[126] Comparable information regarding the sponsored immigrant's eligibility for, or obtaining, naturalization similarly may be blocked. Although USCIS will provide automated information to agencies and entities that will facilitate their enforcing the sponsor's obligation to reimburse the cost of means-tested programs, there is no equivalent exchange of information to a sponsor

123 8 CFR §213a.2(e)(2)(i).

124 8 CFR §213a.2(e)(2)(ii).

125 8 CFR §213a.2(e)(3).

126 5 USC §552a.

defending against those actions or maintenance actions brought by the sponsored immigrant.

The sponsor's or household member's contractual obligations under the affidavit of support do not begin until the intending immigrant obtains LPR status. The affidavit is not binding upon execution and submission. Therefore, the sponsor or household member may withdraw the affidavit at any point before the intending immigrant is granted LPR status based on the submission of the affidavit of support.[127]

Change of Address

Sponsors who change their address have a continuing obligation to inform USCIS and the state where the sponsored immigrant is residing within 30 days of the address change.[128] Those who do not are subject to stiff civil fines. Only persons who execute the Form I-864 are required to file the change of address form—not those who execute the Form I-864A. Potential fines range from $250 to $2,000 for the first failure to report; if the failure is with knowledge that the sponsored immigrant has received a means-tested program, then the fines increase to between $2,000 and $5,000.[129]

USCIS has created a form specifically for this purpose: Form I-865, Sponsor's Notice of Change of Address.[130] The sponsor completes the one-page form and mails it to the appropriate USCIS service center that has jurisdiction over the sponsor's new address.

Where to File

If the visa applicant is applying for adjustment of status, the Form I-864 and supporting documents are filed with the Form I-485. There is no separate filing fee for the Form I-864.

If the applicant is consular processing, the I-864 is filed by the sponsor with the NVC as part of the documentary and form submission process. The NVC notifies the I-130 petitioner of the $120 fee and instructs him or her where and how to file the completed form. The NVC will do a technical review of the completed form and supporting documents—not a determination of whether the 125 percent requirement is satisfied—and forward them to the consulate if they satisfy the requirements.

127 8 CFR §213a.2(e), (f).

128 INA §213A(d)(1); 8 CFR §213a.3(a)(1).

129 INA §213A(d)(2).

130 *See* 8 CFR §213a.3(a)(1).

CHAPTER 9

SELF-PETITIONS FOR ABUSED SPOUSES, CHILDREN, AND PARENTS

Domestic violence occurs in all ethnic communities and at all economic levels, and immigrant women and children are particularly vulnerable to it. For years, abusive U.S. citizens and lawful permanent residents (LPRs) could use immigration as another means of controlling the victim, because only they could initiate the family immigration process. Thus, the abuser might refuse to file a visa petition for his or her spouse or might threaten to withdraw a visa petition if the victim reported the abuse or sought help. The abuser also might threaten to report undocumented victims to the immigration authorities or to separate the victim from his or her children. This presented the victim with two bad options: either leave the abuser and abandon any legal right to remain in the United States or remain in the abusive relationship in the hope that such perseverance would eventually result in obtaining lawful immigration status.

With the Violence Against Women Act of 1994 (VAWA),[1] however, Congress recognized the plight of abused immigrants and their children. VAWA amended the Immigration and Nationality Act (INA) by adding two means for abused immigrant spouses and children of U.S. citizens and LPRs to obtain permanent residence. The first provision allows the abused immigrant spouse or child to self-petition before U.S. Citizenship and Immigration Services (USCIS), rather than having to rely on the U.S. citizen or LPR abusive spouse or parent to file the petition.[2] The second provision allows the abused immigrant to obtain residence by applying for cancellation of removal with the immigration court under relaxed requirements.[3] The applicant must have resided in the United States for three years, rather than for the 10 years required for regular cancellation of removal, and need show only extreme hardship to the applicant or qualifying relatives, rather than the stricter hardship standard applied in regular cancellation. VAWA also mandates the evidentiary standard to be used in evaluating applications for relief by requiring USCIS and immigration judges to consider "any credible evidence" relevant to the self-petition or cancellation application.[4]

Congress has expanded the protections for battered spouses and children in three subsequent pieces of legislation: the Battered Immigrant Women Protection Act of 2000[5] (part of the Violence Against Women Act of 2000 (VAWA 2000)), the

1 Pub. L. No. 103-322, tit. IV, 108 Stat. 1796, 1902–55.

2 INA §204(a)(1)(A)(ii)–(vii), (B)(ii)–(v).

3 INA §240A(b)(2).

4 INA §§204(a)(1)(J); 240A(b)(2)(D).

5 Pub. L. No. 106-386, §§1501–13, 114 Stat. 1464, 1518–37 (Oct. 28, 2000).

Violence Against Women Reauthorization Act of 2005 (VAWA 2005),[6] and the Violence Against Women Reauthorization Act of 2013 (VAWA 2013).[7] It is important to note that because USCIS has not yet issued regulations to implement the 2000 amendments, the existing regulations conflict at some points with current law. Additionally, although VAWA 2005 at section 828 directs that regulations implementing both VAWA 2000 and VAWA 2005 be promulgated within six months of enactment (i.e., by July 5, 2006), to date no regulations have been published.

This chapter will address the requirements and procedure for self-petitions by abused spouses, children, and parents, and for obtaining immigrant visas based on those self-petitions.[8]

Self-Petitioning

Who Can Apply

VAWA amended the INA to allow certain abused spouses, children, and parents to self-petition for permanent residency.[9] The following persons are eligible to self-petition under VAWA:

- Abused spouses of U.S. citizens or LPRs
- Spouses of U.S. citizens or LPRs whose children have been abused by the U.S. citizen or LPR spouse
- Abused "intended spouses"[10] of U.S. citizens and LPRs
- Abused children of U.S. citizens or LPRs
- Abused parents of U.S. citizens who qualify as immediate relatives

Moreover, applicants in the first four of the foregoing categories may include their children as derivative beneficiaries, even if the children are not related to the abuser and even if the children have not been abused.[11]

---

6 Pub. L. No. 109-162, §§3(a), 801–34, 119 Stat. 2960, 2964–71, 3053–77 (Jan. 5, 2006), as amended by Pub. L. No. 109-271, 120 Stat. 750 (Aug. 12, 2006).

7 Pub. L. No. 113-4, 127 Stat. 54 (Mar. 7, 2013).

8 For more information on practice under VAWA, see E. Abriel and S. Kinoshita, *The VAWA Manual: Immigration Relief for Abused Immigrants*, a joint publication of the Catholic Legal Immigration Network, Inc. and the Immigrant Legal Resource Center, available for purchase at www.ilrc.org.

9 INA §204(a)(1).

10 The term "intended spouse" means an alien who married a U.S. citizen or LPR in good faith but then learned that the marriage is not legitimate because the U.S. citizen or LPR was still married to someone else. *See* INA §101(a)(50).

11 8 CFR §204.2(c)(4).

Basic Requirements

A self-petitioning spouse or intended spouse of a U.S. citizen or LPR must demonstrate the following:

- Good moral character;
- Marriage to the U.S. citizen or LPR;
- That the marriage or intended marriage was entered in good faith;
- That during the marriage, the foreign national spouse or his or her child has been battered by, or been the subject of extreme cruelty committed by the U.S. citizen or LPR spouse;
- Residence, past or present, with the U.S. citizen or LPR spouse; and
- Either (1) current residence in the United States, or (2) if living abroad, that the abusing spouse is an employee of the U.S. government or a member of the uniformed services, or subjected the foreign national or the foreign national's child to battery or extreme cruelty in the United States.[12]

Similarly, a self-petitioning foreign national child of an abusive U.S. citizen or LPR must establish:

- Good moral character (presumed for children under age 14);
- Parent-child relationship with the abusive U.S. citizen or LPR;
- Past or present residence with the U.S. citizen or LPR parent;
- Having been subjected to battery or extreme cruelty committed by the U.S. citizen or LPR parent; and
- Either (1) current residence in the United States or (2) if living abroad, that the abusing parent is an employee of the U.S. government or a member of the uniformed services or subjected the child to abuse in the United States.[13]
- A self-petitioning parent of an abusive U.S. citizen must establish:
- Good moral character;
- Parentage of the abusive U.S. citizen (including stepparents and adoptive parents);
- Eligibility to be classified as an immediate relative (indicating that the abusive U.S. citizen must be at least 21 years of age);
- Residence or past residence with the U.S. citizen daughter or son; and

12 INA §204(a)(1)(A), (B).

13 *Id.*

- Having been subjected to battery or extreme cruelty by the U.S. citizen daughter or son.[14]

A major element of the law as it existed prior to October 2000, the requirement that the self-petitioner show that removal would result in extreme hardship to the self-petitioning spouse or his or her child, or to the self-petitioning child, was eliminated by section 1503 of the Battered Immigrant Women Protection Act of 2000.[15]

The statute, regulations, and policy guidance provide the following details on how the self-petition provisions are to be interpreted:

Residence. Prior to the Battered Immigrant Women Protection Act of 2000, the statute required that self-petitioners presently reside in the United States and have resided with the abuser in the United States. These requirements were relaxed in the 2000 amendments. Regarding current residence, either the self-petitioner must currently reside in the United States, or, if the self-petitioner lives outside the United States, the abuser must be an employee of the U.S. government or a member of the uniformed services, or must have subjected the foreign national or the foreign national's child to battery or extreme cruelty in the United States.[16] In addition, although the self-petitioner must have resided with the abuser, that residence need not have been in the United States. Most important, the law does not require that the self-petitioner be currently residing with the abuser. For children, "residence" includes any period of visitation in the United States.[17]

Good-faith marriage. The self-petitioning spouse must establish by a preponderance of the evidence that the marriage or intended marriage was entered into in good faith. For marriages entered into during removal proceedings, however, the standard is the stricter one of clear and convincing evidence.[18] The most important factor in establishing a good-faith marriage is whether the couple intended to establish a life together at the time of the marriage. Conduct after a couple is married—even separation shortly thereafter—is relevant only to establish intent at the time the marriage was entered into. A self-petition will not be denied just because the spouses are no longer living together and the marriage is no longer viable.[19]

Marital relationship. Prior to October 2000, the self-petitioning spouse had to be legally married to the abusing spouse at the time the self-petition was filed, although subsequent termination of the marriage did not affect the self-petition.

---

14 INA §204(a)(1)(A)(vii); USCIS Policy Memorandum, *Eligibility to Self-Petition as a Battered or Abused Parent of a U.S. Citizen: Revisions to Adjudicator's Field Manual (AFM) Chapter 21.15* (Aug.30, 2011), AILA Doc. No. 11090161.

15 Pub. L. No. 106-386, §1503, 114 Stat. 1464, 1518–22 (Oct. 28, 2000).

16 INA §204(a)(1)(A)(v), (B)(iv).

17 INA §204(a)(1)(A)(iv), (B)(iii).

18 INA §§204(g), 245(e).

19 8 CFR §204.2(c)(1)(ix).

The 2000 amendments provide that certain abused spouses whose marriage has been terminated within the past two years may still self-petition. Under those amendments, a foreign national who was a bona fide spouse of a U.S. citizen or LPR within the past two years may self-petition if he or she demonstrates a connection between the legal termination of the marriage within the past two years and battering or extreme cruelty by the U.S. citizen or LPR spouse.[20] In addition, a foreign national who was a bona fide spouse of a U.S. citizen within the past two years and whose spouse died within the past two years may self-petition.[21] Changes in marital status, including divorce or the death of either the U.S. citizen or LPR spouse after the filing of a VAWA petition, do not preclude the granting of the self-petition or the self-petitioner's obtaining permanent residence.[22]

Marriage or remarriage of self-petitioners. The 2000 VAWA amendments provide that the remarriage of a former spouse whose self-petition has been approved or the marriage of a self-petitioning child whose petition has been approved will not serve as a basis for revocation of the approval of the self-petition.[23]

Parent-child relationship. The self-petitioning child must be unmarried and under 21 years of age when the self-petition is filed, with an exception to the filing deadline explained below.[24] He or she must also be the child of the abusive U.S. citizen or LPR parent, but need not be the child of a self-petitioning spouse. The self-petitioning child does not have to be in the abuser's legal custody, nor will changes in parental rights or legal custody affect the status of the child's self-petition.[25]

Derivative children. The self-petitioner's children, including children of self-petitioning children, qualify for derivative status if they are under age 21 and unmarried when the self-petition is filed.[26] These derivative children are not required to have been the victims of abuse, nor do they have to have resided in the United States. Like self-petitioning children, derivative children are eligible for deferred action and work authorization.

Protection against aging out for VAWA self-petitioning and derivative children. VAWA includes several protections against aging out for children.

- First, VAWA 2005 amended the INA by expressly providing that the Child Status Protection Act[27] (CSPA) applies to VAWA self-petitioners and their derivatives. Thus, CSPA rules for determining who is an immediate relative

20 INA §204(a)(1)(A)(iii)(II)(aa)(CC)(ccc), (B)(ii)(II)(aa)(CC)(bbb).

21 INA §204(a)(1)(A)(vi).

22 *Id.*

23 INA §204(h).

24 INA §204(a)(1)(D)(v).

25 8 CFR §204.2(e)(1)(ii).

26 INA §204(a)(1)(A)(iii), (B)(i).

27 Pub. L. No. 107-208, 116 Stat. 927 (Aug. 6, 2002).

specifically apply to VAWA self-petitioners and their derivatives.[28] Similarly, CSPA rules for determining whether individuals are children for purposes of the second family preference also specifically apply to self-petitioners and derivatives of self-petitioners.[29]

- Second, even where CSPA protection doesn't apply, a child whose self-petition is filed or approved before the child turns 21 will be considered, upon turning 21, a petitioner for preference under the family first, second, or third preferences, whichever is appropriate, with the same priority date assigned to the self-petition.[30] No new petition is required, and the self-petitioner is eligible for deferred action and work authorization while awaiting a current priority date and adjustment of status.[31]
- Third, the provision described above applies to derivative children of VAWA self-petitioners, who also are considered VAWA self-petitioners upon turning 21.[32]
- Fourth, the filing deadline for self-petitioning children has been extended to age 25 under certain circumstances. An individual who is 21 years old and who qualified to file a VAWA self-petition before age 21 as a child of a U.S. citizen or as a child of an LPR, but who did not timely file the petition, may file the self-petition prior to age 25 if the abuse was at least one central reason for the filing delay.[33] A central reason is one that is caused by or incident to the battery or extreme cruelty, including situations where: (1) the self-petitioner is subjected to abuse close to turning 21, so that there is insufficient time to submit an application before aging out, or (2) the self-petitioner is so traumatized by abuse that she or he is unable to apply before turning 21.[34]

Citizenship or immigration status of abuser. Prior to the 2000 VAWA amendments, a requirement for self-petitioning for abused spouses or children was that the abusing spouse or parent must have been a U.S. citizen or LPR at the time the self-petition was filed and approved, although subsequent changes in the abuser's citizenship or immigration status would not affect an approved self-petition. Under the 2000 and 2005 amendments, however, abused spouses, children, and parents of U.S. citizens may self-petition within two years after the spouse, parent, or child's

---

28 INA §201(f)(4).

29 INA §203(h)(4).

30 INA §204(a)(1)(D)(i)(I).

31 INA §204(a)(1)(D)(i)(III).

32 INA §204(a)(1)(D)(i)(IV).

33 INA §204(a)(1)(D)(v).

34 USCIS Policy Memorandum, *Continued Eligibility to File for Child VAWA Self-Petitioners After Attaining Age 21; Revisions to Adjudicator's Field Manual (AFM) Chapter 21.14* (Sept. 6, 2011), AILA Doc. No. 11090861.

loss or renunciation of citizenship, if the loss or renunciation was related to an incident of domestic violence.[35] Similarly, abused spouses and children of LPRs may self-petition within two years after the spouse or parent's loss of status if it was because of an incident of domestic violence.[36] Changes in the abuser's citizenship status or loss of the abuser's permanent residence after the filing of a self-petition do not preclude the granting of the self-petition or the self-petitioner's obtaining LPR status.[37] Moreover, if the abuser naturalizes, the previously filed self-petition of his or her spouse or child is reclassified as a self-petition filed by the spouse or child of a U.S. citizen, even if the naturalization occurs after divorce or termination of parental rights.[38]

Death of U.S. citizen abuser. The spouse, child, or parent of a U.S. citizen abuser may self-petition within two years after the death of the U.S. citizen abuser.[39]

Definition of "abuse." To qualify as abuse under the statute, the spouse or child must show that he or she "has been battered or has been the subject of extreme cruelty"[40] perpetrated by his or her spouse or parent. Under the regulations implementing the self-petition provisions, abuse is "any act or threatened act of violence, including any forceful detention, which results or threatens to result in physical or mental injury." It includes psychological abuse, rape, incest, and forced prostitution.[41]

Good moral character. Although the statute does not specify any definite period during which good moral character must be established, the regulations require three years of good moral character preceding the filing of the self-petition.[42] Children under age 14 are presumed to be of good moral character. Legal bars to establishing good moral character are set forth in INA §101(f).

Even if a self-petitioner falls under one of the INA §101(f) statutory bars to good moral character, USCIS nonetheless may find the self-petitioner to be of good moral character if: (1) the act or conviction is waivable for purposes of determining inadmissibility or deportability, and (2) the act or conviction was connected to the abuse suffered by the self-petitioner.[43]

---

35 INA §204(a)(1)(A)(iii)(II)(aa)(CC)(bbb) (spouse of USC); INA §204(a)(1)(A)(iv) (child of USC); INA §204(a)(1)(A)(vii)(I) (parent of USC).

36 INA §204(a)(1)(B)(ii)(II)(aa)(CC)(aaa) (spouse of LPR); INA §204(a)(1)(B)(iii) (child of LPR).

37 INA §204(a)(1)(B)(v)(I).

38 INA §204(a)(1)(B)(v)(II).

39 INA §204(a)(1)(A)(iii)(II)(aa)(CC)(aaa) (spouse of USC); §204(a)(1)(A)(iv) (child of USC); INA §204(a)(1)(A)(vii)(I) (parent of USC).

40 INA §§204(a)(1)(A)(iii)(bb) (spouse of USC); (iv) (child of USC); (B)(ii)(I)(bb) (spouse of LPR); (iii) (child of LPR).

41 8 CFR §204.2(c)(1)(vi), (e)(2)(vi).

42 8 CFR §204.2(c)(1)(vii).

43 INA §204(a)(1)(C).

In a memorandum dated January 19, 2005, USCIS gave guidance for determining good moral character despite a bar.[44] In regard to the first requirement, the memorandum provides that the adjudicator does not need to determine whether a waiver would be granted, but only whether one would be available for filing at the time the adjustment of status application or visa application is filed. In regard to the second requirement, the evidence must establish that the battering or extreme cruelty the self-petitioner experienced compelled or coerced the self-petitioner to commit the act or crime. In other words, the evidence should establish that the self-petitioner would not have committed the act or crime in the absence of the battering or extreme cruelty.[45] In making this determination of connection, the adjudicator should consider "the full history of the domestic violence in the case, including the need to escape an abusive relationship."[46] Finally, even if both requirements are met, the adjudicator must determine whether to exercise discretion favorably.

The memorandum makes special reference to criminal acts or convictions. For acts or convictions that involve a violent or dangerous crime, the memorandum instructs USCIS officers to consult 8 CFR §212.7(d). That provision states that discretion generally should not be exercised favorably in cases involving violent or dangerous crimes, except in extraordinary circumstances. Examples of such extraordinary circumstances include ones involving national security or foreign policy considerations, or where denial of the waiver would result in exceptional and extremely unusual hardship. Regarding aggravated felonies, if the adjudicator determines that the act or conviction is an aggravated felony as defined in INA §101(a)(43), the adjudicator should refer the case for issuance of a notice to appear for removal proceedings. The memorandum applies to all self-petitions pending on or filed on or after October 28, 2000. USCIS attached a chart entitled "Waivable Conduct Contained in the Statutory Bars to Establishing Good Moral Character" to the memorandum. That chart is included as Appendix 9.

The Contents of the Self-Petition Packet

USCIS will consider all credible evidence submitted with the petition before reaching a conclusion.[47] Nonetheless, primary evidence, such as medical, police, or court records, is generally more credible than secondary evidence such as affidavits, so advocates should make every effort to present primary evidence.

The self-petition packet should be paginated consecutively and contain the forms and documents listed below; if the applicant cannot obtain any of the listed documents, then other credible evidence should be submitted in its place.

---

44 USCIS Memorandum, W. Yates, *Determinations of Good Moral Character in VAWA-Based Self-Petitions* (Jan. 19, 2005), AILA Doc. No. 05012561.

45 *Id.*

46 *Id.*

47 INA §204(a)(10)(J).

- *A detailed cover letter with an index*, listing each document contained in the application and the page at which it appears. The index should organize the contents according to the element that each document satisfies. For example, there should be an index subheading for "good moral character," and documents presented to show good moral character should be listed under that subheading.
- *A completed Form I-360,* Petition for Amerasian, Widow(er), or Special Immigrant. Note that the self-petitioner may give a safe address on the application, rather than the location where he or she is residing. This safe address could be the advocate's office or a friend or relative's address. There is no fee for the Form I-360 application.[48]
- *The applicant's detailed declaration*. This is the single most important part of the application. It is an opportunity to show how sympathetic the applicant's case is, as well as to establish credibility through a detailed description of events. The declaration should include the applicant's personal knowledge on each element of the claim. This would include the marriage or other qualifying relationship to the abuser, the abuser's status, battery or extreme cruelty, and good moral character. The applicant should be as involved as possible in drafting the declaration, and even where the advocate assists in the drafting, the declaration should "speak in the client's voice."
- *Evidence of the qualifying relationship to the abuser*:
    - For an abused spouse, the marriage certificate and evidence of termination of all prior marriages by each spouse should be included. For an abused intended spouse whose marriage to the abuser is invalid solely because of the abuser's bigamy, the applicant's declaration should set out these facts, as well as the applicant's good faith in entering into the marriage.[49]
    - For an abused common-law spouse, the applicant should present evidence to establish that the marriage meets the definition of common-law marriage under the law of the state where the marriage occurred.
    - For a son or daughter abused by a U.S. citizen or LPR mother, a copy of the birth certificate, showing the abuser as mother, should be submitted.[50]
    - For a son or daughter born in wedlock who was abused by a U.S. citizen or LPR father, a copy of the birth certificate and a copy of the parent's marriage certificate should be submitted.[51]

---

48 8 CFR §103.7.

49 8 CFR §204.2(c)(2)(ii).

50 8 CFR §204.2(e)(2)(ii).

51 8 CFR §204.2(e)(2)(ii)(B).

- For a son or daughter born out of wedlock who was abused by a U.S. citizen or LPR father, the applicant should submit a copy of his or her birth certificate and documents to show either: (1) legitimation by the father before the son or daughter reached the age of 18 and while in the legitimating parent's custody, or (2) that the father had a bona fide parent-child relationship with the person. Examples of documents to show a bona fide parent-child relationship include statements from the self-petitioner, his or her mother, and other relatives or witnesses concerning the relationship between the father and child, evidence of payment of child support, evidence that the father and child exchanged gifts, photographs, or other mementos, evidence that the father and child did things together, and evidence that the father held the child out as his own.[52]

- For an adopted child, evidence should be submitted to establish that the child was adopted before reaching the age of 16 and that the child has been in the legal custody of and has resided with the adopting parent or parents for at least two years.[53] The two-year legal and physical custody requirement does not apply if the adopted child was abused by the adopting parent or a family member of the adopting parent residing in the same household.[54] Note that the rules and procedures of the Hague Adoption Convention on the Protection of Children and Co-operation in Respect of Inter-Country Adoption apply to adoptions that occur on or after April 1, 2008.[55] Foreign national children adopted on or after this date will not be recognized as having a parent/child relationship with either the abuser parent or self-petitioning parent if applicable Hague Convention procedures were not followed.

- If the abuser is the applicant's stepparent, the applicant should submit his or her birth certificate, together with evidence to show that the marriage creating the relationship of stepparent and stepchild occurred before the stepchild turned 18.[56] For stepchildren, termination of the marriage between the parent and stepparent generally terminates the stepparent/stepchild relationship, unless the stepparent and stepchild continue their relationship after the termination.[57] It may be difficult to show that the relationship has continued in a case involving domestic abuse. However, the VAWA amendments of 2000, providing that divorce after filing a

---

52 8 CFR §204.2(e)(2)(ii)(D).

53 8 CFR §204.2(e)(2)(ii)(F).

54 INA §101(b)(1)(E)(i).

55 8 CFR §204.301.

56 8 CFR §204.2(e)(2)(ii)(E).

57 *Matter of Pagnerre*, 13 I&N Dec. 688 (BIA 1971).

self-petition will not negatively affect eligibility to self-petition, may modify this general rule.

- For the mother of an abusive U.S. citizen, the applicant should submit a copy of the abuser's birth certificate to show the relationship between the abuser and the parent and to establish that the abuser is at least 21 years old, as well as evidence of any change of the abuser's or parent's name.
- For the father of an abusive U.S. citizen, the applicant should submit a copy of the abuser's birth certificate and evidence of any change of name. In addition, if the abuser was born in wedlock, the applicant should submit a copy of the certificate of marriage between the applicant and the abuser's mother. If the abuser was born out of wedlock, then the applicant should submit evidence of legitimation or of a bona fide parent-child relationship between the abuser and the applicant.

- *Evidence of the abuser's U.S. citizen or LPR status.* If the abuser is a U.S. citizen by birth, that status is proved by the abuser's birth certificate showing birth within the United States or its possessions. It could also be established by a certificate of citizenship or a birth certificate showing birth abroad to two U.S. citizen parents or to one U.S. citizen who meets the residential requirements to convey citizenship on his or her children. The status of an abuser who is a naturalized U.S. citizen is shown by the abuser's naturalization certificate.[58] The status of an abuser who is an LPR is shown by the abuser's permanent resident card.

  This evidence very likely will be the most difficult for the applicant to obtain, as it is the evidence most completely under the abuser's control. Government records establishing immigration status generally will not be released to persons other than the party to whom they pertain. Applicants who are experiencing problems obtaining this evidence may want to request assistance from the USCIS Vermont Service Center (VSC). If the self-petitioner is unable to present primary or secondary evidence of the abuser's status, the advocate may ask the immigration authorities to attempt to verify the abuser's citizenship or immigration status from information contained in immigration computerized records and other records.[59] For example, if an abusive U.S. citizen spouse is a citizen through naturalization, or previously filed a petition for a family member, USCIS should have evidence of his or her citizenship status.

  Other evidence that might be sufficient to establish the abuser's status could be the abuser's employment records, such as the I-9 form and copies of

---

58 8 CFR §204.1(g)(1).

59 8 CFR §204.1(g)(3).

the abuser's immigration documents maintained by the employer, although privacy requirements may make these difficult for the applicant to obtain.

If none of the above-mentioned documents is available, secondary evidence such as declarations from persons who know the abuser to be an LPR or U.S. citizen may be presented.[60]

- *Evidence of the applicant's physical presence* in the United States *or* evidence that the abuse occurred in the United States *or* evidence that the abuser is an employee of the U.S. government or a member of the uniformed services.
- *Evidence of good moral character.* Self-petitioners who are 14 years of age or older must provide a copy of police clearance letters from jurisdictions (including jurisdictions in other countries) where they have resided for six months or more during the three-year period preceding the filing of the self-petition.[61] When it was not possible to obtain police clearance letters, self-petitioners have submitted FBI rap sheets or state criminal record reports to satisfy this requirement.
- The applicant's own declaration is crucial in establishing good moral character. If there are no convictions or acts that would establish a statutory or discretionary bar to good moral character, then the applicant may state simply that he or she has never been arrested. A letter or statement from relatives, friends, clergy, or employers attesting to the applicant's good moral character may also be helpful. If there is a statutory bar to good moral character, then the self-petitioner should submit evidence to establish that the act or conviction is waivable under INA §212 or 237 and that there is a connection between the act or conviction and the abuse the self-petitioner suffered. In addition, the applicant should use his or her declaration to show why discretion should be exercised to support a finding of good moral character.
- *Evidence of good-faith marriage.* "Good faith" here means that the applicant married the abuser for the principal purpose of sharing a life together and not solely to obtain an immigration benefit.[62] Evidence could include one or more of the following:
  - The self-petitioner's own detailed declaration
  - Deeds to property or leases showing both spouses' names
  - Bank accounts in both spouses' names or accounts showing one spouse as the beneficiary of the other

---

60 8 CFR §204.1(g)(2).

61 8 CFR §204.2(c)(2)(v) (self-petitioning spouses), (e)(2)(v) (self-petitioning children).

62 8 CFR §204.2(c)(2)(vii).

- Vehicle registration in both spouses' names
- Wills indicating that the parties are married
- Credit card, utility, and other bills in both spouses' names
- Jointly filed income tax returns
- Insurance policies showing one spouse as the beneficiary of the other
- Birth certificates of children born of the marriage
- Evidence of courtship, such as letters and photographs of the couple
- Evidence of the marriage ceremony, such as photographs and invitations
- Declarations from relatives or friends.

- *Evidence of battery or cruel treatment.*[63] The following are examples of evidence that may be submitted for this purpose:
  - The applicant's own detailed declaration
  - Copies of temporary and final protective orders
  - Shelter records and other evidence that the victim sought shelter or protection
  - Counseling records and reports
  - Medical records documenting the abuse
  - Photographs of a visibly injured victim or property damage, supported by affidavits
  - Police reports
  - Criminal court records
  - Declarations of witnesses to the abuse or to the results of violence
  - Letters from clergy to whom the abuse was reported
  - School records reflecting the abuse
- *Evidence of relationship between the self-petitioner and any derivative children*, through birth certificates and other documentation required to establish that the derivative is a "child" under INA §101(b).
- *Form G-28*, Notice of Appearance as Attorney or Representative.

---

63 8 CFR §204.2(c)(2)(iv).

- *Form I-765*, Application for Employment Authorization. This should be included with the self-petition application if the applicant simultaneously is applying for adjustment of status and seeking employment authorization on this basis. Otherwise, the applicant will be issued an employment authorization card upon approval of the self-petition, provided that the applicant checks the box on the updated I-360 form to indicate that she or he is requesting employment authorization.

Intake Interview and Gathering Evidence

The intake interview lays the foundation for obtaining the above information. The following are suggestions for successful interviewing and for gathering corroborative evidence after the initial interview:

- Be aware that you are dealing with an individual who has suffered profound violence and be sensitive to the ways that different cultures deal with such issues.
- If you are doing a general intake interview and are not aware of the applicant's situation, do not overlook a general question that may enable the person to qualify for relief under VAWA. Use open-ended questions to encourage the applicant to disclose any abuse, moving towards increasingly more specific questions.
- Set aside enough time to interview the client. Domestic violence interviews will invariably be lengthy, due to such factors as trauma in reliving painful events, the need to establish a rapport with the client, and translation problems.
- Be aware of the domestic violence syndrome of power and control and the cycle of violence: tension building, explosion, and then the honeymoon phase.
- Frame particular questions. Rather than asking "did you suffer domestic violence?," ask, one at a time, "were you hit, punched, pushed, prevented from working and/or having money, prevented from having friends or contacting your family, insulted, mistreated in front of friends, family, children?"
- It is very important to develop a partnership with the client's domestic violence counselor, who can be very helpful in gathering evidence with the client.
- Think of the battered immigrant's affidavit as similar to an asylum affidavit: it should be detailed, specific, and in the client's own words.
- Before the interview, familiarize yourself with country conditions so that you are aware of the treatment of women in the client's country of nationality. This should enable you to interview the client more effectively.

You may need to obtain information on country conditions and laws of the client's country concerning domestic abuse, particularly if some of the abuse the client suffered took place in his or her country. You may do this by reviewing country reports from the Department of State, Human Rights Watch, Amnesty International, and the United Nations High Commissioner for Refugees. The Human Rights Documentation Exchange is another excellent source of information.

Procedure for Filing

There is no fee for an I-360 VAWA self-petition. The self-petition and supporting documents should be sent to the following address: USCIS, Vermont Service Center, Attn: Humanitarian Unit, 75 Lower Welden Street, St. Albans, VT 05479-0001. Always check the USCIS website for the most up-to-date filing addresses.

The application should be marked on the outside of the envelope, in large red letters: "VAWA Application. Do not open in mailroom." Applications for adjustment of status and for employment authorization should be marked "VAWA Adjustment Application" or "VAWA Employment Authorization Application" at the top in red. This will ensure that the application gets to the VAWA Unit.

Deferred Action and Employment Authorization

When the VSC approves a self-petition, it automatically considers the applicant for deferred action status.[64] The Immigration and Naturalization Service issued a memorandum explaining that self-petitioners generally possess factors that warrant a grant of deferred action.[65] Initial assessments of deferred action will be valid for 15 months, and requests for extensions of deferred action will be granted in increments of 12 months.[66]

Once a self-petition is approved, the self-petitioner is eligible for employment authorization incident to status.[67] As mentioned above, the employment authorization document will be issued on this basis automatically upon application approval, without the need to file an I-765, as long as the self-petitioner marks the checkbox on the I-360 form requesting employment authorization. Self-petitioners granted deferred action are eligible for employment authorization on that basis as well, but must submit an I-765WS to establish economic necessity to work. Applications for employment authorization should be marked in red as "VAWA I-765" to ensure that they are sent to the correct department of the VSC.

---

64 INS Memorandum, P. Virtue, *Supplemental Guidance on Battered Alien Self-Petitioning Process and Related Issues* (May 6, 1997).

65 *Id.*

66 INS Memorandum, M. Cronin, *Deferred Action Determinations for Self-Petitioning Battered Spouses and Children* (Sept. 8, 2000), AILA Doc. No. 01081736.

67 INA §204(a)(1)(K).

Help Down the Road

Adjustment of Status, Inadmissibility Grounds

VAWA self-petitioners adjust under INA §245(a). With the enactment of VAWA 2000, Congress amended INA §245(a) to provide that VAWA self-petitioners are exempt from the requirement of having been inspected and admitted or paroled into the United States. Under INA §245(c), the following statutory bars to adjustment of status do not apply to the adjustment of a self-petitioner: having been employed without authorization; failing to maintain lawful status; having entered as a crewman ("C" nonimmigrant status) or witness in a criminal proceedings ("S" nonimmigrant status); having entered under the visa waiver program; or being deportable as a terrorist. Self-petitioners are not required to pay any adjustment penalty fee. The term "VAWA self-petitioner" includes derivative children.[68]

A 2008 memorandum issued by USCIS to all its district offices confirmed that all approved self-petitioners qualify to use INA §245(a) to adjust status, regardless of manner of entry.[69] Prior to the issuance of this policy guidance, several USCIS district offices were taking the position that self-petitioners applying for adjustment still were subject to the inadmissibility ground of "entry without admission or parole" under INA §212(a)(6)(A), making many self-petitioner adjustment applicants who entered the United States without inspection ineligible to adjust status.

Applying for Adjustment of Status

VAWA self-petitioners who are eligible to file for adjustment of status at the same time they submit their Form I-360 self-petition can file both together (a "one-step" filing) at the VSC. In this circumstance, the self-petitioner and adjustment of status applicant is eligible to seek employment authorization immediately, in the category of "adjustment applicant."

Applications for VAWA adjustment of status that are filed properly with the VSC should be marked "VAWA Adjustment" clearly in red on the outside of the envelope and on the Form I-485 itself, so that the application will be sent to the correct department of the VSC.

Inadmissibility Grounds

VAWA 2000, 2005, and 2014 each provided special exemptions from or waivers of certain inadmissibility grounds for individuals with approved VAWA self-petitions.

---

68 INA §101(a)(51).

69 USCIS Memorandum, M. Aytes, *Adjustment of Status for VAWA Self-Petitioner Who Is Present Without Inspection* (Apr. 11, 2008), AILA Doc. No. 08042161.

First, VAWA self-petitioners are eligible for a discretionary waiver of inadmissibility for misrepresentation (having procured or sought a visa or admission or other immigration benefit by fraud or willful misrepresentation of a material fact) if they demonstrate that removal would cause extreme hardship to themselves or to their U.S. citizen, LPR, or "qualified alien" parent or child.[70] The term "qualified alien" is defined at 8 USC §1641(b), and includes LPRs, asylees, refugees, persons paroled into the country for at least one year, foreign nationals granted withholding of deportation or removal, foreign nationals granted conditional entry under INA §203(a)(7) as it existed prior to April 1, 1980, Cuban and Haitian entrants, VAWA self-petitioners, and abused foreign nationals eligible for VAWA suspension of deportation or cancellation of removal.

Second, VAWA self-petitioners are eligible for a discretionary waiver of certain criminal inadmissibility grounds listed in INA §212(a)(2).[71] The major requirement is that the applicant qualifies as a VAWA self-petitioner; there is no requirement of extreme hardship or a qualifying U.S. citizen or LPR relative. INA §212(h) allows for a discretionary waiver of inadmissibility for crimes of moral turpitude, multiple criminal convictions for which the aggregate sentences to confinement were five years or more, prostitution and commercialized vice, assertion of immunity from prosecution, and for a single offense of simple possession of 30 grams or less of marijuana. Applicants are ineligible for the section 212(h) waiver if they have been convicted of or admitted committing murder, torture, or an attempt or conspiracy to commit those crimes.[72] Persons who entered the United States as LPRs based on immigrant visas obtained at U.S. consulate abroad are not eligible for this waiver if: (1) they have been convicted of an aggravated felony; or (2) they have not resided lawfully and continuously in the United States for seven years prior to the initiation of removal proceedings.[73]

Third, persons with approved VAWA self-petitions are eligible for a discretionary waiver of the inadmissibility ground of having a communicable disease of public health significance, including infection with the etiologic agent for acquired immune deficiency syndrome.[74]

Fourth, the inadmissibility ground arising from reentering or attempting to reenter the United States without admission after having been unlawfully present in the United States for more than one year or having been ordered removed[75] is waivable

---

70 INA §212(i).

71 INA §212(h).

72 *Id.*

73 In *Matter of J–H–J–*, 26 I&N Dec. 563 (BIA 2015), the Board bowed to the weight of federal circuit court decisions and held that a foreign national who adjusted status in the United States, and who has not entered as a lawful permanent resident, is not barred from establishing eligibility for a waiver of inadmissibility under INA §212(h) as a result of an aggravated felony conviction.

74 INA §212(g)(1)(C)

75 INA §212(A)(9)(C)(i).

in the exercise of discretion for certain VAWA self-petitioners.[76] To be eligible for such a waiver, the self-petitioner must show that there is a connection between his or her having been battered or subjected to extreme cruelty and his or her removal, departure from the United States, reentry or reentries to the United States, or attempted reentry into the United States.[77]

Fifth, there are two exceptions for VAWA self-petitioners to the inadmissibility ground of being present in the United States without authorization or parole.[78] Which of the two exceptions applies depends on when the self-petitioner entered the United States. If the self-petitioner first entered before April 1, 1997, he or she need show only status as a VAWA self-petitioner.[79] If the entry was on or after April 1, 1997, however, the VAWA self-petitioner must show also that there was a substantial connection between the entry without inspection and the abuse he or she suffered, or his or her child suffered, by the abusive spouse or parent or a member of the abuser's family residing in the same household.[80]

Sixth, there is a VAWA exception to the three– and ten-year bars for unlawful presence. Under that exception, a VAWA self-petitioner is not subject to the bars if he or she can show a substantial connection between the violation of the person's nonimmigrant visa and the abuse he or she suffered.[81] Although the statutory language indicates that this exception only applies to person who accrued unlawful presence by overstaying a visa, USCIS policy guidance issued in 2009 applies this exception to all self-petitioners who can show a substantial connection between the abuse suffered, the unlawful presence, and the departure from the United States.[82] In addition, some advocates contend that self-petitioners who entered before April 1, 1997, are completely exempt from the three– and ten-year bars and need not show any connection between the visa overstay and the abuse.[83]

---

76 INA §212(A)(9)(C)(iii).

77 *Id.*

78 INA §212(a)(6)(A)(ii).

79 Illegal Immigration Reform and Immigrant Responsibility Act of 1996 (IIRAIRA), Pub. L. No. 104-208, div. C, §301(c)(2), 110 Stat. 3009, 3009–579 (Sept. 30, 1996).

80 INA §212(a)(6)(A)(ii).

81 INA §212(a)(9)(B)(iii)(IV).

82 *Adjudicator's Field Manual* (AFM) ch. 40.9(b)(2)(E), located in 8 *USCIS Policy Manual* pt. O.

83 The exception at INA §212(a)(9)(B)(iii)(IV) is defined in terms of the VAWA exception to unlawful presence, found at INA §212(a)(6)(A)(ii). (The exception applies to "an alien who would be described in [INA §212(a)(6)(A)(ii)] if 'violation of the terms of the alien's nonimmigrant visa' were substituted for 'unlawful entry into the United States' in [INA §212(a)(6)(A)(ii)(III)].") As described above, INA §212(a)(6)(A)(ii) was included in the INA by IIRAIRA, which contained a special provision eliminating the "connection" requirement for persons arriving before its effective date, April 1, 1997. ("The requirements of [INA §§212(a)(6)(A)(ii)(II) and (III)], as inserted by [IIRAIRA §301(c)](1), shall not apply to an alien who demonstrates that the alien first arrived in the United States before [April 1, 1997].") Arguably then, INA §212(a)(9)(B)(iii)(IV) picks up the effective date of the INA §212(a)(6)(ii) exception and eliminates the connection requirement for unlawful presence based on a visa overstay if entry occurred before April 1, 1997.

Seventh, the public charge ground of inadmissibility no longer applies to VAWA self-petitioners.[84]

Domestic Violence Deportability Ground Eased for Abused Persons

The 2000 VAWA amendments also provide for abused persons a waiver of the deportability ground of having been convicted of a crime of domestic violence, stalking, child abuse, child neglect, or child abandonment, or having violated a protection order.[85] For such persons, the attorney general is not limited by the criminal court record and may waive those deportability grounds in the case of a foreign national who:

- Has been battered or subjected to extreme cruelty;
- Is not and was not the primary perpetrator of violence in the relationship; and
- Was either acting in self-defense, or where the crime did not result in serious bodily injury and there was a connection between the crime and the foreign national's having been battered or subjected to extreme cruelty.

In deciding these waiver applications, the attorney general must consider any credible evidence relevant to the application.[86]

The 2000 amendments also expand the waiver for the deportability ground, found at INA §237(a)(1), of having been inadmissible at the time of entry or adjustment of status, insofar as that inadmissibility results from fraud or misrepresentation under INA §212(a)(6)(C). Persons who have approved VAWA self-petitions are now eligible for that waiver.[87]

Applying for Adjustment Before the Immigration Court; Motions to Reopen

Where a self-petitioner is currently in removal or deportation proceedings or has a final order of removal or deportation that has not been effected by a departure from the United States, the self-petitioner may apply for adjustment of status only in immigration court proceedings.[88]

If a final administrative order of removal or deportation has been issued, then the individual will need to file a motion to reopen the proceedings in order to apply for adjustment. The motion to reopen is filed with the last administrative body to have jurisdiction over the proceedings. This would be either the immigration court or,

---

84 VAWA Reauthorization Act of 2013, Pub. L. No. 113-4, §804, 127 Stat. 54, 111 (Mar. 7, 2013).

85 INA §237(a)(7).

86 INA §237(a)(7)(B).

87 INA §237(a)(1)(H).

88 INA §240(a)(3).

if the person appealed the immigration court's decision, the Board of Immigration Appeals (BIA).

There are limitations on the timing and number of motions to reopen that can be filed with the immigration court and BIA, but those limitations are relaxed for VAWA self-petitioners.[89] In general, a motion to reopen must be filed within 90 days of the date of entry of a final administrative order of removal,[90] and an individual may file only one motion to reopen.[91]

There are special provisions for reopening proceedings to apply for VAWA adjustment or VAWA cancellation of removal. First, VAWA 2000 included a provision allowing motions to reopen for persons seeking to reopen *in absentia* removal proceedings to apply for VAWA adjustment or VAWA cancellation of removal.[92] Advocates believed that this was a drafting error and that Congress's intent was to apply the special provisions for VAWA motions to reopen to all VAWA removal cases, not just to *in absentia* proceedings. VAWA 2005 clarified that the reopening provision applies to all removal cases.[93] The motion to reopen must be filed within one year after the final order of removal, except that this time limit may be waived for a foreign national who demonstrates extraordinary circumstances or extreme hardship to the foreign national's child.[94] VAWA 2005 adds the requirement that the foreign national be physically present in the United States at the time of filing the motion.[95] There is no deadline for filing motions to reopen deportation proceedings to apply for VAWA adjustment or VAWA suspension of deportation.

Second, the filing of a motion to reopen and accompanying application for relief stays removal of a "qualified alien," pending final disposition of the motion, including exhaustion of all appeals.[96] A "qualified alien" is someone who has an approved VAWA self-petition, a pending self-petition setting forth a prima facie case for eligibility, an approved application for suspension of deportation or cancellation of removal, or a pending suspension or cancellation application that sets forth a prima facie case for eligibility.[97]

When preparing a motion to reopen, the advocate must comply with the format and content requirements set out in the BIA and immigration court regulations and in any local immigration court rules.

89 INA §240(c)(7)(C)(iv).

90 INA §240(c)(7)(A).

91 INA §240(c)(7)(C).

92 Pub. L. No. 106-386, §1506(c)(1), 114 Stat. 1464, 1528 (Oct. 28, 2000).

93 Pub. L. No. 109-162, §825(a), 119 Stat. 2960, 3063–64 (Jan. 5, 2006).

94 INA §240(c)(7)(C)(iv)(III).

95 INA §240(c)(7)(C)(iv)(IV).

96 INA §240(c)(7)(C) (paragraph following (iv)(IV)).

97 8 USC §1641(c)(1)(B).

Other Relief for VAWA Self-Petitioners in Removal Proceedings

VAWA 2005 also introduced some additional protections for self-petitioners in removal proceedings or subject to reinstatement of removal. These are:

- *Amendment of definition of "exceptional circumstances" for purposes of re- opening in absentia removal orders.* Persons removed *in absentia* who failed to appear for removal proceedings are ineligible for certain forms of relief, including adjustment of status and cancellation of removal, for 10 years after the date of the final order of removal, unless they can show that failure to appear was because of "exceptional circumstances." Exceptional circumstances includes battery or extreme cruelty to the foreign national or any child or parent of the foreign national, as well as serious illness of the foreign national. The amendment applies to failures to appear occurring before, on, or after enactment of VAWA 2005.[98]
- *Encouragement to grant advance permission to reapply for admission.* Congress stated its sense that, in considering an application for permission to reapply for admission after deportation or removal (Form I-212), the secretary of homeland security, the attorney general, and the secretary of state should consider exercising their discretionary authority particularly for VAWA self-petitioners, applicants for VAWA cancellation or suspension, and T and U nonimmigrants.[99]
- *Relief for VAWA self-petitioners who do not timely leave under voluntary departure.* In general, persons who fail to timely depart under an order of voluntary departure are ineligible for 10 years for certain forms of relief, including adjustment of status and cancellation of removal, and also incur civil penalties. Applicants for VAWA adjustment and VAWA cancellation of removal or suspension of deportation, however, will not incur the 10-year bar on relief and civil penalties for failure to timely depart if the abuse they suffered was at least one central reason for the overstay.[100]
- *Certification of compliance with IIRAIRA §384 on notices to appear.* Where an enforcement action leading to a removal proceeding was taken against a foreign national at certain locations, the notice to appear must include a statement that the provisions of IIRAIRA §384 have been complied with.[101] Section 384 contains two major requirements: (1) that immigration authorities keep information in VAWA (and now suspension, cancellation, and T visa) cases confidential; and (2) that Department of Justice (and now presumably Department of Homeland Security) employees make no adverse determination of admissibility or deportability regarding a foreign national

98 INA §240(e)(1).

99 Pub. L. No. 109-162, §813(b)(2), 119 Stat. 2960, 3058 (Jan. 5, 2006).

100 INA §240B(d).

101 INA §239(e)(1).

using information furnished solely by an abuser of that foreign national.[102] The locations triggering the certification requirement are domestic violence shelters, rape crisis centers, supervised visitation centers, family justice centers, victims' services providers, and community-based organizations. Courthouses are included if the foreign national appears in connection with a protection order case, child custody case, or other civil or criminal case relating to domestic violence, sexual assault, trafficking, or stalking in which the foreign national has been battered or subjected to extreme cruelty or if the foreign national is a victim of trafficking or certain crimes.[103] The provision took effect 30 days after enactment of VAWA 2005 and applies to apprehensions occurring on or after that date.[104]

Naturalization

The 2000 VAWA amendments also eased naturalization requirements for persons who have obtained LPR status through a self-petition as an abused spouse or child of a U.S. citizen.[105] Those persons may apply for naturalization after three years of residing continuously in the United States after being lawfully admitted for permanent residence. These amendments also removed the requirement that the naturalizing self-petitioner spouse have been living in marital union with the U.S. citizen spouse. Conditional resident spouses who have been granted a waiver of the joint petition requirement because of having been battered or subjected to extreme cruelty by their U.S. citizen spouse or parent are also eligible to adjust after three years without meeting the marital union requirement.[106]

Special Provisions for Derivative Spouses and Children of Applicants for Adjustment of Status Under the Cuban Adjustment Act, NACARA, and HRIFA

Congress recognized that abused spouses and children of applicants for relief under the Cuban Adjustment Act of 1966 (CAA),[107] the Haitian Refugee Immigration Fairness Act of 1998 (HRIFA),[108] and the Nicaraguan and Central American

102 Pub. L. No. 104-208, §384, 110 Stat. 3009, 3009-652 to 3009-653 (Sept. 30, 1996).

103 INA §239(e)(2).

104 Pub. L. No. 109-162, §825(c)(2), 119 Stat. 2960, 3065 (Jan. 5, 2006).

105 INA §319(a).

106 USCIS Memorandum, W. Yates, *Clarification of Classes of Applicants Eligible for Naturalization under Section 319(a) of the Immigration and Nationality Act (INA), as amended by the Victims of Trafficking and Violence Protection Act of 2000 (VTVPA), Pub. L. 106-386* (Jan. 27, 2005), AILA Doc. No. 05020760.

107 Pub. L. No. 89-732, 80 Stat. 1161.

108 Pub. L. No. 105-277, div. A, §101(h), tit. IX (secs. 901–04), 112 Stat. 2681, 2681-538 to 2681-542 (Oct. 21, 1998).

Refugee Act (NACARA)[109] may incur the same problems as abused spouses of LPRs and U.S. citizens—that is, they may be forced to decide whether to remain in an abusive marriage in order to obtain immigration benefits or to leave the marriage and seek safety. Thus, in VAWA 2000, and again in VAWA 2005, Congress provided remedies similar to VAWA self-petitions for this group of individuals.

- *Relief for abused spouses and children under the Cuban Adjustment Act.* Abused spouses and children of a Cuban eligible for relief under the CAA may apply for adjustment of status without showing current residence with the abusive spouse or parent. In addition, an abused spouse is eligible to apply for adjustment within two years (1) of the death of the Cuban spouse, or (2) termination of the marriage, if the marriage termination is connected to the abuse. In both situations the applicant must have previously lived with the abusive spouse.[110]
- *Relief for HRIFA family members.* Abused spouses, children, and sons and daughters of persons who adjust to LPR status or who are eligible for classification under HRIFA may apply for HRIFA adjustment to LPR status. Thus, an abused spouse, child, or son or daughter may apply for HRIFA adjustment on his or her own even if the principal applicant did not actually adjust under that act.[111] Abused spouses and children do not have to comply with the requirement of having been physically present in the United States since December 1, 1995, as long as they are present at the time of application for adjustment.[112]
- *Relief for NACARA family members.* Abused Nicaraguan and Cuban spouses and children of persons who adjusted status under NACARA or who were eligible for such adjustment were eligible to apply for adjustment under NACARA §202(d)(1) on their own during the 18 months following the enactment of VAWA 2005.[113] Because of the passage of time, this relief is no longer available.
- Under NACARA §203,[114] nationals of El Salvador, Guatemala and former republics of the U.S.S.R. may apply for cancellation of removal or suspension of deportation upon showing continuous presence in the United States since a certain date and meeting other requirements. Dependent spouses, children, and unmarried sons and daughters also may apply for NACARA §203 benefits. VAWA 2000 provided relief for abused spouses

---

109 Pub. L. No. 105-100, tit. II, 111 Stat. 2160, 2193–201 (Nov. 19, 1997).

110 Pub. L. No. 109-162, §823, 119 Stat. 2960, 3063 (Jan. 5, 2006).

111 Pub. L. No. 109-162, §824, 119 Stat. 2960, 3063 (Jan. 5, 2006).

112 Pub. L. No. 106-386, §1511, 114 Stat. 1464, 1531–32 (Oct. 28, 2000).

113 Pub. L. No. 109-162, §815, 119 Stat. 2960, 3060 (Jan. 5, 2006).

114 Pub. L. No. 105-100, §203, 111 Stat. 2160, 2196–200 (Nov. 19, 1997).

and children of principal applicants by eliminating the requirement that the derivative be residing with the principal applicant.[115]

- *Motions to reopen.* The VAWA exceptions to time and number limits on motions to reopen also apply to motions for relief as an abused spouse or child under the CAA and HRIFA.[116]

Special Provisions for Derivative Spouses of Certain Nonimmigrants

VAWA 2005 amended the INA to provide eligibility for employment authorization to battered spouses of nonimmigrants admitted in A, E-3, G, or H nonimmigrant status. In order to qualify, the nonimmigrant spouse must demonstrate that during the marriage he or she or their child was battered or subject to extreme cruelty perpetrated by the principal nonimmigrant spouse. Applications are submitted using Form I-765V. Employment authorization is issued in two-year intervals and may be renewed. Applications are submitted on Form I-765V.

115 Pub. L. No. 106-386, §1510(b), 114 Stat. 1464, 1531–32 (Oct. 28, 2000).

116 Pub. L. No. 109-162, §814, 119 Stat. 2960, 3058–60 (Jan. 5, 2006).

CHAPTER 10

ETHICAL ISSUES IN FAMILY-BASED IMMIGRATION LAW

Attorneys are bound by a code of professional responsibility in their representation of clients. Although nonattorney representatives accredited by the Board of Immigration Appeals (BIA) are not bound in the strict sense by this code, nonprofit agencies would be well advised to adopt and apply the same standards for all staff members who participate in assisting clients in immigration matters. It is in the interests of all practitioners, attorneys, and nonattorneys alike to make their behavior conform to the standards established by the American Bar Association (ABA). No staff member or nonprofit agency wants to be held liable for the consequences of unethical behavior.

Ethical issues arise in many aspects of family-based immigration law. For example, if the attorney is simply giving advice on which immigration form to fill out or how to answer certain questions on the form, a threshold issue is whether an attorney–client relationship has been established. If so, what duties and responsibilities does the attorney owe the client? If the attorney is representing both the petitioner and the beneficiary in a visa petition, and the parties' interests later come into conflict, how can the attorney avoid being caught in the middle? Or, if the attorney discovers that the client has provided false information on an immigration form, what must the attorney do with this information to avoid committing a fraud upon the immigration court or agency while at the same time preserving client confidentiality?

This chapter will cover some of the basic ethical problems that arise in representing clients in family-based immigration cases and provide direction for meeting current ethical standards. The requirements imposed with the affidavit of support involve many potential ethical issues, especially conflicts of interests; these potential ethical issues will be dealt with in some detail.

Sources of Ethics Rules

There is no single comprehensive authority to which immigration lawyers can turn for guidance when confronted with ethical dilemmas. U.S. Citizenship and Immigration Services (USCIS) and Executive Office for Immigration Review (EOIR) regulations at 8 CFR parts 292, 1003, and 1292 address, in part, the discipline of attorneys and nonattorney representatives. But the regulations do not provide guidance on some of the most important and vexing ethics issues faced by immigration lawyers, such as conflicts of interest. Generally, the ethics rules applicable to immigration lawyers are the rules of ethics for the state in which the lawyer is licensed to practice.[1] In addition, most states have statutes regulating business and professions. Of course, state and federal laws regarding fraud apply to all lawyers, irrespective of their area of practice.

This chapter will focus on the ABA Model Rules of Professional Conduct. In 1983, the ABA adopted the Model Rules, which have undergone several subsequent amendments. The Model Rules replaced the prior Model Code of Professional Responsibility, which had been adopted by the ABA in 1969. Since 1983, 48 states and the District of Columbia have adopted some version of the Model Rules as their state ethics rules. Illinois, New York, North Carolina, Oregon, and Virginia have adopted ethics rules incorporating provisions from both the Model Code and the Model Rules.

Establishment of the Attorney-Client Relationship

Lawyers must beware of solicitations to render informal legal advice, no matter how simple the issue may seem. Giving advice, even in the most casual of circumstances, may create an attorney-client relationship and subsequent liability for any advice relied on. The fact that no contract was signed and no fee paid will not necessarily protect a lawyer from liability. Immigration law is so complex, and imposes such severe consequences for even innocent mistakes, that it is unwise to render advice without an in-depth review of the facts directly with the client and a close analysis of the law.

Principles of agency and contract law generally determine whether and when an attorney-client relationship has been established. The relationship begins when the client acknowledges the lawyer's capacity to act on the client's behalf and the lawyer agrees to act for and under the control of the client. Thus, the question of whether an attorney–client relationship exists is one of fact, usually decided using a contract analysis. Typically, the agreement to form an attorney-client relationship is express. The client consults the lawyer. The lawyer agrees to take the case. The parties sign a contract. However, it is possible that the agreement to establish the attorney-client relationship can be implied from the lawyer's actions on the client's behalf or by the client's reasonable reliance.

Whether a person relied on the attorney is a subjective test that focuses on the person's belief that an attorney-client relationship exists. The reasonableness of the client's subjective belief depends on the facts of the case.

> **Example:** Penelope retains an attorney to represent her to petition for her husband's immigration to the United States. Penelope's sister, Theresa, also agrees to complete the Form I-864, Affidavit of Support, and act as a joint sponsor because Penelope cannot meet the income requirements. Penelope brings Theresa

---

[1] *Gadda v. Ashcroft*, 377 F.3d 934 (9th Cir. 2004) (holding federal disciplinary framework for immigration attorneys and representatives does not preempt state laws regulating attorneys).

to her attorney's office. The attorney proceeds to explain the affidavit of support and all of its liabilities to Penelope while Theresa listens. The attorney then explains to Penelope how the Form I-864 should be completed. The attorney hands the blank Form I-864 to Penelope and instructs her to complete it with Theresa and return it to him.

The attorney in the above example may have impliedly established an attorney-client relationship with Theresa. By rendering legal advice in front of Theresa regarding the potential liability under the affidavit of support, Theresa may reasonably believe that an attorney-client relationship exists. Furthermore, by explaining how to complete the Form I-864 in her hearing, the attorney may have led Theresa to believe that the attorney is representing her.

When a lawyer does not wish to take a case, he or she must make this clear to the person seeking counsel. The attorney should notify the person through a nonengagement letter stating specifically that the lawyer is not representing him or her.

The Attorney-Client Relationship and the Affidavit of Support

As the above hypothetical suggests, immigration lawyers face many vexing ethical issues when advising persons regarding the new affidavit of support requirements and liabilities. Form I-864, Affidavit of Support under Section 213A of the INA, purports to be a binding contract. Persons signing the Form I-864 are liable to the immigrating foreign national for maintenance and support and to government entities for reimbursement of any means-tested public benefits provided to the foreign national. Thus, where an immigration lawyer represents a husband and wife to obtain a family-based visa and the couple brings to the office a kind uncle to serve as a joint sponsor because of the couple's low income, it is critical that the lawyer clearly explain, if he or she does not wish to represent the uncle, that the lawyer is not representing the uncle. The lawyer should also advise the uncle to seek counsel regarding liability and obligations under the contract.

However, attorneys representing persons in completing the affidavit of support often face the question of whether they ethically may represent the petitioner, the beneficiary, and other household members or joint sponsors in the same transaction.

In taking on the representation of persons subject to the affidavit of support provisions, the attorney must decide which parties he or she will represent. If representing both the petitioner and sponsored immigrant, the attorney should be very clear with both parties about the potential conflict of interest problems that may arise. If not representing both parties, the attorney also must take pains to explain this to each party. If a joint sponsor is signing a separate affidavit of support, or a "household member" is executing a Form I-864A, Contract Between Sponsor and

Household Member, the attorney also must be clear regarding whether he or she has taken on the sponsor or household member as a client.

When a lawyer does not wish to take a case, he or she must make this clear to the person seeking counsel. The attorney should notify the person through a nonengagement letter stating specifically that the lawyer is not representing him or her.

Fiduciary Duty Even to Nonclients After Initial Consultation

Even when the lawyer decides not to take a case, certain fiduciary duties arise at the first consultation. Model Rule 1.18 outlines an attorney's fiduciary duties to a "prospective client."

Rule 1.18 Duties to Prospective Client

> (a) A person who discusses with a lawyer the possibility of forming a client-lawyer relationship with respect to a matter is a prospective client.
>
> (b) Even when no client-lawyer relationship ensues, a lawyer who has had discussions with a prospective client shall not use or reveal information learned in the consultation, except as Rule 1.9 would permit with respect to information of a former client.
>
> (c) A lawyer subject to paragraph (b) shall not represent a client with interests materially adverse to those of a prospective client in the same or a substantially related matter if the lawyer received information from the prospective client that could be significantly harmful to that person in the matter, except as provided in paragraph (d). If a lawyer is disqualified from representation under this paragraph, no lawyer in a firm with which that lawyer is associated may knowingly undertake or continue representation in such a matter, except as provided in paragraph (d).
>
> (d) When the lawyer has received disqualifying information as defined in paragraph (c), representation is permissible if:
>
>> (1) both the affected client and the prospective client have given informed consent, confirmed in writing, or:
>>
>> (2) the lawyer who received the information took reasonable measures to avoid exposure to more disqualifying information than was reasonably necessary to determine whether to represent the prospective client; and
>>
>>> (i) the disqualified lawyer is timely screened from any participation in the matter and is apportioned no part of the fee therefrom; and
>>>
>>> (ii) written notice is promptly given to the prospective client.

A prospective client is anyone who has consulted with the lawyer about possible representation, even if no attorney-client relationship was formed. With important exceptions, this rule prohibits a lawyer from representing a "client with interests materially adverse to those of a prospective client in the same or a substantially related matter if the lawyer received information from the prospective client that could be significantly harmful to that person in the matter." The rule states two exceptions. First, representation is allowed if the client and prospective client both give informed, written consent.

Second, another lawyer in the same firm can represent the new client if the lawyer who consulted with the prospective client is "timely screened" from the matter, and took "reasonable measures to avoid exposure to more disqualifying information than was … necessary to determine whether to represent [him or her]." In this case, the firm must give the prospective client prompt written notice and must not pay the disqualified lawyer for this matter.

This rule raises the awkward question of what to do if a prospective client innocently discloses harmful information relating to the case of a current, longtime client. Comment 5 to the Model Rule suggests that "[a] lawyer may condition conversations with a prospective client on the person's informed consent that no information disclosed during the consultation will prohibit the lawyer from representing a different client in the case."

The lawyer also has an ethical obligation to preserve confidences gained from a preliminary consultation.

> **Example:** Paul Petitioner consults Ann Attorney regarding a visa petition and adjustment of status application he filed for his wife, Benicia. He tells Ann that although he believes Benicia married him for love, she is now leaving him. He confides that they recently had a fight during which he slapped Benicia. He seeks Ann's assistance to withdraw the petition and inform USCIS that he will not appear at the scheduled adjustment of status interview. Ann gives Paul no advice and informs him that she is not interested in taking his case. A week later Benicia walks into Ann's office and asks for assistance in filing a battered spouse self-petition.

Although Ann was never retained by Paul and, arguably, no attorney-client relationship exists, she has obtained confidential information from Paul that she has a fiduciary duty not to disclose. Ann's fiduciary duty to Paul may interfere with her duty of zealous advocacy to Benicia in convincing USCIS that Benicia is a battered spouse. Thus, Ann would be wise to also decline representation of Benicia.

Immigration lawyers must understand when an attorney-client relationship exists and must communicate clearly with potential clients about the parameters of the relationship for several reasons. First, a lawyer may be disqualified from representing a potential client if the lawyer had an initial consultation with another party regarding a matter adverse to the potential client. Second, the existence of an attorney-client relationship is the threshold element that a plaintiff must prove in a malpractice suit. Most important, a lawyer's ethical obligations and duties are triggered by the establishment of the attorney-client relationship.

Competence and Diligence

Under Model Rules 1.1 and 1.3, attorneys must provide both competent and diligent representation.

> **Rule 1.1 Competence**
> A lawyer shall provide competent representation to a client. Competent representation requires the legal knowledge, skill, thoroughness and preparation reasonably necessary for the representation.

Immigration lawyers are under more pressure than ever to keep abreast of changes to the law, new regulations, and USCIS or Department of State (DOS) policy memoranda. Although the Model Rule seems simplistic and obvious in its requirement of competence, maintaining the level of knowledge and thoroughness necessary to advise clients adequately regarding immigration issues is an increasing challenge. The complexity of immigration law, along with increased penalties for even innocent violations of the law, makes it critical that practitioners research and study the law. The duty of competent representation in matters involving immigration issues attaches to criminal defense attorneys as well. The U.S. Supreme Court's decision in *Padilla v. Kentucky*[2] requires criminal defense attorneys to competently advise clients in criminal proceedings of the immigration consequences of a plea in a criminal case.

A lawyer is expected to be familiar with well-settled principles of law as they relate to the client's case. But what are an attorney's ethical obligations when the law is not well settled and changes rapidly? When rules of law are not commonly known, the lawyer has an ethical obligation to conduct legal research to discover such rules. Thus, it is not enough in immigration law to have access to the statutes, regulations, and case law. A competent attorney must have quick access to interpretations of the laws from the agencies with which the lawyer deals, whether it be USCIS, DOS, or the Department of Labor. In addition, an immigration lawyer must keep informed of the status of legislation and litigation that may affect a client's case.

The ethical duty of competence requires thoroughness and adequate preparation in handling a client matter, particularly considering the drastic consequences of removal on the lives of clients and their families. For the clients of many immigration lawyers, there are often huge matters at stake, involving health, safety and family reunification. Incompetent representation exposes a client to potentially devastating

---

2 559 U.S. 356 (2010).

consequences, including loss of status, family separation, and return to a country where the client's life is at risk.

Rule 1.3 Diligence

A lawyer shall act with reasonable diligence and promptness in representing a client.

The ethical duty of diligence is a lawyer's obligation to perform the work for which the lawyer was hired. Neglect of a client's case is one of the most frequent reasons for complaints to attorney discipline tribunals. Neglect in the immigration law context can cause serious harm to clients because the mere passage of time can cause a missed filing deadline, a visa overstay or violation, or inadmissibility because of accrual of unlawful presence.

Typically, when a lawyer has failed to act diligently, the lawyer aggravates the misconduct by avoiding contact with the client and may even fabricate reports on how the case is proceeding. This results in additional ethical violations involving misrepresentation and failure to communicate with the client. These ethical violations deny the client an opportunity to take other steps to preserve his or her rights.

The ethical obligation of diligence requires the lawyer to carry through to conclusion all matters undertaken for a client. Diligence is required in a case even though the case may become more difficult or relief less likely than expected because of the client's conduct or a change in the law. The duty to complete matters diligently continues until the matter is complete or the relationship has been terminated. For this reason, it is important that lawyers be clear with clients regarding the scope of the representation and when representation has ceased. Otherwise, a client mistakenly may believe that the lawyer is pursuing the client's affairs.

It is good practice to send the client a case-closing letter to clarify when representation ends. Where the scope of the lawyer–client relationship has been expressly limited to particular legal services, the lawyer has no duty to act promptly or diligently about matters outside those defined.

Obviously, an immigration lawyer is ethically required to meet all deadlines imposed by the immigration courts, the BIA, or federal courts. The failure to timely file an adjustment application when visa number retrogression is approaching may be as significant to an immigrant's life as the failure to meet a deadline to timely file a notice of appeal. However, even without a deadline, a lawyer may be disciplined for lack of diligence for taking too long to complete a matter. The ethics rules require not only that a lawyer actually do the work for which the lawyer was hired, but that the lawyer do the work within a reasonable time. Quite often poor office management may cause the lawyer to neglect his duty to the client. Although such an excuse may prevent a court from finding a lawyer guilty of fraud, it will not prevent disciplinary sanctions.

The fact that a client is not actually injured by the lawyer's lack of diligence will not necessarily protect the less-than-diligent lawyer from discipline. In *In re Roche*,[3] the lawyer failed to take any formal action on a client's case for four months after being retained. The court acknowledged that the client had not actually suffered any injury, but suspended the lawyer for 30 days, holding that "[r]espondent's negligent conduct provoked anguish in his client and overall tarnishes the reputation of the legal profession."

Communication

In immigration law, disciplinary tribunals may place a higher duty on lawyers to be careful in management of their offices and staff because clients are often unable to speak English and unfamiliar with the American legal system. Model Rule 1.4 speaks to an attorney's obligations in communicating with his or her clients.

> **Rule 1.4 Communication**
>
> (a) A lawyer shall:
>
> (1) promptly inform the client of any decision or circumstance with respect to which the client's informed consent, as defined in Rule 1.0(e), is required by these Rules;
>
> (2) reasonably consult with the client about the means by which the client's objectives are to be accomplished;
>
> (3) keep the client reasonably informed about the status of the matter;
>
> (4) promptly comply with reasonable requests for information; and
>
> (5) consult with the client about any relevant limitation on the lawyer's conduct when the lawyer knows that the client expects assistance not permitted by the Rules of Professional Conduct or other law.
>
> (b) A lawyer shall explain a matter to the extent reasonably necessary to permit the client to make informed decisions regarding the representation.

The obligation to communicate with the client has been recognized throughout the history of the legal profession. The duty to communicate is rooted in the common-law duty of communication imposed on all agents, including lawyers, and in the lawyer's fiduciary duty of utmost good faith to the client.

Although the duty to communicate with the client is an independent ethical obligation, a client who is happy with the outcome of the case is not likely to file a complaint for lack of communication. Complaints against lawyers for failure to communicate usually are triggered by the client's unhappiness with the case results, and often allege other ethics violations, such as incompetence, lack of diligence, or conflict of interest.

---

[3] 678 N.E.2d 797 (Ind. 1997).

A lawyer has an affirmative duty to keep clients informed of the status of their legal affairs. The duty is personal; thus, the lawyer must communicate directly with the client. Immigration lawyers face the unique problem of having to explain often exceedingly complex legal issues to clients who do not speak or understand English. In some cases, the client may be illiterate or have limited education. But the fact that an immigration lawyer cannot communicate with the client in a common language does not permit the lawyer to delegate all communication with the client to a nonlawyer employee. The lawyer should be present with the interpreter and ensure that he or she provides a full explanation of the client's rights and duties. This includes the scope of the representation, the plan of legal action, filing deadlines, case status, and any and all matters that may affect the client's rights and ability to make informed decisions on legal matters. When the immigration attorney communicates with the client through a family member or friend over the telephone, all significant information should be followed up with a letter in the client's language confirming the conversation.

One of the most difficult things for a lawyer to communicate is the fact that the lawyer has made a mistake in the client's case. This is particularly true in immigration law, where a missed filing deadline may result in years of separation for family members.

Model Rule 1.4(b) states that a lawyer must explain a matter to a client to the extent reasonably necessary for the client to make informed decisions. If a lawyer advises a course of action that may result in adverse consequences to the client, the lawyer also must advise of the risks of that action, of any other options available, and of the risks of those options. A lawyer must become sufficiently educated regarding a case to be able to offer the client meaningful advice about the options. Lawyers must resist the temptation simply to make decisions for the client because the law is "too complicated" to explain or because the law is in flux.

Confidentiality

A lawyer's duty of confidentiality clearly attaches when the lawyer–client relationship begins.

> **Rule 1.6 Confidentiality of Information**
>
> (a) A lawyer shall not reveal information relating to the representation of a client unless the client gives informed consent, the disclosure is impliedly authorized in order to carry out the representation or the disclosure is permitted by paragraph (b).
>
> (b) A lawyer may reveal information relating to the representation of a client to the extent the lawyer reasonably believes necessary:
>
> (1) to prevent reasonably certain death or substantial bodily harm;
>
> (2) to prevent the client from committing a crime or fraud that is reasonably certain to result in substantial injury to the financial interests or property of

another and in furtherance of which the client has used or is using the lawyer's services;

(3) to prevent, mitigate or rectify substantial injury to the financial interests or property of another that is reasonably certain to result or has resulted from the client's commission of a crime or fraud in furtherance of which the client has used the lawyer's services;

(4) to secure legal advice about the lawyer's compliance with these Rules;

(5) to establish a claim or defense on behalf of the lawyer in a controversy between the lawyer and the client, to establish a defense to a criminal charge or civil claim against the lawyer based upon conduct in which the client was involved, or to respond to allegations in any proceeding concerning the lawyer's representation of the client; or

(6) to comply with other law or a court order.

Attorney-client confidentiality is founded on the principle that a lawyer can best advise a client when the client feels free to discuss all information relating to the legal matter, even if embarrassing, without fear of reprisal. Information an attorney learns about a client during representation is presumed to be confidential, without regard to whether the client has requested expressly that the information not be disclosed. Model Rule 1.6 embodies this policy, stating that a lawyer must not reveal information relating to representation of a client, with very limited exceptions, unless the client consents after consultation or the disclosure is impliedly authorized in the representation.

The ethical duty of confidentiality is broader than the protections of communications under the attorney-client privilege. The attorney-client privilege only protects communications *from* the client; the ethical duty of confidentiality applies to all information relating to the representation, regardless of its source. Additionally, the ethical obligation of confidentiality applies in all contexts, not just when information about client communications has been subpoenaed.

Duty of Confidentiality to Former Clients

The duty of confidentiality does not terminate with the attorney-client relationship. The lawyer has an ongoing obligation to maintain confidences of the lawyer's former clients. Model Rule 1.9(c), a provision of the conflicts-of-interest rules, forbids a lawyer from using information relating to a former client's representation to the former client's disadvantage or from revealing a former client's confidential information except as permitted by the rules.

An attorney who once represented parties to obtain an immigrant visa and complete an affidavit of support may face issues of confidentiality later. For example, if a sponsored spouse seeks to enforce the affidavit of support after immigrating, the couple's lawyer may not disclose confidential client information to one former client to use against another former client. However, should litigation erupt between the parties, the prevailing rule is that the attorney-client privilege does not attach between commonly represented parties and will not protect such attorney-client communications if subpoenaed.

Implied Authorization to Disclose

Model Rule 1.6(a) allows a lawyer to disclose client information "impliedly authorized in order to carry out the representation." When authorization is implied, a lawyer need not obtain express consent from the client. However, how does a lawyer know when disclosure is "implied?" The comment to Model Rule 1.6 states that a disclosure is authorized when it is "appropriate in carrying out the representation," such as when a fact that cannot properly be disputed is admitted. The ABA has set forth a foreseeability analysis to permit "impliedly authorized" disclosures that are "necessary to the representation [and that], therefore, must be deemed to have been agreed to when the client hired the lawyer."[4]

Issues of implied authorization may arise with the affidavit of support. Lawyers who counsel persons who agree to be sponsors by signing the Form I-864 or Form I-864A obviously need not get express consent from the sponsor to disclose the sponsor's financial information to USCIS or DOS. Because the form obviously has to be reviewed by USCIS or DOS officials for the visa even to be considered, disclosure should be considered impliedly authorized. In addition, both forms state that USCIS may provide information regarding the sponsor's name and address to any federal, state, local, or private entity providing a means-tested benefit to the sponsored immigrant.

Between the sponsor and the sponsored immigrant, there is no requirement that the contents of the Form I-864 be disclosed.

Practically speaking, though, immigration lawyers often represent both the sponsor and the sponsored immigrant together, and many sponsors have no objection to the sponsored immigrant being privy to the information in the Form I-864. In fact, when the sponsor's income and assets barely meet the required guidelines, the attorney should discuss with the parties whether the sponsored immigrant may be in a better position to convince the consular or USCIS officer that he or she is not likely to become a public charge if the immigrant understands the contents of the affidavit.

In addition, if the sponsored immigrant's income is to be included in the Form I-864, the sponsor and immigrant will have to share information regarding their respective incomes and assets. The Form I-864A also requires both the sponsor and sponsor's household member to sign the contract. Thus, the best practice is for the attorney to explain to the client the need to file the affidavit and/or household

---

4 American Bar Association (ABA) Informal Ethics Opinion 89-1530 (1989).

member contract, the information required by the forms, and the parties who are entitled to access to the contents of the forms. In this way, the client will understand what information must be disclosed necessarily as part of the representation, and to whom it will be disclosed. The client also can discuss with the lawyer whether he or she should share confidential information with other parties, such as a sponsor, cosponsor, or beneficiary.

Client Fraud and Confidentiality

What the lawyer does when protecting client confidences may result in the lawyer unwittingly being used by the client to commit fraud or perjury?

> **Example:** An immigration lawyer represents a client before USCIS. The client has overstayed his tourist visa by one year, but apparently qualifies under INA §245(a) to adjust status through his U.S. citizen son. The lawyer files an adjustment of status application. However, on the way to the adjustment interview, the client informs the lawyer that he recently left the United States and reentered illegally. He admits not disclosing the information previously for fear that the lawyer would not pursue the adjustment of status application. The client insists that the lawyer not disclose the information to USCIS because the client will be put into removal proceedings and prevented from adjusting status by the 10-year bar under INA §212(a)(9)(B).

Whether a lawyer may reveal client confidences to rectify a client's crime or fraud is one of the most controversial issues in legal ethics. Model Rule 1.6 permits disclosure of a client confidence only:

- To prevent imminent death or substantial bodily harm;
- To prevent the client from committing a crime or fraud that will cause substantial injury to the financial interests or property of another, or to rectify such an act; or
- For the lawyer's own benefit in certain kinds of controversies over the lawyer's conduct.

The ABA has said that a lawyer who discovers that the client has used the lawyer's services to perpetrate a fraud must withdraw and may disavow his or her work product to prevent its use in the fraud even though this may involve disclosing confidential information. Moreover, the withdrawal must be accomplished in a manner that limits prejudice to the client's case. "[W]here silence would result in a violation of the lawyer's duty... not to assist a client's ongoing or intended future fraud, ... [t]he duty to keep client confidences must give way...."[5] However,

[5] ABA Formal Ethics Opinion 92-366 (1992).

disclosure should be made only to the extent necessary to avoid assisting the client's fraud, and then only as a last resort.

With respect to how a lawyer should disavow his or her work product, the lawyer must decline to reveal anything about the disaffirmed work product "beyond the simple fact that she no longer stands behind it." It may be necessary for the attorney to request an opinion letter from the state bar concerning the tension between the duty of confidentiality and the need to disavow a client's fraud. Note that state professional responsibility rules differ on how to address this issue, so a lawyer should consult the ethics rules for the state in which he or she is licensed to practice.

Although lawyers may worry that they may be found to have violated the rules of ethics for revealing client confidences in cases involving client fraud, the lawyer must also consider whether the failure to disclose a client's fraud will result in discipline, a charge of contempt, damage liability, accessory criminal liability, or criminal misconduct charges.

Conflict of Interest

Conflicts of Interest Between Existing Clients

Although Model Rule 1.7, which prohibits conflicts of interests between current clients, appears to be very broad, representation of both "sides" does not necessarily mean that a conflict exists. With some exceptions, Model Rule 1.7(a) prohibits representation of a client only if the representation of that client will be directly adverse to another client, or will be materially limited by the lawyer's responsibilities to another.

> **Rule 1.7 Conflict of Interest: Current Clients**
>
> (a) Except as provided in paragraph (b), a lawyer shall not represent a client if the representation involves a concurrent conflict of interest. A concurrent conflict of interest exists if:
>
> (1) the representation of one client will be directly adverse to another client; or
>
> (2) there is a significant risk that the representation of one or more clients will be materially limited by the lawyer's responsibilities to another client, a former client or a third person or by a personal interest of the lawyer.
>
> (b) Notwithstanding the existence of a concurrent conflict of interest under paragraph (a), a lawyer may represent a client if:
>
> (1) the lawyer reasonably believes that the lawyer will be able to provide competent and diligent representation to each affected client;
>
> (2) the representation is not prohibited by law;
>
> (3) the representation does not involve the assertion of a claim by one client

against another client represented by the lawyer in the same litigation or other proceeding before a tribunal; and

(4) each affected client gives informed consent, confirmed in writing.

One of the most common ethics questions asked by immigration lawyers is whether the lawyer may represent both "sides" in an immigration case. For example, may a lawyer ethically represent both spouses in a family-based visa petition? May a lawyer represent both the sponsor and the sponsored immigrant with respect to the affidavit of support? What are the lawyer's obligations if the relationship between the parties sours?

The prohibition against concurrent conflicts of interest is based on two policy considerations. First, the vigor of a lawyer's representation of one client may be diminished in an effort to avoid antagonizing another client. Second, a client must be able to expect the undivided loyalty of the lawyer. As the ABA has expressed it, "[l]oyalty is an indispensable element of a lawyer's relationship with a client."[6]

A lawyer may not terminate one client in favor of another in order to characterize a client as a "former" client and enjoy the looser conflicts test. If clients were *ever* represented concurrently, they are treated as concurrent clients for the purpose of a disqualification motion.

The prohibition against concurrent conflicts of interest is not limited to clients suing each other. It prohibits *any* representation adverse to an existing client. For example, a lawyer represents a man who has filed a visa petition for his wife. During the course of the representation, the man's 15-year-old son consults the lawyer about representing him to obtain a special immigrant juvenile visa, because his father has abandoned and abused the boy. Although the boy's case does not involve filing a complaint or suit directly against the father, pursuit of the boy's case will be adverse to the interests of the father. Thus, the prohibition against conflicts of interest should prevent the lawyer from taking the boy's case.

Concurrent Conflicts of Interest Sometimes Allowed

The general prohibition against concurrent conflicts of interest is subject to a significant exception. Model Rule 1.7 permits a lawyer to represent adverse clients concurrently if:

- The lawyer reasonably believes that he or she can provide competent, diligent representation to each client;
- Such representation is not illegal;
- The clients are not opposing parties in a lawsuit; and
- They give informed, written consent.

---

6 ABA Informal Ethics Opinion 1495 (1982).

Multiple Representation Can Be Appropriate When Conflicts Are Only Potential, Not Actual

In immigration law, conflict of interest issues arise more frequently from representation of multiple parties in the same transaction than from representation of clients whose separate cases are adverse. Multiple representation typically does not involve a situation in which a lawyer's responsibilities to one party will "materially limit" the lawyer's responsibilities to another. Both the petitioner and the beneficiary of the desired visa want the same thing: issuance of a visa. No actual conflict of interest exists. However, there is often potential for conflict between the parties. For example, under the affidavit of support, the sponsoring immigrant is liable for support and maintenance of the sponsored immigrant until the time the immigrant naturalizes or works 40 qualifying quarters under the Social Security Act. A sponsored immigrant may sue the sponsor for this support.

Whether multiple representation is proper when a conflict is only "potential" is a determination made on a case-by-case basis after consideration of the interests involved. A fact-specific analysis accommodates the general reluctance on the part of courts to disqualify counsel for conflicts that are merely potential.

Cases Involving an Affidavit of Support Raise Conflict of Interest Issues

The affidavit of support will raise potential conflicts of interest in every multiple representation, as it provides the sponsored immigrant with a means of legally forcing financial support from the petitioner. Cosponsors or household members signing the Form I-864A may have to share such liability with the petitioner. Even if the sponsored immigrant does not seek enforcement of the contract, the petitioner, cosponsor, or household member may be jointly and severally liable to a federal, state, or private entity seeking reimbursement for certain benefits paid to the sponsored immigrant. Under the Model Rules, it is permissible for an attorney to represent parties whose interests are generally aligned, such as a petitioner, beneficiary, and even cosponsors, because they are all seeking to obtain a family-based visa for the beneficiary, even though there exists some difference of interest among them.

Informed Consent Requires Full Disclosure of Pros and Cons of Common Representation

Model Rule 1.7 allows concurrent conflicts of interest between a lawyer's clients only if they give their "informed consent."[7] "Informed consent" is defined by Model Rule 1.0(e).

---

[7] *See also* Comment 18 to Rule 1.7.

Rule 1.0(e)

> "Informed consent" denotes the agreement by a person to a proposed course of conduct after the lawyer has communicated adequate information and explanation about the material risks of and reasonably available alternatives to the proposed course of conduct.

For a client to give informed consent, the attorney must make full disclosure of the advantages and risks of multiple representation. The attorney has the highest duty to disclose all facts necessary for the parties to make an informed decision regarding the representation, including areas of potential conflicts and the possibility and desirability of obtaining independent legal advice.

For immigration practitioners assisting clients with the affidavit of support requirements, full disclosure includes informing the petitioner, sponsored immigrants, and any cosponsors and sponsoring household members of all potential obligations, penalties, and liabilities in completing and submitting the Form I-864 and the Form I-864A. This should include an explanation of the following:

- The sponsor may be required to support the sponsored immigrants at 125 percent of the current poverty income guidelines;
- The affidavit will be legally enforceable by the sponsored immigrants and by the federal government, a state, or "any other entity" that provides a means-tested benefit for the duration of the validity of the affidavit of support;
- The sponsor's financial information may be disclosed to other entities seeking enforcement of the affidavit;
- The duration of liability on the affidavit; and
- The address-reporting requirements and civil fines for failure to comply.

Full disclosure also requires that the attorney explain the existence of any potential conflict of interest among the petitioner, sponsored immigrant, and cosponsors. This includes an explanation that the sponsors and household members signing the Forms I-864 and I-864A, respectively, may be sued by the sponsored immigrant to enforce the affidavits. The attorney also must explain the ethical limitations of multiple representation. Such limitations include the possibility that the attorney may have to withdraw from representation of all parties should the conflict grow to such an extent that it interferes with the attorney's ability to render adequate representation.

Obtaining Clients' Consent

Once full disclosure has been rendered and the attorney has determined that the representation will not result in an adverse effect on the representation of any of the clients, the attorney must obtain all the clients' consent. Although written consent is not required in all states, consent should be in writing. An attorney's consent form should be tailored to the client's level of sophistication and should include, at least, the following information:

- An explanation of the legal work that will be performed;
- Advantages and disadvantages of multiple representation;
- An explanation of the attorney's obligations regarding client confidences; and
- A recommendation that the parties seek other counsel before agreeing to multiple representation.

If the client is not in a position to know whether he or she will be vulnerable to disadvantage as a result of the representation, consent cannot be valid. In the case of clients who speak limited English, lack familiarity with the U.S. legal system, or are of limited means, the validity of consent may be suspect. In all cases, the lawyer should make full disclosure in writing in the client's native language.

Duty to Withdraw from Representation of All Clients if One Client's Interests Become Adverse to an Existing Client's Interests

If it becomes evident during such multiple representation that the attorney cannot adequately represent the interests of each party, or should any party revoke consent, the attorney must withdraw and thereafter may not represent one party against another on the same matter.[8]

> **Example:** Attorney Smith represents a U.S. citizen mother filing a visa petition for her son. The mother is elderly and not working, so her U.S. citizen daughter agrees to act as a cosponsor. The mother, son, and daughter all consent, after full disclosure, to permit Attorney Smith to represent each of them. While Attorney Smith is preparing the visa petition, the daughter and son have an argument. The daughter calls Attorney Smith and states that she does not want her brother to immigrate to the United States. She states that she revokes her consent to the multiple representation and demands that Attorney Smith immediately return her signed and completed Form I-864 to her.

At the outset of representation in the above hypothetical, Attorney Smith's clients shared an interest in a particular outcome, although there existed a potential conflict in that the daughter could become liable to the son through the affidavit of support. Thus, it was reasonable for Attorney Smith to believe that none of the parties would be adversely affected by the multiple representation. However, because of the potential conflict of interest, Attorney Smith properly obtained consent from each client after full disclosure.

---

8 *See* Comment 29 to Model Rule 1.7.

After Attorney Smith took on the multiple representation, the position of the son and daughter became fundamentally antagonistic. Courts presume that an adverse effect occurs when an attorney represents an interest adverse to an existing client. Consent has been revoked. Attorney Smith therefore cannot continue representation of the parties. If Attorney Smith seeks to pursue the daughter's interests, she will not be able to represent the son and mother competently and diligently, as Model Rule 1.7 requires. Furthermore, Attorney Smith is not permitted simply to drop the daughter as a client and continue representing the mother and son. Otherwise, an attorney could convert a present client into a "former client" by choosing when to cease to represent the disfavored client.

Because continued representation in the above hypothetical will result in violation of Model Rule 1.7, Attorney Smith must withdraw from representing all three parties. Model Rule 1.16 governs withdrawal in circumstances in which a conflict arises after the representation has commenced. The hypothetical demonstrates the importance of full disclosure from the outset to each of multiple clients regarding the potential hazards of multiple representation. In addition to full disclosure, the attorney should reach an agreement with each party from the outset regarding to whom original client papers and documents will be returned in the event withdrawal is required.

Should an attorney proceed with representation of adverse interests in violation of the ethics rules, a client may file a motion to disqualify the attorney from the case. Such disqualification may be used as a basis for the imposition of disciplinary sanctions.

Conflict Between Existing Client and Former Client: Allowed Unless Subject Matter Is "Substantially Related" to Former Case

Model Rule 1.9 governs conflicts of interest between former clients and new or existing clients.

Rule 1.9 Duties to Former Clients

> (a) A lawyer who has formerly represented a client in a matter shall not thereafter represent another person in the same or a substantially related matter in which that person's interests are materially adverse to the interests of the former client unless the former client gives informed consent, confirmed in writing.

A lawyer may not represent a client adverse to a *former* client if the subject matter is "substantially related" to the former case, unless there is written, informed consent. The standard to determine conflict between an existing client and a former client is not as strict as between two existing clients. Disqualification because of conflict of interest is more common when the conflict is between an existing client and a former client. This is probably because conflicts between existing clients are more obvious to lawyers.

Duty of Continuing Loyalty to Former Clients

Although it appears that an immigration lawyer may represent both petitioner and visa beneficiary concurrently as long as the requirements of Rule 1.7 are satisfied, what happens when one of the clients returns to the lawyer after the representation has ended and seeks further representation that may affect the other party?

> **Example**: A lawyer represents a husband, Peter, and wife, Benita, to obtain conditional lawful permanent residence for the wife. Two years later, Benita comes to the office of the lawyer informing the lawyer that Peter has been battering her and she wishes to file for a waiver to remove the condition on her lawful permanent resident status. She also wants advice regarding enforcing the affidavit of support against Peter.

In addition to the lawyer's obligation not to use a former client's confidences against him or her, a lawyer has a duty of continuing loyalty, even after the representation has ended. Clients would feel abused by the legal system if lawyers could later turn against them. Thus, Model Rule 1.9(a) prohibits a lawyer from representing another person in a substantially related matter that is materially adverse to the lawyer's former client, unless the client consents after consultation.

In the above example, Benita may argue that pursuit of the waiver of the condition on her permanent residence is not directly adverse to the interests of Peter and, therefore, poses no conflict. Although a definition of what makes a client's interests adverse is difficult to pin down, generally, the test is whether the former and current client's interests are differing. The interests need not be totally adversarial; it is enough that the two positions are not exactly aligned. It may be a close call whether pursuing the waiver of the condition is adverse to Peter's interests or will cause him detriment. However, enforcement of the affidavit of support against Peter clearly would be adverse. As sympathetic as Benita may be, the best practice for a lawyer in this situation is to decline representation and refer the case to another lawyer. Doubts should be resolved in favor of finding that the representations would be adverse.

Unrepresented Third Party

Where an attorney, for any reason, declines to represent any of the parties involved in the process of obtaining an immigrant visa and completing an affidavit of support, the attorney has certain ethical obligations when dealing with any of them who are unrepresented by another attorney.

> **Rule 4.3 Dealing with an Unrepresented Person**
>
> In dealing on behalf of a client with a person who is not represented by counsel, a lawyer shall not state or imply that the lawyer is disinterested. When the lawyer knows or reasonably should know that the unrepresented person misunderstands

> the lawyer's role in the matter, the lawyer shall make reasonable efforts to correct the misunderstanding. The lawyer shall not give legal advice to an unrepresented person, other than the advice to secure counsel, if the lawyer knows or reasonably should know that the interests of such a person are or have a reasonable possibility of being in conflict with the interests of the client.

The issue of unrepresented third parties will arise when the immigration practitioner is not representing the third-party sponsor signing the Form I-864 or the household member signing the Form I-864A.

> **Example:** Attorney Athena represents a U.S. citizen, Ulysses, in preparing the appropriate consulate documentation to permit his mother to immigrate. Ulysses does not have income or assets sufficient to demonstrate that he can maintain his mother at 125 percent of the poverty income guidelines. However, Ulysses intends to include his son's income on the Form I-864, since his son has lived with him for the past six months. Ulysses asks Attorney Athena for the Form I-864A and requests that Attorney Athena explain the form to him so that he can pass on the instructions to his son.

In the above hypothetical, assuming Attorney Athena does not wish to represent Ulysses' son, she must exercise care not to establish an attorney–client relationship impliedly by rendering legal advice and must avoid giving Ulysses' son the impression that she is disinterested. An unrepresented person, particularly one who is unsophisticated, might assume that an attorney is a disinterested authority on the law, particularly if the attorney attempts to explain the obligations and liabilities of the affidavit of support. Thus, although the attorney can explain the contents and liabilities of the affidavits to her own client, the attorney should make clear that she does not represent the third party and is not disinterested. The attorney should give no advice to the unrepresented third party other than to advise the person to obtain counsel.

Meritorious Claims

Model Rule 3.1 states that a lawyer shall not advocate a claim, defense, or appeal unless there is a basis for doing so that is not frivolous.

> **Rule 3.1: Meritorious Claims and Contentions**
>
> A lawyer shall not bring or defend a proceeding, or assert or controvert an issue therein, unless there is a basis in law and fact for doing so that is not frivolous, which includes a good faith argument for an extension, modification or reversal of existing law. A lawyer for the defendant in a criminal proceeding, or the respondent in a proceeding that could result in incarceration, may nevertheless so defend the proceeding as to require that every element of the case be established.

Infractions of the rules on meritorious claims can result in professional discipline ranging from a reprimand to disbarment. Federal courts may impose monetary sanctions through the use of various statutes, court rules, and the inherent judicial power of the court.

The INA includes provisions sanctioning "frivolous" applications, appeals, or claims.[9] Although the apparent policy behind these provisions was to limit frivolous claims, the practical effect may be to chill lawyers' ability to push novel or creative theories in immigration law. Of course, discouraging frivolous claims is important and such attempts are not limited to immigration law.

INA §240(b)(6) charges the attorney general with defining by regulation what constitutes sanctionable "frivolous behavior" in immigration proceedings before the administrative tribunals. The statute also charges the attorney general with specifying the circumstances in which an administrative appeal would be considered frivolous and summarily dismissed. Possible sanctions under the statute include suspension and disbarment.

There is no uniform definition of a "frivolous" claim, defense, or appeal. The primary difference among the jurisdictions is whether the lawyer's conduct must be judged by a subjective or objective standard. Comment 2 to Model Rule 3.1 requires that lawyers "inform themselves about the facts of their clients' cases and the applicable law and determine that they can make good faith arguments in support of their clients' positions. Such action is not frivolous even though the lawyer believes that the client's position ultimately will not prevail. The action is frivolous, however, if the lawyer is unable either to make a good faith argument on the merits of the action taken or to support the action taken by a good faith argument for an extension, modification or reversal of existing law."

DOJ and DHS Rules on Professional Conduct for Immigration Practitioners

On June 27, 2000, the Immigration and Naturalization Service (INS) and EOIR published a final rule on professional conduct for immigration practitioners, adopting much of the language from the Model Rules.[10] The rule modified 8 CFR parts 3 (now 1003) and 292. The regulations are controversial for several reasons, not the least of which is that sanctions may be levied only against immigrant advocates and not against Department of Homeland Security (DHS) district counsel.

The rules not only outline the authority that EOIR has to investigate and impose disciplinary sanctions against practitioners, but also the authority of DHS to investigate complaints regarding practitioners who practice before it. The rules state that a practitioner may be subject to disciplinary proceedings if he or she engages in frivolous actions that he or she "knows or reasonably should have known … lack

9 INA §§240(b)(6), 274C.

10 65 Fed. Reg. 39513 (June 27, 2000); amended, 75 Fed. Reg. 5225 (Feb. 2, 2010).

an arguable basis in law or in fact, or are taken for an improper purpose, such as to harass or to cause unnecessary delay."[11] However, they also include the proviso that "[n]othing in this regulation should be read to denigrate the practitioner's duty to represent zealously his or her client within the bounds of the law."[12]

In addition, the rules make engaging in "contumelious or otherwise obnoxious conduct which would constitute contempt of court in a judicial proceeding" grounds for sanction.[13] The rules do not define or provide examples of such behavior.

The rules further provide that by signing any document, motion, appeal, or application, the practitioner certifies that he or she has read the document and, after reasonable inquiry, believes that the document is "well-grounded in fact and is warranted by existing law or by a good faith argument for the extension, modification, or reversal of existing law or the establishment of new law."[14] A petitioner is also subject to sanction if he or she "knowingly or with reckless disregard [offers] false evidence. If a practitioner has offered material evidence and comes to know of its falsity, the practitioner shall take appropriate remedial measures."[15] Issues of document fraud will be discussed in the following section.

Sanctions that can be imposed under these rules include expulsion or suspension from practice, or public or private censure.[16] Appeal of an order disciplining an attorney can be made to the BIA.[17]

Document Fraud

The INA also provides penalties for submitting false documents to EOIR or USCIS. The document fraud provisions under INA §274C impose civil and criminal liability on immigration lawyers preparing forms or documents that are falsely made, or failing to disclose that the lawyer assisted in preparing such documents or forms.[18] Submission of such documents is sanctionable not only if it is knowingly done, but also if such documents are submitted "in reckless disregard" of the fact that the document is falsely made.

---

11 8 CFR §1003.102(j)(1).

12 8 CFR §1003.102.

13 8 CFR §1003.102(g). "Contumelious" means "insolently abusive and humiliating." *Merriam-Webster Online Dictionary*, www.merriam-webster.com.

14 8 CFR §1003.102(j)(1).

15 8 CFR §102(c).

16 8 CFR §1003.101(a).

17 8 CFR §1003.106(c).

18 Although the case does not specifically address immigration attorney liability, the Ninth Circuit held that 274C notice forms and procedures violate due process. *Walters v. Reno,* 145 F.3d 1032 (9th Cir. 1998), *cert. denied,* 119 S. Ct. 1140 (Mar. 8, 1999). Thereafter the parties reached agreement on the use of a new, revised form to give notice to individuals who are charged with civil document fraud.

The definition of "falsely made" under INA §274C(f) is troubling in that it does not necessarily require the lawyer to have any intent or knowledge of the falseness of the document offered. A lawyer may be found to have "falsely made" a document if the lawyer prepares a document or application that "has no basis in law or fact, or otherwise fails to state a fact which is material to the purpose for which it was submitted."

What constitutes "reckless disregard" that a document was "falsely made" under INA §274C(a) is not clear. At least one court has stated, however, that an attorney does not have an affirmative duty to investigate the veracity of client representations. In *In re Grand Jury Subpoena*,[19] a private law firm received a grand jury subpoena for files of two clients pursuant to an investigation regarding a sham-marriage conspiracy. The district court quashed the subpoena, holding that the attorney–client privilege and the work product doctrine protected the client files from disclosure absent government proof that any attorney–client communications were made in furtherance of a crime, fraud, or other misconduct.

The district court held that "[a] lawyer is under a professional obligation to represent a client zealously within the bound of the law.... It is fundamentally inconsistent with this obligation to require an attorney to ascertain the truth or falsity of his client's assertions. So long as the attorney does not have obvious indications of fraud or perjury, the attorney is not obligated to undertake an independent determination before advancing his clients' position."

Although an attorney is under no obligation to investigate the truth of a client's assertions, an attorney may not consciously avoid learning the truth when it is obvious the client is engaging in fraud. In *U.S. v. Sarantos*,[20] the defendant attorney instructed clients to sign blank visa petitions that the attorney would later complete and file with the INS. Each petition falsely claimed that the parties were living together as a married couple. The evidence indicated that several of the couples had to communicate with each other through an interpreter at the attorney's office. In other cases, the attorney would execute divorce petitions simultaneously with the INS applications. The district court found that the attorney acted with a reckless disregard for the truth and with a conscious effort to avoid learning the truth, which supported a conviction for aiding and abetting the making of false statements.

Model Rule 3.3 also requires that a lawyer not "offer evidence that the lawyer knows to be false. If a lawyer, the lawyer's client, or a witness called by the lawyer, has offered material evidence and the lawyer comes to know of its falsity, the lawyer shall take reasonable remedial measures, including, if necessary, disclosure to the tribunal."[21] This duty applies "even if compliance requires disclosure of information

19 615 F. Supp. 958 (D. Mass. 1985).

20 455 F.2d 877 (2d Cir. 1972).

21 Model Rules of Prof'l Conduct r. 3.3(a)(3) (Am. Bar Ass'n,).

otherwise protected by Rule 1.6."[22] However, comments to the Model Rule specify that the obligation to rectify false evidence or false statements of law or fact ends with the conclusion of the proceeding.[23]

Terminating Representation Due to Fraud or Other Reasons

When a lawyer must withdraw from representation of a client because of the client's insistence on committing fraud, or for whatever reason, the lawyer must follow certain rules of ethics in accomplishing the termination of the relationship. In certain cases, the rules of ethics require withdrawal. Model Rule 1.16 states that a lawyer must withdraw from representation when:

- The representation will result in violation of the law or rules of ethics;
- The lawyer's health materially impairs the lawyer's ability to represent the client; or
- The lawyer is discharged.

Some of the most common violations of the mandatory withdrawal provisions include violations of the Model Rules. These include Model Rule 1.1 (attorney competence), Rules 1.7 and 1.8 (conflicts of interest), Rule 1.9 (representation adverse to former clients), Rule 3.1 (limits on frivolous claims), and Rule 3.3 (false evidence, client perjury).

What happens, however, when a lawyer wants to withdraw for a reason that does not fall under one of the mandatory clauses? All lawyers have faced the exasperating problem of the client who fails to provide the lawyer with necessary documents and information, neglects to return the lawyer's phone calls, withholds material information, and is chronically late to appointments or fails to show up at all. Although a client can discharge a lawyer at any time and for any reason, lawyers often must provide a justification to "fire" a client. Model Rule 1.16 lists eight circumstances under which a lawyer may seek to withdraw. These are when:

- Withdrawal can be accomplished without a material adverse effect
- The client persists in actions the lawyer reasonably believes are criminal or fraudulent
- The client has used the lawyer's services to perpetrate crime or fraud
- The client insists on taking action that the lawyer considers repugnant or with which he or she has a fundamental disagreement
- The client fails substantially to fulfill an obligation to the lawyer and the client has received a warning that withdrawal may result

---

22 Model Rules of Prof'l Conduct r. 3.3(c) (Am. Bar Ass'n,).

23 Model Rules of Prof'l Conduct r. 3.3, Comment 13 (Am. Bar Ass'n,) (the conclusion of the proceeding occurs when a final judgment has been affirmed on appeal or the time for review has passed).

- The representation will result in an unreasonable financial burden on the lawyer
- The representation has been rendered unreasonably difficult by the client
- There is "good cause."

Thus, the Model Rules do provide for withdrawal when the client's conduct renders representation unreasonably difficult. Rule 1.16 recognizes that lawyers should not be forced to continue to represent a client when effective representation is made impractical by the client's refusal to communicate or cooperate.

Withdrawing from Representation in Affidavit-of-Support Case

During the course of representing a party or parties to obtain an immigrant visa and complete the affidavit of support and/or household member contract, it may become apparent to the attorney that continued representation is not possible because of a conflict of interest that will adversely affect one or more of the represented parties. The most common scenario facing the immigration attorney is one in which the relationship between the spouses sours and the petitioning spouse no longer wishes to pursue the immigrant visa. With the new affidavit-of-support requirements, however, additional ethical issues may arise.

> **Example:** Attorney Tao represents Peter and Benita in filing a Form I-751 petition to remove the conditions on Benita's residence. After filing the Form I-751, but before the interview, Benita calls Attorney Tao and states that she still wants to proceed with the Form I-751 interview, but she has fallen in love with another man and wants to know about the enforceability of the affidavit of support should she decide to leave Peter.

In the above hypothetical, it would appear that Attorney Tao must withdraw from her representation of both Peter and Benita, since continued representation of Benita's interests will be directly adverse to Peter, in violation of the rules regarding conflict of interest. Also, as noted above, Attorney Tao may not simply drop one client in favor of another to eliminate the conflict, because she owes both Peter and Benita a duty of undivided loyalty. There is an exception to this rule if a client consents in advance to the lawyer's continued representation of the other party. However, the lawyer has the burden of proving that the client consented and that such consent is valid. Validity of consent will depend on whether the attorney raised the conflict issue at the earliest possible time and the client is relatively sophisticated in legal or business affairs.

How to Protect Interests of Client During Termination

To terminate representation, an attorney is obligated to take special steps to protect the interests of the commonly represented clients. Model Rule 1.16(d) states that, upon termination of representation, an attorney must take reasonable steps to protect the client's interests. Such steps include the following:

- Give reasonable notice to the clients of termination;
- Allow the clients sufficient time to retain other counsel before ceasing work;
- Cooperate with replacement counsel; and
- Surrender all client papers and property and refund any advance payment of fees that have not been earned.

Even if an attorney has been discharged by the client unfairly, the attorney must take all reasonable steps to mitigate the consequences to the client. If the attorney is representing clients before a judicial or administrative tribunal, the attorney must comply with local court rules regarding withdrawal, which often require obtaining court approval to withdraw.

Conclusion

Lawyers representing immigrants who may be new to the United States and unfamiliar with its language, customs, and legal system have a special duty to ensure that their immigrant clients are fully informed and aware of their rights. Immigration lawyers should require the highest ethical standards, not just of themselves, but also of their colleagues and of lawyers representing the government. With long-term bars for unlawful presence, multiple grounds of inadmissibility, and other severe consequences for failing to comply with immigration laws, practitioners bear a greater responsibility to stay current in immigration law and maintain tight office filing systems. Noncitizens may face severe consequences, including life-long separation from family members and the loss "of all that makes life worth living."[24] Delivery of high-quality and ethical legal services will ensure that justice will be served to this often vulnerable and targeted population.

The affidavit-of-support requirements under INA §213A raise complex ethical concerns for immigration practitioners, especially when multiple representation of parties is involved. Practitioners should take the time before establishing such attorney–client relationships to think through the various ethical issues. As the contractually binding nature of the affidavit raises the possibility of at least a potential conflict of interest in any multiple representation, attorneys must consult their relevant state rules of ethics and, at a minimum, prepare disclosure and consent forms so that clients are fully aware of the implications of such representation. Additionally, attorneys must maintain the confidentiality of client information in the affidavit of support but make clear to the client that disclosure of the information will be made to USCIS or DOS. Finally, the attorney must be vigilant about the

[24] *Bridges v. Wixon*, 326 U.S. 135, 147 (1945).

existence of actual conflicts of interest and take the necessary steps to terminate the representation when undivided loyalty to the client has become impossible.

APPENDIX 1

JUNE 2020 VISA BULLETIN: FAMILY-SPONSORED PREFERENCES

First: (F1) Unmarried Sons and Daughters of U.S. Citizens: 23,400 plus any numbers not required for fourth preference.

Second: Spouses and Children, and Unmarried Sons and Daughters of LPRs: 114,200, plus the number (if any) by which the worldwide family preference level exceeds 226,000, plus any unused first preference numbers:

A. **(F2A)** Spouses and Children of LPRs: 77% of the overall second preference limitation, of which 75% are exempt from the per-country limit;

B. **(F2B)** Unmarried Sons and Daughters (21 years of age or older) of LPRs: 23% of the overall second preference limitation.

Third: (F3) Married Sons and Daughters of U.S. Citizens: 23,400, plus any numbers not required by first and second preferences.

Fourth: (F4) Brothers and Sisters of Adult U.S. Citizens: 65,000, plus any numbers not required by first three preferences.

A. APPLICATION FINAL ACTION DATES

	All Chargeability Areas Except Those Listed	CHINA	INDIA	MEXICO	PHILIPPINES
F1	22MAY14	22MAY14	22MAY14	15NOV97	01FEB11
F2A	C	C	C	C	C
F2B	15MAR15	15MAR15	15MAR15	15FEB99	01SEP10
F3	15APR08	15APR08	15APR08	22JUN96	15APR01
F4	08AUG06	08AUG06	22JAN05	08MAY98	01FEB01

B. APPLICATION FILING DATES

	All Chargeability Areas Except Those Listed	CHINA	INDIA	MEXICO	PHILIPPINES
F1	15FEB15	15FEB15	15FEB15	22DEC99	01SEP11
F2A	01MAY20	01MAY20	01MAY20	01MAY20	01MAY20
F2B	01DEC15	01DEC15	01DEC15	22SEP99	01MAY11
F3	15MAR09	15MAR09	15MAR09	15JUL00	15NOV01
F4	31JUL07	31JUL07	01OCT05	08FEB99	01SEP01

Appendix 2

Request to Reinstate I-130 Petition Based on INA §204(*l*), with List of Supporting Documents

Department of Homeland Security
United States Citizenship and Immigration Services
P.O. Box 10130
Laguna Niguel, CA 92607-1013

[Date]

File No. _______

Dear sir or madam:

I am writing on behalf of my client, ____________, who is seeking reinstatement pursuant to INA §204(*l*) of an I-130 petition filed on his behalf by his _________ [father, mother, etc.]. The petition was filed on _____ and approved on ______. The petitioner died on ______, after the petition was approved and before any application was filed. The approval of the petition was automatically revoked upon the petitioner's death.

INA §204(*l*) provides for the reinstatement of a petition after the death of the petitioner if the beneficiary satisfies certain conditions. The beneficiary must have been residing in the United States at the time the petitioner died and have continued to reside here since his or her death. The beneficiary does not have to establish any humanitarian factors in support of this request.

The following documents are submitted as evidence of eligibility for 204(*l*) relief:

- Copy of the I-130 approval notice
- Copy of the death certificate indicating the petitioner died on ______
- Evidence that the beneficiary entered the United States on ______ [include copy of I-94 or entry stamp if beneficiary was inspected and admitted; if entered EWI, include affidavit of beneficiary describing date, place, and manner of entry to the United States, date of departure from home country, method of travel, and countries traveled through en route to United States]

- Evidence that the beneficiary was residing in the United States on the date the petitioner died and has continued to reside here [include employment or school records; rent, telephone, or utility bills; hospital or medical records; attestations by church, unions, or other organizations; money order receipts; passport entries; birth certificates of children born in the United States; bank accounts or insurance documents; Social Security or Selective Service card; automobile license receipt, title, or vehicle registration; deeds, mortgages, leases, or other contracts to which the beneficiary has been a party; tax receipts; any other relevant document]
- Form I-864, Affidavit of Support, executed by a substitute sponsor, the beneficiary's _____ [LPR or citizen spouse, parent, mother-in-law, father-in-law, sibling, child at least 18 years of age, son, daughter, daughter-in-law, son-in-law, sister-in-law, brother-in-law, grandparent, grandchild, or legal guardian] and proof of relationship
- G-28

Sincerely,

APPENDIX 3

INFORMED CONSENT DOCUMENT FOR INDIVIDUALS SUBJECT TO NTA ISSUANCE

I, [name of client], met with my lawyer/representative, [name of lawyer/representative], and we discussed the following:

1. I am eligible to apply for [identify benefit(s) sought] with U.S. Citizenship & Immigration Services (USCIS).

2. USCIS issued a policy in June 2018 that discusses when noncitizens who apply for immigration benefits with USCIS will be placed into "removal proceedings." Removal proceedings are a process where the U.S. government tries to deport a noncitizen from the United States. Removal proceedings occur in an immigration court where an immigration judge makes the final decision. Removal proceedings can take many months or years to complete and often involve multiple hearings. Some people are detained by ICE during removal proceedings. For these people, the process usually goes much faster. During removal proceedings, the noncitizen can agree to removal or can fight removal. The possible arguments and remedies that may be raised in immigration court depend on the facts of the case.

3. Based on this policy, I understand if I file my application, I may be placed in removal proceedings and I could also be detained during part or all of those proceedings.

4. I understand that my lawyer/representative cannot guarantee any result in my case. My lawyer/representative explained how the USCIS policy could apply to my case, and the risks and benefits of submitting my application. I also understand that there are no guarantees that I won't be placed into removal proceedings if I don't apply. In other words, it is possible that ICE could put me into removal proceedings at any time, even if I don't file this application.

5. If I were placed into removal proceedings, my lawyer/representative [name of lawyer/representative] [WOULD/WOULD NOT] be able to represent me. If not, I understand that it is my responsibility to find a lawyer or representative for any removal case if I want representation.

I understand the above information. My lawyer/representative has answered any questions that I have about the above information. Having been advised of the above, I choose to file an application for [identify benefit(s) sought] with USCIS.

____________________________________ ____________________

[Signature of client] Date

Appendix 4

DOCUMENT CHECKLIST FOR ADJUSTMENT OF STATUS APPLICATION

Type of Document	Requested	Provided or Completed
Proof of Eligible for Adjustment		
Approval Notice for I-130, Petition for Alien Relative		
Contemporaneously Filed I-130, Petition for Alien Relative		
Biographical		
Applicant's Birth Certificate or Other Identity Documents		
Applicant's Marriage Certificate (if derivative)		
Applicant's Divorce Certificate (if derivative, if applicable)		
English Translation or Birth Certificate of Other Identity Documents		
Proof of Inspection and Admission or Parole		
Form I-94 Arrival – Departure Record		
Passport Page with Admission or Parole Stamp		
Border Crossing Card (valid on date of entry)		
Secondary Evidence (examples: plane ticket, bus ticket)		
Written Statements From Applicant and Other(s) with Personal Knowledge of Admission or Parole		
Medical Exam		
Applicant's Form I-693, Medical Examination Report and Vaccination Supplement, Completed by a Designated Civil Surgeon in Sealed Envelope* **Obtain at later date to file in response to RFE or at interview.*		
Other		
Government-Issued Identity Document with Photograph		
2 Passport Style Photographs of Applicant		
Arrest Records* and Certificates of Dispositions from All of Applicant's Arrests, (if applicable) **In many instances arrest records may have information that your client disputes and is not supported by the case disposition. Seek technical assistance in deciding on the submission of arrest records where they contain harmful information about the applicant.*		
Proof for Affidavit of Support		
Photocopy of Sponsor's Tax Returns and W-2s for the Most Recent Tax Year or IRS Tax Transcript for the Most Recent Tax Year		
Photocopy of Sponsor's Previous Tax Returns and W-2s or IRS Tax Transcript for Previous Tax Years (if applicable)		
Letter from Sponsor's Employer on Company Letterhead Stating Sponsor's Employment Title and Start Date, Salary or Hourly Wage, and How Many Hours per Week Sponsor Works (if applicable)		
Sponsor's Pay Stubs for the Last 6 Months (if applicable)		
Schedule C, D, E or F from Most Recent Tax Return if Petitioner is Self-Employed		
Proof of Petitioner/sponsor's Active Military Status		
Documentation of Sponsor's Asset(S) Being Used To Meet Income Requirement Showing Location, Ownership, Date of Acquisition, and Value (if applicable)		
Proof for Joint Sponsor's Affidavit of Support		
Joint Sponsor's U.S. Birth Certificate, U.S. Passport, or Certificate of Naturalization, Consular Report of Birth Abroad or Certificate of Citizenship		
Joint Sponsor's Permanent Resident Card		
Joint Sponsor's Tax Return and W-2s for Most Recent Tax Yr or IRS Tax Transcript for Most Recent Tax Yr		

Photocopy of Joint Sponsor's Previous Tax Returns and W-2s or IRS Tax Transcript for Previous Tax Years (if applicable)		
Letter from Joint Sponsor's Employer on Company Letterhead Stating Joint Sponsor's Employment Title and Start Date, Salary or Hourly Wage, and How Many Hours per Week Joint Sponsor Works (if applicable)		
Joint Sponsor's Pay Stubs for the Last 6 Months (if applicable)		
Schedule C, D, E or F from Most Recent Tax Return if Joint Sponsor Self-Employed		
Documentation of Joint Sponsor's Asset(S) Being Used To Meet Income Requirement Showing Location, Ownership, Date of Acquisition, and Value		
Proof for Contract between Sponsor and Household Member		
Marriage Certificate between Household Member and Sponsor		
Household Member's Birth Certificate		
Sponsor's Birth Certificate		
Household Member's Marriage Certificate		
Lease Showing Sponsor and Household Member Live Together		
Mail Addressed to Same Address for Sponsor and Household Member Addressed to Them Jointly or Separately		
Household Member's Tax Returns and W-2s for Most Recent Tax Year or IRS Tax Transcript for the Most Recent Tax Year		
Previous Tax Returns and W-2s or IRS Tax Transcript for Previous Tax Years (if applicable		
Letter from Household Member's Employer on Company Letterhead Stating Household Member's Employment Title and Start Date, Salary or Hourly Wage, and How Many Hours per Household Member Works		
Household Member's Pay Stubs for the Last 6 Months		
Schedule C, D, E or F from Most Recent Tax Return if Household Member is Self-Employed		
Documentation of Household Member's Asset(S) Being Used To Meet Income Requirement Showing Location, Ownership, Date of Acquisition, and Value		
Proof of 245(i) Eligibility		
Applicant's Approval Notice for an I-130 that Was Filed on or before April 30, 2001		
Applicant's Approved Labor Certification that Was Filed on or before April 30, 2001		
Lease Showing Applicant Resided in the U.S. on December 21, 2000		
Envelopes Addressed to a U.S. Residence and to Applicant on, before, or after December 21, 2000		
Applicant's Medical Records Dated on, before, or after December 21, 2000		
Applicant's Education Records Dated on, before, or after December 21, 2000		
Bills or Invoices for Consumer Activity Addressed to Applicant that occurred on, before, or after December 21, 2000		
Applicant's Bank or Credit Card Statement Dated on, before, or after December 21, 2000		
Declarations from 2 Friends Or Family Members Who Can Attest That Applicant Was In Us On 12/21/2000		
Other: Insert Other Documents Applicant Has To Prove Physical Presence On December 21, 2000		
Fees		
Legal Services Fee: $ Insert Legal Services Fee Amount		
USCIS Filing Fees with Biometrics: $1,225 (if biometrics needed) ($1,140 – I-485, Application to Register Permanent Residence or Adjust Status; $85 – Biometrics Fee)		
USCIS Filing Fees: $1,140 (if no biometrics needed: 79 years or older and under 14 and not filing with a parent ($1,140 – I-485, Application to Register Permanent Residence or Adjust Status)		
USCIS Filing Fees: $750 (if no biometrics needed: under 14 and filing at same time as parent ($750 – I-485, Application to Register Permanent Residence or Adjust Status)		
USCIS Filing Fees with Biometrics and Penalty Fee: $2,225 (if biometrics needed) ($1,140 – I-485, Application to Register Permanent Residence or Adjust Status; $85 – Biometrics Fee, & $1,000 Penalty Fee)		
USCIS Filing Fees and Penalty Fee: $2,140 ($1,140 – I-485, Application to Register Permanent Residence or Adjust Status; $1000 Penalty Fee)		

APPENDIX 5A

NOTICE OF IMMIGRANT VISA CASE CREATION

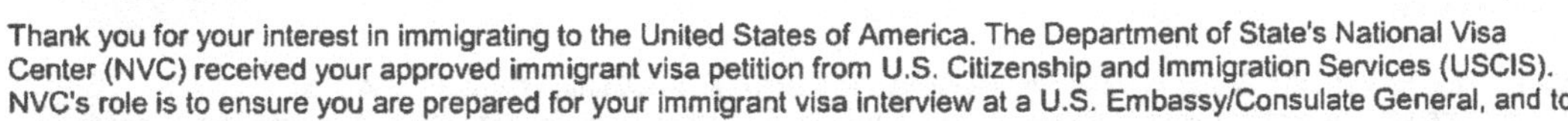

From: National_Visa_Center@state.gov
Sent: Thursday, November 7, 2019 10:55 AM
To:
Subject: Notice of Immigrant Visa Case Creation

Dear

Thank you for your interest in immigrating to the United States of America. The Department of State's National Visa Center (NVC) received your approved immigrant visa petition from U.S. Citizenship and Immigration Services (USCIS). NVC's role is to ensure you are prepared for your immigrant visa interview at a U.S. Embassy/Consulate General, and to schedule your interview appointment.

NVC is responsible for collecting any applicable fees, the Immigrant Visa Application, supporting civil documents, police certificate(s), Affidavits of Support, and financial documents, if applicable, prior to your visa interview at a U.S. Embassy/Consulate General. **Do not mail documents to NVC, even if you received instructions to mail documents to NVC in the past.**

You will need to log on to the Department of State's Consular Electronic Application Center (CEAC) at https://ceac.state.gov/IV to check your case status, pay any necessary fees, upload and submit documents, and read messages from NVC.

If you are logging into CEAC for the first time, please be aware that it can take up to three days (72 hours) from receipt of this notice for your account to be activated. Once activated, you can log into CEAC using the following unique NVC case number and Invoice Identification Number.

NVC Case Number: HCM2007
Invoice ID Number: IVSCA00000

You should keep this information available in a safe place as you will need it every time you log on to CEAC. Please keep in mind that you must use CEAC to provide NVC with the fees and documents that are required prior to your immigrant visa interview. We do not accept these by mail.

Please Note: You must bring the exact original of any scanned document you upload to CEAC that NVC accepts to your immigrant visa interview. Failure to bring the exact original you uploaded to CEAC may delay the processing of your case.

You can find detailed instructions and frequently asked questions at https://nvc.state.gov/ceac. After you complete the steps above, we will review the forms and documents you submit. If something is missing or incorrect, we will tell you how to fix it. Otherwise, we will schedule your case for a visa interview at the U.S. Embassy or Consulate in HO CHI MINH CITY, VTNM.

If you need to contact NVC, please follow the instructions at https://nvc.state.gov/inquiry. NVC may send questions, instructions, and status updates to your CEAC account. If we do this you will receive an email asking you to log into your CEAC account to review a message from NVC.

IMPORTANT: *If you do not log into CEAC or communicate with NVC regarding this immigrant visa case for a period of one year, by law the Department of State must terminate your visa application.*

FINANCIAL SPONSORSHIP RESPONSIBILITIES: Financial sponsors, joint sponsors, and applicants should be aware of the responsibilities arising from a sponsor signing an I-864 and the consequences of a sponsored immigrant's acceptance of federal means-tested public benefits. For more information, visit https://nvc.state.gov/aos.

1

m: National_Visa_Center@state.gov
ıt: Thursday, November 7, 2019 10:55 AM
ɟject: Notice of Immigrant Visa Case Creation

ar

ınk you for your interest in immigrating to the United States of America. The Department of State's National Visa ıter (NVC) received your approved immigrant visa petition from U.S. Citizenship and Immigration Services (USCIS). C's role is to ensure you are prepared for your immigrant visa interview at a U.S. Embassy/Consulate General, and to edule your interview appointment.

C is responsible for collecting any applicable fees, the Immigrant Visa Application, supporting civil documents, police ificate(s), Affidavits of Support, and financial documents, if applicable, prior to your visa interview at a U.S. bassy/Consulate General. **Do not mail documents to NVC, even if you received instructions to mail documents IVC in the past.**

ı will need to log on to the Department of State's Consular Electronic Application Center (CEAC) at s://ceac.state.gov/IV to check your case status, pay any necessary fees, upload and submit documents, and read ssages from NVC.

ıu are logging into CEAC for the first time, please be aware that it can take up to three days (72 hours) from receipt of notice for your account to be activated. Once activated, you can log into CEAC using the following unique NVC case ıber and Invoice Identification Number.

'C Case Number: HCM2007
oice ID Number: IVSCA00000

ı should keep this information available in a safe place as you will need it every time you log on to CEAC. Please keep ıind that you **must** use CEAC to provide NVC with the fees and documents that are required prior to your immigrant ı interview. We do not accept these by mail.

ıse Note: You must bring the exact original of any scanned document you upload to CEAC that NVC accepts 'our immigrant visa interview. Failure to bring the exact original you uploaded to CEAC may delay the cessing of your case.

can find detailed instructions and frequently asked questions at https://nvc.state.gov/ceac. After you complete the ıs above, we will review the forms and documents you submit. If something is missing or incorrect, we will tell you how x it. Otherwise, we will schedule your case for a visa interview at the U.S. Embassy or Consulate in HO CHI MINH Y, VTNM.

ıu need to contact NVC, please follow the instructions at https://nvc.state.gov/inquiry. NVC may send questions, 'uctions, and status updates to your CEAC account. If we do this you will receive an email asking you to log into your \C account to review a message from NVC.

ORTANT: *If you do not log into CEAC or communicate with NVC regarding this immigrant visa case for a period of year, by law the Department of State must terminate your visa application.*

ANCIAL SPONSORSHIP RESPONSIBILITIES: Financial sponsors, joint sponsors, and applicants should be aware of responsibilities arising from a sponsor signing an I-864 and the consequences of a sponsored immigrant's acceptance ederal means-tested public benefits. For more information, visit https://nvc.state.gov/aos.

1

Appendix 5B

Immigrant Visa Case Fee Payment Receipt

Payment Receipts for IV Case RDJ[redacted]
IV Fee Payment Receipt Details

Principal Applicant [redacted]
Payment of Services Initiated 17-OCT-2019 14:23:24
Payment Processed Date 18-OCT-2019
Payment Amount $325.00
Payer [redacted]
Payer Email [redacted]
Transaction ID [redacted]

Applicant	**IV Fee Payment Status**	**Fee Amount**
[redacted]	PAID	$325.00

Next Steps

If your payment status shows that it is IN PROCESS, wait two to three business days for the payment to clear. Then sign into the system again to check for a status update.

If your payment status shows a status other than IN PROCESS or PAID, sign in to the Immigrant Visa Invoice Payment Center page https://ceac.state.gov/CTRAC/Invoice/Signon.aspx and click on Get Help.

If you receive a notice that your case has entered termination, **do not attempt to pay any fees**. You must contact the National Visa Center (NVC). You can find NVC contact information at nvc.state.gov/inquiry.

When the IV fee payment status is PAID, visit nvc.state.gov/260 for instructions on continuing the processing of your immigrant visa petition.

IMPORTANT NOTES:

- If you decide to file Form I-601A, Application for Provisional Unlawful Presence Waiver with USCIS, you must include a copy of this fee payment receipt or USCIS will reject your Form I-601A.
- Please keep this receipt for your records. If you can't print the receipt now, return to the Receipt Screen and email a copy to an address where you can print it later.
- Do not let more than one-year pass from the date your visa becomes available per the Final Action Date for your visa without contacting the NVC about your immigrant visa petition or login to the CEAC portal. If a period of one-year passes from the last date of contact, all submitted forms and fees will expire and you must resubmit them to resume processing.

APPENDIX 5C

IMMIGRANT VISA CASE STATUS UPDATE NOTICE

From: National Visa Center@state.gov
Sent: Saturday, March 14, 2020 1:44 PM
To: [redacted]
Subject: Notice regarding your Immigrant Visa Case

Dear [redacted],

The National Visa Center (NVC) updated the status of your immigrant visa application. Please go to the Department of State's Consular Electronic Application Center (CEAC) at https://nvc.state.gov/ceac. You will need your NVC case number and invoice ID number to log into your account.

Once you have logged into CEAC, please look in your message box or on the Status Chart at the bottom of the page. If NVC has feedback on any items you submitted, there will be a new message with details. If not, please simply follow the updated instructions on your Status Chart to complete your case. If any column says "Pay Now", "Invalid Doc", "Incomplete", or "Re-Opened", that means you must take action by paying a fee, submitting a form, or uploading a corrected/missing document.

Regards,
National Visa Center,
U.S. Department of State
https://nvc.state.gov/ask

Case ID: MRV2014[redacted]
Invoice ID: IVSCA00000[redacted]

NOTE: Please do not reply to this email. This is not a monitored account. If you have questions or need to get in touch with NVC, please follow the instructions at https://nvc.state.gov/ask to call or email us.

Appendix 5D

NOTICE OF FORWARDING IMMIGRANT VISA CASE TO POST

From: National_Visa_Center@state.gov
Sent: Wednesday, April 29, 2020 6:48 PM
To: [redacted]
Subject: Notice regarding your Immigrant Visa Case

Dear [redacted],

The National Visa Center (NVC) received all of the fees, forms, and documents that are required prior to attending an immigrant visa interview at a U.S. Embassy/Consulate General overseas.

NVC will work with the U.S. Embassy/Consulate General in MONROVIA, LIBR to schedule an interview appointment for you. Once we have confirmed an interview date, we will send a notice to you, your petitioner and attorney (if applicable).

Please do NOT make any travel arrangements, sell property, or give up employment until you have received an immigrant visa from the U.S. Embassy/Consulate General.

The U.S. Embassy/Consulate General may require additional documentation at the time of the interview. Please visit https://nvc.state.gov/prep for information about immigrant visa interviews.

Regards,
National Visa Center,
U.S. Department of State
https://nvc.state.gov/ask

Case ID: MRV2014[redacted]
Invoice ID: IVSCA00000[redacted]

NOTE: Please do not reply to this email. This is not a monitored account. If you have questions or need to get in touch with NVC, please follow the instructions at https://nvc.state.gov/ask to call or email us.

APPENDIX 5E

NOTICE OF IMMIGRANT VISA INTERVIEW APPOINTMENT

From:	National_Visa_Center@state.gov
Sent:	Thursday, October 24, 2019 2:36 AM
To:	
Subject:	Immigrant Visa Interview Appointment

OCTOBER 24, 2019

Case Number: HCM2007

Invoice ID: IVSCA0000

 :

The National Visa Center (NVC) completed its processing of your immigrant visa application and forwarded it to the U.S. Embassy/Consulate General, where an immigrant visa interview has been scheduled. Appointment information is located at the bottom of this email.

Important Information:
You submitted forms and supporting documents to the NVC in electronic form. You must present the original forms and documents for review by the consular officer during your interview.

Please promptly read and follow all Interview Preparation Instructions located on the Department of State's web site at: https://nvc.state.gov/interview.

Important information regarding the required medical appointment is also listed on this site. Failure to promptly follow all instructions provided on this site will result in your immigrant visa being refused at the initial interview.

You should present this letter upon arrival at the Embassy/Consulate General.

Those members of your family, named below, must appear at the Embassy/Consulate General on the appointment date.

PRESIDENTIAL PROCLAMATION ON HEALTH CARE: You must be able to demonstrate to the consular officer at the time of interview you will be covered by approved health insurance within 30 days of entry into the United States or have the financial resources to pay for reasonably foreseeable medical costs. Inability to meet this requirement will result in the denial of the visa application. For complete requirements and/or exemptions, visit https://travel.state.gov/healthcare.

What To Do if You Cannot Keep the Appointment:
Some Embassies/Consulates General reschedule interview appointments themselves; others utilize an outside service provider to reschedule appointments. To determine the proper procedure for rescheduling your interview appointment, please go to the Department of State's web site at: https://nvc.state.gov/interview, under "Step 2", select your interview location from the dropdown and click "Download PDF" and follow your Embassy/Consulate General's instructions listed under "Contact Information" on the right.

Reminders:

- Read and follow all interview instructions located at https://nvc.state.gov/interview.
- Bring this letter to your medical examination because the panel physician may need to review it before performing the examination.
- If a sponsor filed an I-864 (Affidavit of Support) AND provided the NVC with proof of an IRS Federal Income Tax Extension in lieu of a Federal Income Tax Return, you must upload this to CEAC or bring the sponsor's most recent Federal Income Tax Return to the visa interview.

1

- Failure to present all necessary documents to the Consular Officer will result in your immigrant visa being refused at the initial interview.

Questions:
The National Visa Center has completed its processing of this case and any further inquiries should be addressed to the U.S. Embassy, Consulate General, or Diplomatic Mission listed below. When communicating with the Embassy/Consulate General by e-mail, letter, or fax, always refer to your name and case number exactly as they appear.

Immigrant Visa Interview Details:

Interview Date/Time: NOVEMBER 21, 2019 at 08:30 AM
Interview Location: THANH PHO HO CHI MINH, VIETNAM
NVC Case Number: HCM2007
Invoice ID: IVSCA00000
Principal Applicant:

HO CHI MINH CITY
VIETNAM
Preference Category: F31-Married Son/Daughter of U.S. Citizen
A #:

Additional Applicants:

Name	A#	Appointment Date/Time
		NOVEMBER 21, 2019 at 08:30 AM
		NOVEMBER 21, 2019 at 08:30 AM
		NOVEMBER 21, 2019 at 08:30 AM
		NOVEMBER 21, 2019 at 08:30 AM

Appendix 5F

MEDICAL EXAM INSTRUCTIONS

All immigrant visa applicants, regardless of age, require a medical examination prior to the issuance of a visa. Only a physician accredited by the U.S. Consulate can perform this examination. It is your responsibility to schedule a medical examination with one of the clinics listed below before your visa interview appointment at the U.S. Consulate. Medical examination results from other physicians will not be accepted.

Authorized panel physicians in Mexico:

CLINICA MEDICA INTERNACIONAL
Ave. Ramon Rivera Lara # 9020
Fracc. Las Lunas
CD. Juarez, Chih.,
Mexico C.P. 32543
Tel: (011-52-656) 227-2800
Toll-free from the U.S.: 1-844-624-9447
Llamada gratuita de México: 01 800 801-8585
Fax: (011-52-656) 227-2808
Website: http://www.clinicamedicainternacional.com.mx/

SERVICIOS MEDICOS DE LA FRONTERA
Prol. Ramon Rivera Lara #8950
Col. Partido Senecu
CD. Juarez, Chih.,
Mexico C.P. 32540
Tel: (011-52-656) 688-2700
Toll-free from the U.S.: 1-844-847-5340
Llamada gratuita de México: 01 800 201-8472
Fax: (011-52-656) 688-2701
Website: www.smf.com.mx

MEDICOS ESPECIALIZADOS INTERNACIONALES
Hamburgo 206, Interior 204, 2nd Floor,
Colonia Juárez, Delegación Cuauhtémoc,
Mexico City 06600
Tel: (55) 2624-0630 or
(55) 5207-3794 ext. 101
Website: www.mei-mexico.com

Please note: Visa applicants who live in the State of Mexico and Mexico City must have their medical examination at Medicos Especializados Internacionales in Mexico City. All other visa applicants can complete their medical examination at any of the three authorized clinics listed above.

Items to bring to your medical examination

You should bring the following items to your medical examination:

- Your visa interview appointment letter,
- Your passport,
- A photocopy of your immunization records,
- If you suffer from chronic illness, have been treated for venereal disease or are under psychiatric care, please bring your current medical file with you to the medical examination.

You must pay all medical examination fees, including x-ray and blood test fees, directly to the examining physician. The examination fee for applicants age 15 years and older is USD $220.00. The fee for applicants between ages 2 and 14 is USD $178.00. Applicants younger than 2 is USD $135.00. A 16% tax will be added to these fees. Cash and credit card (Visa or MasterCard) are the only forms of payment accepted. Any required vaccines or DNA testing will be charged separately.

Please attend a medical examination at least two (2) days before your visa interview appointment if you are age 15 years or older. If you are between ages 2 and 14 years, you should attend an examination at least four (4) business days before your visa interview. You may visit either clinic in Ciudad Juarez between 6:00 a.m. and 11:00 a.m. Monday through Friday; no appointment is necessary. For visa applicants who live in the State of Mexico and Mexico City, you can make an appointment by phone from 9:00 a.m. to 1:30 p.m. and from 2:30 p.m. to 4:30 p.m. The medical clinic in Mexico City accepts appointments from 7:30 a.m. to noon Monday through Friday.

During the medical examination

The medical examination will include a medical history review, physical examination, chest X- ray, urine and blood tests (for applicants 15 years of age or older). The United States also requires tuberculosis (TB) testing for all applicants two years of age and older. Please be prepared to discuss your medical history, medications you are taking, and current treatments you are undergoing. More information on general medical requirements for U.S. immigrants is available here [https://travel.state.gov/content/travel/en/us-visas/Supplements/Supplements_by_Post/CDJ-Ciudad-Juarez.html].

Applicants who show signs or symptoms of tuberculosis or who are HIV/AIDS positive must complete a further medical process in order to comply with the regulations of the Centers for Disease Control (CDC). This process is designed to detect and treat tuberculosis in order to reduce the risk of spreading tuberculosis within the population of the United States. It may take between three and six months before the clinic will be able to complete the final medical exam for these applicants.

As directed by the Centers for Disease Control and Prevention of the United States of America, beginning on October 1, 2018 all immigrant visa applicants whose age is between 2-14 years must provide a blood test for tuberculosis screening. All applicants whose age is 15 years or older must provide a urine sample for gonorrhea screening.

U.S. immigration law requires immigrant visa applicants to obtain certain vaccinations prior to the issuance of a visa. Current immigrant visa vaccination requirements are available here [https://travel.state.gov/content/travel/en/us-visas/Supplements/Supplements_by_Post/CDJ-Ciudad-Juarez.html]. You can also read Frequently Asked Questions about our medical examination requirements online [https://travel.state.gov/content/travel/en/us-visas/immigrate/the-immigrant-visa-process/step-10-prepare-for-the-interview/medical-examination-faqs.html].

After the medical examination

When your examination is completed, the doctor will provide you with exam results in a sealed envelope. DO NOT OPEN THIS ENVELOPE. Instead bring it to your visa interview.

Any x-rays taken will be delivered to you on a compact disc (CD). You DO NOT need to bring the x-rays to your visa interview unless you suffer from tuberculosis (TB). However, you must carry the x-rays with you when you travel to the United States for the first time. The medical examination must be valid for less than 6 months upon entering the United States.

APPENDIX 6A

MENTAL DISORDERS THAT MAY HAVE ASSOCIATED HARMFUL BEHAVIOR

- Mental retardation
- Autistic disorders
- Organic mental disorders (dementias)
- Schizophrenic, paranoid, and other psychotic disorders
- Delusional disorders
- Mood disorders
- Dissociative disorders
- Anxiety-related disorders
- Somatoform disorders
- Personality disorders
- Adult antisocial behavior
- Conduct disorders
- Adjustment disorders
- Sexual disorders
- Impulse control disorders
- Psychoactive substance use disorders
- Other medical disorders

APPENDIX 6B

MENTAL DISORDERS THAT NECESSARILY HAVE ASSOCIATED HARMFUL BEHAVIOR

Medical Condition	Associated Behavior Pattern
1. Antisocial personality disorder	Harmful behavior necessary to establish the diagnosis
2. Impulse control disorders not elsewhere classified • pathological gambling • kleptomania • pyromania • intermittent explosive disorder • impulse control disorder not otherwise specified	Harmful behavior necessary to establish the diagnosis
3. Paraphilias that involve behaviors that harm or intimidate others • exhibitionism • pedophilia • sexual masochism • sexual sadism • zoopilia • voyeurism • some atypical paraphilias (*e.g.*, frotteurism, telephone scatologia)	Harmful behavior necessary to establish the diagnosis
4. Conduct disorders • solitary aggressive type • oppositional defiant disorder • other types	Behavior necessary to establish the diagnosis. If history of serious violation of rights of others or property (*e.g.*, stealing, fire setting)
5. Mood disorders • bipolar disorders • depressive disorders	*E.g.*, in the course of the illness, has assaulted others when manic or attempted suicide when depressed. *E.g.*, in the course of the illness, has attempted suicide; has harmed or neglected children when depressed

Medical Condition	Associated Behavior Pattern
6. Schizophrenic disorders • paranoid disorders • psychotic disorders not elsewhere classified	*E.g.*, in the course of the illness, has engaged in thievery or destruction of property; harmed children
7. Alcohol dependence (alcoholism) *or* Alcohol abuse	Behavior necessary to establish the diagnosis
8. Psychoactive substance disorders (drug abuse)	Behavior necessary to establish the diagnosis
9. Other physical or mental disorders that, in relation to the symptoms of the disorder or its treatments, limit physical attentional or cognitive capacity to perform certain tasks or are otherwise associated with behaviors not controllable by the person (*e.g.*, partial complex seizure disorders)	*E.g.*, in the course of the illness, has assaulted others; has engaged in tasks in which the limitation in capacity has resulted in harm to others, self, or property (*e.g.*, person with transient ischemic attacks or arrythmia with consistent loss of consciousness has continued to drive a motor vehicle until involved in a serious or fatal accident).

APPENDIX 7

QUESTIONS TO ASK QUALIFYING RELATIVE TO ESTABLISH HARDSHIP

Are you a USC or an LPR?

If an LPR, when and how did you immigrate to the U.S.?

If a USC, by birth, derivation, or naturalization?

When were you naturalized?

If provisional waiver, have you decided whether you will relocate or separate from the waiver applicant should that be necessary?

History of Relationship

1) Where did you meet your spouse?

2) How old were you when you met your spouse?

3) When was your first date? What happened afterward?

4) When did you move in together?

5) When did you get married?

6) What was your relationship like at the beginning of the marriage?

7) What is relationship like now?

8) Do you have children? Ages?

9) Explain you and your spouse's relationship with your children.

10) Explain you and your spouse's relationship with your and your spouse's parents.

11) Do you or spouse take care of you or your spouse's parents?

12) If your spouse were to return to his/her native country and separate from you, what would the hardship be to you?

Employment and Economic Prospects

1) How many years of formal education have you had?

2) Describe your job skills and experience?

3) Are you working now? What is your current income?

4) What special skills does your job require, if any?

5) How do you feel about your job and your coworkers?

6) Is it likely you will be able to find employment with these skills in your spouse's country? If not, why not?

7) Will you be able to obtain any employment in spouse's country?

8) What will be your income from this employment?

9) Will you have medical or other employment–related benefits?

10) Describe in detail the consequences of this reduced income on your family's health and welfare?

11) If you will not be able to obtain employment, why not?

12) Describe in detail the consequences to your family's health and welfare of your being unable to find work in your home country?

13) What does your spouse do? What is his/her income?

14) What would the impact be to you without your spouse's income?

Education and Children-Related Questions

1) Will your children be able to attend school if move to your relative's country? If not, why not?

2) What is the quality of education in your relative's country?

3) How would you feel if your children were not educated in the U.S.?

4) Is there a primary school in the city to which you will be returning?

5) Is there a secondary school in this location?

6) How far will your children have to travel to attend school?

7) Will there be any transportation available to them to get to school?

8) Will you have to pay to send your children to school?

9) What will be your costs?

10) Will you be able to afford it?

11) What problems will your children have in adjusting to the educational system in your home country?

12) Do your children speak the native language?

13) Are they able to read and write in the native language?

14) How are they doing in school in the U.S.?

15) Do they have any learning disabilities?

16) Do they receive special services for their disabilities?

17) Are they in special classes for children with disabilities?

18) Are your children especially academically talented?

19) Are they in special classes for gifted children?

20) What are their future educational goals?

21) What are their career goals?

22) How is the U.S. educational system different than the one your children will encounter abroad?

23) What consequences would your children face if uprooted at this time in terms of education (any special study in which they are engaged)?

24) If your children are U.S. citizens, will they go with you abroad or will you keep them in the U.S. with someone else?

25) What will happen to them if they do not go with you abroad?

26) Who will they stay with if you leave them in the U.S.?

27) Who will pay for their expenses in the U.S.?

Health-Related Questions

1) How are the health conditions in the area where you will return?

2) Do you or anyone in your family suffer from a medical condition?

3) What type of treatment are you or someone in your family receiving?

4) How often are you or the person in your family being treated?

5) What type of treatment is being received?

6) How often is the treatment received?

7) What will be the consequences of your treatment being interrupted?

8) Will you be able to obtain the same treatment in your home country? If yes, explain?

9) Do you or any family member receive psychological counseling for any problems?

10) Do you worry about your own or your family members' psychological situation if you relocate with the applicant?

11) Has a psychological evaluation been done on you or any member of your family?

12) Will there be changes in your family's diet if you return to your home country?

13) Will you be able to buy sufficient food for your family?

14) If there is no doctor in your town, how far will you have to travel to see a doctor?

15) Will you have access to maternity care? If yes, will you be able to afford it?

16) Does your family have health insurance in the U.S.? If so, what is the name?

17) If you relocate, will your family be covered by health insurance?

18) Will you be able to afford adequate medical services in the applicant's country? If not, why not?

Housing-Related Questions

1) Do you own or rent your home?

2) How long have you lived at your current address?

3) Will you be able to afford housing in the applicant's home country?

4) If yes, describe what your housing conditions will be like?

5) Will your home have indoor plumbing?

6) Will your home have electricity?

7) Will your home have drainage?

8) How many rooms will your home have?

9) How will your housing compare with your home in the U.S.?

10) How many people will have to live in your house abroad?

11) If you will not be able to afford housing, what will you do? Do you have friends or relatives with whom you could live?

Country Conditions

1) Is there a significant level of violence in the area where you or the applicant would be living?

2) How do you know about the violence (from family, friends, newspapers, or personal knowledge)?

3) Do you know anyone who has been affected by such violence? If so, who are they?

4) What happened to the people you know who suffered violence?

5) If the people you know were injured by violence, do you have any proof of such injury (newspaper clippings, police reports, death certificates, photos of injured people, photos of damaged property)?

6) Do you know the names of any gangs operating in the area?

7) Have you or anyone you know had problems with the gangs in your home country?

8) If so, what were the problems?

9) What would you do to keep yourself and your family safe from gang violence?

10) Is there ongoing political violence in your home country between different political groups? If so, what are the groups?

11) What effect has the political violence had on the place where you or the applicant would be living?

12) Would the violence prevent you from traveling, working, going out at night?

Questions Related to Women

1) In the U.S., women commonly work outside the home. Is that true in the country to which you will be moving/returning?

2) Would you be able to work in your home support your family?

3) What obstacles would you face in finding work?

4) How have your daughters adjusted to life in the U.S.?

5) Would your daughters face unique problems as females in the country to which you will be moving?

6) Are the educational opportunities for girls in your home country similar to those in the U.S? If not, how?

Family and Community Ties in the U.S.

1) Are you involved in your community? If so, how?

2) Do you frequently spend time with family members?

3) What is your relationship with each of them and where do they live?

4) What is their citizenship or immigration status?

5) What kinds of activities do you do with your friends and relatives?

6) How often do you see them?

7) Please describe your daily routine, during the work week, including what you do after work?

8) Please describe what your activities are during the weekend and other free time?

9) Are you involved in any community organization (church groups, sports teams, counseling groups, school groups, labor unions)?

10) Are you active with such groups? How much time do you spend with such groups?

11) Are you in a leadership position with such groups?

12) If you are a member of a church, what is the name of it? How often do you attend?

13) Do you have many close relatives in your home country? If so, where do they live?

14) Do you have many friends in your home country? Have you maintained contact with them?

15) Would your friends or relatives be able to assist you in locating housing and employment abroad? If not, why not?

16) Would the lack of personal contacts make it difficult for you to obtain adequate housing and employment?

Cultural Factors in Applicant's Home Country

If you or the waiver applicant were to relocate, would you face persecution or discrimination due to your sexual orientation, religion, ethnicity, gender or other factors?

Appendix 8

FORM I-864P, 2020 HHS POVERTY GUIDELINES FOR AFFIDAVIT OF SUPPORT

For the 48 Contiguous States, the District of Columbia, Puerto Rico, the U.S. Virgin Islands, Guam, and the Commonwealth of the Northern Mariana Islands:

Sponsor's Household Size	100% of HHS Poverty Guidelines*	125% of HHS Poverty Guidelines*
	For sponsors on active duty in the U.S. armed forces who are petitioning for their spouse or child	***For all other sponsors***
2	$17,240	$21,550
3	$21,720	$27,150
4	$26,200	$32,750
5	$30,680	$38,350
6	$35,160	$43,950
7	$39,640	$49,550
8	$44,120	$55,150
	Add $4,480 for each additional person	Add $5,600 for each additional person

For Alaska:

Sponsor's Household Size	100% of HHS Poverty Guidelines*	125% of HHS Poverty Guidelines*
	For sponsors on active duty in the U.S. armed forces who are petitioning for their spouse or child	For all other sponsors
2	$21,550	$26,937
3	$27,150	$33,937
4	$32,750	$40,937
5	$38,350	$47,937
6	$43,950	$54,937
7	$49,550	$61,937
8	$55,150	$68,937
	Add $5,600 for each additional person	Add $7,000 for each additional person

For Hawaii:

Sponsor's Household Size	100% of HHS Poverty Guidelines*	125% of HHS Poverty Guidelines*
	For sponsors on active duty in the U.S. armed forces who are petitioning for their spouse or child	For all other sponsors
2	$19,830	$24,787
3	$24,980	$31,225
4	$30,130	$37,662
5	$35,280	$44,100
6	$40,430	$50,537
7	$45,580	$56,975
8	$50,730	$63,412
	Add $5,150 for each additional person	Add $6,437 for each additional person

Appendix 9

USCIS MEMO AND CHART ON DETERMINATIONS OF GOOD MORAL CHARACTER

U.S. Department of Homeland Security
20 Massachusetts Avenue, N.W.
Washington, D.C. 20536

HQOPRD 70/8.1/8.2

Interoffice Memorandum

To: Paul E. Novak
Director
Vermont Service Center

From: William R. Yates /S/
Associate Director
Operations

Date: January 19, 2005

Re: Determinations of Good Moral Character in VAWA-Based Self-Petitions

Purpose

On October 28, 2000, the President signed the Victims of Trafficking and Violence Protection Act (VTVPA), Pub. L. 106-386. Title V of the VTVPA is entitled the Battered Immigrant Women Protection Act (BIWPA), and contains several provisions amending the self-petitioning eligibility requirements for battered spouses and children contained in the Immigration and Nationality Act (INA or the Act). Those provisions were established by the Violence Against Women Act of 1994 (VAWA). The purpose of this memorandum is to inform U.S. Citizenship and Immigration Services (USCIS) adjudicators at the Vermont Service Center (VSC) of the change in the law concerning determinations of good moral character made in connection with VAWA-based self-petitions (Forms I-360).

Guidance

Sections 204(a)(1)(A) and (B) of the Act contain the self-petitioning eligibility requirements for battered spouses and children. One of the eligibility requirements is that a self-petitioner must demonstrate that he/she is a person of good moral character. A VAWA-based self-petition will be denied or revoked if the record contains evidence to establish that the self-petitioner lacks good moral character. The inquiry into good moral character focuses on the three years immediately preceding the filing of the self-petition, but the adjudicating officer may investigate the self-petitioner's character beyond the three-year period when there is reason to believe that the self-

Determinations of Good Moral Character in VAWA-Based Self-Petitions
HQOPRD 70/8.1/8.2
Page 2

petitioner may not have been a person of good moral character during that time.[1] A self-petitioner's claim of good moral character will be evaluated on a case-by-case basis taking into account the provisions of section 101(f) of the Act and the standards of the average citizen in the community.[2] Prior to the enactment of the BIWPA, a finding of good moral character could not be made in a battered spouse or child case filed under the VAWA immigration provisions if the self-petitioner committed an act or had a conviction that was included in section 101(f) of the Act. Section 1503(d) of the BIWPA has amended section 204(a)(1) of the Act to make an exception for battered spouses and children in certain circumstances.

Step 1: Determine whether the alien is subject to section 101(f) of the Act.

Section 101(f) of the Act describes the classes of aliens who are statutorily ineligible to be considered persons of good moral character. If the VAWA self-petitioner has committed an act or has a conviction that places him or her into one of the classes contained in section 101(f) of the Act, the adjudicator is barred from making a finding of good moral character unless the self-petitioner demonstrates that the amendments made to section 204(a)(1) of the Act apply to him or her.

Section 204(a)(1)(C) of the Act as amended provides USCIS with the discretion to make a finding of good moral character despite an act or conviction that would be a disqualifying act or conviction under INA§ 101(f) or that would otherwise adversely reflect upon a self-petitioner's moral character. A finding of good moral character may be made if: 1) the act or conviction is waivable for purposes of determining inadmissibility or deportability under INA § 212(a) or § 237(a); and 2) the act or conviction was connected to the alien's having been battered or subjected to extreme cruelty. This change applies to all self-petitioners, including those who file under INA § 204(a)(1)(A)(v) or § 204(a)(1)(B)(iv) as self-petitioners living abroad, despite the fact that these situations are not specifically referenced in INA § 204(a)(1)(C).[3]

Step 2: Determine whether a waiver would be available.

If the adjudicator determines that the self-petitioner has committed an act or has a conviction that renders the self-petitioner inadmissible under section 212(a) of the Act or deportable under section 237(a) of the Act, and that would bar a finding of good moral character, he/she should next determine whether a waiver would be available for the act or conviction. The evidence submitted by the self-petitioner must address whether a waiver would be available for the act or conviction at issue (this includes the waivers created by the BIWPA found at sections 212(h)(1), 212(i)(1),

---

[1] Preamble to Interim Regulations, 61 Fed. Reg. 13065, 13066 (Mar. 26, 1996).

[2] 8 CFR § 204.2(c)(1)(vii). See also, 8 CFR § 316.10(a)(2).

[3] This determination is based on the fact that sections 204(a)(1)(A)(v) and 204(a)(1)(B)(iv) of the Act state that the claimant must be "eligible to file a petition" under section 204(a)(1)(A)(iii) or (iv) of the Act or section 204(a)(1)(B)(ii) or (iii) of the Act, respectively, and that section 204(a)(1)(C) does not specifically preclude a waiver under this provision.

237(a)(7), and 237(a)(1)(H) of the Act). It is important to note that the adjudicator does not have to find that a waiver would be granted, only that one would be available for filing at the time the adjustment of status application (or visa application) is filed.

In situations where an adjudicator questions whether a waiver would be available because the act or conviction involves a violent or dangerous crime, he/she should consult 8 CFR 212.7(d). That provision discusses the circumstances in which a waiver of a violent or dangerous crime may be available. If the adjudicator determines that an act or conviction constitutes an aggravated felony as defined in section 101(a)(43) of the Act, he/she should refer the case for issuance of a notice to appear (NTA) in accordance with the guidelines set out in the Service Center NTA SOP.

Attached to this memorandum as Attachment 1, is a chart indicating which bars to establishing good moral character contained in section 101(f) of the Act are for acts or convictions that may be waived and which are not. This chart is intended to serve as a quick point of reference for adjudicators. Also attached, as Attachment 2, is a quick reference guide for authorities affecting false testimony determinations under section 101(f)(6) of the Act. If the adjudicator is not certain whether a particular act or conviction may be waived, the adjudicator and his/her supervisor should seek legal guidance from the VSC Counsel prior to making a final determination.

Step 3: Determine whether the act or conviction is "connected" to the battering or extreme cruelty.

If the adjudicator determines that a waiver would be available for the act or conviction at issue, he/she should next determine whether the act or conviction is "connected" to the battering or extreme cruelty. In order for an act or conviction to be considered sufficiently "connected" to the battering or extreme cruelty, the evidence must establish that the battering or extreme cruelty experienced by the self-petitioner compelled or coerced him/her to commit the act or crime for which he/she was convicted. In other words, the evidence should establish that the self-petitioner would not have committed the act or crime in the absence of the battering or extreme cruelty. To meet this evidentiary standard, the evidence submitted must demonstrate:

- The circumstances surrounding the act or conviction, including the relationship of the abuser to, and his/her role in, the act or conviction committed by the self-petitioner; and

- The requisite causal relationship between the act or conviction and the battering or extreme cruelty.

In order for a connection to be found, the battering or extreme cruelty must have been perpetrated by the self-petitioner's qualifying USC or LPR spouse, intended spouse, former spouse, or parent. However, self-petitioners are not required to establish that the act or conviction that would bar a finding of good moral character occurred during the marriage to the self-petitioner's qualifying USC or LPR spouse. If the self-petitioner establishes that there was battering or extreme

Determinations of Good Moral Character in VAWA-Based Self-Petitions
HQOPRD 70/8.1/8.2
Page 4

cruelty during the marriage as well as prior to the marriage to the qualifying USC or LPR spouse, the adjudicating officer may find that the self-petitioner has established the required "connection" between the act or conviction, even if it occurred prior to the marriage.

When determining whether a sufficient connection exists between the alien's disqualifying act or conviction and the battering or extreme cruelty suffered by the alien, the adjudicating officer should consider the full history of the domestic violence in the case, including the need to escape an abusive relationship. The adjudicating officer should consider all credible evidence that is in compliance with 8 U.S.C. § 1367 when making this determination. The credibility and probative value of the evidence submitted by the self-petitioner is a determination left to the discretion of the adjudicating officer.

Step 4: Determine whether the self-petitioner warrants a finding of good moral character in the exercise of discretion.

Whether a self-petitioner is a person of good moral character is, in accordance with section 204(a)(1)(C) of the Act, a discretionary determination to be made by the adjudicating officer. For example, even if the evidence submitted by a self-petitioner establishes that (1) a waiver for his or her disqualifying act or conviction is available, and (2) the requisite connection exists between his or her disqualifying act or conviction and the battering or extreme cruelty he or she suffered, the adjudicating officer may nevertheless find that the severity or gravity of the self-petitioner's act or conviction warrants an adverse finding of good moral character in the exercise of discretion.

Further Information

This provision of the BIWPA applies to all self-petitions pending on or filed on or after October 28, 2000. Personnel with questions regarding this memorandum or other VAWA-related issues, please contact Laura Dawkins, Office of Program and Regulations Development by electronic mail.

Attachments

Authorities Affecting False Testimony Determinations
(Attachment 2)

Step #1: Has the self-petitioner ever given "false testimony" for purposes of 101(f)(6):

False written statements that appear in an application, even if the application bears a statement of oath, do not constitute testimony within the meaning of section 101(f)(6). *Matter of L-D-E-*, 8 I&N Dec. 399 (BIA 1959).

False statements uttered orally under oath at a deportation hearing constitute false testimony within the meaning of section 101(f)(6) of the Act. *Matter of Barcenas*, 19 I&N Dec. 609 (BIA 1998).

False oral statements made under oath to an asylum officer can constitute "false testimony" under section 101(f)(6). *In re R-S-J*, 22 I&N Dec. 863 (BIA 1999).

Note: The Ninth Circuit, in which *In re R-S-J* arose, has held that oral statements must be made "to a court or tribunal." *Phinpathya v. INS*, 673 F.2d 1013, 1018-19 (9th Cir. 1981, rev'd on other grounds, 464 U.S. 183 (1984). However, in a more recent case, the Ninth Circuit held that false statements made under oath during a naturalization examination constitute false testimony within the meaning of section 101(f)(6). *Bernal v. INS*, 154 F.3d 1020 (9th Cir. 1998). In deciding *In re R-S-J*, the BIA concluded that an asylum officer is a member of a "tribunal" for purposes of the false testimony bar to establishing good moral character under section 101(f)(6), as that provision has been construed in the Ninth Circuit.

Outside the Ninth Circuit, false statements need not be uttered in administrative or judicial proceedings to constitute "false testimony" under section 101(f)(6), but can include statements made under oath to government officials, including Service officers and consular officials. *Matter of Namio*, 14 I&N Dec. 412 (BIA 1973) (false statement under oath to a border patrol agent); *Liwanag v. INS*, 872 F.2d 684 (5th Cir. 1989) ("false testimony" to a Service officer during an investigation).

Step #2: Was the false testimony material for purposes of 212(a)(6)(C)?

A misrepresentation is material ... if it tends to shut off a line of inquiry which is relevant to the alien's eligibility, and which might have resulted in a proper determination that he be excluded." *Matter of Ng*, 17 I&N Dec. 536 (BIA 1980); see also *Matter of Bosuego*, 17 I&N Dec. 125, 130 (BIA 1979, 1980) (A misrepresentation made in connection with a visa application is material if the misrepresentation tends to shut off a line of inquiry which is relevant to the alien's eligibility and which might well have resulted in a proper determination that he be excluded).

U.S. Citizenship and Immigration Services
January 2005

Waivable Conduct Contained in the Statutory Bars to Establishing Good Moral Character

(Attachment 1)

Provision of INA	**Conduct Prohibiting Finding of Good Moral Character**	**Conduct Waivable?**	**Waiver provision**	**Criteria for waiver**
INA § 101(f)(1)	Someone who is an habitual drunkard.	No		
INA § 101(f)(3)	Someone who engaged in prostitution within the past ten years. [INA § 212(a)(2)(D) ground of inadmissibility]	Yes	INA § 212(h)(1)(C) provides for a waiver of the § 212(a)(2)(D) ground of inadmissibility.	Alien qualifies as battered spouse or child under clause (iii), (iv), or (v) of INA § 204(a)(1)(A) or (ii), (iii), or (iv) of 204(a)(1)(B) AND Sec. of DHS must consent to the waiver (i.e. exercise favorable discretion).
INA § 101(f)(3)	Someone who has ever knowingly encouraged, induced, assisted, abetted, or abided another alien to enter or to try to enter the U.S. in violation of law. [INA § 212 (a)(6)(E) ground of inadmissibility]	Yes	INA § 212(d)(11) provides for a waiver of the § 212(a)(6)(E) ground of inadmissibility.	Aliens seeking adjustment of status as an immediate relative or immigrant under INA § 203(a) may qualify for a waiver only if the alien encouraged, induced, assisted, abetted, or aided only an individual who at the time of such action was the alien's spouse, parent, son, or daughter (and no other individual) to enter the United States in violation of law.
INA § 101(f)(3)	Aliens previously removed from the United States [INA § 212(a)(9)(A) ground of inadmissibility]	No		
INA § 101(f)(3)	Someone who committed or was convicted of either a crime involving moral turpitude or a crime relating to a controlled	Yes for CIMT Waiver for drug offense only available for single	INA § 212(h)(1)(C) provides for a waiver of the212(a)(2)(A)(i)(I) and (i)(II) grounds of	Alien qualifies as battered spouse or child under clause (iii), (iv), or (v) of INA § 204(a)(1)(A) or (ii), (iii), or

U.S. Citizenship and Immigration Services
January 2005

	substance that doesn't fall within one of the exceptions set forth at INA § 212(a)(2)(A)(ii). [INA § 212(a)(2)(A) ground of inadmissibility]	offense of simple possession of 30 grams or less of marijuana.	inadmissibility.	(iv) of 204(a)(1)(B) AND Sec. of DHS must consent to the waiver (i.e. exercise favorable discretion).
INA § 101(f)(3)	Someone who was convicted of two or more offenses (other than purely political offenses), regardless of whether they arose from out of a single scheme or the conviction was in a single trial, for which the aggregate sentences to confinement were 5 years or more. [INA § 212(a)(2)(B) ground of inadmissibility]	Yes	INA § 212(h)(1)(C) provides for a waiver of the 212(a)(2)(B) ground of inadmissibility.	Alien qualifies as battered spouse or child under clause (iii), (iv), or (v) of INA § 204(a)(1)(A) or (ii), (iii), or (iv) of 204(a)(1)(B) AND Sec. of DHS must consent to the waiver (i.e. exercise favorable discretion).
INA § 101(f)(3)	Someone who DHS knows or has reason to believe is, or has been an illicit trafficker in any controlled substance. [INA § 212(a)(2)(C) ground of inadmissibility]	No		
INA § 101(f)(4)	Someone whose present income is derived principally from illegal gambling activities.	No		
INA § 101(f)(5)	Someone who has been convicted of two or more gambling offenses during the period for which good moral character must be established.	No		
INA § 101(f)(6)	Someone who has given false testimony that was material for the purpose of obtaining any benefits under the INA. [INA § 212 (a)(6)(C)(i) ground of inadmissibility]	**NOTE**: Though there is no specific waiver for false testimony, an alien who gives false testimony may come within the ambit of INA § 212(a)(6)(C)(i)	INA §§ 212(i)(1) and 237 (a)(1)(H)(ii) provide for a waiver of the § 212 (a)(6)(C)(i) ground of inadmissibility.	Alien must qualify as battered spouse or child under clause (iii), (iv), or (v) of INA § 204(a)(1)(A) or (ii), (iii), or (iv) of 204(a)(1)(B) and show that refusal of admission would result in extreme

		which bars aliens who procure (or seek to procure) by fraud or willful misrepresentation, a visa, admission, other documentation or benefit under the INA. False testimony that is NOT material does not render an alien inadmissible under INA § 212(a)(6)(C)(i). However, such non-material false testimony DOES statutorily bar USCIS from making a finding of good moral character – i.e., such an "act or conviction" is not "waivable" for purposes of INA § 204(a)(1)(C). Therefore, adjudicators will need to determine two things: 1) whether the self-petitioner has ever given "false testimony"; and 2) if so, whether such testimony was "material." Attached to this chart is guidance to assist in making these determinations.		hardship to the alien or the alien's USC, LPR or qualified alien parent or child [INA § 212(i)(1)] Alien must qualify as battered spouse or child under clause (iii), (iv), or (v) of INA § 204(a)(1)(A) or (ii), (iii), or (iv) of 204(a)(1)(B). This waiver of removal also operates to waive deportation based on the grounds of inadmissibility directly resulting from such fraud or misrepresentation. [INA §237(a)(1)(H)(ii)]
INA § 101(f)(7)	Someone who, during the period for which good moral character must be established, has been confined, as a result of	No		

	conviction, to a penal institution for an aggregate period of 180 days or more, regardless of whether the offense, or offenses, for which she has been confined were committed within or without such period.			
INA § 101(f)(8)	Someone who at any time has been convicted of an aggravated felony, where the conviction was entered on or after 11/29/90 (date of enactment of IMMACT 90).	No		

False statement or claim to U.S. citizenship or registering to vote or voting in Federal, State or local election in violation of lawful restrictions

A person who falsely claims U.S. citizenship in order to vote, who registers to vote or who votes in violation of lawful restrictions is **not** barred from a good moral character finding if:

1) each natural parent is or was a USC;
2) the person permanently resided in the U.S. prior to attaining age 16; and
3) the person reasonably believed at the time of the statement, claim, or violation that he/she was a USC.

This exception was created by the Child Citizenship Act of 2000 (CCA), Pub. L. 106-395, and is retroactively applied as if included in IIRIRA on September 30, 1996. Please refer to a memorandum entitled, "Procedures for Handling Naturalization Applications of Aliens Who Voted Unlawfully or Falsely Represented Themselves as U.S. Citizens by Voting or Registering to Vote," and dated May 7, 2002, for a detailed explanation of the exception described above.

SUBJECT-MATTER INDEX

A